Building Business Intelligence Applications with .NET

Building Business Intelligence Applications with .NET

Robert Ericsson

FIREWAL MEDIA
(An Imprint of Laxmi Publications Pvt. Ltd.)
BANGALORE • CHENNAI • COCHIN • GUWAHATI • HYDERABAD
JALANDHAR • KOLKATA • LUCKNOW • MUMBAI • RANCHI
NEW DELHI

Published by :
FIREWAL MEDIA
(*An Imprint of Laxmi Publications Pvt. Ltd.*)
113, Golden House, Daryaganj,
New Delhi-110002

Phone : 011-43 53 25 00
Fax : 011-43 53 25 28

www.laxmipublications.com
info@laxmipublications.com

Economy Edition Price : **Rs. 350.00** *Only.* *Edition* : 2009

OFFICES

India

✆ **Bangalore**	080-26 61 15 61
✆ **Chennai**	044-24 34 47 26
✆ **Cochin**	0484-239 70 04
✆ **Guwahati**	0361-254 36 69, 251 38 81
✆ **Hyderabad**	040-24 65 23 33
✆ **Jalandhar**	0181-222 12 72
✆ **Kolkata**	033-22 27 43 84
✆ **Lucknow**	0522-220 95 78
✆ **Mumbai**	022-24 91 54 15, 24 92 78 69
✆ **Ranchi**	0651-221 47 64

USA

Boston
11, Leavitt Street, Hingham,
MA 02043, USA

FBU-2807-350-BUILD BUSI INTELL APP .NET **C—17416/09/04**

Printed at : Sanjeev Offset Printers, Delhi.

To Kate, Sophie, Jack, and Ellie.
Thanks for your patience, support, and love.

To Kate, Sophie, Jack, and Lilie
Thanks for your patience, support, and love

Contents

1 Business Intelligence

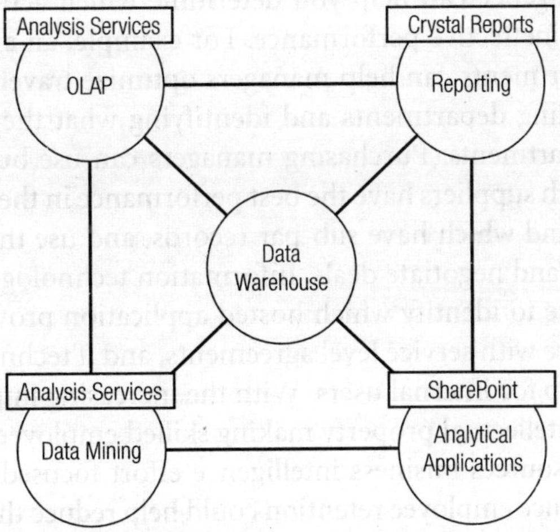

Data is the lifeblood of modern business. As computerized systems have spread throughout all facets of business, the amount of data collected has exploded. Data is captured in almost every one of our daily activities as consumers. Every time we check out at a supermarket, withdraw cash from an ATM, ship a package, or have our cars repaired, data is generated and stored about our activities as consumers. Wal-Mart alone has over 500 terabytes of data in their data warehouse in Bentonville, Arkansas, and it is commonplace for retailers to generate a million or more rows of data per day from their point of sales systems.[1] In addition to the data created by consumers, businesses that sell to other businesses also generate a tremendous amount of data. Most of this data ends up in some kind of transaction processing system as well. However, it has value only if it can be used to make better decisions.

Business intelligence allows you to pull all of this data together to help form a unified view of your enterprise that executives and analysts can use to generate insights and make better decisions. Business intelligence can yield many benefits.

Some of the most obvious uses of business intelligence help increase profitability by increasing product revenues. Little differences can mean a lot to the bottom line. According to consulting firm McKinsey and Company, increasing prices one percent while holding sales volume constant yields an eight percent improvement in operating profits for the average S&P 1500 company.[2] Business intelligence can help marketing managers identify those customers who might be willing to pay more and determine how to raise prices without undermining profitability.

On the cost side, business intelligence can help you determine where the money is really going in your organization, and spot ways to become more efficient. Business intelligence can help you determine which activities have disproportionate costs and ineffective performance. For example, an analysis of the travel costs for sales departments can help managers optimize travel spending by identifying the top spending departments and identifying what they are doing differently than other departments. Purchasing managers can use business intelligence to determine which suppliers have the best performance in the areas of quality and on-time delivery, and which have sub-par records, and use that information to steer procurement and negotiate deals. Information technology managers can use business intelligence to identify which hosted application providers are providing the best compliance with service level agreements, and if technical support is providing adequate help for internal users. With the increasing importance of non-tangible assets and intellectual property making skilled employees more valuable than ever, a human resources business intelligence effort focused on determining the factors that influence employee retention could help reduce the cost of employee turnover. Figure 1.1 contains a simple graph depicting the benefits of business intelligence.

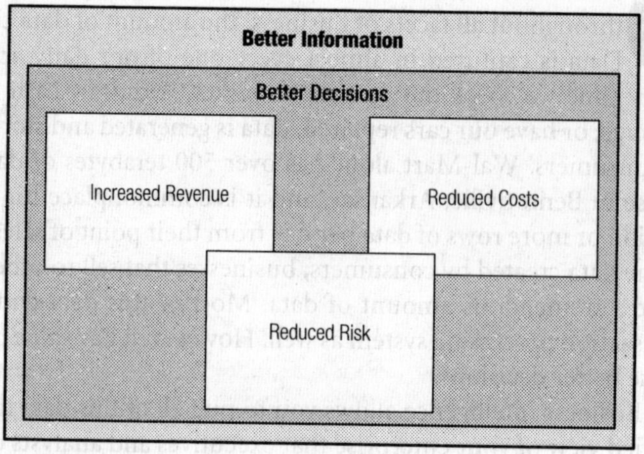

FIGURE 1.1 Benefits of business intelligence.

In addition to the benefits of increased revenues and operational efficiency, one of the most potent benefits offered by business intelligence is improved risk management capability. Whether you like it or not, your company is in the business of risk management. The ongoing transition from a product-driven economy to a service-driven economy, combined with globalization, technological innovation, and shifting regulatory environments, have conspired to accelerate the pace of change for almost every business. Given this increase in velocity, risk management is now vital for the long-term viability of every business. By enabling decision makers to see changes in the underlying business as early as possible, business intelligence provides the foresight to be proactive in the face of risk. This is in contrast to traditional financial reporting, which is focused on what has happened, not on predicting what is likely to happen in the future.

Large financial companies are well aware of the necessity of risk management, so they tend to practice sophisticated techniques such as value at-risk to determine their exposure to different market conditions. *Value at-risk* is a metric of financial risk that calculates the maximum loss for a given time period and level of probability. For example, a bank might calculate that the daily value at-risk of their portfolio is $20 million at a 99% confidence interval. This means that under normal market conditions there is only a 1% chance that the bank could lose more than $20 million. Other types of companies can benefit from a similar kind of analysis. Business intelligence makes that possible by collecting information about the value drivers for a particular business and allowing managers to create "what-if" analyses to see what the effects of changes are to the bottom line. Without the understanding fostered by a solid business intelligence foundation, you would have to guess at the real impact of various events.

There are many types of risks, and solid business intelligence can help manage each one. Traditionally, businesses focused on their financial risks such as uncollectible accounts receivable, obsolete inventory, and unfavorable exchange rate changes. There have been spectacular cases in recent years of large companies being felled by misunderstanding the risks of complex derivatives or rogue traders. Business intelligence can help managers spot financial problems before they have a serious impact on the bottom line. Although business intelligence is no substitute for proper financial control, the ready availability and widespread distribution of analyses makes early detection of errors, omissions, or outright fraud much more likely.

In addition to financial risks, firms face strategic risks that could imperil their very existence. A *strategic risk* is one of pursuing the wrong goals in the face of changing conditions. Causes of strategic risks include changes in laws and regulations, mergers and acquisitions, and actions by competitors. Failing to properly react to changes in these circumstances can result in considerable losses and possibly even an inability to continue as a viable independent business. Business intelligence can be used to help identify risks and create leading indicators that can be used to spot the emergence of events related to the risk before they affect the bottom line.

A third type of risk is operational risk. An *operational risk* is one of doing the right things in a suboptimal way. You may have a great strategy, but saddle your results with poor execution. Common operational risks are of plant capacity limitations or excesses, production accidents, and product development errors. Business intelligence focused on operational areas can help spot problems in those areas before they become critical.

Lastly, you may face *informational risks*. Without accurate and timely information, you may be flying blind, oblivious to the real issues that confront your business. The informational risks of having inaccurate information, unreliable access to information, and misleading reports can compound other risks and result in losses all on their own if these numbers are reported as correct when, in fact, they are not. Instituting a solid business intelligence platform is a very good start to improving the overall accuracy and relevancy of information provided to decision makers.

Because of the benefits that business intelligence can provide on the top and bottom lines, it represents an area of increasing importance for many businesses. Although there have been companies selling business intelligence applications for many years, recently, business intelligence has become much more pervasive. The business intelligence market has been very hot for a number of years, with the overall market growing from about $500 million in 1994 to about $3.3 billion in 2001.[3] Although this growth rate slowed down in 2002, it still grew during a period of overall contraction in information technology spending.

This strong rate of growth isn't surprising considering the impressive financial returns possible for enterprises implementing business intelligence solutions. IDC has found that business-analytics applications have an average five-year return on investment of 431 percent, with 63 percent of projects achieving payback within a two-year period.[4] Although these results must be taken with a grain of salt, they do indicate the high financial value of a successful business intelligence program.

Also fueling the growth of business intelligence has been the spread of enterprise application integration and e-business. Enterprise application integration tools make it much easier to integrate information between disparate systems and have reduced the risk and expense of business intelligence projects. The ability to conduct transactions with business partners has made it much more feasible to share knowledge gleaned from business intelligence with business partners, thus multiplying the beneficial effects of business intelligence. Retailers are especially strong in this area, with many retailers sharing extensive information about current and future demand and inventory levels with their suppliers. By making the whole supply chain more efficient, retailers and their close partners benefit.

BUILDING A BUSINESS INTELLIGENCE PLATFORM

To generate business intelligence you need to be able to collect, access, analyze, and share information. As in any other information technology project, business intelligence goes through a life cycle of eliciting the requirements, designing a solution, implementing that solution, and finally deploying that solution. However, for business intelligence, more effort needs to be spent constructing a platform for analysis rather than solving specific analytical problems. After the platform is constructed, the analysts and decision makers use the platform to gain insight into the reality of the business. Instead of a specific application, the focus is on creating a business intelligence platform. By constructing a business intelligence platform, you are essentially creating tools for knowledge workers to better understand the state of the business. The business intelligence platform will need to evolve to fit their goals and needs. Instead of a discrete project, business intelligence has the flavor of an ongoing program. Business intelligence has open-ended user goals: the user gains understanding about a particular topic.

This is in contrast to transactional applications that process the day-to-day activities of the business. Transactional applications tend to have closed-ended goals with very specific functions and requirements. There are many differences between constructing a typical transactional line-of-business application and those of a business intelligence platform. The primary difference is that with a transactional application, you know more about the entire process and the exact steps to be taken. The requirements for a transactional application tend to be more concrete and closed-ended. For example, a user of an order entry application needs to be able to perform a set of specified tasks (such as create an order, add items to the order, inquire on ship dates, and so on.) There may be some flexibility in the order of operations for creating an order, but in the end, the same steps need to be followed to create a complete order that can be filled and billed.

The differences between business intelligence applications and transactional applications are summed up in Figure 1.2.

STEPS TO SUCCESSFUL BUSINESS INTELLIGENCE

To create a successful business intelligence platform, there are five essential steps: understand the problem, collect the data, analyze the data, share the results, and act on the information. Of course, it isn't as easy as just following steps; you need to apply all of your technical, managerial, and political skills. In the following paragraphs, we will cover these five steps at a high level and revisit them in more detail as we proceed through the book.

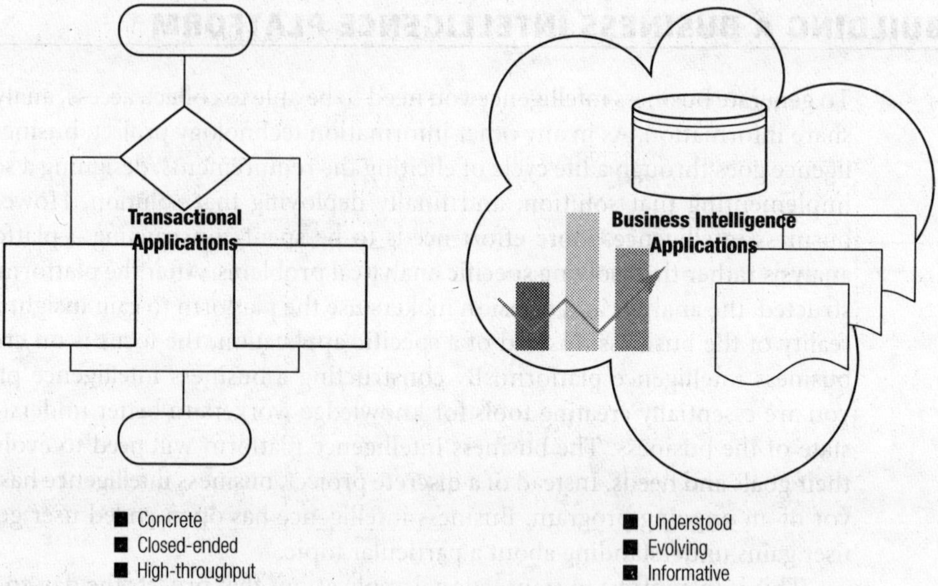

FIGURE 1.2 Comparison of business intelligence applications and transactional applications.

Understand the Problem

The first order of business in developing a business intelligence platform is to understand the priorities of the business. The kinds of questions that are important for a retailer are different than those for a manufacturer. Mapping the existing data flows and structures in your company is a great place to start. This will allow you to start to collect and identify the elements that are most important for your operations. Working closely with the business decision makers, you will need to determine where the greatest needs are. After determining the areas of most crucial need, focus on those elements first, with the goal of establishing a successful business intelligence platform in that area. A smaller project will reduce the time-to-benefit and provide a more immediate return on investment. From that beachhead of success, you can extend the platform into other operational areas in the order of importance to the business.

Collect the Data

The next thing to do is create a plan for collecting the data. To produce business intelligence, you have to have data. Not just any data, but accurate and timely data. Quality data is a critical success factor for a business intelligence platform. Most business data is in a lot worse shape than expected. Even if the transactional applications that have been collecting data have proper constraints and business rules, constant changes and incorrect but valid data undermine accuracy. The simplest example of incorrect but valid data is in address and contact information for customers. A well-written transactional application that collects this kind of data will know the relevant format for street addresses for the customer's country and region, but will not usually be able to determine if the data entered is correct. Simple transposition and data entry errors can turn 1234 Mockingbird Lane into 1324 Mockingbird Lane without the transactional system complaining about the error. Or a customer might move without informing the company, resulting in data inaccuracies.

Poor quality data undermines trust in the system. If decision makers don't trust the underlying data, they won't use the system, no matter how well designed. In addition to problems with data quality, you will need to grapple with integration issues among various systems in your enterprise. Most companies have a wide variety of applications that have evolved to meet various business needs over time. Important data can reside anywhere from a mainframe application to an Excel spreadsheet on a salesperson's laptop. Companies want best-of-breed applications and don't always coordinate purchasing across the board. Sometimes, executives want functionality that wasn't available at the time, so IT staffs have built custom applications. Often, these homegrown applications are preserved long after similar functionality is available in the marketplace. Divisions that were acquired (and even some of those that have always been with the company) often have different financial and operational applications than the rest of the company. In many cases, these systems will have different meanings for common terms such as "customer." In one system, a customer is simply any entry in the customer table. In another, a customer must have outstanding orders. Resolving definition issues among systems and departments can be a very time-consuming and potentially politicized undertaking. It is very important to have a total commitment from top executives before embarking on such a project. There will be situations when you will need their clout to break deadlocked impasses.

In addition to the more mundane complexities of sharing information among systems, you may encounter legal barriers as well. In many instances it is illegal or unethical to share customer transaction information across multiple systems. In these cases, the data might still be usable for analytical purposes if it is sufficiently redacted to make customers anonymous. The European Union has much stricter privacy and information-sharing laws than those of the United States. Any program designed to share customer information between European and US divisions of a corporation requires special scrutiny.

One of the most difficult things about a business intelligence initiative is gathering the metadata. *Metadata* is simply the data that describes your data. For example, the definition of a customer identifier as a nine digit number generated sequentially based on the date the customer was entered in the system would be a form of metadata. Without accurate metadata that is agreed upon by all the relevant parties, decision makers won't be able to discern the specific meaning of a given analysis correctly. Are sales gross or net? Does cost of goods sold include allocated overhead or not? Understandably, metadata is notoriously hard to define and track down. Attaining and keeping a consistent definition of enterprise metadata requires the full support and cooperation of your organization's subject matter experts and executives.

Analyze the Data

Next, you need to provide a way to analyze the data. This means understanding the users of your business intelligence platform. Most users will be primarily consumers of intelligence. A minority of users will produce most of the content consumed by the others. Although some data analysis tasks might be reserved for specialists, the tools to analyze the data should be placed as broadly as possible through the organization to get the most benefit. Those who really know the business are most able to benefit from access to business intelligence. This is in contrast to the older, more centralized style of decision support systems that were targeted at directing information up the chain to the executive suite so that good decisions could be handed back down the chain. In today's world of flattened hierarchies and empowered employees, the information and tools to analyze it need to be spread throughout the organization.

Share the Results

In addition to providing widespread access to the data, you need to provide the means to publish and share the results of analysis. The value of business intelligence is subject to strong network effects: it is more valuable the more people in the organization know about it. In addition, creating conduits for sharing and discussing the analysis makes the organization more capable of reacting to change.

Act on the Information

The whole purpose of business intelligence is to support better decision making. This means that the information needs to be in a format that is easily actionable and that facilitates change in the organization. Ideally, the same systems that give you the information for a decision allow you to act on it. Unfortunately, this is only rarely the case right now. But there is a strong trend underway to integrate the sources of business intelligence with the enterprise systems that are the nervous system of modern organizations. Often, this integration is taking place in portals that are increasingly becoming the centralized gateway to corporate intranets.

OVERCOMING OBSTACLES

Many opportunities to make use of information are missed. Much of the business intelligence infrastructure in use today is focused on static reports and was built to handle much lower volumes of data than is currently being generated. Many legacy decision support systems are too rigid to respond to rapid changes in business conditions. Often, reports are generated that answer questions that are no longer relevant. Much of this inadequacy is due to the gulf between information technology managers and line-of-business managers. Too often, technology managers don't understand the business well enough to produce applications that meet with the true business need for better information. On the other side, line managers often don't have a clear understanding of the possibilities and limitations of business intelligence. Both of these sides need to come together to successfully develop a winning business intelligence platform.

Business intelligence needs to satisfy decision makers and produce real business results. Many executives are not satisfied with the way information is currently delivered. According to a survey of executives at Global 3500 companies by the technology research firm Forrester, most are unsatisfied with the way they currently receive analytic information. Thirty percent of those surveyed thought their analytic software has significant gaps in usability. Twenty-two percent cited lack of detail as an issue, and 20 percent said data access and accuracy were not satisfactory.[5]

One of the easiest mistakes to make with any business information is to get too focused on the data and lose sight of where it fits in within the entire corporate value chain. The information needs to be presented in a way that makes sense to managers in the context of business process. Managers want the presentation of the data to be clear, attractive, and easy to understand. Managers are measured on their business competency, not on their ability to tease information out of an arcane business intelligence system, so careful attention to usability needs is critical. Keeping the learning curve flat, especially initially when people are kicking the tires on the new system, is essential. Of course, you will want to provide advanced capabilities for business analysts, but it is probably a good idea to hide that complexity from most managers until after they have experienced the value of the system. Then they might be willing to spend the time to learn how to get more value from the system.

It is also essential that the results of business intelligence allow decision makers to understand the story behind the numbers and produce insights into the true direction of the business. Business intelligence should highlight the significant trends and allow the juxtaposition of different elements to develop hypotheses. Simply deluging people with numbers is not adequate. Many people discern patterns much more readily from a well-designed graphical view of data than a simple tabular layout. At a minimum, highlighting of textual or numeric elements that are in some way out of the expected range will help decision makers gain insight into the true state of the business.

One common trap that business intelligence projects often fall into is that of describing what has happened, but offering very little in the way of predictions to help spot what might happen in the future. Many companies are in effect steering the ship by looking backwards at the information generated by their financial reporting. Financial reporting is usually one of the last things to happen in a business process. A careful selection of leading indicators to be measured and reported on can help spot trouble on the horizon well before it becomes a crisis. The goal in selecting leading indicators is to choose variables that are easily measured and have some logical connection to activities in the future. The goal is not to be 100 percent accurate, which is not even possible since we are talking about predictions of the future, but to detect consistent and predictable relationships between the leading indicator and the variable of interest.

The best business intelligence platforms don't come right out of a box, despite what some vendors would have you believe. There is a considerable effort involved in understanding the business environment and constructing a business intelligence platform suitable for your business. The specifics of implementation will differ for each organization and depend on the kind of information to be analyzed and acted upon, the quantity and quality of that information, and the budget that is available for creating a solution. As we have discussed, there are many technical, organizational, legal, and other issues that need to be dealt with to produce a comprehensive and useful business intelligence infrastructure for an organization.

Business intelligence applications, by their very nature, have huge amounts of data associated with them. In some cases, the amount of data that is stored and analyzed is truly staggering. Even though the data is stored in a way that is optimized for analysis, the sheer volume of data involved means that business intelligence processing requirements can be very intense. Decision makers don't want to be held up by their tools, and one of the biggest user frustrations with business intelligence solutions is slow performance. Even worse is the mistrust that can be engendered by unplanned downtime. Even planned downtime for data loading can be a big impediment to user acceptance of a business intelligence system. Since business intelligence applications and their primary users are so demanding, infrastructure should be carefully planned with respect to both availability and performance.

The overall difficulty of building a business intelligence solution is reflected in a finding by the David Consulting Group that says the delivery rate measured in function points per person-month of data warehousing applications was less than one half the rates of e-business applications.[6] Although this doesn't necessarily imply business intelligence applications are twice as difficult to build as e-business applications, it reinforces the fact that business intelligence applications tend to be complex to analyze, design, construct, and deliver.

MANAGERIAL CONTROL SYSTEMS

An essential change that business has undergone in the recent past and continues to experience is an overall acceleration of the pace of change. The forces of globalization and technological change have conspired to make the speed of business much faster than it was in the recent past. Just as a car needs a more sophisticated control system to be driven at high speeds if it is to avoid a potentially catastrophic crash, a business needs a more sophisticated control system if it is to be operated at a high speed to avoid calamity.

Managerial control systems are designed to use information to make strategic and control decisions, to encourage positive employee behavior, and to assess performance against goals. A managerial control system is closely aligned with a business intelligence platform. A managerial control system is focused more on the business controls and coordination that goes beyond the information systems that provide the information. That being said, it is virtually impossible to create an effective managerial control system without the use of business intelligence technologies. The goals of a managerial control system are to:

- Convey goals.
- Direct employee and partner actions.
- Communicate results of action.
- Facilitate evaluation of strategy.

The first piece of the managerial control system is to communicate the goals of the organization. Managers at the executive level decide on the strategic goals and the measures used to judge performance. Lower-level managers take the executive direction and determine a set of goals that can be done on a day-to-day basis by the employees of the organization. The results of these day-to-day activities are measured and compared to the plans to see what is going well and what isn't. A simplified schematic of a managerial control system is shown in Figure 1.3.

There are many variants on the managerial control system that could be used to effectively run an organization in a fast-paced market, but one thing they all share is the common theme of performance measurement.

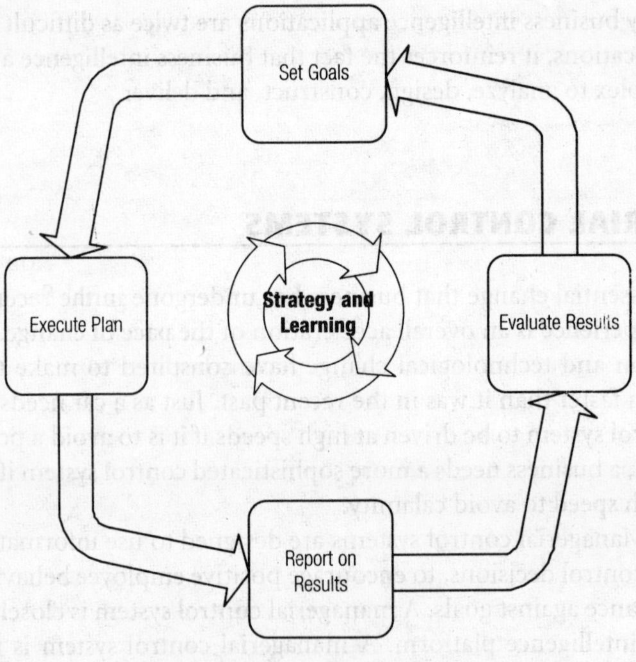

FIGURE 1.3 The feedback loop of a managerial control system.

Performance Measurement

You can't improve what you don't measure. Performance measurement is vital for the long-term success of any endeavor. In our complex world, everyone has multiple goals and mechanisms for reaching them. For example, in addition to financial performance goals, many firms place great importance on employee satisfaction and community contribution. Good performance measures are

Relevant: Related to the strategic and tactical goals of the company
Balanced: Balanced between short-term and long-term goals
Understandable: Easily comprehended by those it affects
Objective: Measurable without significant bias
Consistent: Used on a regular basis
Actionable: Affected by actions of employees

Both financial and nonfinancial goals are important. Financial measures tend to be lagging indicators, and by the time trouble is indicated by the financial results, it may be too late to recover. A focus on nonfinancial measures helps give a leading indicator of the firm's future health. Superior financial performance usually follows from good execution on nonfinancial areas first. One technique that can help achieve an equitable focus on both financial and nonfinancial measures is the balanced scorecard.

Balanced Scorecard

The *balanced scorecard* is a management technique that was developed in the late 1980s and early 1990s by Robert Kaplan and David Norton.[7] The balanced scorecard was designed to correct some of the managerial flaws that are created that come from too strict a focus on the financial aspect of a business, sometimes to the exclusion of all other aspects of company health. Instead of strictly focusing on the financial aspects of an organization, the balanced scorecard is designed to provide a view of the organization that takes into account more than just the financial measures. A balanced scorecard allows a company to translate strategy into action by setting goals and measuring activity from a variety of viewpoints. A balanced scorecard should start with the strategy of the firm and be aligned with the goals of the firm. What the balanced scorecard allows is the measurement and management of critical aspects of the company that contribute towards meeting strategic goals and objectives. Traditional financial measures fall short in this area because they are focused on the past. Typical financial measures answer questions about what happened last quarter. Relying solely on financial measures is like driving a car by looking at the rearview mirror; you have a great idea about where you have been but absolutely no clue about what you are about to run into. A balanced scorecard should include financial measures as well as leading indicators that point to the direction the firm is headed and how well the company is meeting its strategic goals. There are four perspectives in the canonical balanced scorecard:

- Learning and growth perspective
- Business process perspective
- Customer perspective
- Financial perspective

These four perspectives are related, and ultimately translate into strategic success. The organizational learning and adaptability fostered by the goals and measures in the learning and growth perspective drive business process improvements. The business process improvements that reduce cycle times, activity costs, and defects enable customers to be more satisfied with the company. Customer satisfaction, in turn, creates demand for the company's products, and engenders financial success as measured by earnings before interest and taxes (EBIT), and product-line profitability. In addition to the bottom line benefits, satisfactory financial results enable a company to invest in both people and processes to continue the virtuous cycle of improvement. The relationship between the different elements of the scorecard is illustrated in Figure 1.4.

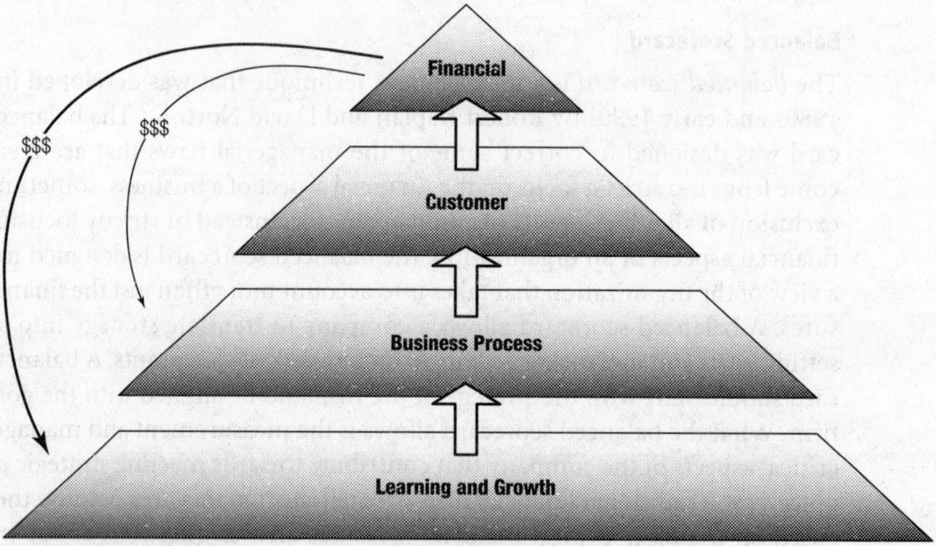

FIGURE 1.4 The relationship between the levels of the scorecard.

Learning and Growth Perspective

The learning and growth perspective looks at the knowledge contained within the company and the corporate cultural attitude towards learning and improvement. In the era of the knowledge worker, placing emphasis on the capacity of the organization to foster learning and improvement is vital. In a knowledge economy, the most valuable assets walk out the door each night. Retaining and enhancing the capabilities of workers is vital to achieving and maintaining a competitive advantage. The learning and growth of a company directly impacts the ability to achieve other company goals. Without a smart and motivated workforce, it is difficult to establish a business process that will enable customer satisfaction that will drive financial performance. Some typical measures that one might find in a growth and learning scorecard include training time, staff turnover, and staff satisfaction scores.

Business Process Perspective

The business process perspective looks at what the business does and how well the essential process is accomplished. Some typical measures that one might find in a business process scorecard include cycle time, defects, and activity costs.

Customer Perspective

The customer perspective evaluates how well the company is satisfying the needs and desires of its customers. If they are not being satisfied, they will eventually go somewhere else. Without customers, there is no company. Some typical measures one might find in a customer scorecard include market share, customer satisfaction scores, and number of customer complaints.

Financial Perspective

Finally, we have the financial perspective. Without proper attention to the needs of shareholders, a company cannot continue to exist. This includes both the traditional financial measures that are mostly historically focused, as well as forward-looking measures such as risk exposure and value at risk. The point of the balanced scorecard is not that financials are unimportant, just that they need to be evaluated in the context of everything else. Some typical measures one might find in a financial scorecard include contribution margin, cash flow, and order backlog.

Balanced Scorecard Success Factors

As a management tool, the most important aspects of implementing a balanced scorecard are non-technical.* However, automating the measurement and presentation of the scorecard is vital to the long-term success of the program. There are a surprising number of companies that can describe their strategies very well in terms of innovation, customer service, and the great people they have, but don't have the business intelligence capabilities to measure and create reward systems based on nonfinancial measures.

BUSINESS INTELLIGENCE TECHNOLOGIES

A business intelligence platform is made up of many interconnected technologies. Depending on the kind of knowledge to be gained and how it is to be acted upon, one technology might be more appropriate than another. In many cases, multiple technologies can be brought to bear on the same problem to yield even better results. In our tour of business intelligence technologies, we will cover many of the

*The most important aspect to the success of a balanced scorecard is that it is aligned with company strategy; corresponds with incentive programs, and has full commitment from top management. Achieving these goals is vital to the success of implementing a balanced scorecard. However, in this book we will focus on the technical facets of implementing a balanced scorecard. Excellent references about the managerial facets of implementing a balanced scorecard include *The Balanced Scorecard: Translating Strategy into Action* by Robert Kaplan and David Norton, and *Balanced Scorecard Step-by-Step: Maximizing Performance and Maintaining Results* by Paul Niven.

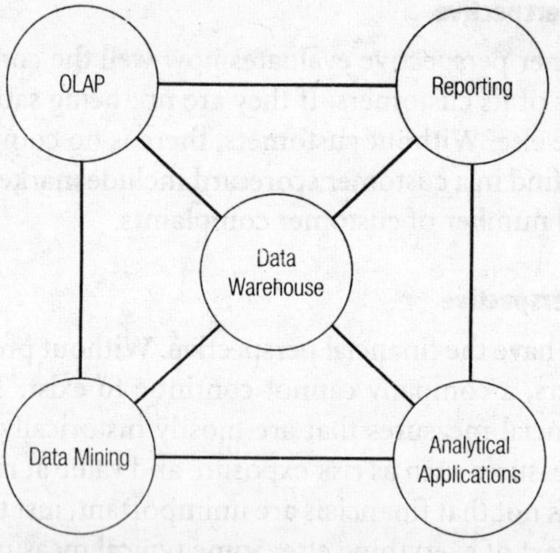

FIGURE 1.5 Business intelligence technologies.

basic building blocks for business intelligence. These are the elements of functionality that are common in many different business intelligence infrastructures. This is not a litmus test for business intelligence that says if you don't have an OLAP database you can't possibly be effectively applying business intelligence, just simply that these are some of the more commonly seen elements in business intelligence solutions today.

Although there are a multitude of possible taxonomies for business intelligence technologies, we will take the approach of discussing them in an order that is somewhat cumulative for building a business intelligence infrastructure. We will focus on the following technologies: data warehousing, OLAP, reporting, data mining, and analytical applications. In the balance of this chapter, we will introduce the technologies and begin to show how they fit together and into .NET.

Data Warehouse

A *data warehouse* is a foundation for business intelligence. The purpose of a data warehouse is to be a repository for consolidated and organized data that can be used for analysis. This data can come from a large variety of sources including online transaction processing (OLTP) databases, legacy systems, spreadsheets, and external sources. Data warehouses range from very, very large with many terabytes of data to smallish collections of a few megabytes. A *data mart* is a subset of a data warehouse that is focused on a specific area of interest. The term "data warehouse" is often used broadly to encompass both of these meanings. Bill Inmon defines a data warehouse as a collection of data that is subject-oriented, integrated, time-variant, and non-volatile. Its purpose, according to Inmon, is to enhance management's decision making ability."[8]

Subject oriented means that the data warehouse is organized around particular subjects instead of ongoing operations. For example, a data warehouse might have a section organized for the analysis of sales by date, product, and region. Contrast this to a database organized around ongoing operations. Operational data would have this same information stored in a set of transactional tables supporting point-of-sale and inventory applications. In general, the format of this data will be very suitable for the transactional applications that use it, but much less so for analysis outside of those applications.

A data warehouse is integrated because it contains data gathered from a variety of sources merged into a coherent view. Primarily, this means that data is collected from all of the transactional systems in the enterprise that have relevance to the subject. Even if a company has distinct sales systems across different divisions, in order to get a holistic view of company sales, all of that data needs to be brought together in the data warehouse. In addition to data collected inside the enterprise, sometimes data from outside the enterprise is included in the warehouse to improve the quality and analytical value of the data. Continuing with our sales example, the sales data might be augmented with external market research or demographic data to assist in analyzing and understanding sales patterns.

Time variant simply means the data is related to a particular time period. So, our sales data will have a date attached to it either directly taken from the transactional systems or as it is inserted into the data warehouse.

Nonvolatile refers to the static nature of the data after it is copied into the data warehouse. Unless a data error is found, the data isn't typically modified in the data warehouse. Instead, the data is maintained in the transactional systems, then copied to the data warehouse in a process called extraction, transformation, and loading (ETL).

A *data mart* is conceptually similar to a data warehouse. However, instead of being based on data across the entire enterprise, a data mart is a subset of corporate data that is targeted for a specific business department or set of users. This subset can be extracted directly from enterprise system data or from a larger data warehouse.

On-line Analytical Processing (OLAP)

Online analytical processing (OLAP) provides analysts with tools for exploring patterns and trends in multidimensional business data. OLAP analysis is often used to get a better understanding of patterns and trends in historical data and to analyze business performance across a variety of metrics and functional areas. Using OLAP tools, analysts can drill deep into data and find answers to complex and changing business problems. Multidimensional information or *cubes* can be organized into hierarchies that reflect business reality. For example, a sales organization might be broken down into regions and each region into a sales office. The reporting period for a company might be broken down into years, quarters, months, and weeks. Given those hierarchies, we should be able to answer business questions such as which sales office reported the highest total sales in the last quarter and which region had the largest increase in sales over this quarter last year.

In some cases, OLAP is provided by a relational database that has specially designed partitions and summaries to support queries. In other cases, OLAP is provided by a specialized data store that contains the data organized and summarized into multidimensional structures. Constructing a multidimensional store of your business data is a complex process, but also allows analysts to more easily answer questions about the business. For example, we might have a Sales cube that contains the information summarized around the hierarchies of sales regions and time. This would allow analysts to look at sales information that is broken down into any combination of sales regions and time that might make sense. If a promotion was run in the Southern region last summer, a query can be run to see if sales were higher in the Southern region last summer than in previous summers and if the percentage change in the Southern region was greater than changes in other regions. In this way, we can tell whether the promotion was a success or failure.

The hierarchy of categorizations is the *dimensions* of a cube. Although the term "cube" is used to describe the dimensions, this does not mean that you are limited to three dimensions as in a physical cube. Virtual cubes can have a large number of dimensions organized into hierarchical levels. Each level of a dimension is of a finer grain than its parent. Multiple hierarchies can exist for each dimension. In our sales example, the sales region dimension could be broken up into two hierarchies: the region-by-office hierarchy, which breaks down sales by region and sales office, and the region-by-country hierarchy, which breaks the sales down by region and country. These dimensions can be shared among different cubes to provide a common basis among the cubes. This is commonly done with dimensions sucn as Time so that monthly, quarterly, and annual reporting is consistent among different hierarchies.

The numerical elements that you are interested in gaining knowledge about are called *measures.* In our Sales cube, we might have measures for price, cost, and quantity. Measures are treated as a special kind of dimension that can be referenced as the "Measures" dimension. A *member* is an element in a dimension. A *calculated member* is a member with a value calculated at runtime based on the existing data in the cube.

Reports

The most basic level of business intelligence is provided by reports. Reports are the traditional backbone of conduits to communicate business information to decision makers. Back in the days when information systems were little more than back office data processing systems, inflexible "green bar" reports printed out from monolithic mainframe applications were the primary source of information for business decision makers. Things have gotten much better, and today, reports are much more flexible and useful.

The reason that reports are still important is that, despite the increasing velocity of the changes in the world, many of the decisions made in a business are fairly predictable and require predictable views of enterprise information. For example, no matter how sophisticated a business is, it is still useful to know how much cash came in the door during a specified period of time. Reports deliver these predictable business-focused views of critical information to broad user bases. In many systems, reporting on up-to-the-minute information is available on demand. But there are some needs that require reporting only at scheduled intervals—think of an end-of-day receipts report. The predefined reporting model allows a core set of report designers to create a base layer of content that provides information for common business processes. To provide some level of customization for reports, it is common to have report parameters that control the specific data set returned in the report. Parameters such as today's date can be set automatically or supplied by the user before viewing the report. Report design tools are used in the process of accessing data, applying business logic, and formatting the results to produce predefined or parameterized reports. Report design transforms raw data into information that can be understood and used by decision makers.

Data Mining

Data mining uses statistical techniques and artificial intelligence algorithms to discover patterns that are hidden deep in your data. Data mining can be a very deep and complex subject, but there are relatively simple algorithms that can be used to generate meaningful information out of a sea of data. Data mining enables you to discover previously unknown facts present in your business data. Statistical analysis, OLAP queries, and reports are used mostly to answer specific questions of your data, such as "Did our sales grow last quarter?". With data mining, you can sort through the data in search of frequently occurring patterns and detect trends in your data without having an *a priori* hypothesis about it. There are a variety of techniques used to mine data including associations, sequential patterns, and classifiers. You can extract both predictive and descriptive information via data mining. Predictive information can be used to tell you about future events you are interested in. For example, if you have a large quantity of information about your customers and what their buying patterns are, you can generate a predictive model that tells you what customers are likely to buy in the near future. In fact, this kind of predictive assessment is made about you all of the time. Credit scoring is a technique used by banks and other creditors to determine an individual's credit risk. It involves reviewing your personal and credit histories to come up with an assessment of how likely you are to default on a loan. Auto insurance companies have discovered that a credit score is also very predictive of your driving safety—those who are more likely to pay back loans are also more likely to be safe drivers. This relationship, and the discount that auto insurance companies offer to those with good credit, was discovered through data mining. Descriptive information can be used to more fully understand data. Descriptive data mining applies some structure to the data, allowing one to create descriptions of the data based on patterns and similarities.

Analytic Applications

Analytic applications are designed to automate data-intensive business processes, assisting end users with complex data analysis and manipulation. These applications help speed the process and increase the reliability and availability of information for decision-making purposes. Analytic applications are domain-specific solutions that enable decision makers to access, analyze, and act on information in the context of a specific business area. Often, they have a strong statistical basis and use industry-specific models. For example, the insurance industry will have detailed models that show their ratio of premiums to payouts and how those would be affected by various price changes and events. These applications typically use data warehouses and other analytical tools, and, for maximum effectiveness, should be integrated into enterprise systems to allow decision makers to act on their analyses in a seamless fashion. Building the analytical application is similar to building any other business application. However, given the strong visual nature of most analytical applications, and the potential of a broad user base, you need to pay special attention to usability. This requires more time and consideration than is given typically to line-of-business applications with a limited user audience. For example, a typical business case for a line-of-business application will be to enter a customer order. While an interface to support that activity needs to be well designed and well thought out, the number of possible paths is relatively limited. A business case for an analytical application might involve investigating the performance of various vendors. A business intelligence application like this involves many more paths for the user to take. For example, the application needs to have sufficient complexity to be capable of determining if an order is acceptable.

.NET BUSINESS INTELLIGENCE

We have defined a business intelligence platform as those components that, taken together, enable decision makers to do more with the information collected by the company. Not surprisingly, Microsoft® has products that provide the essential technologies for business intelligence. Throughout the rest of this book, we will look more in depth at each one of the key areas of business intelligence and what Microsoft .NET has to offer in each of these areas.

One of the trends in the history of the evolution of computing systems has been that application features tend to migrate to the operating system. For example, in the early 1980s, the operating systems of the day were text based with very primitive graphical display features. Some applications needed to have a more sophisticated appearance, so the developers of those applications built their own libraries for drawing menus, windows, and dialog boxes. Building a graphical library was difficult work, and it would often take as much effort to build the graphical libraries as it would to build the applications they were supporting. These applications would run directly on the text-based operating system and use their custom libraries for the display. Gradually, operating system vendors such as Apple®, Microsoft, and IBM developed graphical user interface (GUI) libraries that could be incorporated by application developers to save them the time and effort of writing their own GUI libraries. This trend has continued into the present day with the inclusion of more and more services into the base operating systems, with the result that developers can spend less time developing infrastructure and more time focusing on solving business problems.

A few things happened along the way that changed the dynamics of application infrastructure. The first, and most obvious, is the emergence of the Internet as the primary platform instead of the operating system. Companies started to build custom infrastructure to provide solutions on the Internet, similar to what had been done with GUI libraries in the early 1980s. In many cases, these custom solutions were for operations that could be performed across many companies such as searching, payment processing, and authentication. Initially, it was very difficult to reuse the solutions across different applications. To do so, you basically needed to hack a way to send the request for a search, for example, to the search engine site, and then bring the results back, parse them, and display them in the browser. This process would need to be repeated for each service you wanted to integrate into your Internet application. This was a very convoluted and complex process that was neither scalable nor reliable.

Instead of being supplied by operating system suppliers, the infrastructure for developing Internet-based services developed in the form of standards. In the late 1990s, standards to discover and connect to infrastructure services were evolving quite rapidly. These standards include XML (eXtensible Markup Language), SOAP (Simple Object Access Protocol), and UDDI (Universal Description, Discovery and Integration). To a large degree, XML is the linchpin of all the new breed of infrastructure standards. XML allows the expression of data in a standard format that is simple to parse and understand. SOAP uses XML to describe interfaces. UDDI is a way to discover and use interfaces available over the Internet. These standards make it much easier to use shared infrastructure across the Internet, but that does not take them the last mile to integrate with internal corporate systems. For that, software to translate SOAP messages into method calls on an operating system had to be developed. Initially, this software was developed independently and packaged separately from the operating system. Now, Internet services are being integrated into the very fiber of the operating system, much as GUI frameworks before them.

One of the main goals of .NET is to make it very easy to develop applications that can take advantage of Web Services. .NET allows Web Services to use the same component-oriented programming model followed by internal services. This means that the properties, events, and methods implemented by a Web Service can be used as if they were local. .NET allows programmers to use legacy applications wrapped in Web Services with ease. The developer no longer has to focus on the infrastructure behind the service. This allows greater attention to understanding and solving real business problems.

The kind of environment provided by .NET is ideally suited for the development of a business intelligence platform. By its very nature, business intelligence involves getting data out of heterogeneous systems and bringing it together. Web Services are an excellent way to provide some abstraction from the specifics of different systems and allow them to simply work together.

In addition to Web Services, other components of .NET include Smart Clients, servers, and development tools. The idea behind Smart Clients is to enable the creation of rich client interfaces that allow flexible access to information on PCs and other devices to give people the ability to get to and act on information at anytime, anywhere. Smart Clients allow you to build applications that can take advantage of all of the features of Windows®.

Microsoft .NET servers provide support for XML Web Services by providing an infrastructure for deploying and managing them. Microsoft includes just about every server product they ship in the list of .NET servers. For the purposes of a business intelligence platform, the most important Microsoft servers are SQL Server™ 2000, SharePoint™ Portal Server 2001 and Host Integration Server 2000.

We will cover SQL Server in depth as a centerpiece of a data warehousing effort. SQL Server 2000 is the primary technology for data warehousing in the .NET platform. SQL Server 2000 comes bundled with Microsoft Analysis Services, which is the core Microsoft technology for providing OLAP. In addition to providing multidimensional analysis, Analysis Services also allows you to create data mining models from both multidimensional and relational data sources.

We will discuss using SharePoint as a means to publish, share, and find information. Share Point provides a very flexible portal interface that can be customized to provide each user with a personalized view of the information that is important to him. In addition to the portal features, Share Point delivers document management, content indexing, and team collaboration features.

We will not cover other .NET Servers even though they can play a role in a business intelligence platform. In particular, Host Integration Server is an excellent way to allow you to build on legacy systems by providing easy data access to mainframes. BizTalk® server may also have a role in some business intelligence applications by enabling conversions from existing data formats to formats that would be easier to integrate with other systems.

The last element of .NET are the development tools and platform. Microsoft Visual Studio® .NET and the .NET Framework allow the quick construction of XML Web Services that integrate enterprise applications. Although we won't be discussing these tools in depth or providing a tutorial on their use, we will be using Visual Studio .NET to construct some of our sample applications. Visual Studio .NET comes bundled with a copy of Crystal Reports, which provides a good starting point for the development and deployment of reports. In addition, you can create your own custom Windows- or Web-based reporting tools quite readily with the tools available in Visual Studio .NET. The flexible interface and data access capabilities possible with Visual Studio .NET assists the creation of useful and compelling analytical applications. Knowledge management applications can take advantage of the excellent facilities provided for creating Web-based applications.

The components of .NET map quite well to the business intelligence technologies outlined earlier (data warehousing, OLAP, reporting, data mining, analytical applications, and knowledge management). In addition to the components that are more formally a part of .NET, Microsoft Office can make important contributions to a business intelligence platform. Office is an ingrained part of the daily lives of our users, and offers many capabilities that can be quite useful in the analysis of information. A diagram of how the .NET components map to our business intelligence taxonomy appears in Figure 1.6.

To weave the story together, we will create a .NET business intelligence platform for a fictitious specialty food manufacturer called Chocolate Pretzel Company. Chocolate Pretzel Company is a manufacturer of fine chocolate pretzels (no surprise there) that are sold in small food shops throughout the East Coast. The products for such a company are relatively familiar to most of us and we can readily comprehend the value chain of a simple manufacturing operation. This will allow us to discuss the technologies at hand without having to spend an undue amount of time explaining the business. This is not to say that food manufacturing is simple or easy to do well, but that it is more understandable to most people than say life insurance or pharmaceuticals. As we go through the book, we will continue to add detail to the operations of Chocolate Pretzel Company and the problems faced by management.

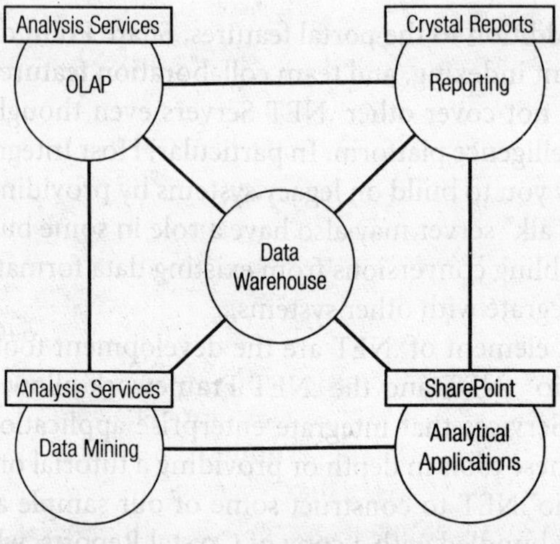

FIGURE 1.6 .NET business intelligence technologies.

We will begin by describing how we can create a data warehouse for the company in SQL Server. We will construct some ETL tools using .NET to automate the process of gathering Chocolate Pretzel Company data. After showing the ETL tools, we will construct an OLAP cube for analysis. Next, we will create an OLAP application that uses the data in the data warehouse and MDX (Multidimensional eXpression Language) to answer complex business questions and monitor key performance indicators. Building upon that core, we will build a reporting application using .NET and Crystal Reports. Lastly, we will tie things together by showing how to use a Web portal for distribution to decision makers throughout the enterprise.

SUMMARY

This initial chapter laid the groundwork for the balance of the book. We explored the importance of data analysis in today's business environment and showed how using business intelligence can contribute to the top and bottom lines of an organization. We also discussed how business intelligence plays a crucial role in managing risk by allowing the discovery of trends in data before the situation becomes critical. After covering these reasons for the rapid rate of growth in business intelligence solutions, we explored the steps it takes to create business intelligence in any organization: understand the problem, collect the data, analyze the data, share the results, and act on the information. Next, we moved to a discussion of some pitfalls in creating a business intelligence solution and an overview of the basic technologies used to create business intelligence. Finally, we closed with a high-level view of the business intelligence capabilities provided by .NET. The next chapter will explore in more depth one of the crucial technologies in business intelligence: the data warehouse.

END NOTES AND REFERENCES

1. Thomas, Owen, "Lord of the Things," *Business 2.0*, 2002. Available online at *http://www.business2.com/subscribers/articles/mag/0,1640,37760,00.html* (25 August 2003)
2. Marn, V.; Roegner, Eric V.; and Zawada, Craig C., "The Power of Pricing," *The McKinsey Quarterly*, 2003 Number 1, pp. 26–39.
3. Pendse, Nigel, "Market share analysis," *The OLAP Report,* 2003. Available online at *http://www.olapreport.com/Market.htm* (25 August 2003)
4. "IDC Study Finds Analytics Projects Yield 431% Average ROI." *IDC.* 2002. *http://www.idc.com* (25 August 2003)
5. Butt, Joseph L. Jr., "Turning Data Into Dollars," *Forrester,* 2001. Available online at *http://www.forrester.com/ER/Research/Report/0,1338,11283,00.html* (25 August 2003)
6. "Industry Data," *The David Consulting Group,* 2002. Available online at *http://www.davidconsultinggroup.com/indata.htm#productivity* (25 August 2003)
7. Kaplan, Robert and Norton, David, *The Balanced Scorecard: Translating Strategy into Action,* Harvard Business School Press, 1996.
8. Inmon, Bill, "Definition of a Data Warehouse," *Inmon Associates.* Available online at *http://www.inmoncif.com/library/articles/dwdef.asp* (25 August 2003)

2 The .NET Data Warehouse

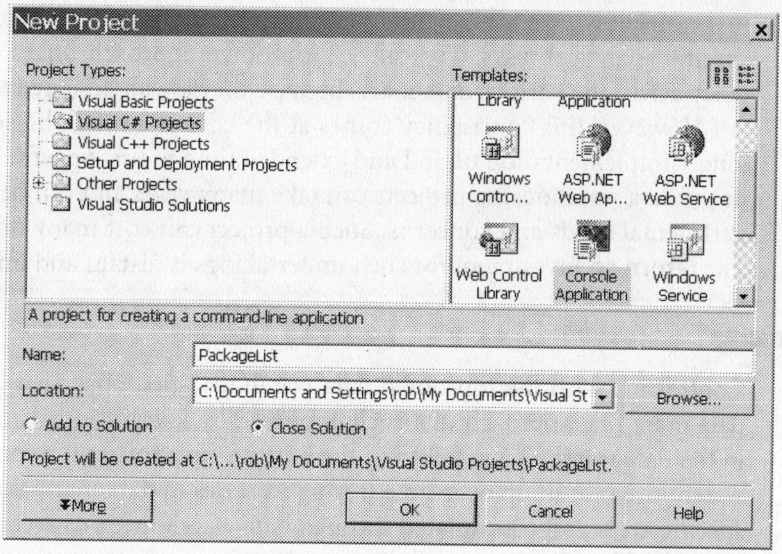

As we discussed in Chapter 1, one of the foundations of a business intelligence platform is a data warehouse. The data warehouse is crucial to a successful business intelligence effort because it is the location of the cleansed and standardized data. In this chapter, we will discuss data warehousing and then show how the tools provided with Microsoft SQL Server can be used to develop a data warehouse.

TOP-DOWN VERSUS BOTTOM-UP

In almost any complex endeavor, there are differences in opinion among practitioners and experts. Like system design in general, data warehousing has a historical divide into two camps: top-down and bottom-up.

Top-down

On the top-down side, we have the unified data warehouse advocates who believe that the proper way to construct a data warehouse is to create one centralized repository for the entire enterprise. Bill Inmon, the man who coined the phrase "data warehouse," is the leader of this group with his vision of a "Corporate Information Factory" that places the data warehouse at the center of all business intelligence activities.[1] This data warehouse, typically designed as a normalized enterprise data model, provides a single version of the truth and is very robust against changes in the business. From this central repository, dimensional data marts are created for specific analytical tasks. Typically, a top-down approach offers excellent consistency across the various data marts because they are all designed together.

However, this consistency comes at the cost of a much bigger project with a longer implementation period and extended time to first benefit. Monolithic, top-down data warehousing projects can take many years and can be inflexible to departmental needs and concerns. Such a project can cost many millions of dollars. The return on investment for such undertakings is distant and uncertain.

Bottom-up

Contrasting with the top-down data warehouse-first approach is the bottom-up data mart-first approach that is championed by Ralph Kimball, another luminary in the data warehousing field.[2] In the bottom-up approach, a comprehensive data warehouse is built up over time through a series of data marts that are focused on specific areas and coordinated through data warehouse bus architecture. Creating a standard bus for the overall data warehousing environment means that different data marts can be plugged together. The bus analogy stems from the usage of the term in personal computer hardware, where the inception of the ISA and subsequent PCI bus standards made it much easier to assemble pieces made at different times by different manufacturers in one personal computer.

Starting with a relatively limited and focused scope provides a way to kick-start a business intelligence platform. Since each data mart is a relatively small project, they can begin to deliver value more quickly than a larger data warehouse project. Once the data marts have begun to prove their worth to the enterprise, it is much easier to justify an ongoing investment in developing additional marts. Each additional application or process focus that is added will benefit the value of the whole through the network effect—each additional element adds perspective and insight to the other elements. This more evolutionary approach has the advantage of producing more immediate results at the long-term risk of not achieving successful integration among the data marts.

However, the fragmentation engendered by the bottom-up approach, if not managed properly, can lead us back to the bad old days of isolated stovepipe reporting systems and information confusion. Less structured and comprehensive business intelligence efforts are great for getting immediate return and matching investments to returns. But, eventually, the incongruities between departmentally focused efforts will stifle the flow of information across the entire enterprise and reduce the competitive advantage gained from business intelligence.

Hybrid Approach

These sides have come much closer in recent years. The top-down approach has accepted that it is necessary to deliver value more quickly and the bottom-up approach recognizes that a failure to adequately plan for future integration can be a costly mistake. The difference in these views is a little more than just semantic, but they do want to achieve the same end result: a flexible data repository that adapts to business changes and provides a single version of the truth. Finding a middle ground between these two approaches is essential. To make sure that these focused applications don't become isolated silos, careful attention needs to be paid to making sure that the strategic goal of providing information for the entire enterprise is not compromised.

To do this, you need to pay careful attention to developing enterprise-wide metadata. Be sure to establish and maintain a core list of common elements. Make sure to design a solid and extensible staging area for collection, cleansing, and distribution of your enterprise data. In addition to simply providing the means for business intelligence, make sure to measure utilization and results to establish return on investment. To help build and maintain momentum, publicize successes that are made possible by improved business intelligence.

DATA WAREHOUSE VS. TRANSACTIONAL SYSTEMS

A data warehouse is much different than a transactional system. Most of this difference derives from the different purposes of the two systems. Transactional systems focus on updating and adding single records, with the key element being fast and efficient processing of transactions. Data warehouses provide access to many records with a key element being very quick access to information for reporting and analysis. Since form generally follows function, the differences in design are not surprising. Many people coming to data warehouse design from transactional system design make the classic mistakes of ignoring these distinctions. Or, they make the even worse mistake of using a transaction system directly as a data warehouse.

To most effectively design a data warehouse, dimensional modeling is used to optimize the data for fast retrieval. *Dimensional modeling* is the process of creating a logical model that is optimized for query and analysis performance. In many cases, a data schema produced by a dimensional model of a system is much simpler than the schemas of the transactional databases supporting the same system. Although many people believe that dimensional modeling is a recent development, it has actually been around for quite some time. The first known references to what we now understand as dimensional modeling are from a joint General Mills and Dartmouth University research project in the 1960s.[3]

One reason for this relative simplicity is that data warehouses don't need to support transactions. Transactions greatly complicate the design of a database because of the critical properties that must be met to support transactions. The four properties that are generally agreed upon to be necessary to support transactions are:

- Atomicity
- Consistency
- Isolation
- Durability

Taken together, these properties are commonly referred to by their acronym: ACID. Systems professionals often say, referring to these properties, that their transactional systems have "passed the ACID test." It is no simple matter to design a system to properly support ACID transactions, and the resulting databases are less than optimal for generating reports of meaningful business phenomena.

Atomicity

Atomicity means that a transaction either completes in its entirety or not at all. There is no possibility that only a part of a transaction is completed. If only part of a transaction can be completed, then the whole transaction is undone. The canonical example of the importance of atomicity is the example of doing a transfer in a banking system. In such a system, the first account in debited and the second one is credited. If a customer attempts to transfer money from one account to another, there would be big problems if the transaction was left in a half-completed state. Either the customer would have the first account debited without the corresponding credit to the second account, which would make the customer unhappy. Or, the second account would be credited without the corresponding debit, which would make the bank unhappy.

Consistency

Transactions must preserve the internal consistency and integrity of the database. If the database satisfies all of its integrity constraints before the transaction, it must also satisfy those conditions after the transaction. Although there are many kinds of integrity constraints that are possible for a database depending on the type of application it supports, some constraints such as uniqueness of primary keys and referential integrity are consistently applied across all applications.

Isolation

A transaction must act as if it is running entirely on its own, even though there might be thousands of other transactions occurring nearly simultaneously. Basically, this means that the system behaves as if all of the transactions are conducted in series. In most cases, the isolation of transactions is supported by database locks. Managing table locking is a very important and complex part of the job of a transactional database system.

Durability

Durability means that the results of the transaction will not be lost in a system failure. Since many transactions in a database are performed between an enterprise and its customers, this is an important property. You would not want to charge customers twice for the same transaction, nor would you want to not charge them at all. This typically requires that the transactions be recorded to a disk immediately after they are completed, in the form of a log that can be restored in the event of a system failure.

Performance Impact

In most cases, transactional databases are in a highly normalized form that requires multiple joins to get to elements that are meaningful to business users. Although these joins make transactions more efficient by reducing the size of the tables that need to be locked for a given transaction, the presence of joins makes typical business intelligence activities, such as creating reports and analyses, more difficult and complex. Instead of dealing with tables that represent business entities, a strong knowledge of SQL is required to piece together business facts from a series of normalized tables.

In addition to the complexity of extracting business facts from normalized tables, reporting directly from transactional databases imposes a large performance penalty. Running complex queries on a live transactional system to support reporting and analysis can have a devastating effect on transaction throughput of the system. The biggest performance problems arise from database locking. As discussed earlier, the purpose of database locking is to prevent a record from being accessed simultaneously by two different database tasks. A long-running query might prevent transactional tasks from being processed and cause system bottlenecks, or a transaction might stop queries from being processed. Either way, the contention caused by additional queries will result in suboptimal response time for transactions.

Indexing is another area where the priorities of transactional processing and data warehousing collide. Since indexes add time to insertions and deletions (as much as 20%), databases designed primarily for transactional processing tend to have minimal indexes—potentially only on primary and foreign keys. Data warehouses, on the other hand, can benefit from many more indexes to facilitate retrieval of data. The drawback of slowed insertions and deletions does not impact data warehousing very much.

Different Uptime Requirements

In addition, due to their different usage in the enterprise, data warehouses and transactional systems often have different uptime requirements and backup and restore strategies. Transactional systems often have elaborate support for on-the-fly backup of the transactions (the D in ACID). Organizations spend great amounts of money ensuring that their transaction logs are backed up, often keeping mirrored systems that can resume operations almost immediately in the event of a failure.

On the other hand, data warehouses, since they operate with static historical data, can simply be backed up on a regular schedule. There is little chance that sales data from three years ago are going to be updated in the normal course of business. This means that there is little need to perform full backups on a data warehouse very often. Instead, it makes much more sense to use incremental backups when data is updated, and rely on periodic full backups. This might mean that recovery from a complete failure of the data warehouse would require a year's worth of incremental backups to be restored. But, this might be a cost-effective solution in many cases. Imposing unnecessary reliability requirements on data warehousing applications can result in increased cost that doesn't add value.

Operational Data Store

Transactional systems and data warehouses have dramatically different requirements, designs, and implementations. The *operational data store* represents a middle ground between these two extremes. An operational data store is typically a set of tables that support near real-time reporting on operations. A typical example of this is in a call center where customer data is stored in an easily retrievable de-normalized format to expedite the process of servicing customer inquiries. Although this isn't a full data warehouse, it does facilitate some analysis. Most importantly, an ODS removes the burden of supporting queries from the transactional system. Figure 2.1 shows how an operational data store might fit in with a call center application.

The operational data store is sort of halfway between a transactional system and a data warehouse. In general, they are designed to directly support operations and

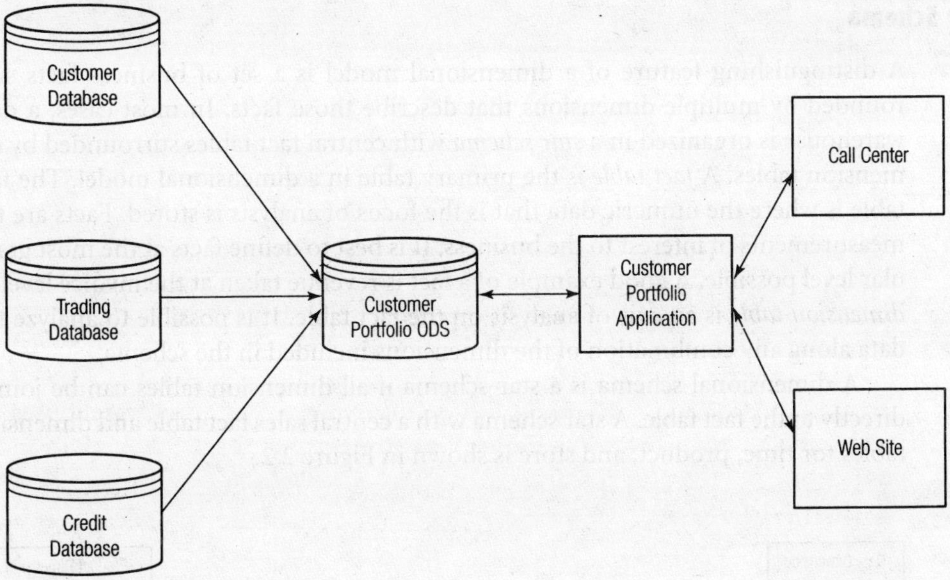

FIGURE 2.1 Operational Data Store.

not perform ad hoc analysis. But they are often an excellent source of data for a data warehouse since they are typically a first level extract of data from a transactional system and contain information that is directly related to the business. We won't focus on operational data stores in this book, but if you do have one in your organization, you should be aware that it can be very useful as a starting point for building a data warehouse.

DIMENSIONAL MODELING

Now that we've highlighted the differences between transactional systems and data warehouses, we will explore dimensional modeling in some more depth. As noted earlier, dimensional modeling is the process of creating a logical model that is optimized for query and analysis performance and ease of use. Dimensional models are the foundation for a well-constructed data warehouse. They have proven to be very robust over time, and, because they are organized around elements that are important to the business, they provide decision makers with an understandable and flexible platform for ad hoc queries and analyses. This simplicity and understandability is one of the best features of the dimensional model.

Star Schema

A distinguishing feature of a dimensional model is a set of business facts surrounded by multiple dimensions that describe those facts. In most cases, a data warehouse is organized in a *star schema* with central fact tables surrounded by dimension tables. A *fact table* is the primary table in a dimensional model. The fact table is where the numeric data that is the focus of analysis is stored. Facts are the measurements of interest to the business. It is best to define facts at the most granular level possible. A good example of a fact is revenue taken at the invoice level. A *dimension table* is an axis of analysis on the fact table. It is possible to analyze the data along any combination of the dimensions included in the schema.

A dimensional schema is a star schema if all dimension tables can be joined directly to the fact table. A star schema with a central sales fact table and dimension tables for time, product, and store is shown in Figure 2.2.

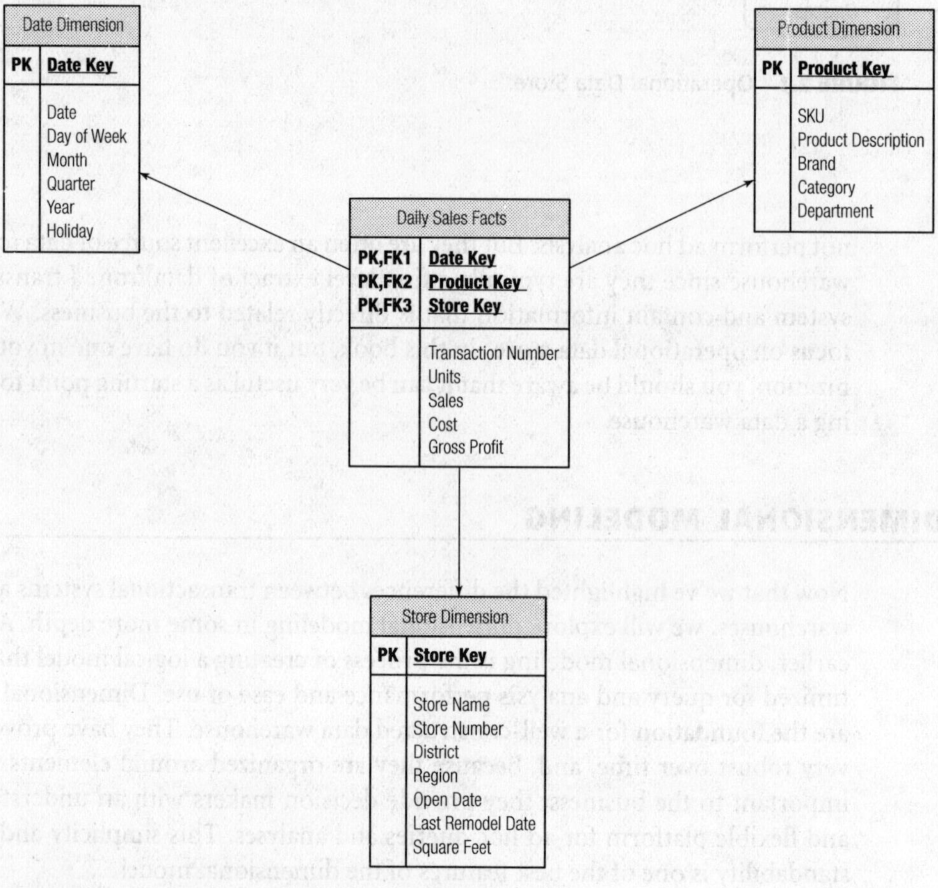

FIGURE 2.2 A simple star schema for retail sales.

In Figure 2.2, note that the central fact table has multiple foreign keys that join the facts directly to the primary keys of the dimension table. The facts themselves are specific numeric columns in the fact table. It would be possible to lump everything together into one table by collapsing all of the dimensions into one flat table, but this would be a very broad table that is less flexible in the face of change. Quite often, it becomes necessary to add dimensions after the fact table has already been constructed, but the single table approach would make this much more difficult. The dimensions are usually thought of as independent facets of a transaction. The dimensions are rarely strongly statistically independent, but are instead logically independent. For example, customer and store would often be statistically correlated because shoppers would tend to shop at the same stores. However, they are logically independent in that an analyst might be interested in partitioning by customers or stores or both.

Sometimes, a transaction in the fact table will have one or more dimensional elements missing. For example, if you have a promotions dimension, some products may be sold without an associated promotion. In this case, instead of setting the promotions foreign key in the fact table to null, it is preferable to add a "No Promotion" record in the dimension table and set the foreign key to point to that record. This makes the representation of no value consistent with the rest of the data and makes querying and analysis easier.

Slowly Changing Dimensions

These dimensions have a tendency to evolve over time. This phenomenon is called *slowly changing dimensions*. Slowly changing dimensions present a problem because the axes of analysis can change over time. A common change is a reorganization of the sales structure. For example, if the sales regions are changed, then salespeople may be reassigned across those different regions. So an analysis of the "new" Eastern region might not include sales from the same salespeople as the "old" Eastern region.

The word "slowly" refers to the speed of change compared to the fact table. Fact tables typically change with every update to the data warehouse. Dimensional changes, however, occur on a periodic basis. Although a change such as a sales force reorganization may occur all at once, the structure of the sales force dimension still changes more slowly than the data in the sales fact table.

Ralph Kimball, in *The Data Warehouse Toolkit: The Complete Guide to Dimensional Modeling*, proposes three different strategies for handling changing dimensions. He categorizes the solutions into three types, which he calls Type One, Type Two, and Type Three.

The strategy for *Type One* is to simply replace the data in the dimension table with the new data. Replacing the data is very appropriate if the old data was erroneous or it is unlikely that the changes will materially affect important analyses.

However, simply replacing the data makes it impossible to do an apples-to-apples comparison of old data vs. new data. So, following the sales example, it would be impossible to analyze sales in the old sales structure since it would no longer be present in the database.

The second strategy, *Type Two*, adds the new data into the dimension table while preserving the old data. In this case, we would add a new row to the sales table for the new Eastern region and record new sales data against it. This preserves the old structure and allows analysis of the old vs. new structure. This strategy can lead to a lot of data in dimension tables, since the old records are kept in the table. Since dimensional tables are orders of magnitude smaller than fact tables, this is not usually a huge problem.

Type Three preserves a version of the history by adding it to the dimension record. For example, to preserve the category changes for a product, you would have a field for the old category and the date it was changed. This strategy has the advantage of preserving the old data for analysis across one change, but can't support multiple changes in the data. In addition, queries to analyze data across old and new values can be complex.

Each strategy for handling slowly changing dimensions has its place. For correcting erroneous entries or information that does not need to be tracked over time, the simplicity of the Type One solution has the most appeal. For changes that are separable over time, a Type Two solution is the most sensible. Finally, for changes necessitating the ability to find the previous values and analyze them, a Type Three solution is appropriate.

Shared Dimensions

It is a typical analysis requirement to provide consistent dimensions across different subjects. For example, it is useful to be able to query on sales and purchase orders over the same time and product dimensions. Since sales and purchase orders are different business processes and have different facts, they will be stored in different fact tables, but would share the time and product dimensions. Careful modeling of your bus architecture will result in the sharing of as many dimensions as possible. Sharing dimensions over multiple fact tables is sometimes called a fact constellation. In a very complex organization composed of multiple fairly-independent business units, it might not be possible to cover the entire organization with a large set of shared dimensions. Some might not share any other dimensions except time, which can usually be consistently mapped among different subjects.

Sometimes, dimensional designers are tempted to create snowflake schemas. A *snowflake schema* is like a star schema, except one or more dimension tables are not joined directly to the fact table. Instead, they must be joined through other dimension tables. A schema that has been snowflaked along the product dimension is shown in Figure 2.3.

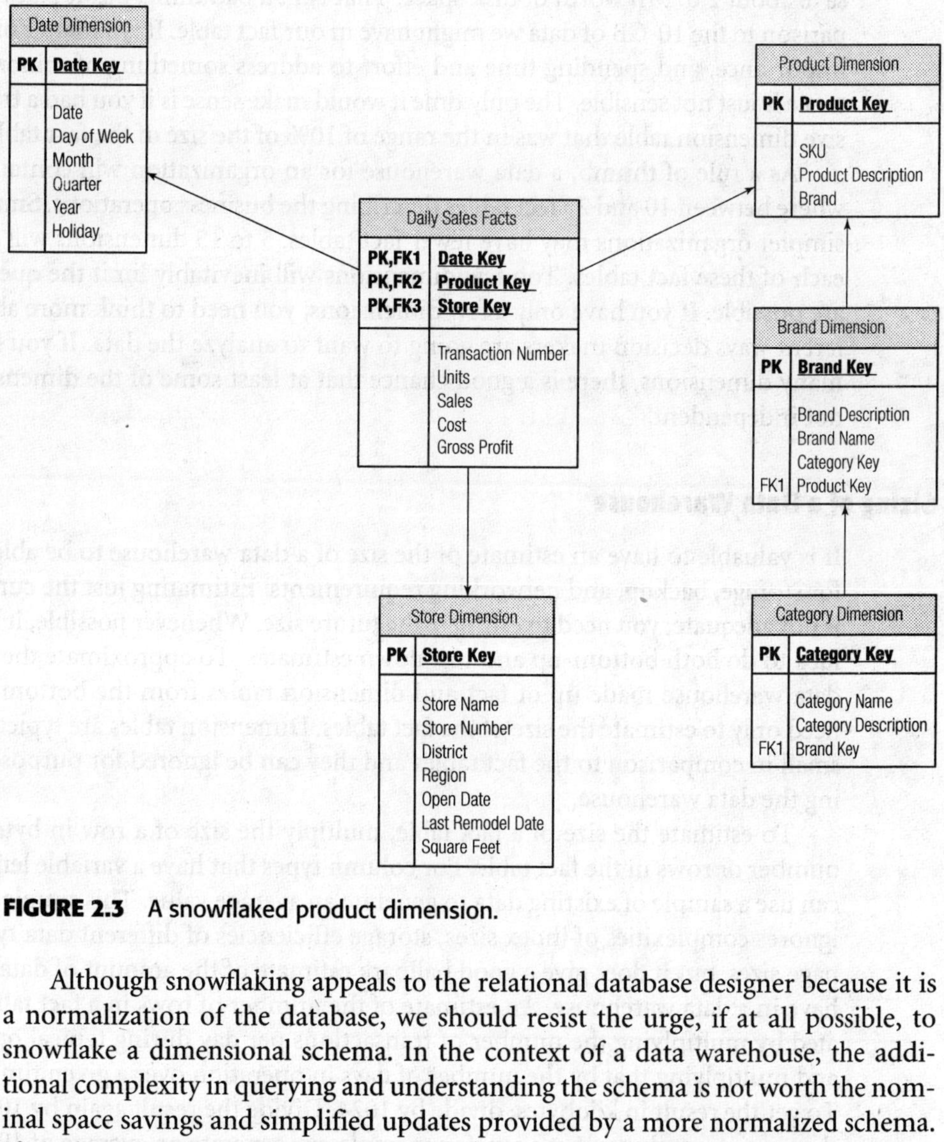

FIGURE 2.3 A snowflaked product dimension.

Although snowflaking appeals to the relational database designer because it is a normalization of the database, we should resist the urge, if at all possible, to snowflake a dimensional schema. In the context of a data warehouse, the additional complexity in querying and understanding the schema is not worth the nominal space savings and simplified updates provided by a more normalized schema. If you have a subject matter expert look at a pure star schema, he will almost always be able to identify the process that is captured in the design. The same is not true for a heavily snowflaked design. Database experts have no problem understanding multiple levels of foreign keys, but the abstract concept of keys tends to confuse most business decision makers.

Compared to the sizes of the fact tables, the size of the dimension tables is inconsequential. If we have a 100,000-row product dimension table and we save 28 bytes per row by replacing a 30-byte category description with a 2-byte code, we will save about 2.67MB worth of disk space. That isn't a bad thing, but it pales in comparison to the 10-GB of data we might have in our fact table. It is a matter of relative importance, and spending time and effort to address something of minor importance is just not sensible. The only time it would make sense is if you had a truly massive dimension table that was in the range of 10% of the size of the fact table.

As a rule of thumb, a data warehouse for an organization will contain somewhere between 10 and 25 fact tables describing the business operations. Smaller and simpler organizations may have fewer fact tables. 5 to 15 dimensions will describe each of these fact tables. Too few dimensions will inevitably limit the queries that are possible. If you have only a few dimensions, you need to think more about different ways decision makers are going to want to analyze the data. If you have too many dimensions, there is a good chance that at least some of the dimensions are not independent.

Sizing of a Data Warehouse

It is valuable to have an estimate of the size of a data warehouse to be able to plan for storage, backup, and networking requirements. Estimating just the current size is not adequate; you need to estimate the future size. Whenever possible, it is a good idea to do both bottom-up and top-down estimates. To approximate the size of a data warehouse made up of fact and dimension tables from the bottom up, you need only to estimate the size of the fact tables. Dimension tables are typically fairly small in comparison to the fact tables and they can be ignored for purposes of sizing the data warehouse.

To estimate the size of a fact table, multiply the size of a row in bytes by the number or rows in the fact table. For column types that have a variable length, you can use a sample of existing data to generate an average value. This simple estimate ignores complexities of index sizes, storage efficiencies of different data types, and page sizes, but it does give a good ballpark estimate of the amount of data you will have in a data warehouse. An estimate of the number of rows in a fact table is created by multiplying the number of transactions per day during typical operations and multiplying that by the number of days in operation over a given time period. To get the result in kilobytes, divide by 1024. Divide the result again by 1024 to get the size in megabytes. Let's say, for example, we generate an average of 10,000 line items of point-of-sale data every day. For the design we just put together for the central fact table, an average line of point-of-sale data is 316 bytes in length, so each day we are generating 3,160,000 bytes of data, or a little over 3-MB. If we operate

365 days a year, that amounts to approximately 1095-MB per year, or a bit over 1-GB of data.

A different way of calculating the size of a data warehouse that is related directly to sales information is to start with the top line financial number for a given unit of time and divide by the amount of the average sale. As an example, let's say we have top-line revenue of $50 million per year with an average point-of-sale line item of $15. That means we generate approximately 3,333,333 line items of data per year. Multiplying by the same length we used before, 316 bytes, we arrive at a total of 1,053,333,333 bytes, which is close enough to our bottom-up estimate that we can feel pretty comfortable that we are talking about storing about 1 GB of new data per year.

EXTRACTION, TRANSFORMATION, AND LOADING (ETL)

Source data from transactional systems is brought together in data warehouses though the process of extraction, transformation, and loading (ETL). ETL tools are responsible for the cleansing and translation of raw data from its native format in transactional systems and loading it into data warehouses. Basically, they convert the raw inputs from the transactional systems into something that can be analyzed in a data warehouse. An overview of the ETL process is presented in Figure 2.4.

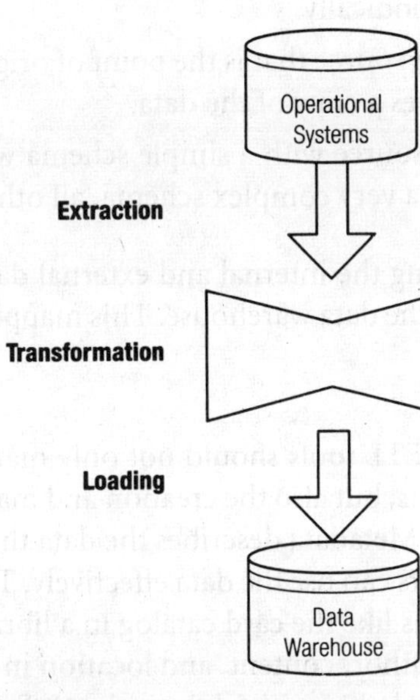

FIGURE 2.4 The ETL process.

As corporate information systems have become more complex, so has ETL. In many cases, ETL tools need to support many different systems and applications spanning from large-scale Enterprise Resource Planning (ERP) and Customer Relationship Management (CRM) systems, to electronic commerce applications to homegrown operational applications. In addition, ETL tools need to support obtaining data from external sources. External sources can add a lot of analytical value to a data warehouse by providing information on industry benchmarks and standard performance. This information can be used in comparing performance against industry norms or augmenting the analysis that is possible with internal data only. An example of useful external data is financial information from credit scoring bureaus such as Dun and Bradstreet. Incorporating this data into a customer table would enable analysis of the data by customer revenue, credit rating, and other categories.

The first step to ETL is identifying the sources and the data that they provide. If there are multiple sources for the same data you will need to evaluate each of the sources on the basis of the following:

Correctness: Some systems have more accurate data than others.

Completeness: Some sources contain an entire fact or dimension table, while others might contain just a subset. It is easier to work with systems that contain all of the data.

Timeliness: A source that is updated continually is better than one that is updated only periodically.

Origination: A source that is the point of origination for the data is better than one that receives a copy of the data.

Simplicity: A source with a simple schema will have simpler conversion code than one with a very complex schema, all other things being equal.

After identifying the internal and external data sources, you will need to map the source data to the data warehouse. This mapping is part of the role of metadata.

Metadata

A complete set of ETL tools should not only manage the integration of heterogeneous environments, but also the creation and management of metadata. Metadata is data about data. Metadata describes the data that exists in the data warehouse so that decision makers can use the data effectively. The usual analogy used to describe metadata is that it is like the card catalog in a library. The cards describe the books in terms of their author, content, and location in the stacks. Without the card catalog (or its modern computerized equivalent), finding a book in a library would be a hopeless task. How would you know which books addressed a certain subject? If you could find out which books were relevant, how would you locate them in the library? Searching for the proper book would be a tedious process of trial and error.

In terms of business intelligence, metadata has nothing to do with books, but it does provide the same benefits as a card catalog. Instead, the metadata describes the data kept in the data warehouse and in transactional systems. The information captured about the data is everything from technical details such as size and data type to the definition in terms of the business. The metadata helps people understand which information to use for which purposes and where to find it. For example, what does net profit on a line of point-of-sale data mean? Is it just the cost of goods subtracted from the selling price or is some element of allocated costing used in the calculation? Without metadata, the only way to know would be to recalculate it yourself and compare the results, or dig through source code to see how it was calculated. Neither of these methods is very efficient or appealing.

Metadata has been around for a very long time in the form of database schemas and data-flow diagrams, but the emergence of widespread business intelligence has made metadata a much more visible and important factor. Metadata used to be predominantly technical metadata that provided developers and technical staff information on where the data comes from and how it is to be maintained. It was essential to the ongoing operation of the data warehouse. Examples of technical metadata include:

- Logical data models
- Physical data models
- Transactional systems feeding data warehouse
- Identification and mapping of source system fields
- Transformations performed on source data
- Security information
- Program names and descriptions
- Versioning information
- Extraction schedules and logs

Business metadata, on the other hand, provides business users with a roadmap for accessing data in the data warehouse. Solid business metadata allows the decision makers to make better use of the information by reducing the search times for specific data and increasing the trust level in the data. Examples of business metadata include:

- Subject areas
- Table names with business definitions
- Field names with business definitions

- Description of field mappings and transformations from source system
- Confidentiality and security rules
- Data owner
- Data refresh dates and schedules

Metadata is very difficult to gather, organize, and maintain. The gathering of metadata is a very time-intensive task and, to be done right, requires interviewing business users to find out how the data is calculated and used. Information systems departments being what they are, there is always a search on for a silver bullet that will protect us from having to talk to actual business users, but there is no substitute for directly interviewing subject matter experts when it comes to creating metadata.

Even after the metadata is gathered and codified, it tends to change at the speed of the business. New business models and systems change the calculation and use of the metadata continuously. A common pitfall is to come out of the gate at the beginning of a data warehousing project and create an excellent initial repository of metadata that becomes outdated as soon as the excitement of the new project wanes. Outdated metadata is often irrelevant, or even worse, misleading.

Data Preparation and Cleansing

Data cleansing is an important factor in a successful data warehouse. Data cleansing checks data for errors such as duplication, incorrect spelling, and unrecognized abbreviations. As data volumes have grown, so has the volume of errors in data. Business intelligence, just as most systems, follows the "garbage in, garbage out" principle. Even the best software solution can be made irrelevant by presenting bad data. As soon as decision makers lose faith in the accuracy of a business intelligence system, the system becomes worthless. It is difficult to recover a reputation for accuracy once it is lost. Unfortunately, it is very easy to introduce poor quality data into a data warehouse.

If you enter your source data into a transactional system with 97% accuracy on each field, with a customer record consisting of 10 elements (first name, last name, first address, second address, city, state, zip code, phone number, fax number, and e-mail address), you will have 300 errors per 1000 customer records. And that is not the worst of it. Despite your best efforts, data is a perishable good and it will spoil over time. For example, about two percent of customer records become obsolete in a month because people move, change marital status, die, and/or experience other changes to their contact information.[4] The same dynamic applies to inventory and point-of-sale information, as vendors add new products and discontinue old ones.

In addition to the dynamic nature of data, business rules and systems change over time, resulting in even more inconsistencies in data. Some of these may be inconsequential, but others can cause real problems. The Data Warehousing Institute has estimated that poor quality customer data alone costs $611 billion a year in excess postage, printing, and staff overhead.[5] In addition to those direct costs, the costs of misaligned promotions and lost customer loyalty could be even greater.

Before data can be added to a data warehouse from a transactional system, it must be prepared and cleansed. One of the easiest ways to facilitate this operation is to create a database that is separate from the data warehouse, to use as a data preparation area. This holding area is where you can start to transform the data from transactional data to warehouse data.

Some common issues encountered when moving data from transactional systems to a data warehouse include:

Date mapping: Date fields need to be mapped into date dimension tables.

Field lengths: Different transactional systems might have different field lengths for common fields. The data warehouse needs to use a common length.

Data types: The same field can be stored as different types in different databases. The data warehouse needs to use one data type.

Encodings: Transactional systems might map values to different codes. For example, some use T and F for true and false, and some use 1 and 0.

Units of measure: Transactional systems might deal in different units. A warehouse application might deal in cases, while a point-of-sales system might work with individual units.

Duplicates: Transactional systems might have duplicates of some data. These need to be reconciled.

Capitalization: Transactional systems might use different standards of capitalization.

Missing data: Systems might use different conventions for missing data.

These are by no means the only errors that might be encountered when moving data from transactional systems to a data warehouse. In fact, data transformation for a data warehouse is one of the most challenging tasks in a data warehousing project, sometimes taking more than half of warehouse-development efforts.

Transformation can involve some manual steps to reconcile inconsistent or ambiguous entries. These should be avoided if at all possible since they tend to be an avenue for errors and can be a great expense in the ongoing operations of the data warehouse. A significant number of manual interactions is a good indicator that the source data might be too rough for use in the data warehouse without changes to the source system.

If the data is in poor condition, it might be easier to make changes to the source systems than to try to fix all of the problems in the ETL process. However, attempting to fix transactional systems might be a potent distraction to the primary purpose of a data warehousing effort and should be done only as a last resort. It is usually easier to attack the problem by using ETL tools. However, sometimes the problems are intractable and must be remedied at the level of the transaction system. Since this will halt progress on the data warehousing project until the problems are resolved, this is definitely a risk to keep in mind when planning a data warehousing project.

Loading Data

After you have decided on your data sources and created your transformation and cleansing processes, you are ready to load the data into the data mart. It makes the most sense to load the dimensional data first and then load the fact table that references the dimensional data through foreign keys. You have to make sure to preserve database integrity when loading a data mart, so if you are using a bulk loading facility such as SQL Server's Bulk Copy Program (BCP), you should make sure it is configured to enforce referential integrity on inserting data. As data is loaded, the indexes will need to be recalculated. If you are loading more than 10 to 15 percent of the rows, it makes sense to drop the indexes to facilitate quick inserts and then rebuild the indexes after the data has been loaded. It usually makes sense to load data marts one at a time during off hours so that you impact performance of transactional systems as little as possible.

There are different techniques available for the sometimes difficult task of detecting data changes for the purpose of updating data warehouse data. Some of these are:

Snapshot: Compare source data with a prior copy.

Trigger: Use a trigger to update the data warehouse as transactions occur.

Transaction: Use the transaction log as the basis for updates to the data warehouse.

Full: Create a complete new copy of the source data.

DATA TRANSFORMATION SERVICE

Microsoft SQL Server includes a tool that supports data extraction, translation, and loading called Data Transformation Service (DTS). Although there are competing stand-alone products that offer a more complete ETL solution, DTS does a good job of providing support for relatively simple data warehouse migration tasks.

In many cases, DTS will be up to the task of creating an ETL solution that will meet your needs.

DTS provides capabilities to import, export, and transform data among one or more data sources. DTS can connect to any data source that is supported by OLE DB (Object Linking and Embedding DataBase), a common standard for data access. Any data source that supports ODBC (Open Database Connectivity) can be accessed through the OLE DB Provider for ODBC.

DTS solutions are bundled as *packages*. A package can contain any of the four types of objects:

Connections: Specify the source and destination for the data to be moved with DTS.

Tasks: Specify the actions that occur during the package execution.

Transformations: Map data from the source to the destination.

Workflow: Specifies the precedence and constraints of the tasks in the package.

Import/Export Wizard

A DTS package can be built in a number of different ways. The first and easiest way of creating a DTS package is to use the DTS Import/Export Wizard. The tool takes you through the process of creating an import or export between diverse data sources in a step-by-step fashion. The steps in the Import/Export Wizard are shown in Figure 2.5.

The Import/Export Wizard can use many different kinds of data sources and destinations:

- SQL Server
- OLE DB and ODBC
- Text files
- Microsoft Excel spreadsheets
- Desktop databases including Access, Visual® FoxPro, dBase, and Paradox®

The data to be copied can be either from entire tables in the source, or taken from a query. In addition to simply copying the data to the destination, you can perform custom transformations using scripts. Scripts are a powerful and simple way to perform transformations. In many cases, script transformation will be all that you will need to create your ETL applications.

The non-compiled nature of scripting is a double-edged sword when it comes to transformations: the simplicity with which you can create and update the script is counterbalanced by slow execution. If you have a need for greater performance

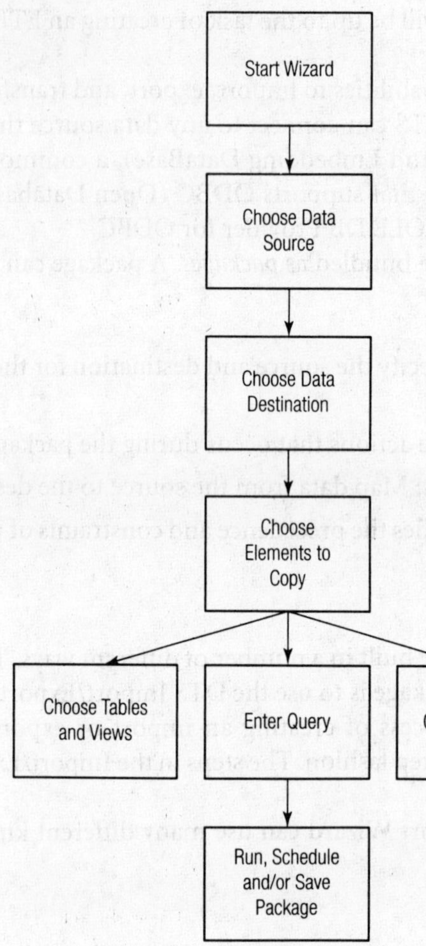

FIGURE 2.5 Import/Export Wizard steps.

in your transformations, you will probably want to write some custom code using the DTS object model. We discuss that option in an upcoming section.

When you have finished running the Import/Export Wizard, you can execute the package immediately or schedule it for execution in the future. You must save the package if you want to execute it in the future. You can save a DTS package in one of the following file formats:

- SQL Server database
- SQL Server Meta Data Services
- Structured Storage file
- Microsoft Visual Basic file

SQL Server Database

Saving it to the SQL server database is the default option. This allows you to store packages on any instances of SQL Server on your network and keep track of packages in SQL Server Enterprise Manager. In addition to the convenience and security of having the packages stored in SQL Server, the format allows you to manipulate and keep track of multiple versions of the package. The packages are located in the Data Transformation Services folder under the Local Packages entry as shown in Figure 2.6.

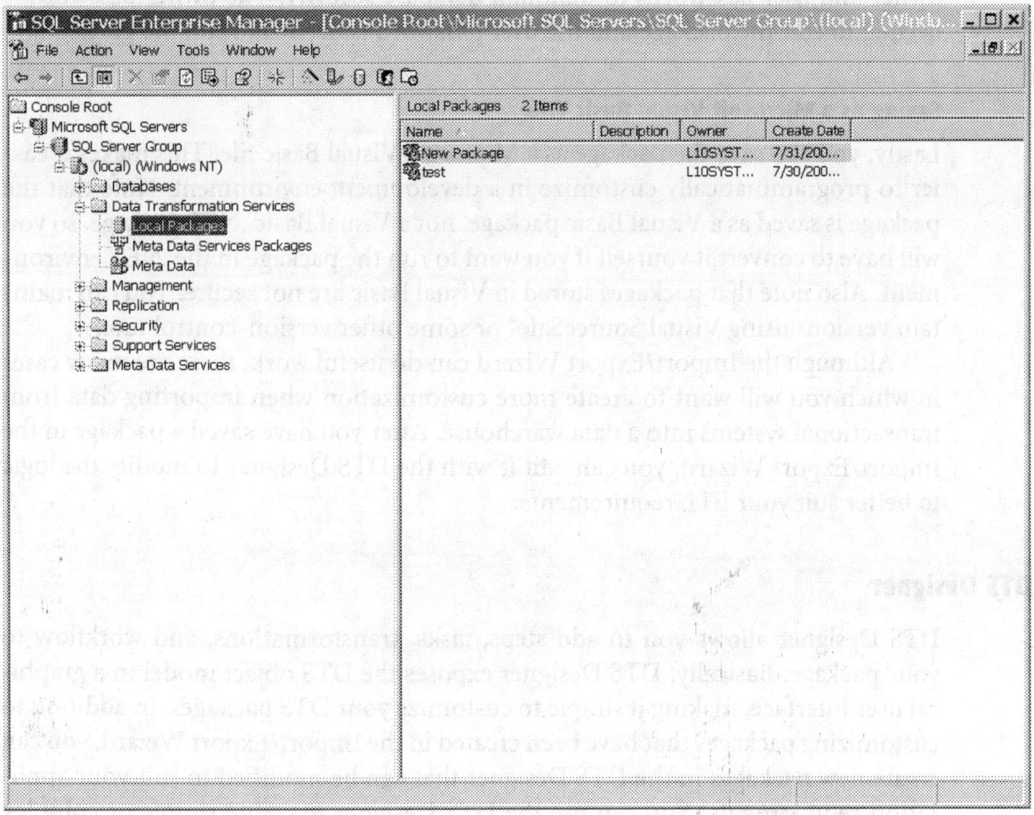

FIGURE 2.6 Local Packages.

Saving in SQL Server Meta Data Services

Saving in SQL Server Meta Data Services allows you to maintain historical information about the data manipulated by the package. You can track the columns and tables that are used by the package as a source or destination. You also can use the data lineage feature to track which version of a package created a particular row.

However, Meta Data Services and the repository database are optional elements in a SQL Server installation and you have to make sure that they are available to you. Meta Data services maintain security in much the same way as SQL Server.

Saving in Structured Storage Files

Structured storage files allow you to maintain the package in the disk file system instead of SQL Server. It supports multiple packages and multiple versions of the same package in the structure file. You can protect the structured storage file with owner and user passwords to maintain database security. The owner password is needed to edit the package and the user password is needed to run the package.

Saving as a Microsoft Visual Basic File

Lastly, you can save the package as a Microsoft Visual Basic file. This makes it easier to programmatically customize in a development environment. Note that the package is saved as a Visual Basic package, not a Visual Basic .NET package, so you will have to convert it yourself if you want to run the package in the .NET environment. Also note that packages stored in Visual Basic are not secure. You can maintain versions using Visual SourceSafe® or some other version-control tool.

Although the Import/Export Wizard can do useful work, there are many cases in which you will want to create more customization when importing data from transactional systems into a data warehouse. After you have saved a package in the Import/Export Wizard, you can edit it with the DTS Designer to modify the logic to better suit your ETL requirements.

DTS Designer

DTS Designer allows you to add steps, tasks, transformations, and workflow to your package. Basically, DTS Designer exposes the DTS object model in a graphical user interface, making it simple to customize your DTS packages. In addition to customizing packages that have been created in the Import/Export Wizard, you can create new packages in the DTS Designer that can be modified to suit your application requirements. You can use the DTS Designer to create simple or complex packages that do many different kinds of event-driven and conditional tasks by simply dragging them from the tool palette on the left to the work area in the middle of the window.

To open the DTS Designer, open the SQL Enterprise Manager and select the SQL Server you want to work with. Drill down to the Data Transformation Services folder under the SQL Server you have chosen and right-click and choose New Package. This will open up a new DTS Package in the Designer. The DTS Designer is shown in Figure 2.7.

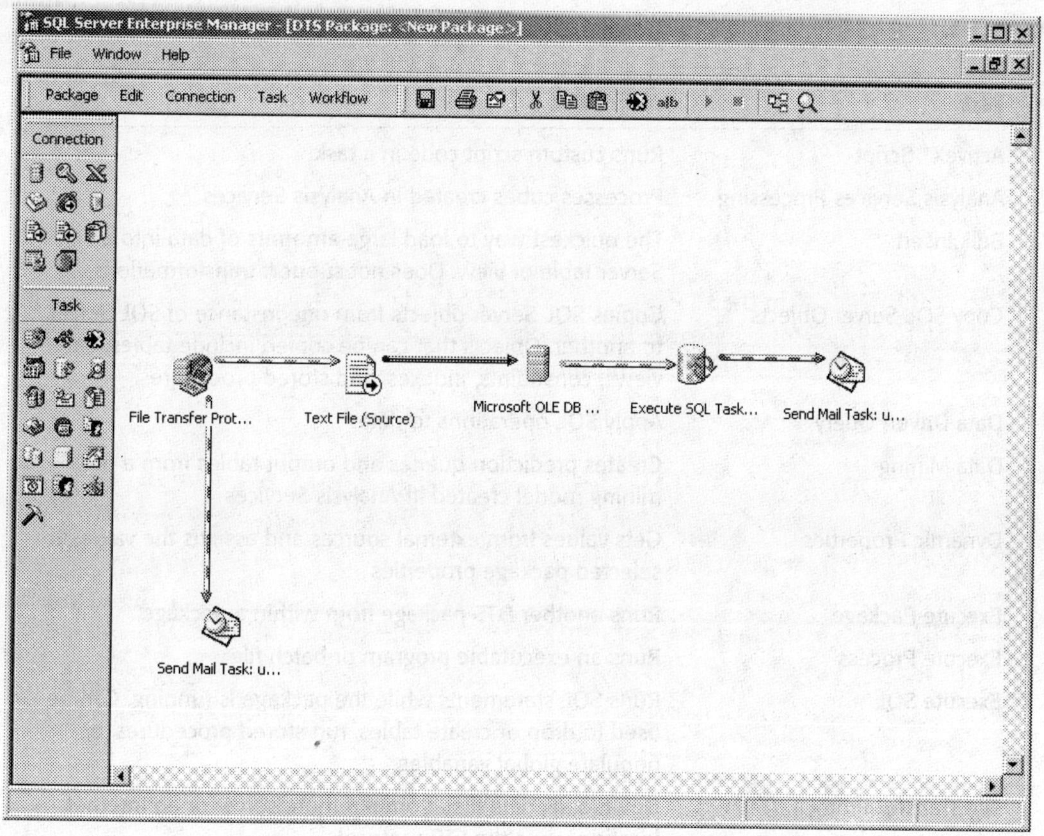

FIGURE 2.7 The DTS Designer.

Almost every task available in DTS is available through the DTS Designer and it can create quite complex DTS packages that cover many possible workflows. The tasks that are available in the DTS Designer are described briefly in Table 2.1.

In addition to the tasks, we can create a variety of data connections in the DTS Designer to provide both data inputs and destinations. The connections available in the DTS Designer are the same as those available in the Import/Export Wizard:

- SQL Server
- OLE DB and ODBC
- Text files
- Microsoft Excel spreadsheets
- Desktop databases including Access, FoxPro, dBase and Paradox

TABLE 2.1 Available tasks in DTS Designer.

Task	*Description*
ActiveX® Script	Runs custom script code in a task
Analysis Services Processing	Processes cubes created in Analysis Services
Bulk Insert	The quickest way to load large amounts of data into a SQL Server table or view. Does not support transformations.
Copy SQL Server Objects	Copies SQL Server objects from one instance of SQL Server to another. Objects that can be copied include tables, data, views, constraints, indexes, and stored procedures.
Data Driven Query	Apply SQL operations to data.
Data Mining	Creates prediction queries and output tables from a data mining model created in Analysis Services
Dynamic Properties	Gets values from external sources and assigns the values to selected package properties
Execute Package	Runs another DTS package from within a package
Execute Process	Runs an executable program or batch file
Execute SQL	Runs SQL statements while the package is running. Can be used to drop or create tables, run stored procedures, or populate global variables.
File Transfer Protocol (FTP)	Downloads data files from a remote server or an Internet location using the FTP protocol
Message Queue	Sends and receives messages from Microsoft Message Queues
Send Mail	Sends e-mail messages via MAPI (Messaging Application Programming Interface)
Transfer Database	Copies entire database from one instance of SQL Server to another
Transfer Error Messages	Copies user-specified error messages from one instance of SQL Server to another
Transfer Jobs	Copies jobs from one instance of SQL Server to another
Transfer Logins	Copies logons from one instance of SQL Server to another
Transfer Master Stored Procedures	Copies stored procedures written in a master database from one instance of SQL Server to another
Transform Data	Applies transformations and moves data between a source and destination

Simply creating tasks and data connections is not enough to specify a workflow. You also need to be able to specify an order of operations. The DTS Designer provides some simple elements to provide a workflow between the tasks that have been created. The workflow is indicated by a series of arrows that link the tasks together based on the condition of the processor. The arrows used to indicate the workflow are distinguished by color. In the example shown in Figure 2.8, we start our DTS Package with an FTP task. If the FTP task fails (the striped red line), we send an e-mail. If it succeeds (the striped green line), we open up a Text File connection and then transform the data (the solid black line) into a SQL Server database. If that succeeds, we execute a SQL task and then send an e-mail on completion (the striped blue line).

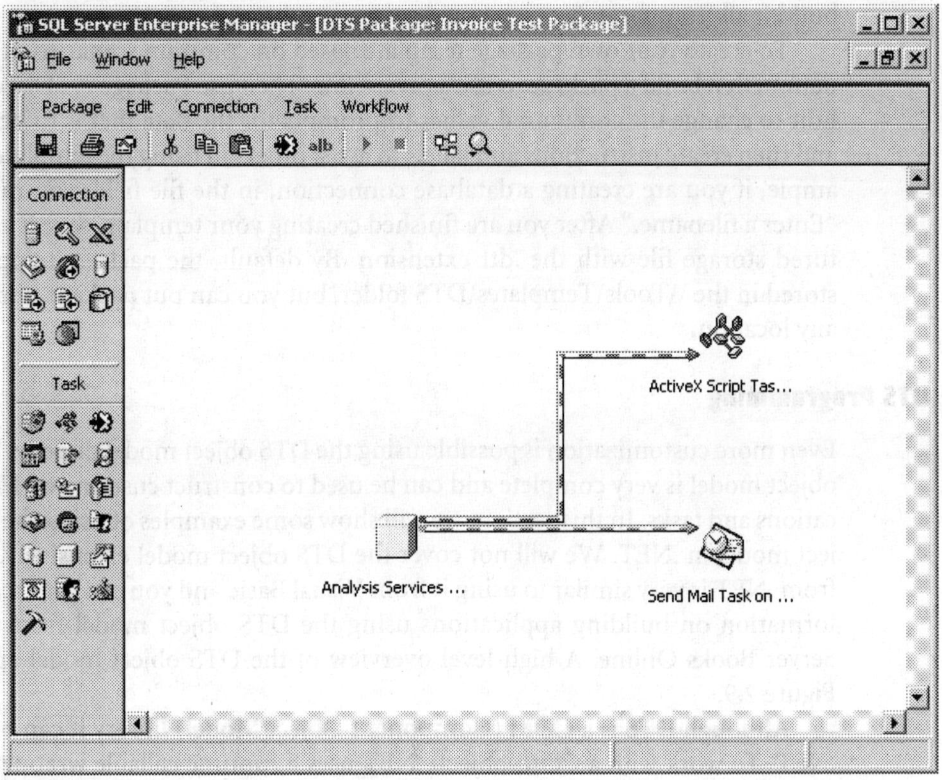

FIGURE 2.8 DTS workflow.

As with the DTS Import/Export Wizard, you can save the DTS package to the SQL Server database, to SQL Server 2000 Meta Data Services, as a structured storage file (.dts file), or as a Microsoft Visual Basic file. Even though the DTS Designer offers considerable power, it also offers some ways to make the task of creating multiple DTS packages easier.

Package Templates

In addition to creating a DTS Package from scratch in the designer, you can use a package template to create a partial solution for common DTS scenarios. To open a package template, open the SQL Server Enterprise Manager and right click the Data Transformation Services folder. In the context menu, select All Tasks, and then select Open Template. This will show a Select File dialog box where you can choose the template (.dtt file) you want by double clicking it. After you have opened the package template, it will be displayed in the DTS Designer and you can complete the template by populating the tasks and workflow without having to build it all from scratch.

To create your own package template based on common scenarios in your situation, first build a package to use as a baseline. Then use Package . . . Disconnected Edit to change the configured values to prompts for the data that is to be entered, and then create instructions and labels to assist others in using the template. For example, if you are creating a database connection, in the file field, you might type "Enter a filename." After you are finished creating your template, save it as a structured storage file with the .dtt extension. By default, the package templates are stored in the \\Tools\Templates\DTS folder, but you can put package templates in any location.

DTS Programming

Even more customization is possible using the DTS object model directly. The DTS object model is very complete and can be used to construct customized ETL applications and tasks. In this section, we will show some examples of using the DTS object model in .NET. We will not cover the DTS object model extensively. Using it from .NET is very similar to using it from Visual Basic and you can get excellent information on building applications using the DTS object model from the SQL Server Books Online. A high-level overview of the DTS object model appears in Figure 2.9.

Although DTS is a COM (Component Object Model) library it can be used in .NET. To work with a COM object, .NET uses a runtime callable wrapper (RCW) that exposes the wrapped COM object to the .NET framework and marshals function calls between managed and unmanaged code. The use of COM objects from .NET is often called COM interoperability or *interop*.

There are a couple of options to creating an RCW for COM objects. First, you can use the references in Visual Studio .NET to reference a COM object. This will create a default RCW and allow you to access it in your applications. However, this

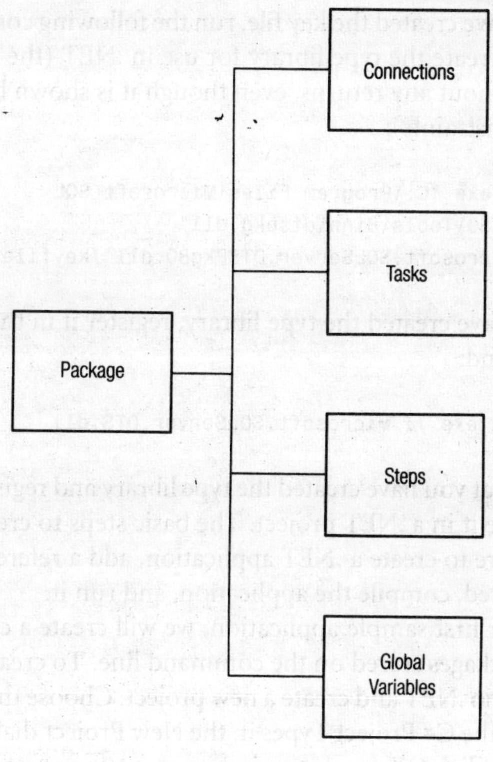

FIGURE 2.9 DTS object model.

simple method has some disadvantages. The primary issue is that importing references in Visual Studio .NET does not allow you to create signed RCW classes. Signed RCW classes are required for anything that will be added to the Global Assembly Cache (GAC).

In many cases, using an unsigned RCW is not a problem. However, for our examples, we must be able to add our .NET classes to the GAC, so we will use the second method of creating an RCW. This method makes use of the command-line Type Library Importer tool from the .NET SDK, which supports creating strongly-named libraries that can be added to the GAC. To create a signed RCW, we first use the Strong Name tool to generate a key file. So, first we open up a command prompt and navigate to a folder for the library. In this example, we will call that folder DTS, but it can be anywhere on your machine. Switch to the DTS folder and type the following at the command prompt:

```
sn.exe -k DTSPkg.snk
```

After you have created the key file, run the following command from the command prompt to create the type library for use in .NET (the command should be all on one line without any returns, even though it is shown below on multiple lines due to space constraints):

```
tlbimp.exe "C:\Program Files\Microsoft SQL
Server\80\Tools\Binn\dtspkg.dll"
/out:Microsoft.SQLServer.DTSPkg80.dll /keyfile:DTSPkg.snk
```

After you have created the type library, register it in the GAC by using the following command:

```
gacutil.exe /I Microsoft.SQLServer.DTS.dll
```

Now that you have created the type library and registered it in the GAC, you are ready to use it in a .NET project. The basic steps to create a .NET application that uses DTS are to create a .NET application, add a reference to the DTS package we just registered, compile the application, and run it.

For our first sample application, we will create a console application that just lists the packages stored on the command line. To create this application, open up Visual Studio .NET and create a new project. Choose the Console Application template from the C# Project Types in the New Project dialog. Name the project PackageList and click OK (as shown in Figure 2.10).

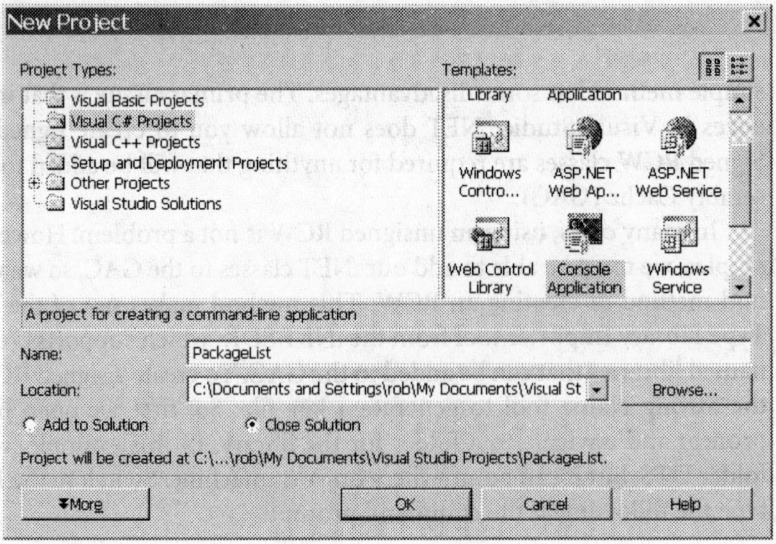

FIGURE 2.10 Create the PackageList application.

After creating the application, select Project . . . Add Reference from the menu. This will open the Add Reference dialog window. Click the Browse button and find the Microsoft.SQLServer.DTSPkg80.dll we just created and select it. After it appears in the selection list on the Add Reference dialog, click the OK button to close the dialog and add the reference to your project.

After you have added the reference, add the following code to the Class1.cs file and compile the application.

```
using System;
    using Microsoft.SQLServer.DTSPkg80;

    namespace PackageList
    {
        class Class1
        {
            static void Main(string[] args)
            {
                if (args.Length != 3)
                {
                    Console.WriteLine
                     ("Please enter a server, user and password.");
                    return;
                }

                // create the application
                ApplicationClass app = new ApplicationClass();

                PackageSQLServer pkgSQLServer = app.GetPackageSQLServer
                   (args[0],
                    args[1],
                    args[2],
                    DTSSQLServerStorageFlags. .DTSSQLStgFlag_Default);
                PackageInfos packages =
                   pkgSQLServer.EnumPackageInfos("", false, "");
                PackageInfo package = packages.Next();
                // loop through the packages
                while (! packages.EOF)
                {
                    Console.WriteLine(package.Name);
                    package = packages.Next();
                }
                // clean up the application
                app = null;
```

```
            }
        }
    }
```

After you have compiled the application, run it from the command line, supplying the name of a SQL Server, a SQL Server user, and password as the command line arguments. You will receive a list of the DTS packages that have been stored on the server.

The next example will show how you can load and execute a DTS package from a C# application. To create this sample application, create a new project as we did in the previous sample and name it PackageLoad. Add the reference to the DTS library as we did before and add the following code to the Class1.cs file:

```
using System;
using Microsoft.SQLServer.DTSPkg80;

namespace PackageLoad
{
    class Class1
    {
        static void Main(string[] args)
        {
            if (args.Length != 4)
            {
                Console.WriteLine
                ("Enter a server, user, password and package name.");
                return;
            }
            // create an empty package
            Package2Class package = new Package2Class();
            object pVarPersistStgOfHost = null;
            // load the package from the SQL Server
            package.LoadFromSQLServer(args[0], args[1], args[2],
                DTSSQLServerStorageFlags.DTSSQLStgFlag_Default, null,
                null, null, args[3], ref pVarPersistStgOfHost);
            // run the package
            package.Execute();
            // release the package
            package.UnInitialize();
            // clean up
            package = ;
```

For our last example of using the DTS object model, we will save a package to the SQL Server. To create this sample application, create a new project as we did in the previous sample and name it PackageSave. Add the reference to the DTS library as we did before and add the following code to the Class1.cs file:

```
using System;
    using Microsoft.SQLServer.DTSPkg80;

    namespace PackageSave
    {
        class Class1
        {
            static void Main(string[] args)
            {
                if (args.Length != 4)
                {
                    Console.WriteLine
                     ("Enter a server, user, password and package name.");
                    return;
                }
                // create the new package
                Package2Class package = new Package2Class();
                // assign the package name
                package.Name = args[3];

                // create a step in the package
                Step step = package.Steps.New();
                // create a ActiveX script task
                Task task = package.Tasks.New("DTSActiveScriptTask");
                // get the ActiveScriptTask interface from the task
                ActiveScriptTask script =
                  task.CustomTask as ActiveScriptTask;
                // assign the script name and a simple script
                script.Name = "Script_task";
                script.ActiveXScript = "Function Main()\n" +
                     "MsgBox( \"Hello\" )\n" +
                     "Main = DTSTaskExecResult_Success\n" +
                     "End Function";
                // assign the step task name and name
                step.TaskName = script.Name;
                step.Name = script.Name;
                // add the step to the package
                package.Steps.Add(step);
                // add the task to the package
```

```
                package.Tasks.Add(task);
                package.FailOnError = false;
                // create a reference to hold a return value (not used)
                object pVarPersistStgOfHost = null;
                // save the package to SQL Server
                package.SaveToSQLServer(args[0], args[1], args[2],
                    DTSSQLServerStorageFlags.DTSSQLStgFlag_Default,
                    null, null, null, ref pVarPersistStgOfHost, true);

                // clean up
                package = null;

            }
        }
    }
```

As you can see in the code in SavePackage, the package we save contains a simple ActiveX Script task that displays just a "Hello" message box. Extending the application to create a more complex script would be straightforward.

In addition to creating applications that use the tasks built into SQL Server, you can create your own custom DTS tasks in .NET. To implement a custom DTS task, you need to implement the CustomTask interface. The methods that must be implemented for the CustomTask interface are:

- `Execute`
- `RegisterServer`
- `UnregisterServer`

`Execute`, not surprisingly, is the method that is called when the task is invoked in a DTS package. `RegisterServer` and `UnregisterServer` manage the registry keys necessary for a custom task when the task is installed and uninstalled, respectively.

In addition to the methods, CustomTask requires you to implement some properties as well:

- `Name`
- `Description`
- `Properties`

`Name` and `Description` are string properties that identify the task. The `Properties` collection exposes the custom properties that might be used by the task.

If you implement only CustomTask, the UI for your custom task in the DTS Designer will be a simple default properties sheet. If you want to provide a more advanced interface for your task, you will also need to implement the CustomTaskUI interface. The following example will use the default interface.

Creating a DTS custom task is similar to creating a DTS application. The first step is to create a new Class Library project. After creating the new project, add the DTS library reference as we did in the previous examples. Next, rename the Class1.cs file to SimpleTask.cs and copy the following code into that file:

```
using System;
using System.Runtime.InteropServices;
using System.Windows.Forms;
using Microsoft.Win32;
using Microsoft.SQLServer.DTSPkg80;

[assembly:ClassInterface(ClassInterfaceType.AutoDual)]
namespace SampleCustomTask
{
    [Guid("D41B2CC3-221F-4082-B88B-A0294747897F"), ComVisible(true)]
    [ProgId("SampleCustomTask.SampleTask")]
    public class SampleTask : CustomTask
    {
        private string _name;
        private string _description;

        public SampleTask()
        {
            _name = "";
            _description = "SampleTask description";
        }

        public string Description
        {
            get
            {
                return _description;
            }
            set
            {
                _description = value;
            }
        }

        public string Name
        {
```

```
        get
        {
            return _name;
        }
        set
        {
            _name = value;
        }
    }

    public void Execute(object pPackage, object pPackageEvents, _
        object pPackageLog, ref DTSTaskExecResult pTaskResult)
    {
        //Assume we fail
        pTaskResult = DTSTaskExecResult.DTSTaskExecResult_Failure;
        try
        {
            MessageBox.Show(_description);
        }

        catch(System.Exception e)
        {
            Console.WriteLine(e);
        }
        //Return success
        pTaskResult = DTSTaskExecResult.DTSTaskExecResult_Success;
    }

    // implementation of CustomTask.Properties
    public Properties Properties
    {
        get
        {
            return null;
        }
    }

    [System.Runtime.InteropServices.ComVisible(false)]
    override public string ToString()
    {
        return base.ToString();
    }
```

```
//Registration function for custom task.
[System.Runtime.InteropServices.ComRegisterFunctionAttribute()]
static void RegisterServer(Type type)
{
    try
    {
        const string key =
         "Software\\Microsoft\\
         Microsoft SQL Server\\80\\DTS\\Enumeration\\Tasks";
        const string CATID_DTSCustomTask =
            "{10020200-EB1C-11CF-AE6E-00AA004A34D5}";
        string guid = "{" + type.GUID.ToString() + "}";
        guid = guid.ToUpper();

        Console.WriteLine("RegisterServer {0}", guid);

        RegistryKey root;
        RegistryKey registryKey;
        RegistryKey subKey;

        // Add the proper COM Category in HKEY_CLASSES_ROOT
        root = Registry.ClassesRoot;
        registryKey =
          root.OpenSubKey ("CLSID\\"
          + guid
          + "\\Implemented Categories",
          true);
        subKey = registryKey.CreateSubKey(CATID_DTSCustomTask);
        subKey.Close();
        registryKey.Close();
        root.Close();

        // Add the key to DTS Cache in HKEY_CURRENT_USER
        root = Registry.CurrentUser;
        registryKey = root.OpenSubKey(key, true);
        subKey = registryKey.CreateSubKey(guid);
        subKey.SetValue("", type.FullName);
        subKey.Close();
        registryKey.Close();
        root.Close();

        // add the class id
        root = Registry.ClassesRoot;
        registryKey = root.OpenSubKey("CLSID\\" + guid, true);
```

```
            registryKey.SetValue("DTSTaskDescription",
              "SampleTask description");
            subKey.Close();
            registryKey.Close();
            root.Close();

        }
        catch(Exception e)
        {
            System.Console.WriteLine(e.ToString());
        }
    }

    //Unregistration function for custom task.
    [System.Runtime.InteropServices.ComUnregisterFunctionAttribute()]
    static void UnregisterServer(Type type)
    {
        try
        {
            const string key =
              "Software\\Microsoft\\
                Microsoft SQL Server\\80\\DTS\\Enumeration\\Tasks";
            string guid = "{" + type.GUID.ToString() + "}";
            guid = guid.ToUpper();

            Console.WriteLine("UnregisterServer {0}", guid);

            RegistryKey root;
            RegistryKey registryKey;

            // Delete key in HKEY_CURRENT_USER
            root = Registry.CurrentUser;
            registryKey = root.OpenSubKey(key, true);
            registryKey.DeleteSubKey(guid, false);
            registryKey.Close();
            root.Close();
        }
        catch(Exception e)
        {
            System.Console.WriteLine(e.ToString());
        }
    }
```

```
    }
}
```

After you have copied the code there are a few more steps to take before you compile. As with the DTS library, we want to create a strong name for the task library so we can add it to the GAC. To do this, we will run the Strong Name tool to create a key in the project folder from the command line:

```
sn.exe –k SampleCustomTask.snk
```

After creating the key in the project folder, we need to make sure that the assembly is signed with the key. To do this, edit the AssemblyInfo.cs file in the SampleCustomTask project by replacing the existing line:

```
[assembly: AssemblyKeyFile("")]
```

with

```
[assembly: AssemblyKeyFile("..\\..\\SampleCustomTask.snk")]
```

After you have made those changes, you are ready to compile the project.

After compiling, we are ready to add the assembly to the GAC. To do this, open a command line in the folder where the assembly was compiled and run the following command:

```
gacutil.exe /I SampleCustomTask.dll
```

Now that the assembly has been added to the GAC, we are ready to register it by running this command:

```
regasm.exe SampleCustomTask.dll
```

Now, we are ready to run the DTS Designer to see the custom task in action. To do this, start the SQL Server Enterprise Manager and navigate to the Data Transformation Services folder on your SQL Server. Create a new package and add your custom task to the main window. Execute the package and you will see the name you have assigned to the task displayed in a dialog.

These examples just scratch the surface of what is possible by writing custom DTS code in .NET. For more information on this topic, you can consult the SQL Server Books Online. Translating examples from Visual Basic or C++ to .NET is straightforward and offers a lot of opportunities for custom ETL solutions.

CREATING A CUBE IN ANALYSIS SERVICES

Chocolate Pretzel Co. makes and sells quality chocolate pretzels in the eastern United States. The product line is fairly limited with a focus on quality. There is one pretzel manufacturing facility in each of the sales regions, and each plant can produce the entire line of pretzels. The distribution model is pretty simple. Salespeople sell to specialized retail outlets that sell the product to consumers. Invoices for orders are sent to the retail outlets on net 30 terms for those customers with good credit. Payment is due on receipt for those customers with less than good credit.

The sales force is divided up into regions (North, Central, and South). Products are distributed from warehouses that are assigned to the sales regions. Most of the time, the salespeople deliver the pretzels themselves from the local warehouse as they do their routes. In some special situations, pretzels are shipped in from a different warehouse. The company runs promotions that offer discounts to the retailers and, typically, runs ads in media outlets for the promotions. These promotions are managed on a regional basis. Each region is its own profit center with responsibility for both revenue and cost.

Chocolate Pretzel Co. has a simple IT infrastructure and has done a good job of standardizing the IT services across the regions. Every day, the transactional data from the regions is sent to the corporate headquarters for ETL into the data warehouse system.

The first area of the data warehouse is invoice analysis. This can yield some powerful insights into buying patterns of customers and allow management to make better decisions to improve sales and profitability by looking at the top-line revenue numbers in great detail. Manufacturing costs are recorded and assigned to each order. Overhead is assigned to each line item of an invoice of $5 plus $0.25 per carton. This is just an attempt to cover some of the fixed and variable nonmanufacturing costs. A diagram of the invoice analysis star schema is shown in Figure 2.11.

To create a cube from the Chocolate Pretzel Co. data warehouse, we first create a new database in Analysis Services. To do this, open the Analysis Manager and select the server you want to use. After you have selected the server, select Action . . . New Database from the menu. Populate the Database dialog that is presented with the name and description you want to give to your database. In this case, we will name the database "Pretzel."

After creating the database, we will create a data source for our cube. The data source specifies the tables that contain the source data for our cube. A data source can use any OLE DB provider to connect to a variety of databases and file formats. To create a data source in the database we just created, right click on the Data Sources folder in the database and select New Data Sources from the shortcut menu. The sample data is stored in an Access .mdb file, so on the first tab of the

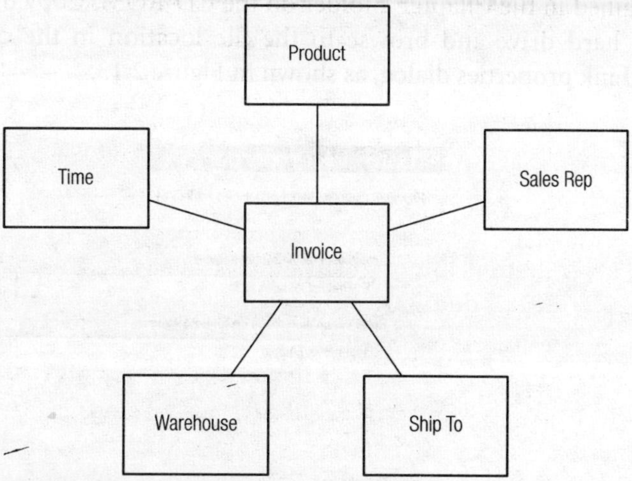

FIGURE 2.11 The invoice star schema.

DataLink properties dialog, select the Microsoft Jet 4.0 OLE DB Provider, as shown in Figure 2.12.

After we have selected the OLE DB Provider, we will select the file to be used as the source data. The file containing the sales information is called sales.mdb and is

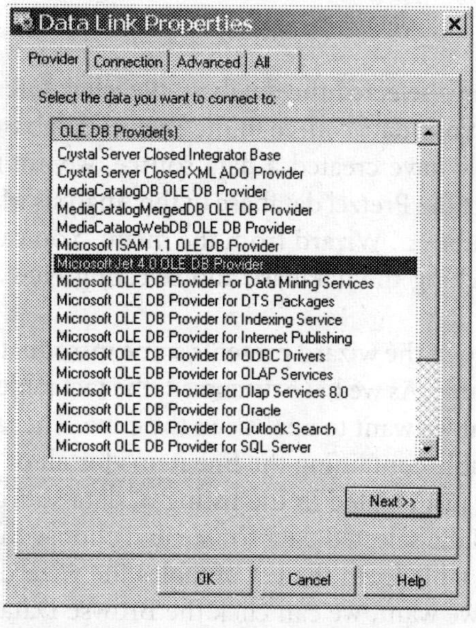

FIGURE 2.12 Selecting an OLE DB provider.

contained in the Chapter 2 folder on the CD-ROM. Copy the file to a location on your hard drive and browse to the file location in the connection tab of the DataLink properties dialog, as shown in Figure 2.13.

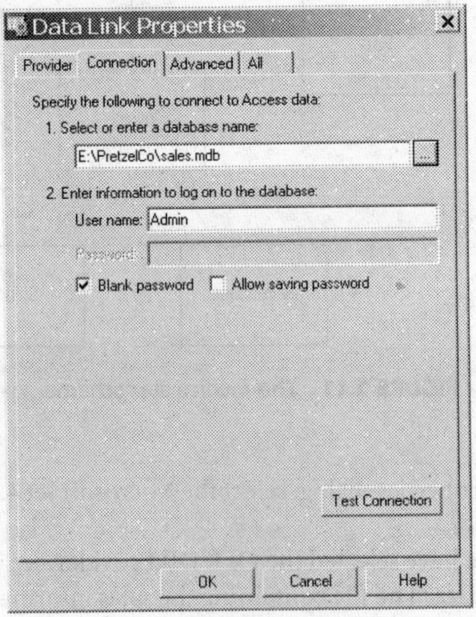

FIGURE 2.13 Selecting the source database.

After you have selected the database file, click OK on the DataLink properties dialog to create your data source in the Pretzel database.

Now that we have created a data source, we are ready to create our invoice cube. First, select the Pretzel database in the Analysis Manager and then choose Action . . . New Cube . . . Wizard from the menu. You can also get to the Cube Wizard by right clicking the database and selecting New Cube . . . Wizard from the context menu.

The first step in the wizard presents some introductory information. Click Next to select a fact table. As we have discussed, the fact table consists of the fine-grained transactions that we want to analyze in the cube. The fact table we are interested in is the Invoice table containing the line items for all of the invoices. Select the data source we have just created in the listing of data sources on the first screen of the wizard. Expand the selected data source and choose the Invoice table. After selecting the Invoice table from the list of tables the wizard should appear as shown in Figure 2.14. If we want, we can click the Browse Data button to see what the underlying data looks like.

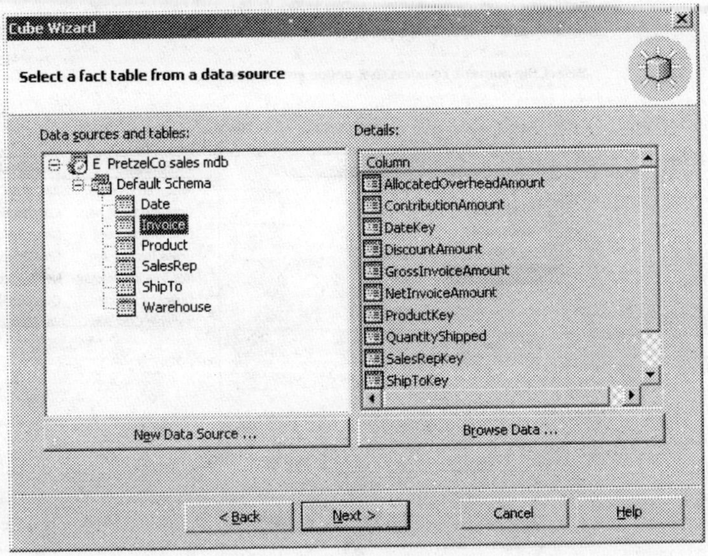

FIGURE 2.14 Selecting the Invoice fact table.

Clicking Next will take us to the next screen in the wizard. In this screen, we are selecting the numeric columns for the cube measures. Measures are the information that the users are interested in analyzing. In the case of the invoice table, we are going to select the following fields to be used as measures:

- AllocatedOverhead
- ContributionAmount
- DiscountAmount
- GrossInvoiceAmount
- NetInvoiceAmount
- QuantityShipped
- VariableCostAmount.

After selecting these columns as measures, the screen should look like Figure 2.15.

Clicking Next takes us to the Wizard screen to create dimensions. Since we haven't yet created any dimensions in our cube, we will click the New Dimension button that launches the Dimension Wizard. The first screen in the Dimension Wizard contains some introductory information. Clicking Next on the introduction screen takes us to the screen where we can set the type of hierarchy for the dimension. We can choose one of a Star Schema, Snowflake Schema, Parent-Child, Virtual Dimension, or Mining Model. We have already discussed star and

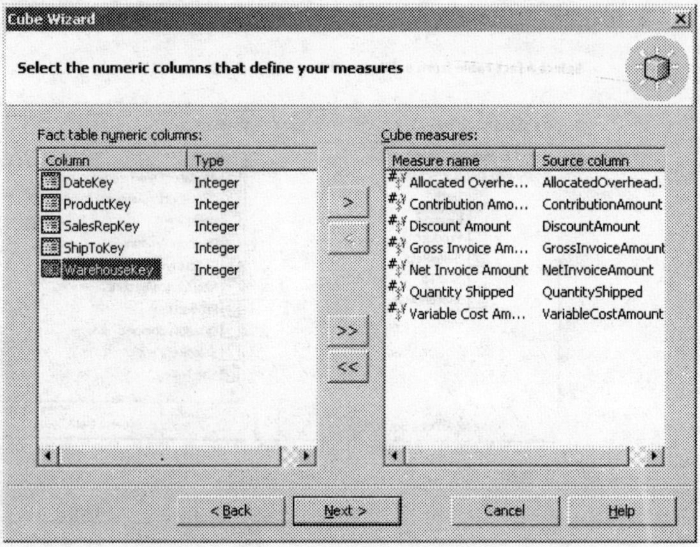

FIGURE 2.15 Selecting the Invoice measures.

snowflake schemas earlier in this chapter. To recap briefly, recall that a star schema has a single table associated with each dimension and a snowflake schema has a normalized set of tables representing the dimension hierarchy. The Parent-Child option allows the schema to be constructed from two columns in the same table with one identifying the members and the other identifying the member's parents that are selected later in the Wizard. For example, if you have a product family and product name in the same table, they can be used to create a parent-child dimension. A *Virtual Dimension* is one that is derived from another dimension, selected later in the wizard. A *Mining Model* creates a dimension that can be used as an input or output for a mining model. This kind of dimension is discussed in more detail in Chapter 8.

In this case, we will choose Star Schema and click Next. The next screen allows us to select the dimension table to be used as the basis for the hierarchy. In this case, we will choose the date table and the screen will show us the columns in the table as in Figure 2.16. As with the fact table, if we want, we can click the Browse Data button to see what the underlying table looks like.

Clicking Next allows us to select the dimension type, choosing between Standard and Time. In this case, we are creating a Time dimension, so we choose that option as shown in Figure 2.17 and click Next. Later on, we will create a Standard dimension.

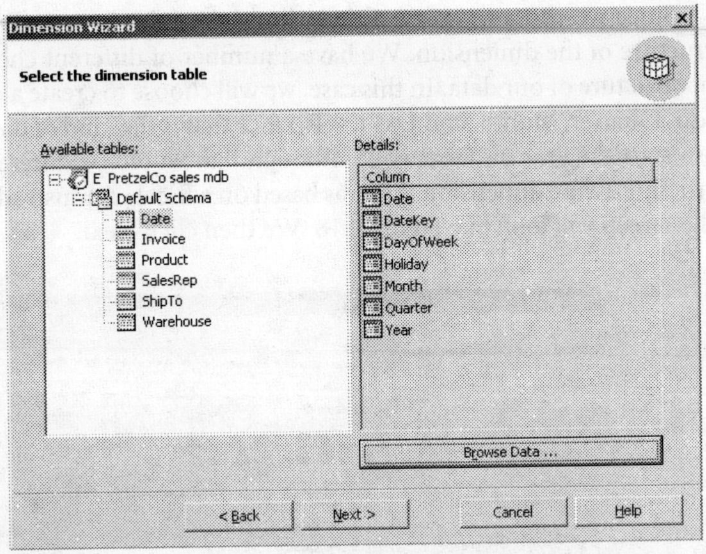

FIGURE 2.16 Selecting the dimension table.

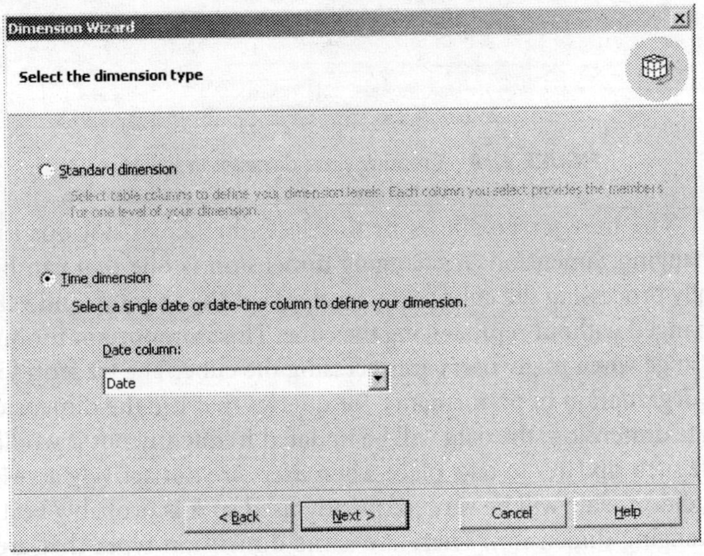

FIGURE 2.17 Selecting the dimension.

Since we chose to create a time dimension, the next step prompts us for the structure of the dimension. We have a number of different choices depending on the structure of our data. In this case, we will choose to create a dimension that has Year, Quarter, Month, and Day levels, since that is the kind of data we have. We will also start the year on January 1, although that would be different if we were constructing a time dimension that was based on a fiscal year instead of a calendar year. The screen will look like Figure 2.18. We then click Next.

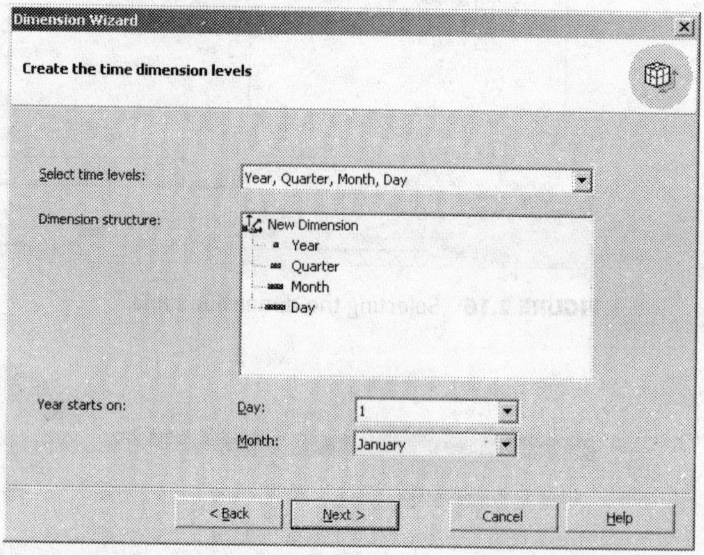

FIGURE 2.18 Creating time dimension levels.

The next screen allows us to select whether or not our time dimension is a changing dimension. A changing dimension is one that can be updated without fully processing the cubes. Any level except the very top and very leaf levels can be changed without reprocessing the cube. This is important for information that will change when many users are accessing the cube. The tradeoff for this convenience is degradation in performance for queries that use the dimension. In the case of a date dimension, the data will be updated frequently but it would be easy to schedule such updates to take place when users are not actively accessing the system. In addition, date will be very frequently used so it is probably best to not label it as a changing dimension. There are some dimension types that are always labeled as changing dimensions including virtual dimensions, parent-child dimensions, and dimensions that use ROLAP (Relational OnLine Analytical Processing) storage.

So, we don't change any values on the Advanced screen. We then click Next, which takes us to the final screen in the Dimension Wizard. We name the dimension "Time" and mark it as a shared dimension so that we can use this same time di-

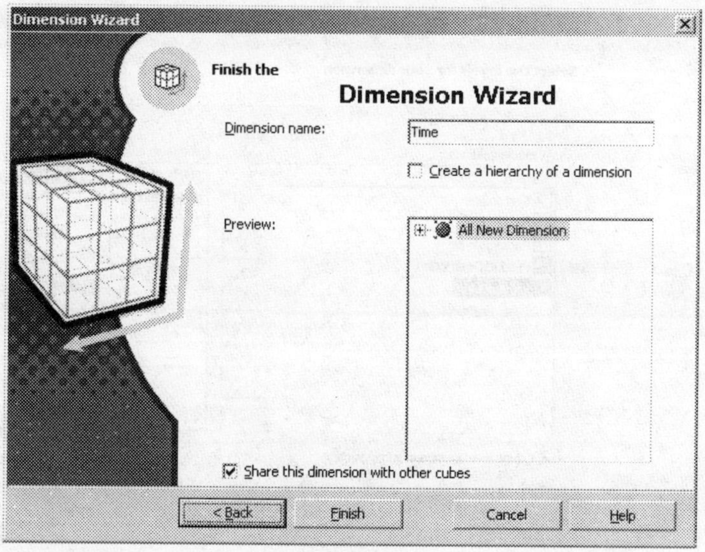

FIGURE 2.19 Saving the dimension.

mension across different cubes. The screen will appear like Figure 2.19. We click Finish, and that will return us to the Cube Wizard at the dimension selection screen.

Next, we will create a standard dimension for the products. So here we invoke the Dimension Wizard again using New Dimension. Skipping over the introduction screen, we choose Star Schema from the hierarchy selections and click Next. In the Select dimension table screen, we choose Product and click Next. The following screen allows us to choose the levels for the dimension. Here we choose the Product Group as the first level and the Product Description as the second level. After we have chosen our two levels, the screen will appear like Figure 2.20.

After we have chosen the columns for our dimensions, we specify the member keys that correspond to our level members. In this case, we will accept the defaults and click Next.

The next page lists the advanced options for the cube. The first option is for a changing dimension, which we have already discussed in the creation of the time dimension. The product dimension doesn't change all that often, so we leave that option cleared. The next option is for the "Ordering and uniqueness of members," which basically allows the sorting of the members. We will select this option. The last option is for the "Storage mode and member groups," which allows you to specify the storage of the dimension to be outside of the cube in a relational database (ROLAP). Note that if you have a very large dimension (more than 5 million members), you must store the data in a separate relational database. However, our Product dimension here is small and we will leave this option cleared. After our selections, the screen will look like Figure 2.21 and we then click Next.

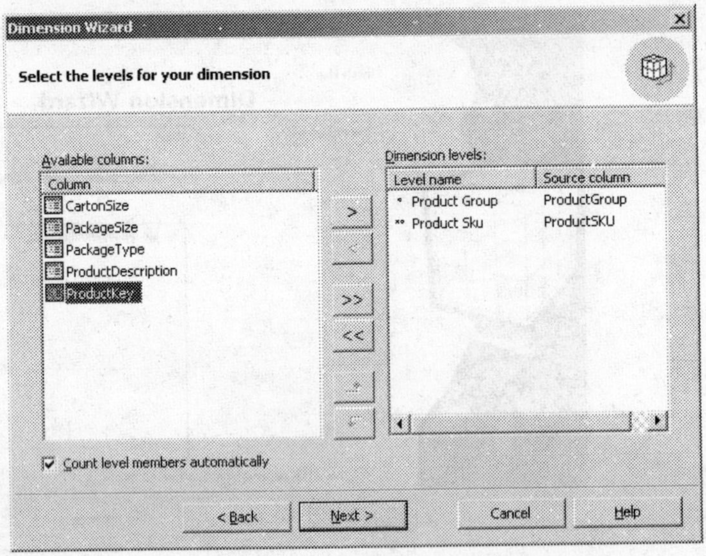

FIGURE 2.20 Saving the dimension.

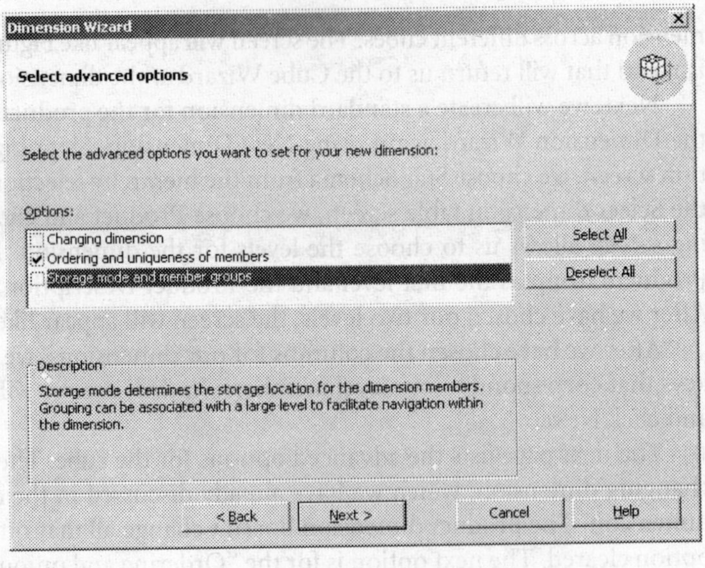

FIGURE 2.21 Advanced dimension options.

Since we selected the option to enforce order and uniqueness, the next screen allows us to specify the ordering and uniqueness for each level. We can order by name, key, or column. We can enforce key uniqueness in the dimension or among the level members. We can enforce name uniqueness in the dimension, among the level members, among siblings, or not at all. In this case we will choose the defaults as shown in Figure 2.22 and move to the next, and last, step of the Dimension Wizard.

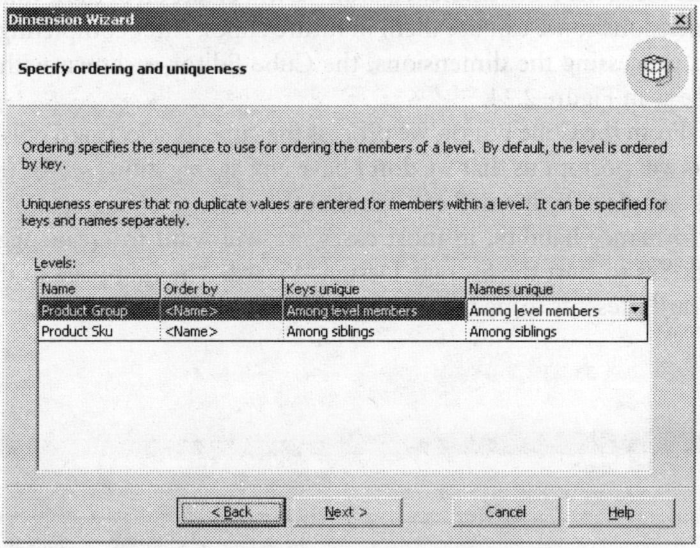

FIGURE 2.22 Specifying the ordering for a level.

The last step we take in the Dimension Wizard is to name the dimension and specify sharing among other cubes. We will name the dimension "Product" and share it to other cubes as shown in Figure 2.23.

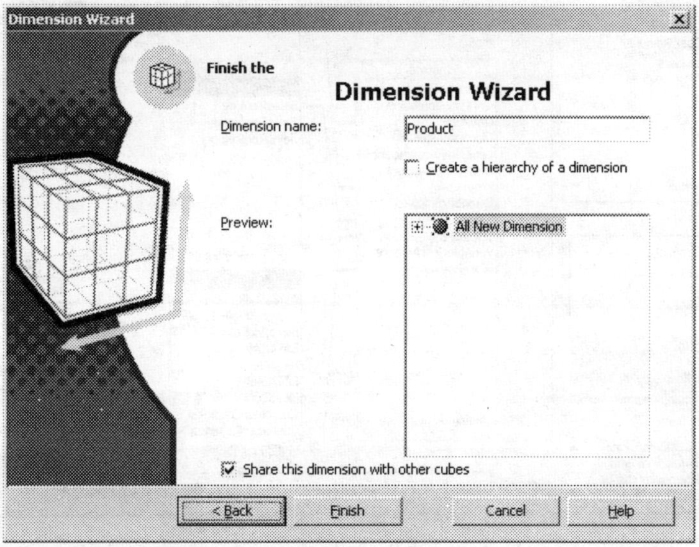

FIGURE 2.23 Saving the dimension.

In addition to the Time and Product dimensions, we will create dimensions for the Sales Rep, Warehouse, and Ship To in a similar fashion to the first two dimensions using the Dimension Wizard. We will create all of these dimensions as shared dimensions so we can use them in future cubes. After completing the Cube Wizard and processing the dimensions, the Cube Editor is shown with our new Invoice cube as in Figure 2.24.

From the Cube Editor, we process the cube by selecting Tools . . . Process Cube. This will prompt us that we don't have any aggregations set for the cube. Although this sample cube is small enough that the absence of aggregations will not be a big performance liability, in most cases, we will want to create aggregations. So, we click Yes to start the Storage Design Wizard. The first page in the Storage Design Wizard presents some introduction and we click Next.

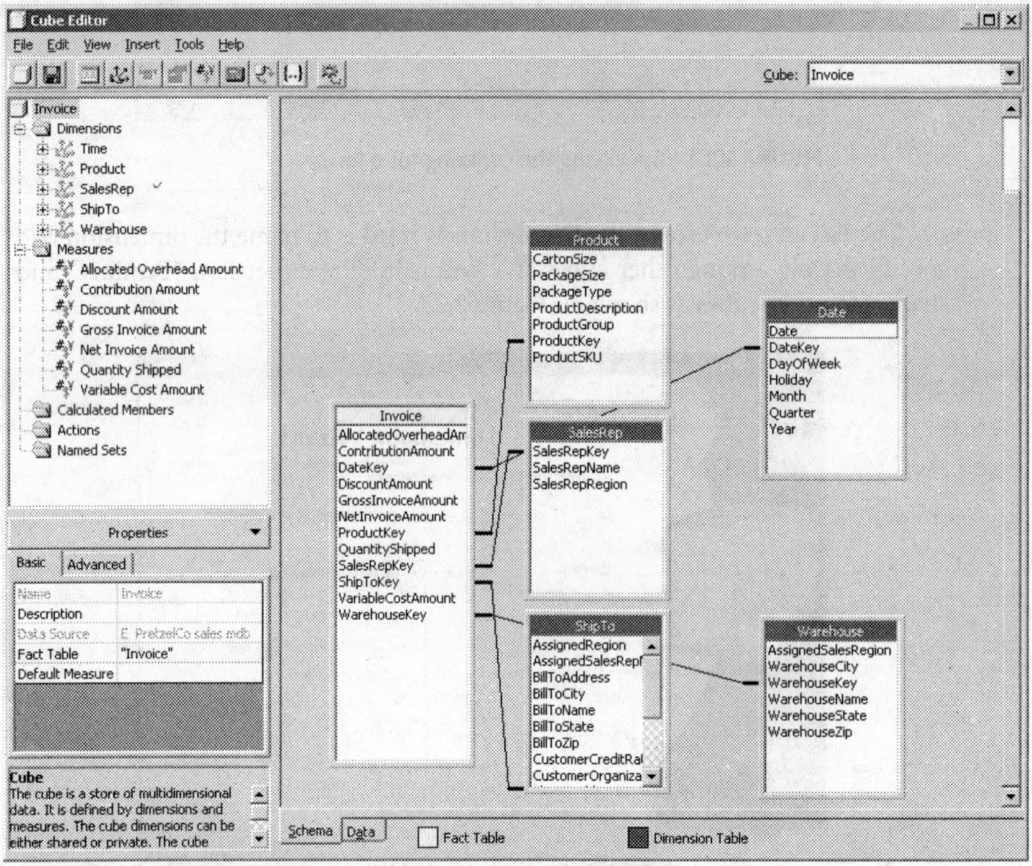

FIGURE 2.24 Viewing the cube in the Cube Editor.

On the following page, we choose how the data will be stored. Our options are MOLAP (Multidimensional OLAP), ROLAP, and HOLAP (Hybrid OLAP). Descriptions of these storage choices appear later in this chapter. We will select MOLAP, as shown in Figure 2.25 and click Next.

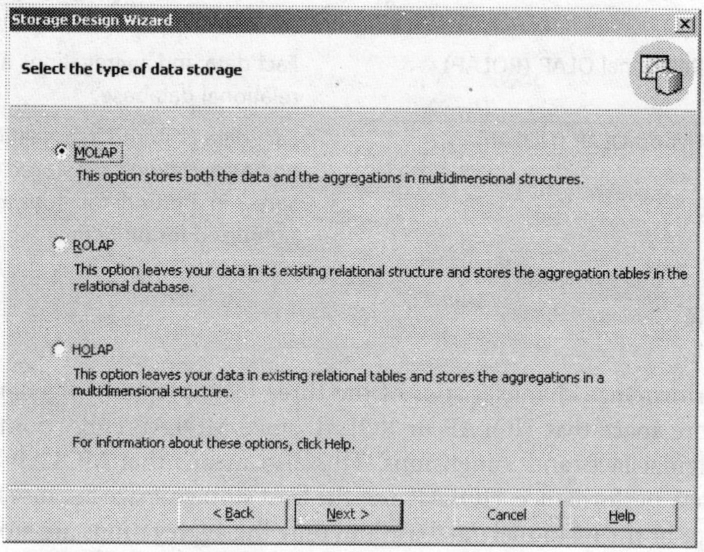

FIGURE 2.25 Selecting the type of data storage.

The way a cube is stored in Analysis Services has a big impact on performance. The more aggregations that are stored with the data, the faster the query response time will be. But, a greater number of aggregations creates a larger database and slows down cube updates. Understanding this tradeoff is vital to optimizing the performance and maintainability of your business intelligence applications.

Also affecting the storage size and performance of a cube are the different technologies used to store cubes in OLAP Services. There are three ways that OLAP Services stores cubes: as multidimensional database files (MOLAP), as tables in a relational database (ROLAP), or as a hybrid of multidimensional database files and relational tables (HOLAP). Each of these storage types has different strengths and weaknesses. A description of the different storage techniques is presented in Table 2.2.

Each of these technologies has different characteristics with respect to the amount of storage space that is used and the time it takes to process the cubes and query performance. An article entitled "Analysis Services: Optimizing Cube Performance Using Microsoft SQL Server 2000 Analysis Services" on the MSDN Web site (*http://msdn.microsoft.com/library/default.asp?url=/library/en-us/dnsql2k/html/olapunisys.asp*) offers an excellent detailed breakdown of the different storage and

TABLE 2.2 Analysis Services storage options.

Storage mode	***Description***
Multidimensional OLAP (MOLAP)	Fact data and aggregations are stored on the OLAP server in a proprietary format that is optimized for multidimensional use.
Relational OLAP (ROLAP)	Fact data and aggregations are stored in a relational database.
Hybrid OLAP (HOLAP)	Fact data is stored in a relational database and aggregations are stored on the OLAP server in a proprietary format that is optimized for multidimensional use.

performance characteristics of the three technologies. In general, MOLAP takes more space that HOLAP or ROLAP since MOLAP cubes contain a copy of the original facts and dimensions. This also means that MOLAP cubes have better query performance. HOLAP uses the least storage space because the original data is kept in the relational database and only the aggregations are stored in the proprietary multidimensional format. Testing reveals that MOLAP and HOLAP use about the same amount of storage space with a low to moderate level of aggregation. As the level of aggregation increases over that level, ROLAP uses more storage space than HOLAP and takes much longer to process cubes. Deciding which storage technology to use for your cubes is an important choice that requires careful consideration of the available options and priorities for your business intelligence application.

The next screen in the Storage Design Wizard is where you set the level of aggregation. This is a classic performance versus size tradeoff with larger, more heavily indexed cubes yielding faster query performance. In this case, we will aggregate until the performance gain reaches 50%. After we click Start, the wizard will begin to calculate and will return a screen that looks like Figure 2.26. Click Next and we will be at the end of the Storage Design Wizard. Leave the Process Now option button selected and click Finish. The cube will process in a few seconds and return some results like those shown in Figure 2.27. Clicking Close on this dialog box will return us to the Cube Editor.

Now that we have created a very simple Invoice cube, we can analyze it to glean fundamental insights about the buying patterns of Chocolate Pretzel's customers. Even just simply browsing the data in the Analysis Manager can yield some interesting information. To do this, select the Invoice cube and then click the Data tab.

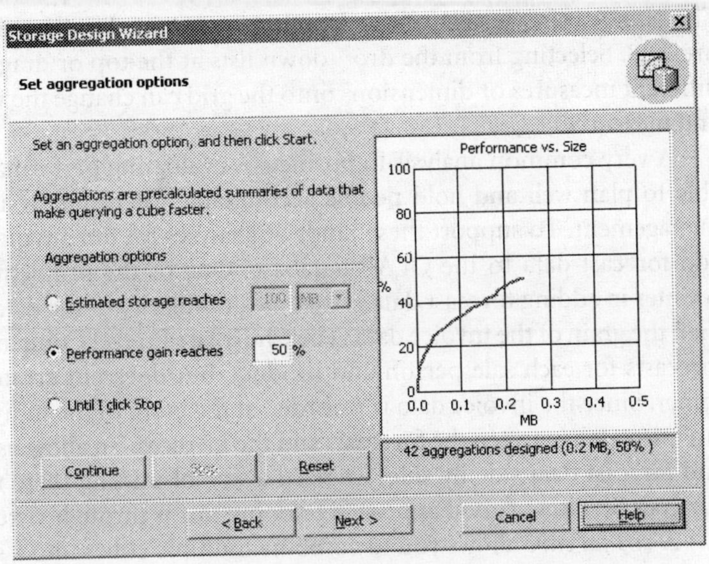

FIGURE 2.26 Setting the level of aggregation in the cube.

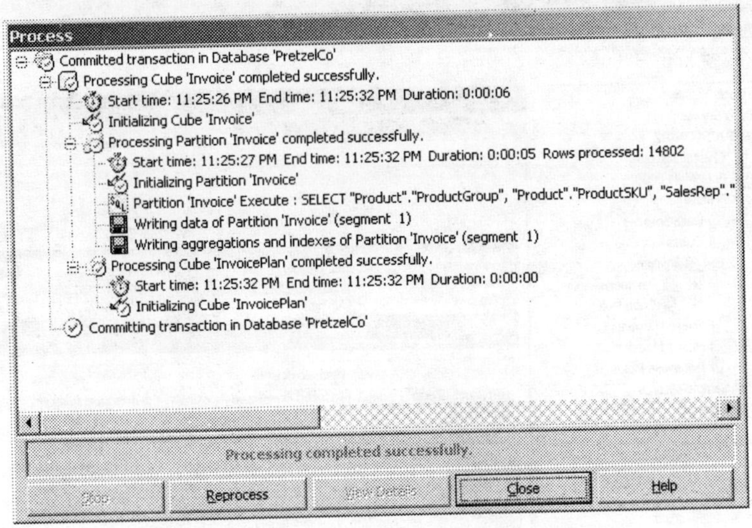

FIGURE 2.27 Results of processing the cube.

This shows a simple view of the data that is contained in the cube as shown in Figure 2.28. Selecting from the drop-down lists at the top or dragging and dropping different measures or dimensions onto the grid can change the various dimensions and measures.

A very common analysis in business is evaluating performance to plan. Being able to plan well and hold people accountable for results is a hallmark of good management. To support these kinds of analyses for our Invoice cube, we need to add forecast data to the OLAP database. One of the problems that we will encounter in adding forecast data is that the granularity of the data is a little different than the grain of the invoice data. The Chocolate Pretzel Company creates monthly forecasts for each salesperson and product, but does not create forecasts by customer. Since the invoice data is recorded at the grain of the individual stores, there is a mismatch between the forecasts and the invoices. To allow us to analyze invoice and forecast data side by side, we need a way of putting these things together. In Analysis Services, a good approach to doing this is through virtual cubes.

A *virtual cube* allows you to combine multiple cubes into a single logical cube. It is analogous to a relational database view that allows you to combine tables into a virtual table. To create a virtual cube, we select the measures and dimensions from

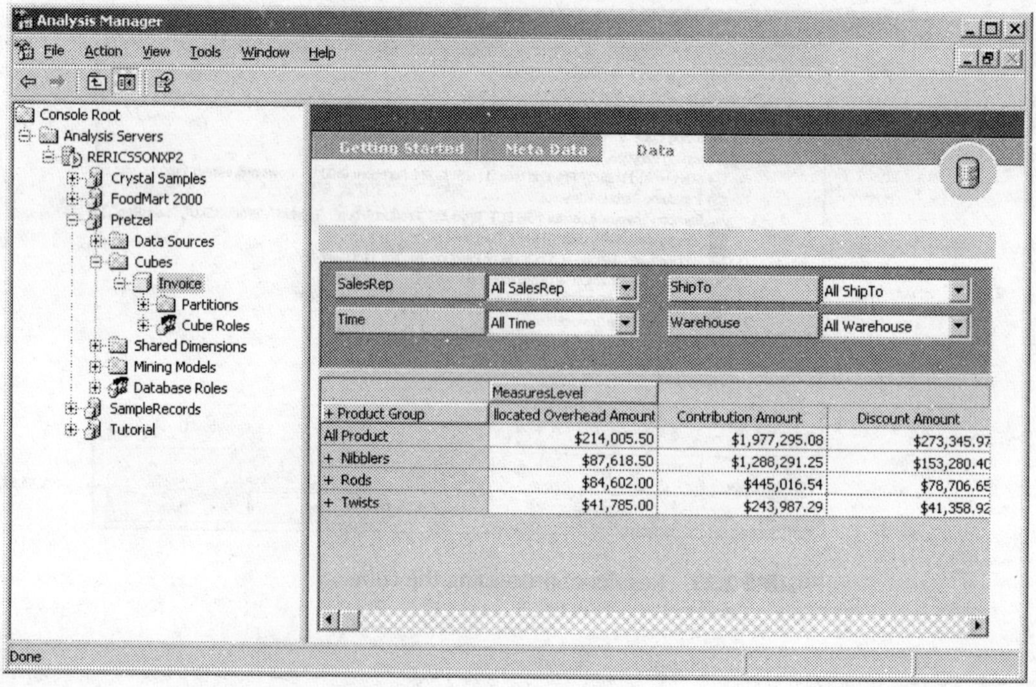

FIGURE 2.28 Browsing data in Analysis Manager.

the set of all of the dimensions and measures in the cubes that it combines. So, we can combine the invoice and forecast information into a virtual cube that can be used to evaluate our performance to plan.

Before we add a virtual cube that combines the invoice and forecast information, we need to create a cube to contain the forecasts. The basic steps to create a cube with forecast information is similar to the steps followed to create the invoice cube. To begin, select the Pretzel database in the Analysis Manager and then choose Action . . . New Cube . . . Wizard from the menu. Skipping over the first step of the wizard, we select a fact table for our cube. After selecting the Plan table in the Wizard, the screen will look like Figure 2.29.

After selecting the Plan fact table, we click next and move to the measures selection screen. For the plan table, we will select the following fields to be used as measures:

- Allocated Overhead Planned
- Contribution Planned
- Discount Planned
- Gross Invoice Planned
- Net Invoice Planned
- Quantity Planned
- Variable Cost Planned

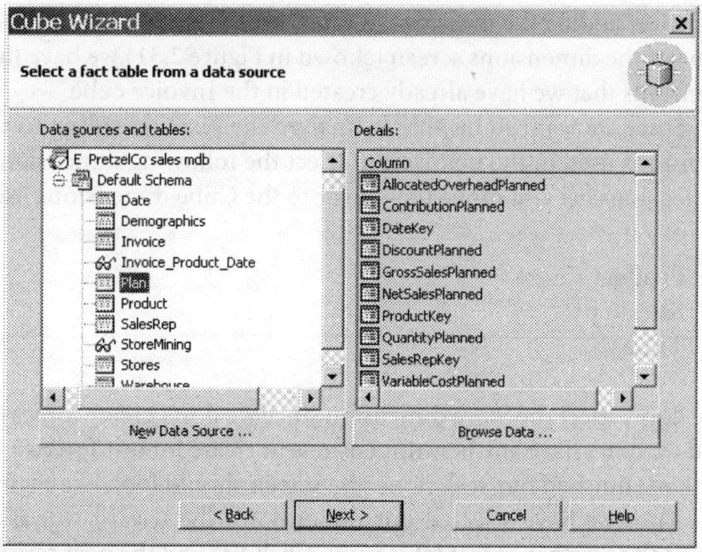

FIGURE 2.29 Selecting the Plan fact table.

After selecting these measures, your screen will look like Figure 2.30. Note that the measures selected for the plan correspond to the measures selected for the invoice in Figure 2.15.

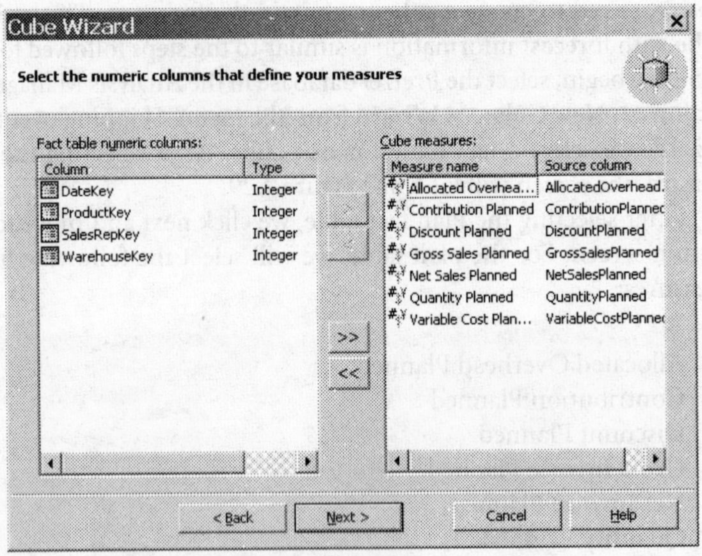

FIGURE 2.30 Selecting the Plan measures.

After adding the measures, we next set the dimensions for the cube. On the left pane of the dimensions screen (shown in Figure 2.31) we have the list of shared dimensions that we have already created in the Invoice cube.

Since we want to be able to analyze the plan according to the same set of dimensions used in the invoice, we select the following dimensions from the Shared dimensions list and move them over to the Cube dimensions list:

- Product
- SalesRep
- Time

We don't select the Store dimension since we don't create forecasts at the store level and we don't have any new dimensions to create for our forecast information. After we have finished our selections, the screen should look like Figure 2.32.

After we have selected our dimensions, the wizard will ask us if we want to count the number of fact table rows. Click Yes and the next screen will be where we name our newly created cube, the last step in the Cube Wizard. Enter "Plan" as the

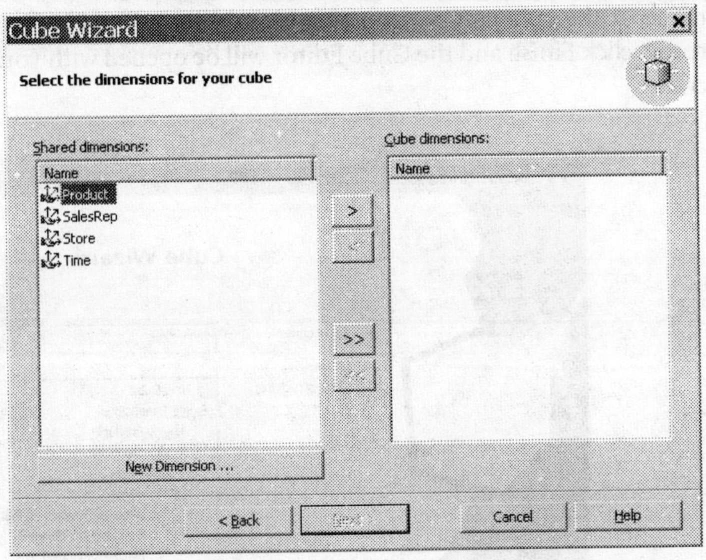

FIGURE 2.31 The shared dimensions.

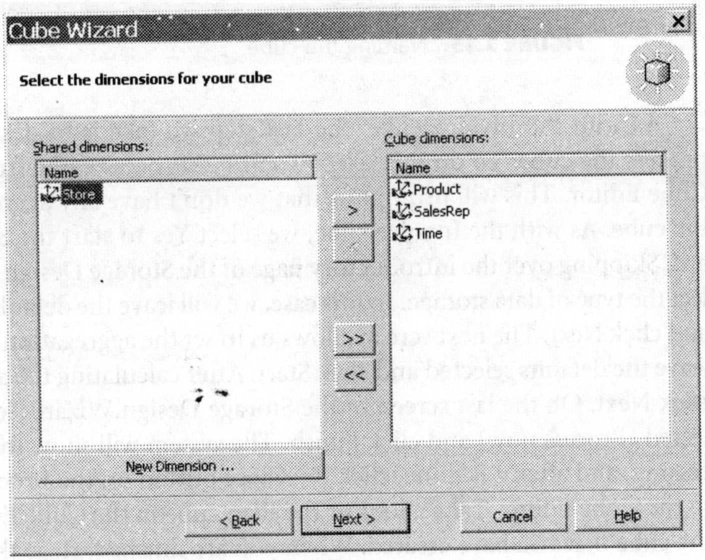

FIGURE 2.32 The Plan dimensions.

name of the cube and your screen should look like Figure 2.33. When you are ready, click Finish and the Cube Editor will be opened with your newly created Plan cube.

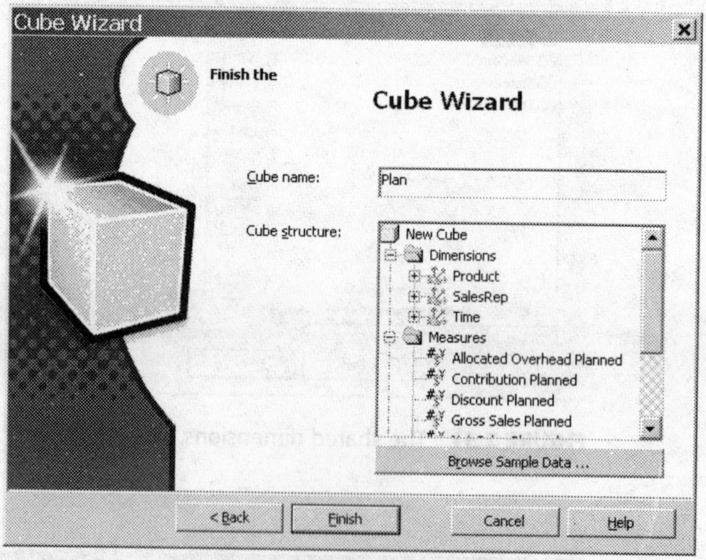

FIGURE 2.33 Naming the cube.

As with the Invoice cube, the last step we take is to design the storage and process the cube. To do this select Tools . . . Process Cube from the menu of the Cube Editor. This will prompt us that we don't have any aggregations defined for the cube. As with the Invoice cube, we select Yes to start the Storage Design Wizard. Skipping over the introductory page of the Storage Design Wizard, we then select the type of data storage. In this case, we will leave the default selected (MOLAP) and click Next. The next screen allows us to set the aggregation options. Again, just leave the defaults selected and click Start. After calculating the aggregations, we can click Next. On the last screen of the Storage Design Wizard, leave the defaults selected (Process now) and click Finish. The system will show the results of the processing, and after it is done, click the Close button on the Process dialog to return to the Cube Editor. Take a look at the Plan cube in the Cube Editor to understand the cube that you have created. When you are finished, close the Cube Editor.

Now that we have created our Plan cube, we are ready to create a virtual cube that will allow us to analyze invoices against the Plan. To begin, select Action . . . New Virtual Cube from the Analysis Manager menu. This will start the Virtual Cube Wizard. The first screen contains some introductory information about virtual cubes. After you have read it, click Next.

The next screen in the Virtual Cube Wizard allows you to select the cubes that will be used in the virtual cube. We have two cubes available in our Pretzel database. Select them both and move them over to the Virtual cube includes list box on the right side of the screen as shown in Figure 2.34. After you have done this, click Next to continue.

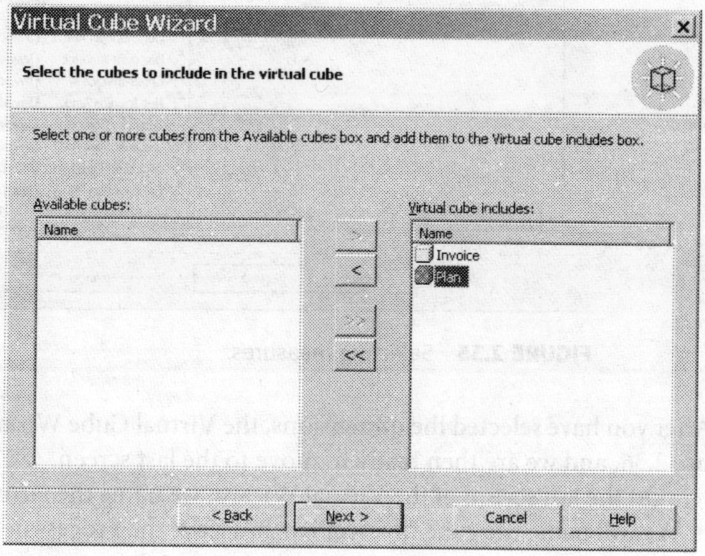

FIGURE 2.34 Selecting cubes.

On the next screen, we choose the measures that will be available in our virtual cube. Since we want to be able to compare all of the aspects of our performance against plan, we will choose all of the measures from both cubes to be included in the virtual cube. After you have moved all of the measures from the Available Measures list to the selected measures list, your screen will look like Figure 2.35 and you can click Next to continue.

Next, we select the dimensions that will be available in our virtual cube. Since we don't do forecasts by store, it would not be useful to include that dimension in the virtual cube. Select the following dimensions from the Available dimensions list and move them to the Selected dimensions list:

- Product
- SalesRep
- Time

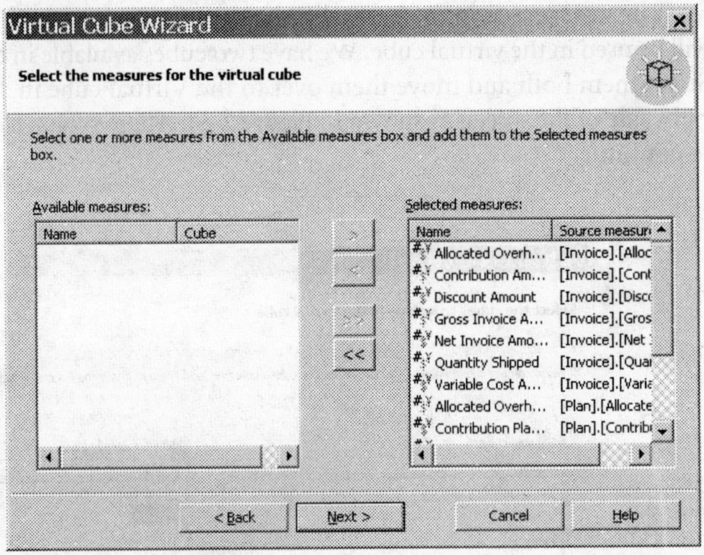

FIGURE 2.35 Selecting measures.

After you have selected the dimensions, the Virtual Cube Wizard will look like Figure 2.36, and we are then ready to move to the last screen.

On the last screen of the Virtual Wizard, we name the virtual cube and process it. We will name the cube InvoicePlan and leave the Process now option button se-

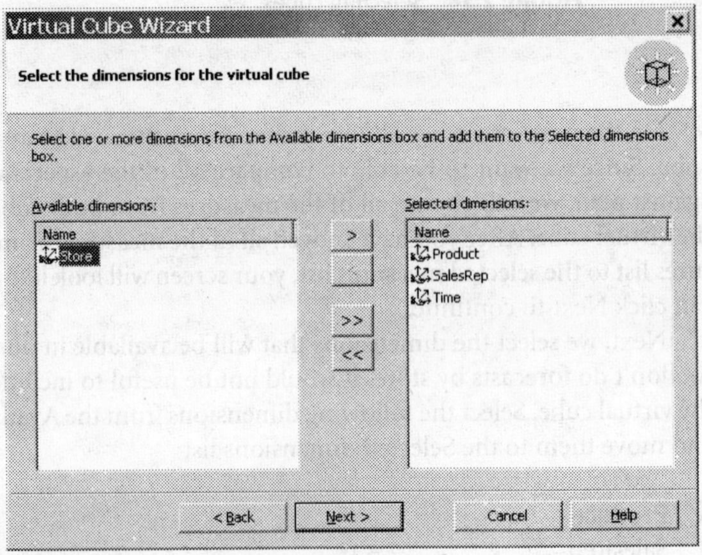

FIGURE 2.36 Selecting dimensions.

lected and click Finish. Analysis Services will process the cube and show us the Process dialog with the progress. After the cube has been processed, close the Process window to see the Cube Editor for the virtual cube we just created. As with the other cubes we have created, you can view the data in the virtual cube. One difference is that you cannot edit the dimensions or members directly in a virtual cube as you can with a regular cube. To change the dimensions or members in the virtual cube, you must change them at the source cube. When you are finished examining the InvoicePlan cube, close the Cube Editor to return to the Analysis Manager.

Adding a few more dimensions to allow analysis on promotions, customer satisfaction, and other aspects important to the business would allow even greater insight. The limitations to your analysis are basically imposed by the availability of data. The more and better data you have, the more and better analyses you can perform. In the next chapter, we will show how to query cubes and get data out in a more customizable way.

SUMMARY

In this chapter, we have discussed data warehousing and how it fits into a business intelligence platform. We have covered the top-down and bottom-up approaches to creating a data warehouse and showed how a plan that is a hybrid of the two, which focuses on rapid time to benefit with an overall plan for warehouse integration, is the best approach. We have compared transactional systems to data warehouses to show how they are very distinct types of systems with transaction systems focused on managing records that are being updated and data warehouses concerned with querying data that is loaded through a batch process. We have discussed some of the basics of dimensional modeling as the foundation for creating a simple and robust schema for data analysis using star schemas. We touched on the topic of moving data from your transactional systems into your data warehouse. Lastly, we showed how to create a cube for analysis in Analysis Services from the data collected by the data warehouse. In the next chapter, we will discuss OLAP with a focus on using Microsoft Analysis Services to perform analysis on the data that we have inserted into the data warehouse.

END NOTES AND REFERENCES

1. For more information, see Inmon, W.H., Inhoff, Claudia, and Sousa, Ryan, *Corporate Information Factory, 2nd Edition,* John Wiley & Sons, 2000.

2. For more information, see Kimball, Ralph, and Ross, Margy, *The Data Warehouse Toolkit: The Complete Guide to Dimensional Modeling,* John Wiley & Sons, 2002.
3. Ibid. pp16.
4. Eckerson, Wayne, "Data Quality and the Bottom Line," The Data Warehousing Institute, 2002, pp.5
5. Ibid. pp.10
6. Bernstein, Philip, and Newcomer, Eric, *Principles of Transaction Processing,* Morgan Kaufmann, 1997.

3 OLAP Cubes

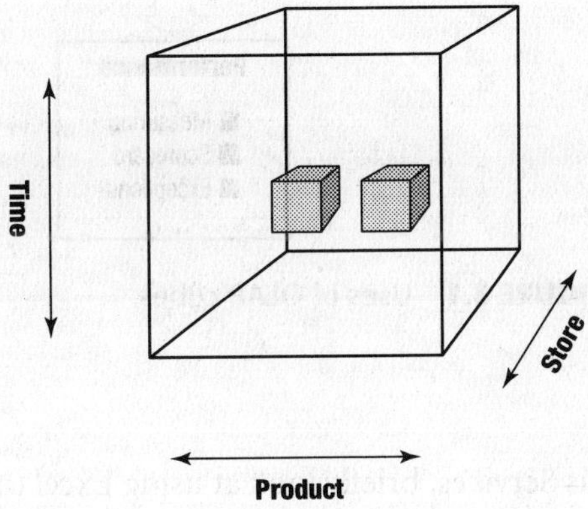

As we have discussed in the previous chapter, *on-line analytical processing* (OLAP) is a crucial technology for business intelligence applications. OLAP cubes are well suited to many business intelligence applications. Executive users want to get information about key performance measures of the business, and about exceptions and variances from benchmarks and budgets. Financial analysts can use OLAP cubes for ad hoc examination of financial and operational data. Another common usage of OLAP is in sales and marketing applications to analyze product sales and profitability. In addition, OLAP cubes can be used in a wide range of operational analyses, including manufacturing throughput and efficiency, supplier performance, and product cost analysis. In short, OLAP is useful for many different kinds of business analysis and intelligence gathering. Figure 3.1 shows many uses of OLAP cubes.

In this chapter, we will discuss OLAP in more depth with a specific focus on the capabilities and use of Microsoft Analysis Services. OLAP Services is a huge topic in itself. We will cover some of the concepts required to work with OLAP data in Mi-

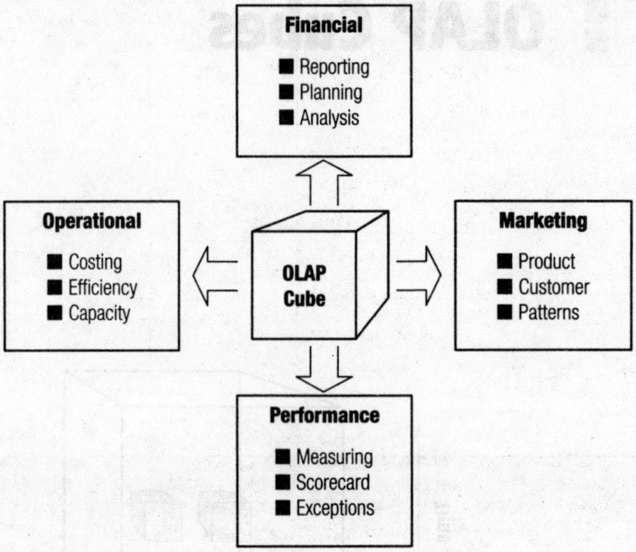

FIGURE 3.1 Uses of OLAP cubes.

crosoft Analysis Services, briefly look at using Excel to view cube data, and dip into *multi-dimensional expressions* (MDX), the query language used to access cubes in Analysis Services.

CUBE CONCEPTS

Analysis Services stores data in cubes. These cubes store various levels of summarized data in data structures highly optimized for user queries using MDX. In addition to simple user queries, cubes support intricate numeric analyses. Using the statistical and numeric functions built into MDX as well as functions called from outside libraries, cubes can produce everything from simple summary sales reports to complex cost allocation algorithms.

One of the strongest features of OLAP cubes is the intuitive data model that users can easily understand. Using tools that users are already familiar with, such as Microsoft Excel, OLAP cubes allow flexible data viewing, analysis, and navigation. Users can drill down and drill up through various levels of summarized data to better analyze and understand the causes of top-level trends as well as manipulate the axes of analysis to get a different view of the data.

Defining a Cube

Cubes are the logical storage structures for OLAP databases. They combine dimensions and measures into a model that users can query. A cube defines a set of related dimensions that form an *n*-dimensional grid or cube. Each cell contained in the cube holds a value or set of values called *measures*, which we will discuss in depth later in this chapter. For now, we can think of the measures for each cell as being the intersection of specified members of the dimensions. For example, consider a cube that contains values for unit sales and dimensions for stores, time, and products. We can envision such a cube as looking like the cube shown in Figure 3.2, which has product on the x-axis, time on the y-axis, and stores on the z-axis.

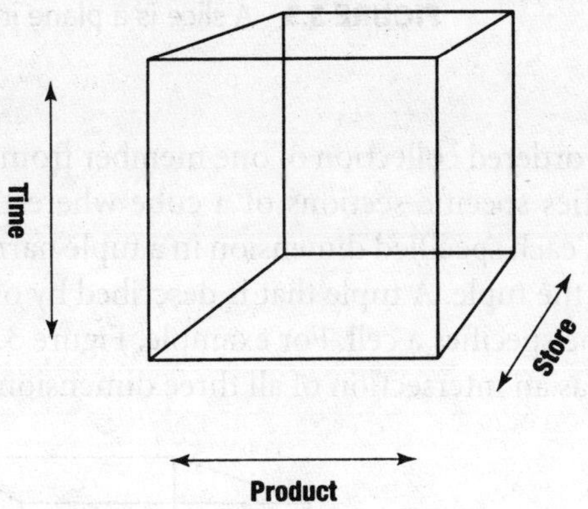

FIGURE 3.2 A three-dimensional cube with products, times, and stores.

Slices

To retrieve a total for a particular product, find that product on the x-axis and sum up the values across all of the members of the time and store axes with which it intersects. This is called *slicing*. A slice consists of a member or group of members that are evaluated across other dimensions. You can think of a slice as being a subset of a cube. In this simple case, the slice is a plane that is perpendicular to the x-axis at the location of the selected product, as shown in Figure 3.3.

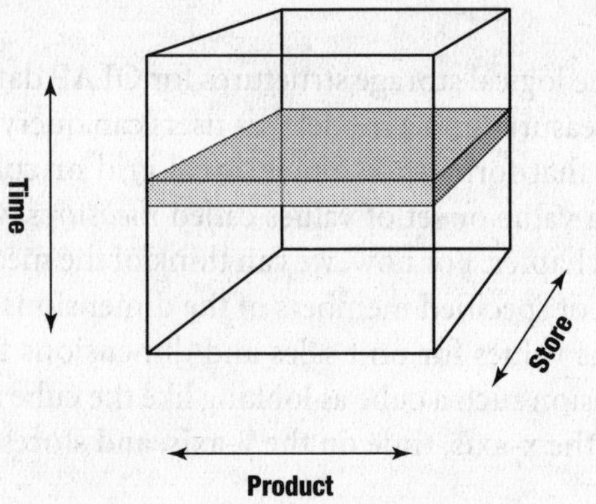

FIGURE 3.3 A slice is a plane in a cube.

Tuples

A *tuple* is an ordered collection of one member from one or more dimensions. The tuple identifies specific sections of a cube where these dimensions intersect. In other words, each specified dimension in a tuple narrows down the records that are members of the tuple. A tuple that is described by one member from each dimension of a cube specifies a cell. For example, Figure 3.4 illustrates a specific cell that is described as an intersection of all three dimensions.

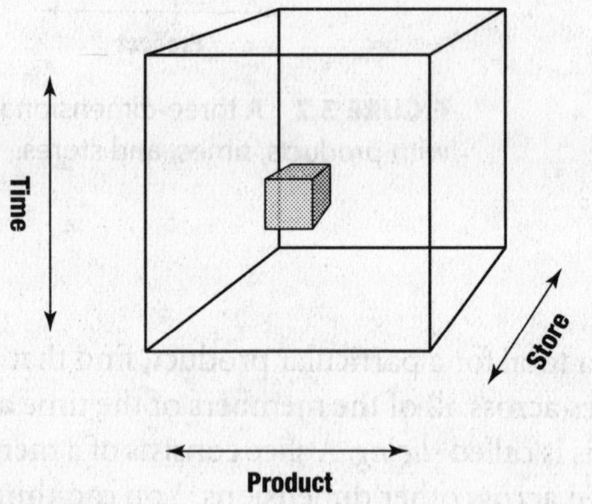

FIGURE 3.4 A tuple defined by all three dimensions.

Sets

A set is simply an ordered collection of tuples. A set can contain zero tuples, in which case it is an empty set. Sets can be defined either by explicitly listing the member tuples or by using one of the many MDX functions that return a set (see Appendix A for a list of MDX functions). A set can define an axis of a cube. The order that tuples are listed in a set is important—the order determines the nesting order for that axis dimension. For example, Figure 3.5 shows a set containing two distinct tuples.

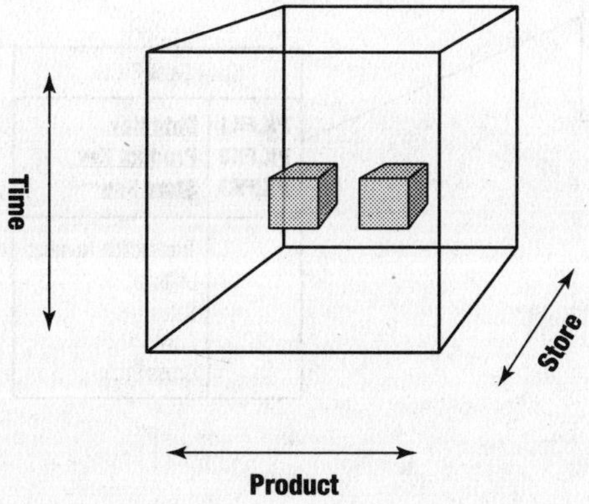

FIGURE 3.5 A set containing two distinct tuples.

Sets and tuples are not interchangeable in MDX functions. It is important to know that a set composed of a single tuple is not a tuple and cannot be used in place of a tuple. However, you can create a set that has a single tuple.

Measures

One of the most fundamental concepts is the measure. Measures are the numerical data values, or facts, that users analyze. Examples of measures include Sales, Units, and Cost of Goods Sold. Every cube must contain at least one measure, but cannot have more than 1,024. Measures are usually numeric. OLAP Services supports measures based on both additive and non-additive columns. Additive columns can be meaningfully summed across all dimensions. For example, a sales measure is additive. Non-additive columns cannot be summed meaningfully. For example, a customer identifier is non-additive.

Every measure in a cube specifies an aggregate function. The aggregate function determines how measure values for child members are aggregated to produce a value for the parent measures. The most commonly used and generally useful aggregate function is Sum. In addition to Sum, OLAP Services supports Min, Max, Count, and Distinct Count. Additive measures can be aggregated by any of these functions. Non-additive measures are summarized by the Count or Distinct Count aggregate functions.

A fact table from the data warehouse is used as the basis for a cube and the measures in the cube correspond to fact table facts. Each measures comes from a column in this fact table. As an example of this, consider the fact table in Figure 3.6.

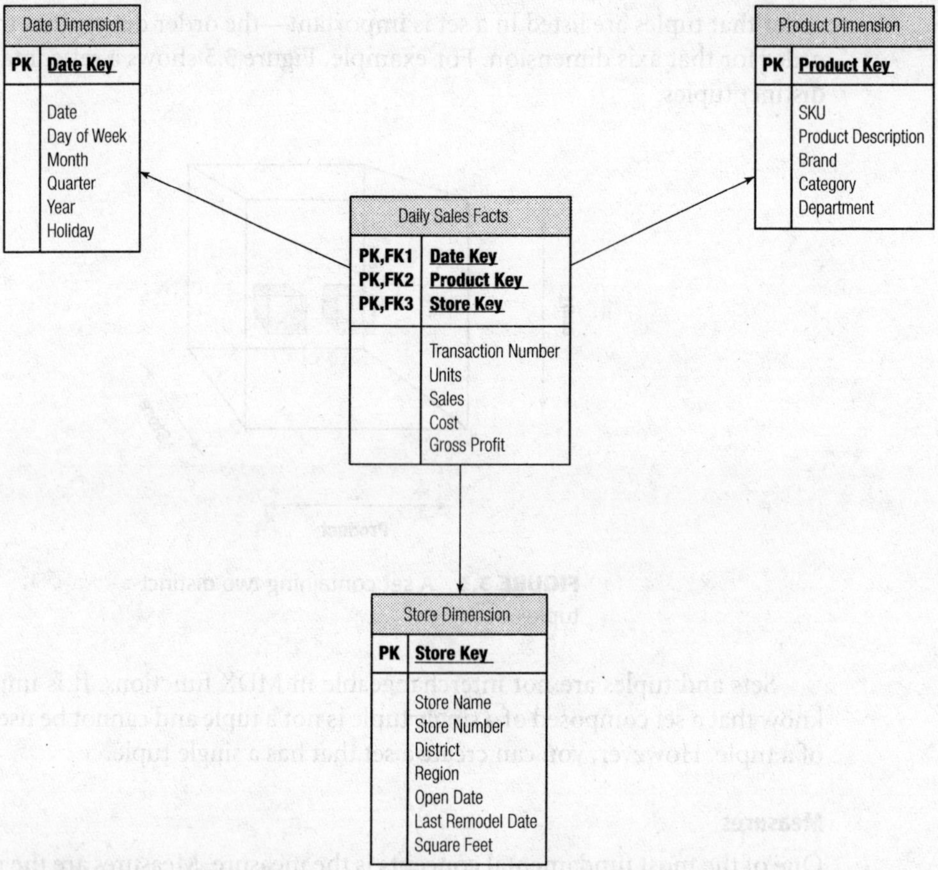

FIGURE 3.6 Sales fact table used to create a sales cube.

This fact table would directly support the creation of measures for Units, Sales, Cost, and Transaction Number in the sales cube. Units, Sales, and Cost are additive measures. Transaction Number is a non-additive measure. If we add more facts to the fact table, we can add more measures to the cube.

In addition to the measures that are taken directly from the fact table, it is possible to create members that are calculated from multiple measures. For example, the Gross Profit measure we just described can be computed from the Sales and Cost measures. These calculated members can be stored in the cube or calculated on demand when needed. If they are calculated on demand, they are called *calculated members*.

Calculated members allow you to add members and measures to a cube without increasing its size. Only the definition of a calculated member is stored in the cube. Although calculated members must be based on data (such as members) that already exists in the cube, you can create complex expressions by combining this data with arithmetic operators, numbers, and a variety of functions. Analysis Services includes a library of over 100 functions and allows you to register and use other function libraries. We will more fully describe the functions that are available in the upcoming MDX section.

In many cases cubes do not have data for all intersections. This is called a *sparse cube*. Sparse is not a negative term; it means simply that there are missing data points for a majority of the cells. This is a very common case for all kinds of data. Consider a cube that is looking at the dimensions of Product, Time, and Promotion. Since at any given time only a relatively few products are associated with a Promotion, the resulting cube would contain mostly missing data values. It is important that these values are properly handled when we are calculating aggregates across the dimension, a subject we address more fully in the MDX section.

Dimensions

Dimensions represent the categories that provide context to the numeric measures. These categories should be derived from the classifications that are important to your business. For example, it makes sense for a Sales cube to have a Product dimension to facilitate analysis in the context of products.

A dimension is made up of levels and members. A *level* is a group of dimension members that share a common meaning. Levels map to dimension table columns. A *member* is a discrete value in a dimension. Members map to dimension table values in a level's column. The dimensions are organized levels and members in a hierarchical tree structure.

Hierarchy

As a hierarchy, it makes sense to describe relationships between members and between levels of a dimension in family terms. Member with no children are said to be at the *leaf level*. Members with no parent are at the *root level*. All other members have at least one parent and at least one child and may have *descendants*, *siblings*, and *cousins*. For example, consider the dimension hierarchy shown in Figure 3.7. In this hierarchy we would say that:

- North America is the *parent* of East.
- East and West are *children* of North America.
- New York, Atlanta, and Toronto are *descendants* of East.
- East and North America are *ancestors* of New York.
- East, Midwest, and West are *siblings*.
- New York and Vancouver are *cousins*.

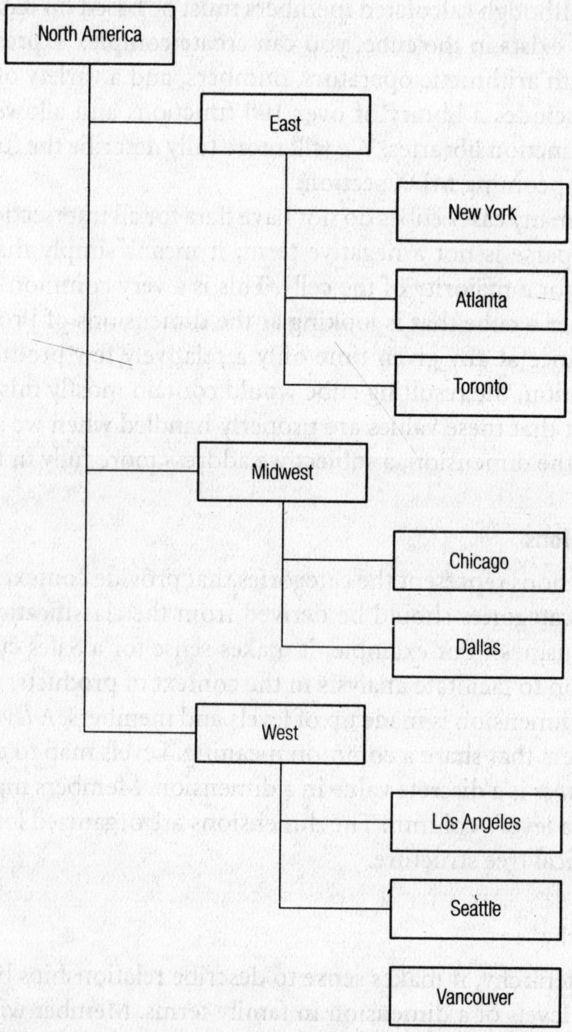

FIGURE 3.7 OLAP hierarchy is described in family terms.

All dimensions contain a hierarchy, and for most dimensions, the hierarchy consists of multiple levels. The multiple levels of a hierarchy allow you to drill up and down along a particular path. In other words, a hierarchy is a way in which the members of a dimension can be aggregated or "rolled up" to higher levels. Dimensions can have multiple hierarchies, representing different paths of aggregation. For example, the Time dimension can have a Calendar and a Fiscal hierarchy to represent different ways of aggregating through time. Note that these hierarchies do not have to have matching levels. So the Calendar hierarchy could have Year, Quarter, Month, Week, and Day levels while the Fiscal hierarchy had Year, Quarter, and Day levels.

When you drill down on a member, you see all the children of that member in the same hierarchy. Drilling down allows you to focus on specific data to explore details that underlie a higher-level member. When you drill up on a member or group of members in a hierarchy, you collapse the detail so that you see only the summary information for the parent. Drilling up allows you to see a bigger picture with fewer details.

Most of the time, data is viewed from the perspective of only a few dimensions. In our natural environment, people live in a four-dimensional world—the three dimensions of space and the forward moving dimension of time. Most people, with the possible exception of mathematicians, have great difficulty understanding and manipulating dimensional orders that are greater than four.

One way to better understand cubes is to think of how they can be viewed in something that we are all familiar with—a spreadsheet. In this section, we will use the PivotTable feature in Microsoft Excel to view the sample FoodMart 2000 sales cube and understand how dimensions can be mapped to a spreadsheet. Although a spreadsheet can't display as many dimensions as a well-constructed graphical representation, it is easy to understand at relatively low levels of dimensionality. For example, let's suppose a cube has two dimensions: Stores and Time. The cube stores sales across all stores and time periods. A two-dimensional view of this cube can easily be represented in a spreadsheet. Figure 3.8 shows a spreadsheet with the di-

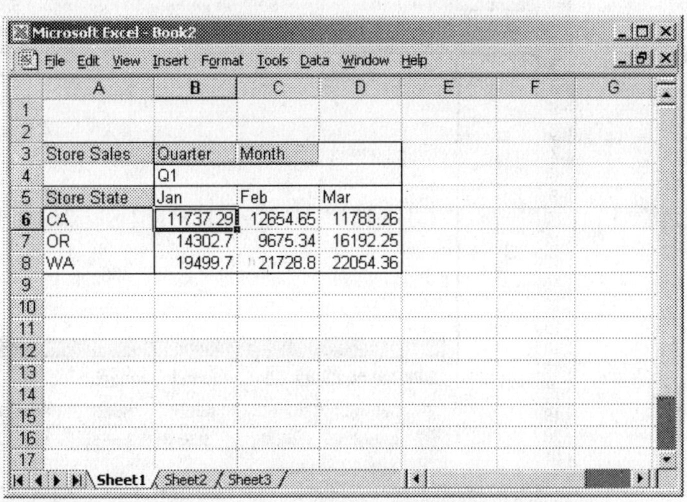

FIGURE 3.8 Two-dimensional cubes can be represented as a spreadsheet.

mensions Stores and Time that was constructed using the PivotTable Wizard in Excel.

Excel is a very good tool for analyzing multidimensional data stored in Analysis Services. Creating a PivotTable using Excel is a three-step process. First, you select the "Data" option from the Excel main menu and choose the "PivotTable and PivotChart report . . . " option. This will present you with the step-one dialog to choose the type of data you want to analyze and the type of report you want to create. To construct the simple example in Figure 3.8, we picked "External data source" as our data source and "PivotTable" as our type of report. In the second step, you select the source of the data. To use data from Analysis Services, choose the OLAP Cubes tab. If the cube you want to use for your report is not present in the list of existing data sources, you can create a new one. To create a new connection, you need to know the name of the Analysis Server that you want to use and the name of the cube. After you have finished creating or selecting the data source, you click Next to decide where you want to place the PivotTable in your workbook, set any desired options, and click Finish. The PivotTable will be put in the worksheet you selected (it will look like Figure 3.9) and it is ready to populate using the PivotTable toolbar. Dragging the desired dimensions and measures to the spreadsheet will populate the PivotTable with data.

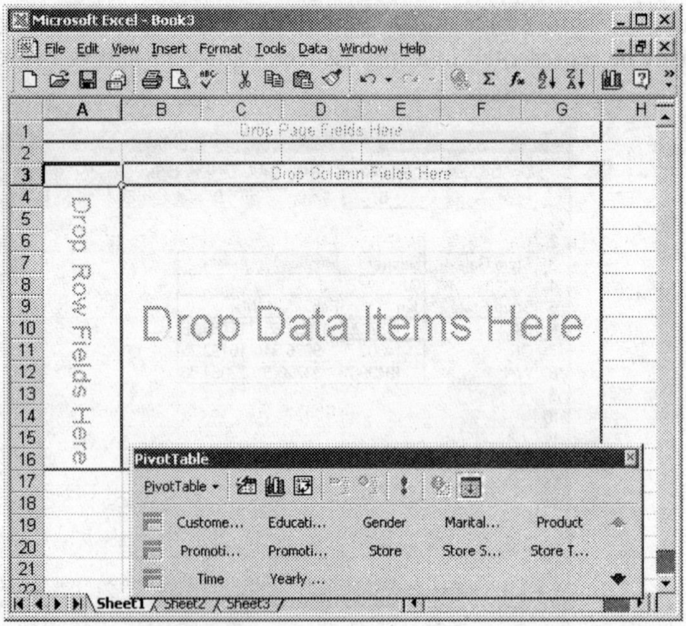

FIGURE 3.9 PivotTable ready to be populated with fields.

If you want to consider only two dimensions (as in Figure 3.8), you need only to select dimensions for the rows, columns, and measures for the data items. Things get more interesting when we are considering three or more dimensions. You can add more dimensions in a couple of different ways. The first way is to add a dimension to the pages field that will create different PivotTable pages for each of the members in that dimension. For example, suppose we are interested in focusing on three product groups: Drink, Food, and Non-consumables. This three-dimensional model can be shown with multiple pages in which each page in the PivotTable shown in Figure 3.10 represents one of these products.

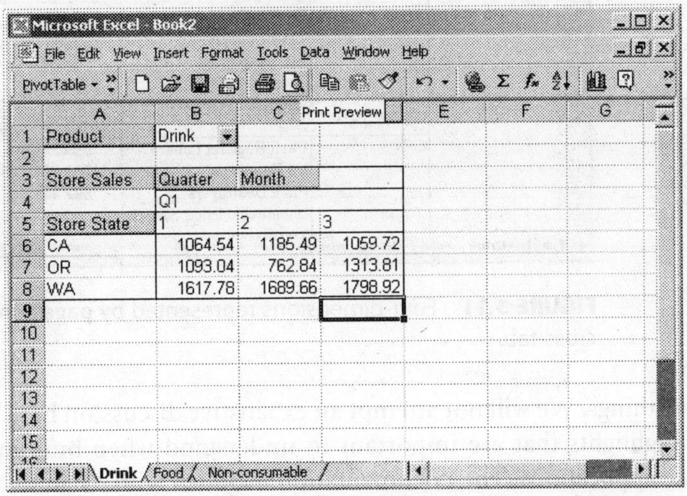

FIGURE 3.10 Three-dimensional cubes can be represented by multiple pages.

Another way to consider another dimension in a PivotTable is to create a cross-tab with an existing dimension. So, if we wanted to consider Promotions, we can drag it from the PivotTable tool bar to the row field area to get the results shown in Figure 3.11.

As we have seen, Excel provides flexible capabilities to view data stored in cubes. However, there are some significant limitations to relying on Excel as your sole interface to cubes. In the next section, we will explore MDX as a way of querying your cubes.

Querying with MDX

The key technology for working with multidimensional data in Analysis Services is MDX. MDX is a full-featured query language that is designed specifically to work with multidimensional data. MDX is a very powerful language that can do many,

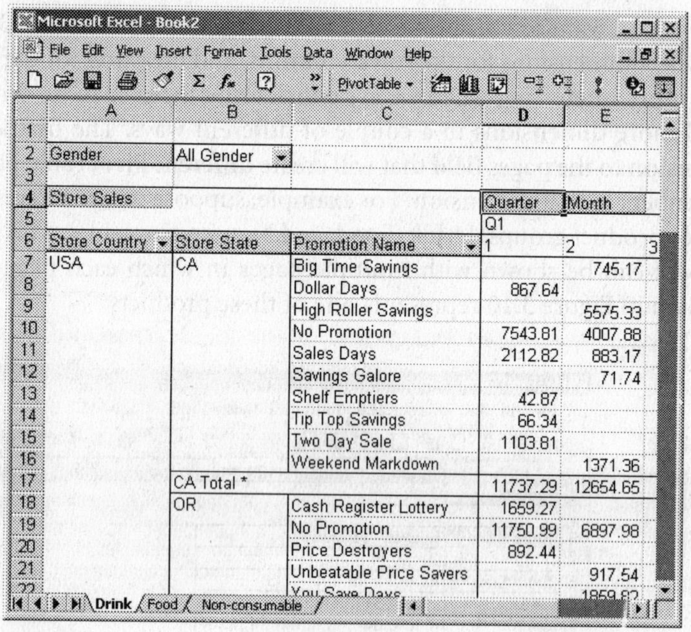

FIGURE 3.11 Four-dimensions represented by pages and cross-tab.

many things. We will not attempt an exhaustive discussion here but instead hit just the highlights that are important to understand when building business intelligence applications. The documentation included with Analysis Services is very detailed and includes good descriptions of the available features. To augment this documentation, we have provided a detailed listing of the functions with examples in Appendix A.

We will begin our discussion on MDX with a very basic MDX query from the FoodMart 2000 cube sample that comes bundled with Analysis Services. One of the simplest queries that we can create is the following:

```
SELECT {[Store]} ON COLUMNS,
{[Product]} ON ROWS
FROM Sales
```

This query returns the aggregation of the default measure across all of the stores and all of the products in our Sales cube. In this case, the default measure is Unit Sales. So that query is equivalent to:

```
SELECT {[Store].[All Store]} ON COLUMNS,
{[Product].[All Product]} ON ROWS
```

```
FROM Sales
WHERE (Measures.[Unit Sales])
```

In general, the format of a simple MDX query is the following:

```
SELECT {[axis specification]} ON COLUMNS,
{[axis specification]} ON ROWS
FROM [cube name]
WHERE ([slicer specification])
```

The basic MDX statement consists of the `SELECT`, `FROM`, and `WHERE` clauses, much like a SQL statement. There are similarities between SQL and MDX. They both allow you to create and process a query that returns results. Many of the same things that can be done in MDX can also be done with SQL (albeit with considerable cost in complexity and performance). But, MDX and SQL are also different. The syntax, although sharing the same words, has different semantics. To make it easier for readers who already know SQL, where possible, we will attempt to explain these differences in terms that will take advantage of your SQL knowledge.

The `SELECT` *Statement*

Returning to our canonical simple MDX statement, we first have the `SELECT` statement. The `SELECT` statement includes a set specification to choose the members for the selected axis. As we have discussed previously, a set is an ordered collection of tuples that can be defined either through an explicit list of the tuples comprising the set or by an MDX function that returns a set. For example,

```
{Measures.Sales}
```

is a valid definition for a set consisting of a single tuple. To define multiple tuples in a set, something like the following can be done:

```
{Measures.Sales, Measures.Cogs}
```

Note that the set defined by the previous statement is different from the set defined by this statement:

```
{ Measures.Cogs, Measures.Sales}
```

Order is important when defining a set and it determines the order in which the results are returned in the result set.

The colon operator is very useful in constructing sets of multiple tuples in their natural order without specifying each explicitly. So, the set defined by

```
{[Time].[All Time].[2000].[Quarter 1]:
  [Time].[All Time].[2000].[Quarter 3]}
```

is identical to the set defined by

```
{[Time].[All Time].[2000].[Quarter 1],
  [Time].[All Time].[2000].[Quarter 2],
  [Time].[All Time].[2000].[Quarter 3]}
```

Axes can be either named or numbered. The named axes, in order, are COLUMNS, ROWS, PAGES, CHAPTERS, and SECTIONS. Numbered axes are indicated by AXIS(index), where index is a zero-based numbering scheme. So, COLUMNS can also be called AXIS(0), ROWS can be called AXIS(1), and so on.

The FROM *Statement*

Next, we have the FROM clause, which contains a cube name. The cube name is simply the name of the cube where the query is to be run. This is analogous to the SQL FROM statement with a key difference being that an MDX FROM statement can reference only one cube. Although MDX as specified in the OLE DB for OLAP specification allows for multiple cubes in a FROM statement, there is no concept of joins between cubes in an MDX statement in Analysis Services. The most prevalent way to join cubes together in Analysis Services is to create a virtual cube. For more information on how to build a virtual cube, see the Analysis Server help topic "Building a Virtual Cube."

The WHERE *Statement*

Finally, we have the WHERE statement. The WHERE clause defines the slicer from which the results will be taken. In MDX, a tuple for a slicer can be constructed in a two different ways. First, and most commonly, the members that define the tuple can be explicitly listed. If the tuple is very simple and consists of only one member from one dimension, the tuple can be constructed by simply specifying that dimension member, for example, [Measures].[Sales] or [Time].[All Time].[2000].

If a tuple is more complex and composed of members from more than one dimension, the members must be enclosed by parentheses, for example, ([Measures].[Sales], [Time].[All Time].[2000]). It is also acceptable to put a simple tuple in parentheses, and it is a good practice to keep your MDX queries consistent. The second way of defining a tuple is by using the return value of one of the functions that return tuple values, such as Current, Item, or StrToTuple.

The slicer determines which member or set of members are evaluated across the dimensions specified on the axes. Unlike the WHERE clause in SQL, the WHERE clause in MDX does not affect the selection of the members on the axes. Instead of restricting the returned members, the WHERE clause in MDX determines the values that go into the selected members. For example, if we wanted to get the Unit Sales instead of the Sales measure, we would use the following:

```
SELECT {[Store].[All Store]} ON COLUMNS,
{[Product].[All Product]} ON ROWS
FROM Sales
WHERE (Measures.[Units])
```

The last thing we want to note about a simple MDX statement is the punctuation used to define the various terms. MDX uses curly braces to enclose sets of dimension elements. Although the curly braces are not required if there is just one element in the set in a SELECT clause, we will use them consistently in the book. In addition to the curly braces, square brackets are used in names of the dimension elements. These are required only if the name has spaces in it, but to be consistent, we will always enclose the names in square brackets.

It is also possible to create a query that returns just one cell from a cube. This can be useful for some business intelligence applications in which it is desired to present just one number. For example, an executive dashboard might display the profit for the current year using the MDX query:

```
SELECT FROM Sales
WHERE ([Measures].[Profits], [Time].[2003])
```

This query returns just a single cell for the given slicer containing the total profits for 2003.

In addition to the Measures dimension, we can also specify other dimensions to use as part of the slice. For example, if we were interested only in Sales for January 2000, we can combine the requested measure with a Time member to restrict our results as in the following query:

```
SELECT {[Store]} ON COLUMNS,
{[Product]} ON ROWS
FROM Sales
WHERE (Measures.[Sales],
  [Time].[2000].[Quarter 1].[January])
```

In addition to the measures that are available in a cube, it is possible to create a calculated member using MDX. Calculated members are very flexible and easy to create in MDX. SQL has an analogous capability to create calculations using the AS keyword. For example, a SQL query that creates a simple calculated column might be something like:

```
SELECT unit_sales, total_sales, total_sales - total_cost
AS profit
```

To perform more complex calculations across multiple dimensions in SQL, it is usually necessary to create temporary tables. To create a calculated member in MDX you use the following construction:

```
WITH MEMBER [member name] AS '[member-formula]'
```

This `WITH` statement comes at the beginning of an MDX statement, before the `SELECT`. The `WITH` section creates members that can be used in the rest of the query. The simplest construction for a calculated member builds a new member from already existing measures. The MDX equivalent of that SQL statement is as follows:

```
WITH MEMBER [Measures].[Profit]
AS '[Measures].[Total Sales] - [Measures].[Total Cost]'
SELECT
  {[Measures].[Unit Sales], [Measures].[Total Sales],
   [Measures].[Profit]}
ON COLUMNS,
{[Time].Children}
ON ROWS
FROM Sales
```

Notice that the Member we created using the `WITH` statement is referenced in the selection of the members.

Another way of using the `WITH` statement is to define sets for a use in an MDX query. Sometimes, it is useful to be able to disentangle the logic to create a set from the rest of the query. For example,

```
WITH SET Actuals AS
'Filter([Time].[Month].members,
  NOT([Measures].[Actual] = 0))'
SELECT
  {CROSSJOIN([Business Unit].Members, Measures.AllMembers)}
ON COLUMNS,
{Actuals } ON ROWS
FROM [Key Performance Indicators]
```

This query returns a result set for the actual and budgeted results only for those months in which actual results have been recorded.

Standard Operators

An operator is a symbol specifying an action that is performed on one or more expressions. As you would expect, MDX provides a set of standard operators that are similar to those provided by SQL. These include the most commonly used arithmetic, comparison, and logical operators such as addition (+), subtraction (–), multiplication (*), division (/), equals (=), greater-than (>), less-than (<), less-than-or-equal-to (<=), greater-than-or-equal-to (>=), `NOT`, `AND`, `OR`, and `XOR`. More details on these operators is available in Appendix C.

Built-in Functions

In addition to the standard operators, MDX supplies a large selection of built-in functions. These functions can be categorized into logical functions, numeric functions, string functions, set functions, tuple functions, *member functions,* and *utility functions.* These functions are readily usable from within an MDX statement without any special considerations. As mentioned at the beginning of the section, details of each of the MDX functions and examples of their use are provided in Appendix A.

Registered Functions

In addition to the functions directly supported by MDX, Analysis Services allows access to functions provided by Microsoft Visual Basic for Applications Expression Services and Microsoft Excel if it is installed on the computer with Analysis Services. Most of the mathematical and logical operations from these two libraries are supported. Most of the functions that manage application instances, file handling, error handling, user interface, or refer to other elements of a worksheet are not supported. For more details on the exact list of functions that are supported see the Analysis Services help topic on "Registered Function Libraries."

Libraries as an Alternative to MDX

As an example, we will use the `SetToArray()` function in MDX to pass an array to the Excel `Max()` function to calculate the maximum unit sales for a given set. `SetToArray()` takes a given set and converts it to a Variant array that Excel can work with. When you are calling functions in an external library that have the same name as internal MDX functions, you must preface the function call with the library name and an exclamation point. So, our example looks like:

```
WITH MEMBER [Measures].[Max] AS
'Excel!Max(SetToArray({[Measures].[Unit Sales]}))'
SELECT
{[Time] }
```

```
ON COLUMNS,
{[Product].[Product Family].members}
ON ROWS
FROM Sales
WHERE [Measures].[Max]
```

The results of this MDX statement are shown in Table 3.1.

TABLE 3.1 Results of the preceding MDX statement.

	1997
Drink	24597
Food	191940
Non-Consumable	50236

The same results can be achieved in pure MDX by using the internal `Max()` function as follows:

```
WITH MEMBER [Measures].[Max] AS
   'Max({[1997]},[Measures].[Unit Sales])'
SELECT
{[Time]} ON COLUMNS,
{[Product].[Product Family].Members}
ON ROWS
FROM Sales
WHERE [Measures].[Max]
```

Complex Functions

In addition to functions that can be used as alternatives for existing MDX functions, Excel and VBA provide a broad range of functions for which there are no analogues in MDX, especially in the areas of date manipulation and mathematics. For example, if you believe that a time-series being observed, for example, sales, is not following a strictly linear relationship, then it can be appropriate to use a nonlinear transformation on the data to better approximate the true growth pattern. So, if we assume that unit sales growth over time is a constant percentage, we can write an equation describing sales as

$$y_1 = Ae^{rt}$$

where *t* represents the time period, *r* is the rate of growth per period, and *A* is the intercept. An exponential growth curve showing the pattern resulting from constant percentage increases over time appears in Figure 3.12.

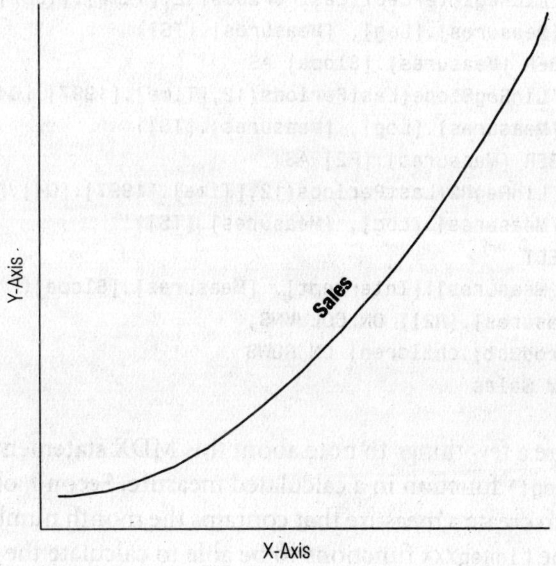

FIGURE 3.12 An exponential growth curve shows constant percentage increases over time.

To estimate the parameters for the exponential growth model with linear regression, we take the log of both sides to get:

$$\log y_t = \log A + rt$$

Since MDX does not have a native log function, we will need to use an external library to transform the y-values so we can fit the equation. The log transformation can be performed using the Excel library like so:

```
WITH MEMBER [Measures].[Log]
AS 'Excel!Log([Measures].[Unit Sales])'
```

After transforming the y-values using the Excel `Log()` function, we can use the `LinRegXXX` functions in MDX to calculate the regression coefficients.

```
WITH
MEMBER [Measures].[Log]
  AS 'Excel!Log([Measures].[Unit Sales])'
```

```
MEMBER [Measures].[TS]
  AS 'StrToValue(Time.CurrentMember.Name)'
MEMBER [Measures].[Intercept]
  AS
   'LinRegIntercept(LastPeriods(12,[Time].[1997].[Q4].[12]),
   [Measures].[Log], [Measures].[TS])'
MEMBER [Measures].[Slope] AS
   'LinRegSlope(LastPeriods(12,[Time].[1997].[Q4].[12]),
   [Measures].[Log], [Measures].[TS])'
MEMBER [Measures].[R2] AS
   'LinRegR2(LastPeriods(12,[Time].[1997].[Q4].[12]),
   [Measures].[Log], [Measures].[TS])'
SELECT
  {[Measures].[Intercept], [Measures].[Slope],
[Measures].[R2]} ON COLUMNS,
{[Product].children} ON ROWS
FROM Sales
```

There are a few things to note about this MDX statement. First, note the use of the `Excel!Log()` function in a calculated measure. Second, observe how `CurrentMember` is used to create a measure that contains the month number. These two combine to allow the `LinRegXXX` functions to be able to calculate the regression coefficients for a non-linear growth model. This could not be done without using an external function.

User-defined Functions

In addition to being able to use the functions in the VBA and Excel libraries, you can create your own libraries that provide functions to Analysis Services. User-defined functions are a Component Object Model (COM)-based feature, and they can be created by any tool that can construct a COM library. We will create a user-defined function library using Visual Studio.NET.

First, let's cover how to call a user-defined function from an MDX statement. The `USE LIBRARY` statement allows you to specify a library to register with the following syntax:

```
USE LIBRARY "<library_path_and_file_name>" | <program_ID>
  [,"<library_path_and_file_name>" | <program_ID>...]
```

For example,

```
USE LIBRARY "c:\functions\library.dll"
```

If you want to register multiple libraries, you can specify each in a comma-delimited list.

After the library has been registered, calling a user-defined function from it is very simple. Basically, you can just reference the name of the function and pass in any arguments. This is where the various `ToStr` and `StrTo` functions come into play. Also important is the `SetToArray` function, which is used to pass a set to an external function via an array.

Solve Order

An important consideration for members that are calculated over more than one dimension is the solve order. The solve order determines what should be done when the calculation formulas over different dimensions overlap. As a simple example of this let's consider what might happen if we were calculating the margins over some different product categories. In Table 3.2, we have two formulas on different dimensions. On the measures dimension (Sales and Cost) we are calculating margin with:

$$\frac{(Sales - Cost)}{Sales}$$

On the product dimension (Apples and Oranges), we are calculating the difference between apples and oranges by subtracting the sales of oranges from the sales of apples and the cost of oranges from the cost of apples. The number calculated in the bottom right-hand corner depends on the calculation order of the formulas. If we calculate the margin after calculating the difference, we get 50% in that cell ((100 – 80) – (70 – 60) / (100 – 80)). If we calculate the difference after calculating the margin, we get 5%. Since there is a big difference in the results based on the order of operations, it is important to be able to specify the order in which the formulas are applied.

TABLE 3.2 Different results from different calculation orders.

	Sales	***Cost***	***Margin***
Apples	100	70	30%
Oranges	80	60	25%
Apples to Oranges comparison	20	10	????

The order that MDX solves is determined by a setting called, appropriately enough, the solve order. Every calculated member has a solve order priority. A calculated member with a lower solve order is calculated before a member with a higher solve order. By default, a calculated member has a solve order of 0, but you can assign a solve order to a calculated member with the `SOLVE_ORDER` keyword. The solve order is relative and can be any integer (although Analysis Services imposes a lower limit of –8191.) For example, if we had the situation described in Figure 3.12, we could write the following MDX statement to ensure that the margin was calculated before the difference:

```
WITH
MEMBER [Measures].[Margin] AS
  '([Measures].[Sales] -   [Measures].[Cost]) /
  [Measures].[Cost]',
  FORMAT_STRING = '#.00%', SOLVE_ORDER = 0
MEMBER [Product].[Apples to Oranges] AS
  '[Product].[Apples] - [Product].[Oranges]',
  SOLVE_ORDER = 1
  SELECT
    {[Measures].[ Sales], [Measures].[Cost],
    [Measures].[Margin]} ON COLUMNS,
    {[Product].[Apples], [Product].[Oranges],
    [Product].[Apples to Oranges] } ON ROWS
FROM Sales
```

Note that it would have been possible to leave out the `SOLVE_ORDER = 0` from the `[Measures].[Margin]` calculated member because that is the default value. Also note the use of the `FORMAT_STRING` property to indicate to MDX that the value of the calculated member is to be returned as a percentage.

Empty Tuples

In many cases, an MDX query will return a result set that contains many empty tuples. To remove these tuples from the result set, MDX has the `NON EMPTY` keyword. For example, the following query returns a substantial number of empty tuples as shown in the result set for the query in Table 3.3.

```
SELECT
{[Product].[All Products].[Drink].
[Alcoholic Beverages].[Beer and Wine].
[Beer].[Good].Children}  ON COLUMNS,
{[Store].[All Stores].[USA].[WA].Children} ON ROWS
FROM [Sales]
WHERE ([Time].[1997].[Q2])
```

TABLE 3.3 Result set with empty tuples.

	Good Imported Beer	Good Light Beer
Bellingham		
Bremerton	12.00	3.00
Seattle	4.00	
Spokane	3.00	5.00
Tacoma	3.00	4.00
Walla Walla		
Yakima		

To remove the empty tuples, we include the NON EMPTY keyword:

```
SELECT
{[Product].[All Products].[Drink].
[Alcoholic Beverages].[Beer and Wine].
[Beer].[Good].children}  ON COLUMNS,
NON EMPTY {[Store].[All Stores].[USA].[WA].children} ON ROWS
FROM [Sales]
WHERE ([Time].[1997].[Q2])
```

which returns the following results:

Note that there are still some empty cells included in the result set for this query in Table 3.4. This is because the NON EMPTY keyword works at the tuple level, not at the cell level. For example, the sample results show that there were sales of the product in Q1 but not in Q2. Because of the sales in Q1, the tuple is not empty and is included in the result set. In general, empty cells are treated as if they are zero for the purpose of numerical computations, and as an empty string for string manip-

TABLE 3.4 The same query using the NON EMPTY keyword on the rows.

	Good Imported Beer	Good Light Beer
Bremerton	12.00	3.00
Seattle	4.00	
Spokane	3.00	5.00
Tacoma	3.00	4.00

ulation. If we wanted to further process the empty cells, we can use the `IsEmpty()` function, which is detailed in Appendix A.

Properties

MDX provides access to custom and intrinsic properties that are defined on dimensions, levels, member, and cells. The intrinsic properties provide basic information about the position, name, and value of a member. Custom properties provide flexible attributes for members that can hold almost any value. Custom member properties can be added to a specific named level in a dimension (with the exception of the (All) level). The easiest way to add custom properties is to use the Dimension Editor in Analysis Manager.

To return properties in an MDX result set, you use the `PROPERTIES` keyword. For example, consider the following query:

```
SELECT
CROSSJOIN([Time].[Year].Members, [Store].children)
ON COLUMNS,
Product.[Product Name].members
DIMENSION PROPERTIES
Product.SKU ON ROWS
FROM Sales
```

The results of this query will include the SKU property of the Product Name members in each row.

SUMMARY

In this chapter, we covered the concepts necessary to understand and work with OLAP data in Microsoft Analysis Services, took a brief look at using Excel to view cube data, and discussed the highlights of MDX. In the next chapter, we will build on the content in this chapter and explore other client options for accessing and displaying cube data from Analysis Services.

REFERENCES

SQL Server Online Help, available by opening the Help menu from within the program. This is also available, along with other useful resources, online at *http://www.microsoft.com/sql/techinfo/productdoc/2000/default.asp.*

Information about MDX is available online at *http://msdn.microsoft.com/library/default.asp?url=/library/en-us/olapdmad/agmdxbasics_04gg.asp.*

4 Analysis Service Clients

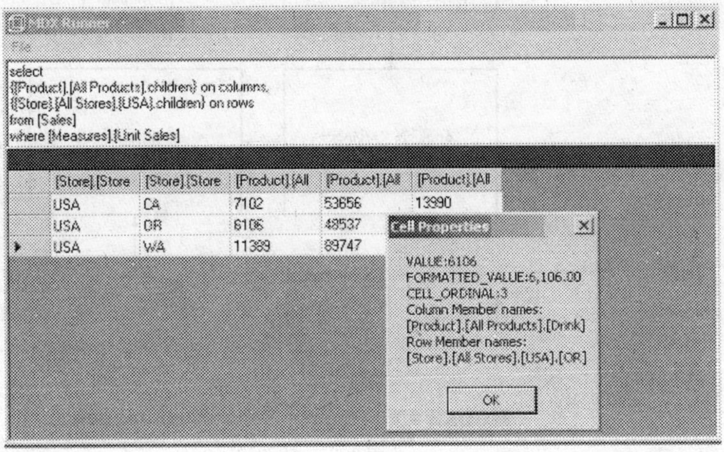

Analysis Services is a middle-tier server for OLAP and data mining. There are two distinct but overlapping tools for supporting these functions included in Analysis Services: OLAP Services and Data Mining Services. Our focus in this chapter is on OLAP Services, with coverage of Data Mining Services deferred to Chapter 8.

OLAP Services manages multidimensional cubes of data for analysis and client access to that information. OLAP Services imports data from a data warehouse, calculates aggregations, and responds to queries. PivotTable Service, an OLE DB data provider, provides client access. Microsoft Excel and other OLAP client applications retrieve data from the server using the PivotTable Service. These client applications present this information to the user, or can create local data cubes for offline analysis. A schematic of how these components fit together is shown in Figure 4.1.

In addition to the client objects used to manipulate data, there is an object model that is designed for the management of the metadata stored in Analysis Services. This object model is called *Decision Support Objects*, and we will show how

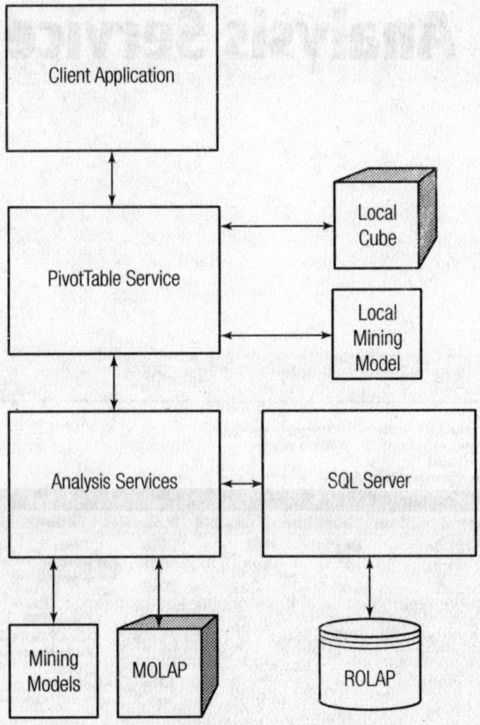

FIGURE 4.1 Analysis Services components.

this technology can be used to create applications that programmatically administer Analysis Services.

CLIENT TECHNOLOGIES

There are a variety of ways to create applications using Analysis Services in .NET. At the lowest level, we have the standard library exposed by OLE DB for OLAP. Building on that foundation, we have *ActiveX Data Objects Multi-dimensional (ADOMD)* and *XML for Analysis (XMLA)*. In the sections that follow, we will discuss building applications using ADOMD. The next chapter will cover XMLA.

OLE DB for OLAP

OLE DB for OLAP is published by Microsoft and establishes an Application Programming Interface (API) standard for multidimensional data access that is broadly used for OLAP on the Windows platform. OLE DB for OLAP consists of a set of objects and interfaces that extends the relational database access provided by

OLE DB to include multidimensional data. The use of OLE DB as the core of OLE DB for OLAP allows the reuse of the interfaces that provide common data handling and manipulation, and minimizes the number of multidimensional specific objects and interfaces that have to be added to the architecture. The language used to access data through OLE DB for OLAP is MDX, which we covered in the last chapter. The architecture of OLE DB for OLAP and the relationship to OLE DB is shown in Figure 4.2.

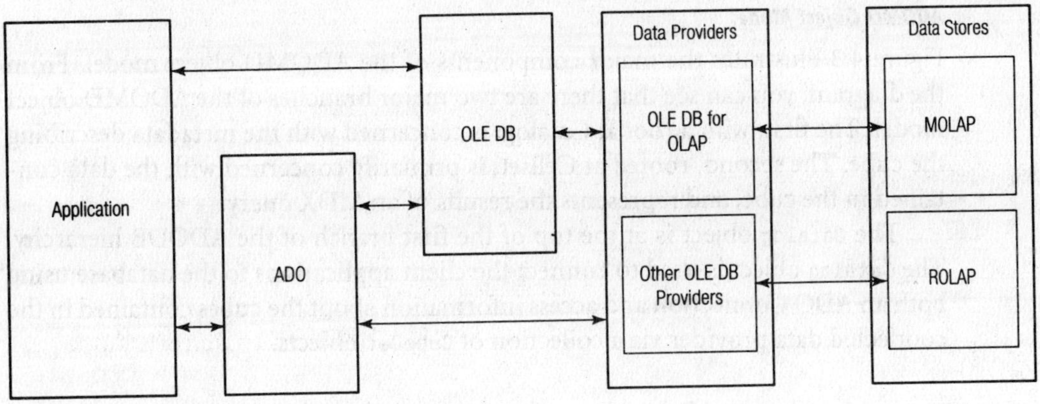

FIGURE 4.2 OLE DB for OLAP architecture.

We will not cover creating an application using the OLE DB for OLAP interfaces directly. OLE DB for OLAP is a powerful set of interfaces, but it is relatively low-level and working with it directly would be overkill for most business intelligence applications. Instead, we will discuss creating applications using the higher-level abstractions of ADOMD in this chapter and XMLA in the following chapter.

ADOMD

ADOMD provides a set of COM objects that can be used to manipulate multidimensional data. ADOMD is based on the OLE DB for OLAP specification, which defines a set of COM objects and interfaces to allow OLE DB to access multidimensional data stores.

ADOMD uses an OLE DB for OLAP provider to gain access to data and provide a common library for accessing the underlying data. Although it is not a native .NET component, ADOMD can be used in .NET applications via COM Interop in .NET. To simplify the transition to .NET and preserve the large amount of code that has been written to take advantage of COM, the Microsoft .NET Framework provides a strong interoperation layer that allows calls to be made to and received from ActiveX components, COM components and Win32 API functions. It is not, however, our objective here to cover all of the .NET interoperability features.

As you expect from the name, ADOMD is related to ADO. In fact, ADOMD depends on ADO for connections and some other services. Both can be used to access Analysis Services to retrieve data and metadata. ADO, as it is designed for relational databases, returns tabular views of cube data or metadata, which can be very useful when you want to bind data to a simple grid or other flattened display. ADOMD is organized as a hierarchy that matches the structure of a cube in Analysis Services, and retrieves cube data and metadata in a richer form.

ADOMD Object Model

Figure 4.3 illustrates the major components of the ADOMD object model. From the diagram, you can see that there are two major branches of the ADOMD object model. The first, with a root at Catalog, is concerned with the metadata describing the cube. The second, rooted at Cellset, is primarily concerned with the data contained in the cube, and represents the results of an MDX query.

The `Catalog` object is at the top of the first branch of the ADODB hierarchy. The `Catalog` object is used to connect the client applications to the database using both an ADO Connection and access information about the cubes contained in the connected data provider via a collection of `CubeDef` objects.

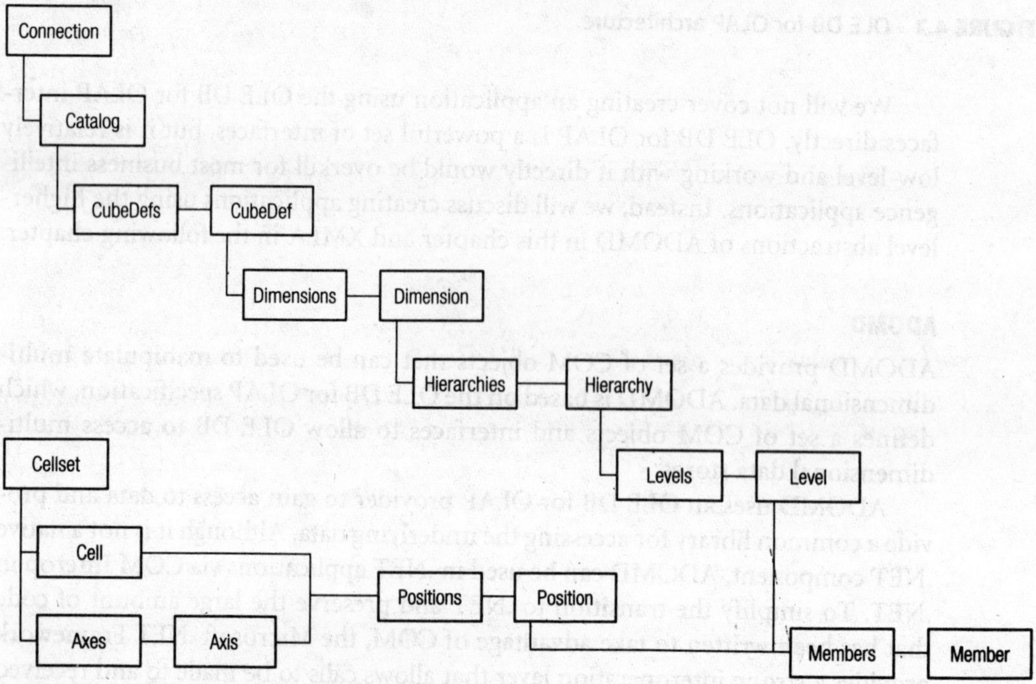

FIGURE 4.3 The ADOMD object model.

Each `CubeDef` object contains the name and description of the cube, in addition to some other properties, and allows access to the structure of the cube contained in the Dimensions collection. Each Dimension object contains the name and description of the dimension, other properties, and the Hierarchy objects that make up the dimension via the Hierarchies collection. A Hierarchy object has a name and description as well as other properties, and the collection of Levels in the hierarchy. Each Level contains a name and a description, other properties, and a Members collection. The Member objects can differ depending on the context in which they are used. As a member of a Level, Member has a Children property that returns the Members on the next lower level of the hierarchy, and a Parent property that can be used to navigate up the hierarchy.

The cube data is retrieved through the `Cellset` object. The `Cellset` is retrieved as the results of an MDX query and contains the collection of Cells organized into Axes and Positions, which can be retrieved in the form of a multidimensional array or by navigating down the axes. The `CubeDef` and the `Cellset` come together at the Members. When used in context of a `Position`, the `Children` and `Parent` properties of a `Member` are empty, so you cannot navigate the `CubeDef` hierarchy. However, it has two properties that are useful in displaying multidimensional data: `DrilledDown` and `PreviousSameAsParent`. `DrilledDown` returns `true` if there is at least one child member on the same axis, and `false` otherwise. `PreviousSameAsParent` returns `true` if the immediately preceding member on the same axis is the member's parent, and `false` otherwise.

Using ADOMD in .NET

As in any COM library, to use ADOMD in a .NET application you must first import it and add references to ADO and ADOMD to your project. Thanks to the strong COM interoperability provided in .NET, this is not difficult. To add a COM reference in Visual Studio .NET, open the Project menu and choose Add Reference. In the Add Reference dialog box that is displayed, select the COM tab; find the entry for "Microsoft ActiveX Data Objects (Multi-dimensional) 2.7 Library," and click the Select button or double-click the entry to move it into the Selected Items list box. Next, find "Microsoft ActiveX Data Objects 2.7 Library" in the component list and move it to the Selected Items list box. The screen should look like Figure 4.4. After both libraries have been selected, click OK. Visual Studio .NET will create all of the necessary plumbing for you to use these libraries in your C# project.

After you have imported the libraries, you will next establish an ADO connection to the Analysis Server. The syntax to do this looks much like the syntax used to connect to a relational database in ADO:

```
using ADODB;
Connection conn = new ConnectionClass();
```

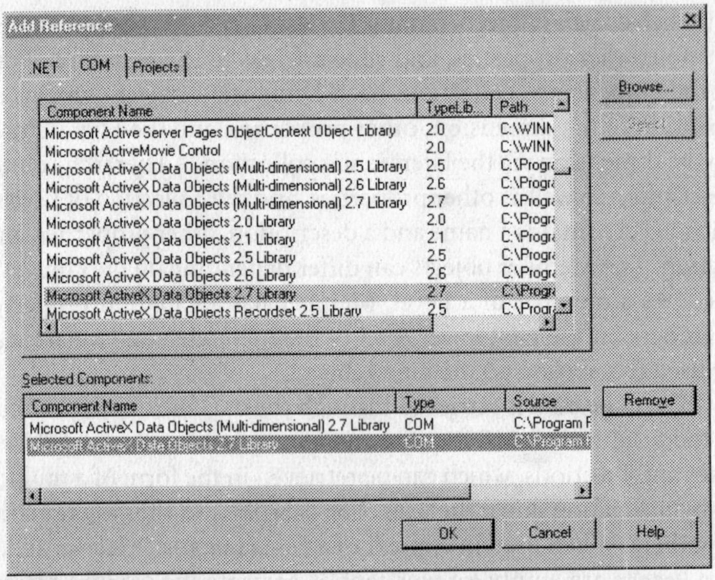

FIGURE 4.4 Importing the ADO and ADOMD libraries.

```
conn.Open(
   "Provider=MSOLAP;Data Source=localhost;
    Initial Catalog=FoodMart 2000;","", "",
   (int)ConnectOptionEnum.adConnectUnspecified);
```

`Connection` is a COM interface defined in ADODB and we create an instance of the `ConnectionClass` to be used through that interface. Note that we have included the `using` keyword with our imported ADODB library. After doing this, we can use the local name of the objects contained in the libraries instead of using the ADODB.Connection syntax, which is equivalent, but more verbose.

Using ADO for Metadata

After we have connected to the database, we can use ADO to return the schemas information about the cubes that are contained in the database. To do this we use the `OpenSchema` method with the following syntax:

```
recordset = connection.OpenSchema(QueryType, Criteria, SchemaID)
```

`OpenSchema` returns a `Recordset` object containing descriptive information for a part of the metadata, based on the `SchemaEnum` argument that used in their query type. So, the line:

```
Recordset rs =
  (Recordset)conn.OpenSchema(SchemaEnum.adSchemaCubes,
   Missing.Value,
   Missing.Value);
```

will return a `Recordset` object that we can navigate through to get the cubes available in the database. Because `adSchemaCubes` doesn't require any criteria, we have used the `Missing.Value` for the second argument in `OpenSchema`. Because of the strongly typed nature of C#, missing values are not allowed in a function call. The System.Reflection namespace provides the `Missing` class that allows C# to call a method with the default arguments, so that is what we use here. The structure of the rowset that is returned appears in Table 4.1.

TABLE 4.1 Contents of the `adSchemaCubes Recordset`.

Column name	***Type***	***Description***
CATALOG_NAME	string	Name of the catalog
SCHEMA_NAME	string	Name of the schema
CUBE_NAME	string	Name of the cube
CUBE_TYPE	string	The cube type, which is one of the following: • "CUBE" • "VIRTUAL CUBE"
CUBE_GUID	GUID	The Cube GUID. `Null` if unknown
CREATED_ON	Time stamp	Time stamp of cube creation. `Null` if unknown.
LAST_SCHEMA_UPDATE	Time stamp	Time stamp of last schema update. `Null` if unknown.
SCHEMA_UPDATED_BY	string	UserID of last person to update the schema. `Null` if unknown.
LAST_DATA_UPDATE	Time stamp	Time stamp for last update. `Null` if unknown.
DATA_UPDATED_BY	string	UserID of last person to update cube. `Null` if unknown.
DESCRIPTION	string	Description of the cube
ANNOTATIONS	string	Notes on the cube

It gets a little bit more complicated if we want to use a `SchemaEnum` that requires arguments. Then we have to create an argument for the *Criteria*. The code to get the dimensions from the Sales cube is as follows:

```
Recordset rsdim = (Recordset)conn.OpenSchema
  (SchemaEnum.adSchemaDimensions,
  new Object[]{"FoodMart 2000", null, "Sales"},
  Missing.Value);
```

This returns a `Recordset` that contains information about the dimensions in the Sales cube in the FoodMart 2000 database, which is described later. For this call, we have populated the *Criteria* argument with an array of type object to limit the results we get back to just the dimensions in the Sales cube in the FoodMart 2000 catalog.

The order of the objects passed in the object array is important. What we are doing with this array is creating a row of a particular type that is passed in to limit the resulting `Recordset`. In this case, we are passing in a row from the Dimensions rowset, which has the structure shown in Table 4.2.

TABLE 4.2 Dimension Rowset Structure.

Column name	*Type*	*Description*
CATALOG_NAME	string	Catalog name
SCHEMA_NAME	string	Schema name
CUBE_NAME	string	Cube name
DIMENSION_NAME	string	Dimension name
DIMENSION_UNIQUE_NAME	string	Dimension unique name
DIMENSION_GUID	GUID	GUID for the dimension
DIMENSION_CAPTION	string	Dimension caption
DIMENSION_ORDINAL	integer	Dimension ordinal number
DIMENSION_TYPE	enum	One of the following values: • MD_DIMTYPE_TIME for a Time dimension. • MD_DIMTYPE_MEASURE for a Measures dimension. • MD_DIMTYPE_OTHER for a dimension that is neither Time nor Measure. • MD_DIMTYPE_UNKNOWN for an unclassified dimension.
DIMENSION_CARDINALITY	integer	Approximate number of members in the dimension
DEFAULT_HIERARCHY	string	Default hierarchy for the dimension
DESCRIPTION	string	Description of the dimension
ANNOTATIONS	string	Notes on the dimension

With the object array we have specified (`new Object[]{"FoodMart 2000", null, "Sales"}`), we are limiting the `Catalog` name and the `Cube` name, but not the `Schema` name or any of the other values. Note that any of the values that we do not pass in explicitly are treated as `null`.

By using the different schema enumerations and filtering, you can get any piece of Analysis Services metadata via ADO. Although you can use any of the valid ADO Schema enumerators, the possible values that are specific to ADOMD data include:

- `adSchemaCubes`
- `adSchemaDimensions`
- `adSchemaHierarchies`
- `adSchemaLevels`
- `adSchemaMeasures`
- `adSchemaMembers`

We have seen how `adSchemaCubes` and `adSchemaDimensions` are used. The use of the other ADO Schema enumerators is very similar, except with respect to the specific criteria that are used in the call to `OpenSchema`. A list of the schemas that are available and the fields that can be used as constraints is available in Appendix E.

Using ADOMD for Metadata

Although retrieving the metadata through ADO is not terribly difficult, the organization of the results does not reflect the hierarchy of the data. To get the data back in a hierarchical form, we can use ADOMD. For example, to retrieve the list of cubes as we just did in ADO, the equivalent ADOMD would be:

```
Catalog cat = new Catalog();
cat.ActiveConnection = conn;
CubeDefs myCubeDefs = cat.CubeDefs;
```

Using the returned `CubeDefs` collection, we can navigate through the entire ADOMD tree to retrieve any additional metadata that is required.

Getting Data in a `Recordset`

Retrieving data from Analysis Server with ADO is very simple. Basically, you can run an MDX query and return the results as a `Recordset`. For example,

```
Recordset rs = conn.Execute(mdx, out records, 0);
```

ON THE CD

returns the set of records specified by the MDX query in the first argument to `Execute`. This result can be used as a flattened `Recordset`, meaning it can be directly bound to a grid without any special considerations. As a simple example of this, the following code from the Mdequis sample in the Chapter 4 folder on the CD-ROM binds the results of an MDX query to a grid displayed in a form. The complete code is available in the project.

```
private void RunQuery()
{
    try
    {
        Connection conn = new ConnectionClass();
        conn.Open("Provider=MSOLAP;Data Source=localhost;
            Initial Catalog=FoodMart 2000;","","",0);
        string mdx = textBoxQuery.Text;

        object records = 0;

        Recordset rs = conn.Execute(mdx, out records, 0);

        OleDbDataAdapter myDA = new OleDbDataAdapter();
        _gridDS = new DataSet();

        myDA.Fill(_gridDS, rs, "MyTable");

        dataGrid1.SetDataBinding(_gridDS, "MyTable");

        conn.Close();
    }
    catch (Exception ex)
    {
        MessageBox.Show(ex.Message);
    }
}
```

There are some limitations when retrieving multidimensional data in a flattened `Recordset`—because it is retrieved as a flat set of data, you don't access to the metadata. To retrieve properties and perform useful tasks such as drill up and down, you need to know the structure of the data. If you plan on creating an application that will use the metadata, you'll probably want to retrieve the data in the form of a `Cellset`.

Getting Data in a Cellset

Retrieving the data from an MDX query in the form of a `Cellset` is just as easy as retrieving a `Recordset`. We simply create an instance of a `Cellset` and call the `Open` method with the MDX statement and the connection to the data source:

```
Cellset cst = new CellsetClass();
cst.Open(mdx, conn);
```

This code will populate the `Cellset` with data from the MDX query. This data can then be navigated to retrieve Axis and Member information.

Putting It All Together

Using both an ADO `Recordset` with an ADOMD `Cellset` together can be useful. For example, in our Mdequis example we use the ADO `Recordset` as an easy way to bind flattened MDX results to a `DataGrid` control. We then combine it with an ADOMD `Cellset` retrieved from the same query to access property and axis information when the cells in the `DataGrid` are clicked. The code to do this appears here:

```
private void ShowCellProperties(int row, int column)
    {
        // figure out the number of columns to offset
        int offset = _rs.Fields.Count –
            _cst.Axes[0].Positions.Count;
        // if in the data section, show the cell properties
        if (column - offset >= 0)
        {
            object[] indexer = {column - offset, row};
            Cell cell = _cst.get_Item(ref indexer);

            foreach(Property p in cell.Properties)
            {
                Debug.WriteLine(p.Name + ":" + p.Value);
            }

            foreach(Member m in
                _cst.Axes[0].Positions[column - offset].Members)
            {
                Debug.WriteLine(m.UniqueName);
            }
            foreach(Member m in
                _cst.Axes[1].Positions[row].Members)
            {
                Debug.WriteLine(m.UniqueName);
            }

        }
    }
```

You can see the results of the `ShowCellProperties` by clicking on a cell in the `DataGrid`. A screenshot of the results appears in Figure 4.5. First, we calculate an offset value to reflect that some of the columns in the `DataGrid` are populated with the names of the row members. So we simply take the total number of columns in our

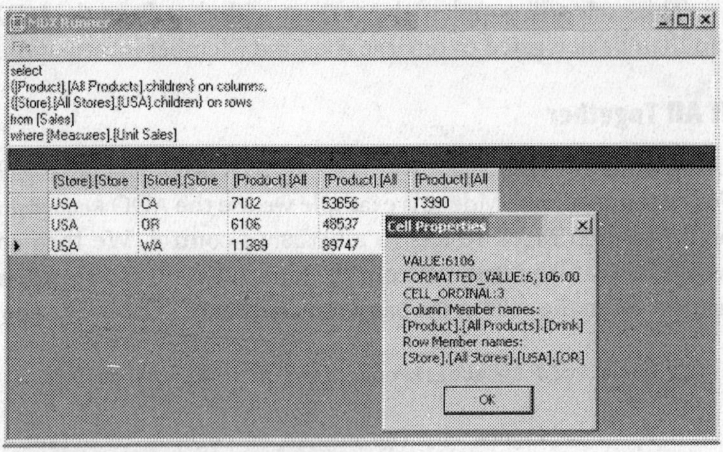

FIGURE 4.5 MDX Runner displaying the properties for a selected cell.

`Recordset` (`_rs.Fields.Count`) and subtract the number of `Positions` in our column `Axis` (`_cst.Axes[0].Positions.Count`). Next, we make sure that the calculated offset indicates that we are in a data cell, and we retrieve the `Cell` in that position in the `Cellset` with the lines:

```
object[] indexer = {column - offset, row};
Cell cell = _cst.get_Item(ref indexer);
```

The indexer is an array of type object that we build from the index of the column and row that we would like to retrieve. Notice that the indexer orders the indexes in the same order that ADOMD numbers `Axes` (columns are 0, rows are 1, etc.) and that this is the opposite of the row-major way that we deal with the `DataGrid`. Now that we have the `Cell`, we can retrieve the `Cell.Properties` collection. After we have the cell properties, we want to display the member name for the `Cell`'s column and row position. To do this, we retrieve the appropriate Axis from the `Cellset`: `Axes[0]` gives us the columns and `Axis[1]` gives us the rows and gets the `Members` at the position of the cell we clicked.

Using Decision Support Objects

The last client technology we will discuss in this chapter is *Decision Support Objects (DSO)*. As we have shown, ADO and ADOMD can be used to access and display metadata in a straightforward manner. However, they do not provide a means to easily manage the metadata. DSO is a COM-based library used to manipulate the metadata in Analysis Services. DSO does not require the PivotTable services to be present since it accesses interfaces provided directly by Analysis Services. The DSO object model parallels the structure of the metadata, as it is stored in Analysis Services. As such, it is the best way to programmatically administer Analysis Services. Using DSO, you can manipulate servers, databases, cubes, dimensions, mining models, and roles. A diagram of the DSO object model is shown in Figure 4.6.

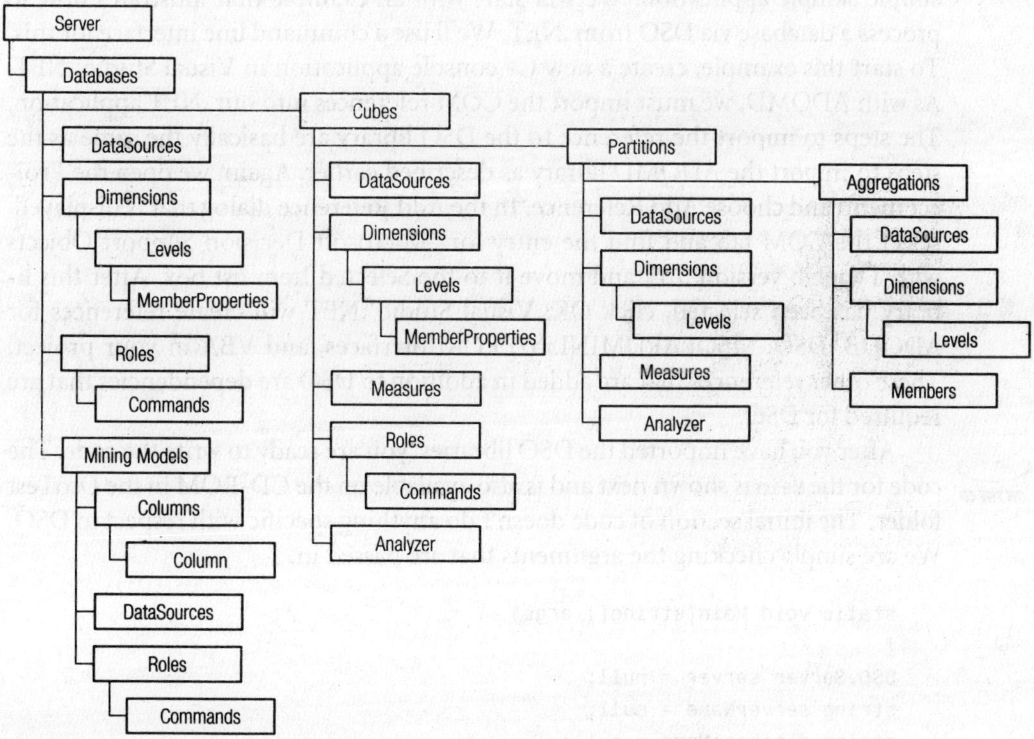

FIGURE 4.6 The DSO object model.

The DSO object model is fairly straightforward, but there are some important considerations that should be understood when developing a DSO application. The top level of the hierarchy, the `Server`, is used to connect to the Analysis Services server. Once connected, the `Server` can be used to start and stop Analysis Services, retrieve information about the server, and retrieve a collection of `Database` objects. A `Database` can be used to create, edit, and delete all of the objects that are contained in a database such as cubes, dimensions, and mining models. A `Cube` can be used to create, edit, and delete all of the objects that are contained in a cube such as data sources, dimensions, measures, partitions, and roles. The `Cube` object can also process the cube, which updates the cube data and structure.

One of the features of the DSO object model is the use of the `MDStores` collection as the root for the collections of databases, cubes, partitions, and aggregations.

Each of these is represented by a common interface, `MDStore`. To create an instance of one of these objects, you must reference the containing `MDStores` collection and add the item there. For example, to create an instance of a cube, you would reference the `MDStores` collection of a database and create it there.

To help understand DSO and how it can be used in .NET, let's take a look at a simple sample application. We will start with an example that illustrates how to process a database via DSO from .NET. We'll use a command line interface for this. To start this example, create a new C# console application in Visual Studio .NET. As with ADOMD, we must import the COM references into our .NET application. The steps to import the reference to the DSO library are basically the same as the steps to import the ADOMD library as described earlier. Again, we open the Project menu and choose Add Reference. In the Add Reference dialog that is displayed, select the COM tab and find the entry for "Microsoft Decision Support Objects with TypeLib version 5.1" and move it to the Selected Item list box. After this library has been selected, click OK. Visual Studio .NET will create references for ADODB, DSO, MSOLAPDMINLib2, POMInterfaces, and VBA in your project. These other references that are added in addition to DSO are dependencies that are required for DSO.

ON THE CD

After you have imported the DSO libraries, you are ready to write the code. The code for the `Main` is shown next and is also available on the CD-ROM in the DsoTest folder. The initial section of code doesn't do anything specific with respect to DSO. We are simply checking the arguments that are passed in.

```
static void Main(string[] args)
{
DSO.Server server = null;
string serverName = null;
string databaseName = null;
try
{
    // check the arguments
    if (args.Length != 2)
    {
        Console.WriteLine
            ("Usage: DsoTest <servername> <database>");
        return;
    }
    // read the arguments
    serverName = args[0];
    databaseName = args[1];
```

After assigning the `serverName` and `databaseName` arguments, we are ready to connect to the server. First, we create an instance of the server and connect to the name given in the command line.

```
// create an instance of the server
server = new DSO.ServerClass();
// attempt to connect to the server
Console.WriteLine
  (String.Format("Connecting to {0}", serverName));
server.Connect(serverName);
```

After we have connected to the server, we retrieve the collection of databases. This is in the form of a collection of `MDStore` interfaces. From this collection, we select the database name that was provided in the command line.

```
// get the collection of databases
DSO.OlapCollection collection = server.MDStores;
// get the specified database from the collection
Console.WriteLine(String.Format("Retrieving database {0}",
  databaseName));
DSO.MDStore db = collection.Item(databaseName) as
  DSO.MDStore;
// if we don't have a database, throw an exception
if (db == null) throw
  new Exception
   (String.Format("Cannot retrieve database: {0}",
    databaseName));
```

After we have selected the database, we are ready to process it. Here we are going to do a full processing of the database. Once the processing is complete, the `finally` clause will close the connection and we are ready to quit the application.

```
// process the cube
Console.WriteLine("Processing database. Please wait.");
db.Process(DSO.ProcessTypes.processFull);

}
catch(Exception e)
{
    // report on the exception
    Console.WriteLine(e.Source);
    Console.WriteLine(e.Message);
}
finally
{
    // close server if we opened it
    if (server != null)
        server.CloseServer();
    // wait for enter to continue
```

```
        Console.WriteLine("Press enter to continue");
        Console.ReadLine();
    }
```

This simple application just scratches the surface of what can be done using DSO, but it does give a flavor of how DSO works in .NET and how it can be used to administer Analysis Services programmatically.

SUMMARY

In this chapter, we discussed building client applications using ADOMD and DSO in .NET. Thanks to the strong interoperability with COM that is provided by the .NET Framework, using the COM-based ADOMD and DSO is not difficult. For managing metadata in Analysis Services, DSO is the best technology overall. However, there are some significant disadvantages when using ADOMD to access OLAP data in .NET. ADOMD is dependent on the presence of the PivotTable Service and requires that the proper libraries be installed on all of the clients. The distribution and maintenance of a large number of DLLs is never painless. Second, ADOMD is a COM technology, so you will need to work through the interoperability layer wherever it is used from .NET. Although this is not difficult, it does make your applications that much more complex by adding another layer. In addition, you lose the benefits of running managed code exclusively in your application.

Instead of using ADOMD in your OLAP applications in .NET, you should strongly consider using XML for Analysis (XMLA) as the basis for your client applications in .NET. Using XMLA offers some significant advantages for .NET applications, as we will explore in Chapter 5.

REFERENCES

SQL Server Online Help, available by opening the Help menu from within the program, and online at *http://www.microsoft.com/sql/techinfo/productdoc/2000/default.asp*.

MSDN Library, available online at *http://msdn.microsoft.com/library/default.asp?url=/library/en-us/startsql/getstart_4fht.asp* or for download at *http://www.microsoft.com/sql/techinfo/productdoc/2000/books.asp*

Information about Analysis Services is available online at *http://msdn.microsoft.com/library/default.asp?url=/library/en-us/olapdmad/agmdxbasics_04qg.asp*.

5 XML for Analysis

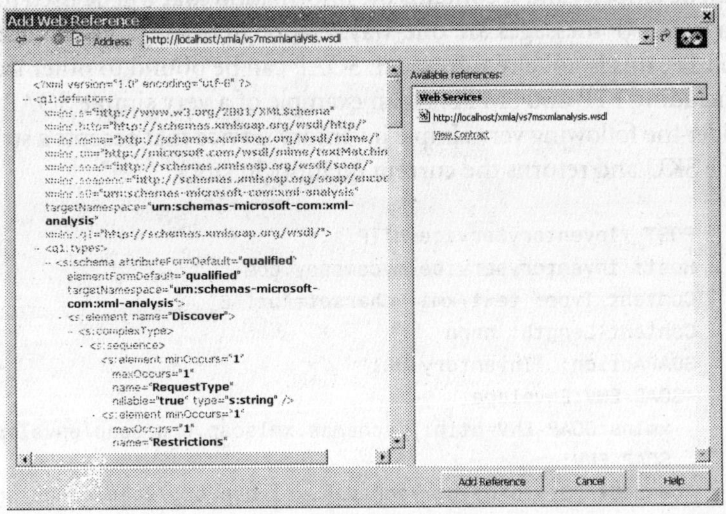

OVERVIEW

XMLA is a standard proposed and supported by Microsoft, Hyperion®, and SAS to provide an XML schema that can be used to standardize the way OLAP services are called over the Internet or intranet. XMLA is based on the Simple Object Access Protocol (SOAP), and is usable from any client that can call standard SOAP methods. SOAP is a lightweight XML-based protocol for exchanging structured and type information on the Web. Because the overall goal is to keep SOAP as simple as possible, it is very modular and easily extensible to new types of applications. By using Internet standards, SOAP is able to easily integrate with many existing systems. The .NET Framework has excellent support for both creating and using Web Services and we will make use of them as we build applications that use XMLA to create business intelligence.

SOAP

Before we cover XMLA, lets cover the basic technology that XMLA uses: SOAP. A SOAP message is an XML document that consists of a SOAP envelope, an optional SOAP header, and a SOAP body. The *SOAP envelope* is the root element of the XML document, and may contain namespace declarations and other attributes that are specialized for the SOAP provider. The optional *SOAP header* must be the first element in the document if it is present, and is typically used to include security, transactions, and other extensions. The *SOAP body* must be present (although it can be empty), and it contains the information that will be used to process the message. SOAP messages are one-way. Although SOAP is most commonly used with HTTP, this is not a requirement. SOAP can be bound to other transport protocols including FTP and SMTP. As an example of a very simple SOAP interaction, consider the following very simple inventory service that accepts a string parameter for the SKU and returns the current quantity in stock:

```
POST /InventoryService HTTP/1.1
Host: inventoryservice.mycompany.com
Content-Type: text/xml; charset="utf-8"
Content-Length: nnnn
SOAPAction: "Inventory-URI"
<SOAP-ENV:Envelope
  xmlns:SOAP-ENV=http://schemas.xmlsoap.org/soap/envelope/
  SOAP-ENV:
  encodingStyle=http://schemas.xmlsoap.org/soap/encoding/
/>
<SOAP-ENV:Body>
   <m:GetInventory xmlns:m="Inventory-URI">
       <sku>BK-4556-A</sku>
   </m:GetInventory>
</SOAP-ENV:Body>
</SOAP-ENV:Envelope>
```

The first part of this message is the HTTP header that tells the receiver where this information should be sent. The SOAPAction header field indicates the intent of the SOAP HTTP request with a Uniform Resource Identifier (URI) of the application that should receive the request. The next part is the SOAP envelope, containing a body with the request to the `GetInventory` method with a value for the requested SKU.

A response to this request might look like this:

```
HTTP/1.1 200 OK
Content-Type: text/xml; charset="utf-8"
```

```
Content-Length: nnnn

<SOAP-ENV:Envelope
  xmlns:SOAP-ENV=http://schemas.xmlsoap.org/soap/envelope/
  SOAP-ENV:
  encodingStyle=http://schemas.xmlsoap.org/soap/encoding/
/>
<SOAP-ENV:Body>
   <m:GetInventoryResponse xmlns:m="Inventory-URI">
       <QuantityInStock>241</QuantityInStock>
   </m: GetInventoryResponse>
</SOAP-ENV:Body>
</SOAP-ENV:Envelope>
```

Goals

Building on SOAP and OLE DB for Analysis, XMLA extends the reach of OLAP applications across the Internet or intranet. A diagram of an implementation from the XMLA specification is shown in Figure 5.1.

There have been two versions of XMLA released: Version 1.0 was published on April 23, 2001, and Version 1.1 was released on November 21, 2002. Version 1.0 is the version that is implemented by the Microsoft XML for Analysis SDK, which is the basis for the example in this book. Version 1.1 was an incremental update to 1.0, and was the first version to be created by members of the XMLA Advisory Council, a standards group that was formed after Hyperion and Microsoft released Version 1.0 in 2001. The two specifications are so similar they are nearly interchangeable. However, there are some significant changes between the two, so applications written using one version of the specification will not work with applications written using the other. The samples in this chapter were written with the XMLA 1.0 provider in the XML for Analysis Software Development Kit. Details on how to get and install the SDK are provided later in this chapter.

According to the XMLA Specification, the design goals of XMLA include:

Providing a standard API: Providing a standard data access API to remote data access providers that can be used universally on the Internet or intranet for multidimensional data

Stateless architecture: Optimizing a stateless architecture, requiring no client components for the Web, with minimal round trips

Technology independence: Supporting technologically independent implementations using any tool, programming language, technology, hardware platform, or device

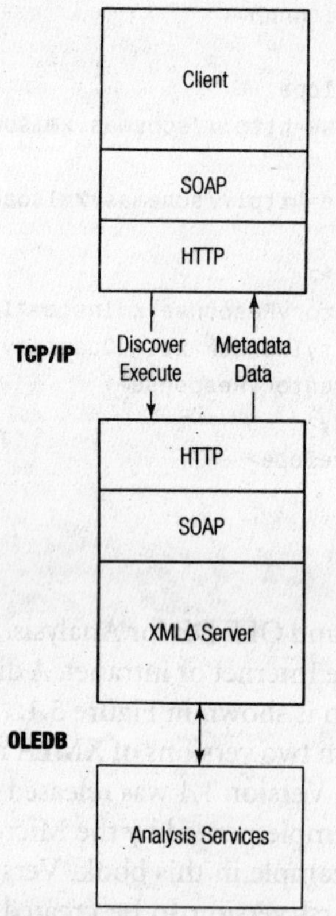

FIGURE 5.1 A reference implementation of XMLA.

Being standards based: Building on open Internet standards, such as SOAP, XML, and HTTP

Making use of OLE DB: Using and reusing successful OLE DB design concepts, so that OLE DB for OLAP applications and OLE DB providers can be easily enabled for XML for Analysis

Efficiency: Working efficiently with standard data sources, such as relational OLAP and data mining

Methods

One of the beauties of XMLA is its simplicity. XMLA has only two specified methods: `Discover` and `Execute`. `Discover` is used to retrieve metadata about the data provided by a particular Web Service, including a list of available data sources and what properties are supported. `Discover` can be used to dynamically determine what services a particular XMLA provider supports. The specific data that is retrieved by the `Discover` method depends on the parameters that are used in the method call. The second method in XMLA is `Execute`. `Execute` is used to run MDX queries against a data source and retrieve the results. In the following sections we explore both of these methods.

Discover

The method call for `Discover` looks like:

```
Discover (RequestType, Restrictions, Properties, Results)
```

The `RequestType` parameter determines the type of information to be returned. The `RequestType` parameter is taken from one of the `RequestType` enumeration values listed in Table 5.1.

The `Restrictions` parameter allows filtering of the data that is returned in the `Results`. The type of results requested by the `RequestType` determines the fields that

TABLE 5.1 `RequestType` enumeration values.

Enumeration value	*Description*
DISCOVER_DATASOURCES	Returns a list of data sources available on the server or Web Service
DISCOVER_PROPERTIES	Returns a list of information and values about the requested properties that are supported by the specified data source
DISCOVER_SCHEMA_ROWSETS	Returns the names, values, and other information of all supported RequestType enumeration values, and any additional provider-specific values
DISCOVER_ENUMERATORS	Returns a list of names, data types, and enumeration values of enumerators supported by a specific data source's provider
DISCOVER_KEYWORDS	Returns a rowset containing a list of keywords reserved by the provider
DISCOVER_LITERALS	Returns information about literals supported by the data source provider
Schema Rowset Constant	Returns the schema rowset that is defined by the constant

can be filtered. The specific list of fields that can be used to limit results in each RequestType are listed in Appendix D. This parameter is required, but it may be empty if you wish to retrieve all of the available results from the RequestType.

The Properties field provides additional information that controls the format data returned by Discover or the connection to the XMLA server. For example, the AxisFormat property specifies that the results should be in tabular format and the Password property is used to provide a password for the connection to the server. Properties can be provided in any order and the properties can be empty if the defaults will suffice for the current request. The list of properties available in the XMLA Provider for Analysis Services appears in Table 5.2.

The results parameter is used to contain the XML returned by the server. The contents of the results will be determined by the other three parameters.

The following example shows what the Discover call looks like when requesting a list of data sources from the server:

```
User-Agent: Mozilla/4.0
  (compatible; MSIE 6.0;
  MS Web Services Client Protocol 1.0.3705.209)
Content-Type: text/xml; charset=utf-8
SOAPAction:
  "urn:schemas-microsoft-com:xml-analysis:Discover"
Content-Length: 421
Expect: 200
Connection: Keep-Alive
Host: localhost

<?xml version="1.0" encoding="utf-8"?>
<soap:Envelope
  xmlns:soap="http://schemas.xmlsoap.org/soap/envelope/"
  xmlns:xsi="http://www.w3.org/2001/XMLSchema-instance"
  xmlns:xsd="http://www.w3.org/2001/XMLSchema">
<soap:Body>
  <Discover xmlns="urn:schemas-microsoft-com:xml-analysis">
    <RequestType>DISCOVER_DATASOURCES</RequestType>
    <Restrictions xsi:nil="true" />
    <Properties xsi:nil="true"/>
  </Discover>
</soap:Body>
</soap:Envelope>
```

The Discover XML element contains XML elements for the RequestType, Restrictions and Properties. The Restrictions XML element contains the RestrictionList element that lists the restrictions that should be applied the request type. In this case,

TABLE 5.2 XMLA Provider for Analysis Services available properties.

Property	***Default Value***	***Description***
`AxisFormat`	`TupleFormat`	The format for the `MDDataSet` `<Axis>` element. The choices are `TupleFormat` or `ClusterFormat`.
`BeginRange`	–1 (all cells)	An integer value corresponding to a `CellOrdinal` attribute value used to restrict an OLAP dataset returned by a command to a specific range of cells
`Catalog`	Empty string	The catalog on which to connect
`Content`	`SchemaData`	An enumerator that specifies the type of data returned in the result set **None:** Allows the structure of the command to be verified, but not executed **Schema:** Contains the XML schema for the query results **Data:** Contains only the data for the query results **SchemaData:** Returns both the schema information and the data
`DataSourceInfo`	Empty string	A string containing the information needed to connect to the data source, such as the server name
`EndRange`	–1 (all data)	An integer value corresponding to a `CellOrdinal` used to restrict an OLAP dataset returned by a command to a specific range of cells
`Format`	Tabular for `Discover` Multidimensional for `Execute`	An enumerator specifying the format of the returned results. Values include: **Tabular:** A flat or hierarchical rowset **Multidimensional:** MDDataSet format
`Password`	Empty string	A string containing password information required for the connection
`ProviderName`	Empty string	The XML for Analysis Provider name
`ProviderVersion`	Empty string	The version number of the XML for Analysis Provider
`StateSupport`	None	Provider state support. Values include: **None:** No support for stateful operations. **Sessions:** Sessions are supported.
`Timeout`	Undefined	A numeric time-out specifying in seconds the amount of time to wait for a connection to be successful
`UserName`	Empty string	A string containing user name information required for the connection

we are passing in a null value for the `Restrictions` (`<Restrictions xsi:nil="true" />`) so that we get the list of all the available data sources. The `Properties` element contains the `PropertyList` element that contains each of the properties that is to be used for the request. In this case, we are passing a null value in and accepting the default property values. Finally, we close the `Body` and `Envelope` and the request is ready to send.

After the request is received and processed, the XMLA provider will respond with the list of data sources in a SOAP reply. The namespace information in the XML tags has been removed and the schema has been truncated to make the structure of the `Discover` response message more visible.

```
HTTP/1.1 200 OK
Server: Microsoft-IIS/5.1
Date: Fri, 02 May 2003 19:49:59 GMT
Connection: close
Content-Type: text/xml

<?xml version="1.0"?>
<SOAP-ENV:Envelope>
<SOAP-ENV:Body>
    <m:DiscoverResponse>
    <return SOAP-ENV>
    <root>
    <xsd:schema>
        <xsd:element name="root">
            <xsd:complexType>
                <xsd:sequence
                    minOccurs="0"
                    maxOccurs="unbounded">
                    <xsd:element name="row"
                        type="row"/>
                </xsd:sequence>
            </xsd:complexType>
        </xsd:element>
        <xsd:complexType name="row">
            <xsd:choice
                maxOccurs="unbounded" minOccurs="0">
                <xsd:element name="DataSourceName" />
                <xsd:element
                    name="DataSourceDescription" />
                <xsd:element name="URL" />
                <xsd:element name="DataSourceInfo" />
                <xsd:element name="ProviderName" />
```

```
                <xsd:element name="ProviderType">
                    <xsd:complexType>
                        <xsd:sequence
                         maxOccurs="unbounded"
                         minOccurs="0">
                            <xsd:any
                             processContents="lax"
                             maxOccurs="unbounded"/>
                        </xsd:sequence>
                    </xsd:complexType>
                </xsd:element>
                <xsd:element
                    name="AuthenticationMode" />
            </xsd:choice>
        </xsd:complexType>
    </xsd:schema>
    <row>
        <DataSourceName>
            Local Analysis Server
        </DataSourceName>
        <DataSourceDescription>
            local machine
        </DataSourceDescription>
        <URL>http://localhost/xmla/msxisapi.dll</URL>
        <DataSourceInfo>
            Provider=MSOLAP;Data Source=local
        </DataSourceInfo>
        <ProviderName>
            Microsoft XML for Analysis
        </ProviderName>
        <ProviderType><TDP/><MDP/><DMP/></ProviderType>
        <AuthenticationMode>
            Unauthenticated
        </AuthenticationMode>
    </row>
    </root>
    </return>
    </m:DiscoverResponse>
</SOAP-ENV:Body>
</SOAP-ENV:Envelope>
```

As usual, the first XML element in the SOAP message is the envelope that contains the body of the message. The `DiscoverResponse` element in the body contains the return value, which contains the root element. In the root element, we first have the XSD schema that defines the schema for the data that follows. In this case, the data follows the tabular schema that lists the rows containing XML elements for each of the data values. Finally, we close the `DiscoverResponse` element, the body, and the envelope.

Execute

In addition to `Discover`, XMLA supports the `Execute` method. The method call for `Execute` looks like:

```
Execute (Command,Properties,Results)
```

The `properties` argument in `Execute` has a similar purpose to the `Properties` argument in `Discover`. It defines the type of data that will be returned or some attribute of the connection. `Properties` must be included, but it may be empty if the defaults will suffice for the current request. The `results` parameter represents the SOAP document returned by the server. The contents of `results` are determined by the other two parameters. The following is an example of the `Execute` method that contains an MDX `SELECT` statement:

```
SOAPAction: "urn:schemas-microsoft-com:xml-analysis:Execute"
Content-Length: 670
Expect: 200
Host: localhost

<?xml version="1.0" encoding="utf-8"?>
<soap:Envelope>
<soap:Body>
<Execute xmlns="urn:schemas-microsoft-com:xml-analysis">
<Command>
<Statement>select {[Product].children} on rows,
  {[Store].children} on columns from Sales
</Statement>
</Command>
<Properties>
<PropertyList>
<DataSourceInfo>
  Provider=MSOLAP;Data Source=local
</DataSourceInfo>
<Catalog>FoodMart 2000</Catalog>
<Format>Multidimensional</Format>
<AxisFormat>TupleFormat</AxisFormat>
</PropertyList>
</Properties>
```

```
</Execute></soap:Body>
</soap:Envelope>
```

As we can see here, the SOAP request for `Execute` is similar to the request sent for `Discover`. We have XML elements for the `Command` and `Properties`. The `Command` XML element contains the MDX query that is to be run on the server and the `Properties` element contains the `PropertyList` element that contains the properties that are to be used for the request. In this case, we have `DataSourceInfo`, `Catalog`, `Format`, and `AxisFormat` specified in the `PropertyList`. Finally, we close the `Body` and `Envelope` and the request is ready to send.

After the request is received and processed, the XMLA provider will respond with the resulting data in a SOAP reply. The namespace information in the XML tags has been removed and the schema has been truncated to make the structure of the `Execute` response message more clear to human readers.

```
HTTP/1.1 200 OK
    Server: Microsoft-IIS/5.1
    Date: Fri, 02 May 2003 20:19:46 GMT
    Connection: close
    Content-Type: text/xml

    <?xml version="1.0"?>
    <SOAP-ENV:Envelope>
    <SOAP-ENV:Body>
    <m:ExecuteResponse>
    <return>
    <root>
    <xsd:schema
      xmlns="urn:schemas-microsoft-com:xml-analysis:mddataset">
    ...
    </xsd:schema>
    <OlapInfo>
    <AxesInfo>
    <AxisInfo name="Axis0">
    <HierarchyInfo name="Store">
    <UName name="[Store].[MEMBER_UNIQUE_NAME]"/>
    <Caption name="[Store].[MEMBER_CAPTION]"/>
    <LName name="[Store].[LEVEL_UNIQUE_NAME]"/>
    <LNum name="[Store].[LEVEL_NUMBER]"/>
    <DisplayInfo name="[Store].[DISPLAY_INFO]"/>
    </HierarchyInfo>
    </AxisInfo>
    <AxisInfo name="Axis1">
```

```
<HierarchyInfo name="Product">
<UName name="[Product].[MEMBER_UNIQUE_NAME]"/>
<Caption name="[Product].[MEMBER_CAPTION]"/>
<LName name="[Product].[LEVEL_UNIQUE_NAME]"/>
<LNum name="[Product].[LEVEL_NUMBER]"/>
<DisplayInfo name="[Product].[DISPLAY_INFO]"/>
</HierarchyInfo>
</AxisInfo>
<AxisInfo name="SlicerAxis">
<HierarchyInfo name="Measures">
...
</HierarchyInfo>
<HierarchyInfo name="Time">
...
</HierarchyInfo>
<HierarchyInfo name="Promotion Media">
...
</HierarchyInfo>
<HierarchyInfo name="Promotions">
...
</HierarchyInfo>
<HierarchyInfo name="Customers">
...
</HierarchyInfo>
<HierarchyInfo name="Education Level">
...
</HierarchyInfo>
<HierarchyInfo name="Gender">
...
</HierarchyInfo>
<HierarchyInfo name="Marital Status">
...
</HierarchyInfo>
<HierarchyInfo name="Store Size in SQFT">
...
</HierarchyInfo>
<HierarchyInfo name="Store Type">
...
</HierarchyInfo>
<HierarchyInfo name="Yearly Income">
...</HierarchyInfo>
</AxisInfo>
</AxesInfo>
<CellInfo>
```

```
<Value name="VALUE"/>
<FmtValue name="FORMATTED_VALUE"/>
</CellInfo>
</OlapInfo>
<Axes>
<Axis name="Axis0">
<Tuples>
<Tuple>
<Member Hierarchy="Store">
<UName>[Store].[All Stores].[Canada]</UName>
<Caption>Canada</Caption>
<LName>[Store].[Store Country]</LName>
<LNum>1</LNum>
<DisplayInfo>131073</DisplayInfo>
</Member>
</Tuple>
<Tuple>
<Member Hierarchy="Store">
<UName>[Store].[All Stores].[Mexico]</UName>
<Caption>Mexico</Caption>
<LName>[Store].[Store Country]</LName>
<LNum>1</LNum>
<DisplayInfo>131078</DisplayInfo>
</Member>
</Tuple>
<Tuple>
<Member Hierarchy="Store">
<UName>[Store].[All Stores].[USA]</UName>
<Caption>USA</Caption>
<LName>[Store].[Store Country]</LName>
<LNum>1</LNum>
<DisplayInfo>131075</DisplayInfo></Member>
</Tuple>
</Tuples>
</Axis>
<Axis name="Axis1">
<Tuples>
<Tuple>
<Member Hierarchy="Product">
<UName>[Product].[All Products].[Drink]</UName>
<Caption>Drink</Caption>
<LName>[Product].[Product Family]</LName>
<LNum>1</LNum>
<DisplayInfo>131075</DisplayInfo>
```

```
</Member>
</Tuple>
<Tuple>
<Member Hierarchy="Product">
<UName>[Product].[All Products].[Food]</UName>
<Caption>Food</Caption>
<LName>[Product].[Product Family]</LName>
<LNum>1</LNum>
<DisplayInfo>131087</DisplayInfo>
</Member>
</Tuple>
<Tuple>
<Member Hierarchy="Product">
<UName>[Product].[All Products].[Non-Consumable]</UName>
<Caption>Non-Consumable</Caption>
<LName>[Product].[Product Family]</LName>
<LNum>1</LNum>
<DisplayInfo>131077</DisplayInfo>
</Member>
</Tuple>
</Tuples>
</Axis>
<Axis name="SlicerAxis">
...
</Axis>
</Axes>
<CellData>
<Cell CellOrdinal="2">
<Value xsi:type="xsd:double">24597</Value>
<FmtValue>24,597.00</FmtValue>
</Cell>
<Cell CellOrdinal="5">
<Value xsi:type="xsd:double">191940</Value>
<FmtValue>191,940.00</FmtValue>
</Cell>
<Cell CellOrdinal="8">
<Value xsi:type="xsd:double">50236</Value>
<FmtValue>50,236.00</FmtValue>
</Cell></CellData>
</root>
</return>
</m:ExecuteResponse>
</SOAP-ENV:Body>
</SOAP-ENV:Envelope>
```

Looking at the SOAP response for `Execute`, we first have the usual `Envelope` and `Body` tags that contain the results for the query. The first element in the root is the XSD schema describing the results, followed by the data itself in `MDDataSet` format.

There are two possible formats that the results from `Execute` can be returned in: `Rowset` and `MDDataSet`. `Rowset` is a very simple tabular structure that contains rows and columns that contain the data elements. `MDDataSet` is the format used to contain multidimensional results returned by `Execute`. `MDDataSet` has three major sections: `OLAPInfo`, `Axes` and `CellData`.

OLAPInfo

`OLAPInfo` defines the structure of the results. The first section of `OLAPInfo` is `CubeInfo`. `CubeInfo` contains a simple listing of the cubes where the results come from. This is an addition to the specification in Version 1.1 and in Version 1.0 there is no easy way to determine the originating cube for the results. The second section of `OLAPInfo` is the `AxesInfo` section that defines the list of axes that are contained in the results. `AxesInfo` contains an `AxisInfo` element for each of the returned axes. Within each `AxisInfo` element, the hierarchies and their members and properties are listed. The standard properties for each hierarchy are `Uname`, `Caption`, `Lname` and `Lnum`. The last section in `OLAPInfo` is the CellData section, consisting of a set of `CellInfo` elements that contain the properties for the cells, including standard and custom properties. The standard properties for `CellInfo` are `Value`, `FmtValue`, `ForeColor` and `BackColor`. These properties or others may or may not be included depending on the query used to retrieve the data.

Another element that is possible in the `AxisInfo` or `CellInfo` section is the definition of default values for specific properties. This is used to provide a smaller results set if the value is uniform or nearly uniform across the result set. To define a default value, the `Default` element is added to the `AxisInfo` or `CellInfo` section.

To make the `OLAPInfo` section more understandable, we will walk through an example with results based on the query:

```
select
{[Product].children} on rows,
{[Store].children} on columns
from Sales
```

resulting in the `AxesInfo` shown here:

```
<AxesInfo>
  <AxisInfo name="Axis0">
    <HierarchyInfo name="Store">
      <UName name="[Store].[MEMBER_UNIQUE_NAME]" />
```

```
        <Caption name="[Store].[MEMBER_CAPTION]" />
        <LName name="[Store].[LEVEL_UNIQUE_NAME]" />
        <LNum name="[Store].[LEVEL_NUMBER]" />
        <DisplayInfo name="[Store].[DISPLAY_INFO]" />
      </HierarchyInfo>
    </AxisInfo>
    <AxisInfo name="Axis1">
      <HierarchyInfo name="Product">
        <UName name="[Product].[MEMBER_UNIQUE_NAME]" />
        <Caption name="[Product].[MEMBER_CAPTION]" />
        <LName name="[Product].[LEVEL_UNIQUE_NAME]" />
        <LNum name="[Product].[LEVEL_NUMBER]" />
        <DisplayInfo name="[Product].[DISPLAY_INFO]" />
      </HierarchyInfo>
    </AxisInfo>
    <AxisInfo name="SlicerAxis">
      <HierarchyInfo name="Measures">
        ...
      </HierarchyInfo>
      <HierarchyInfo name="Time">
        ...
      </HierarchyInfo>
      <HierarchyInfo name="Promotion Media">
        ...
      </HierarchyInfo>
      <HierarchyInfo name="Promotions">
        ...
      </HierarchyInfo>
      <HierarchyInfo name="Customers">
        ...
      </HierarchyInfo>
      <HierarchyInfo name="Education Level">
        ...
      </HierarchyInfo>
      <HierarchyInfo name="Gender">
        ...
      </HierarchyInfo>
      <HierarchyInfo name="Marital Status">
        ...
      </HierarchyInfo>
      <HierarchyInfo name="Store Size in SQFT">
        ...
      </HierarchyInfo>
      <HierarchyInfo name="Store Type">
```

```
    ...
  </HierarchyInfo>
  <HierarchyInfo name="Yearly Income">
    ...
  </HierarchyInfo>
 </AxisInfo>
</AxesInfo>
```

The query returns two Axes, columns (Axis0) and rows (Axis1). The AxesInfo section determines which properties are returned for the hierarchies in each Axis. In this case, there is only one hierarchy on each Axis, Store and Product for Axis0 and Axis1, respectively. After the two dimensional axes, the slicer axis with all of the hierarchies that do not appear in the dimensional axes and their properties are returned. This information can be used to show what other hierarchies are available for analysis in a given cube.

It is interesting to compare those results with the results of a cross-join query, which adds a hierarchy to an axis. The query:

```
select {crossjoin({[Product].children}, {[Time].children})} on rows,
{[Store].children} on columns
```

returns a dimensional AxesInfo section that looks like:

```
<AxesInfo>
  <AxisInfo name="Axis0">
    <HierarchyInfo name="Store">
      <UName name="[Store].[MEMBER_UNIQUE_NAME]" />
      <Caption name="[Store].[MEMBER_CAPTION]" />
      <LName name="[Store].[LEVEL_UNIQUE_NAME]" />
      <LNum name="[Store].[LEVEL_NUMBER]" />
      <DisplayInfo name="[Store].[DISPLAY_INFO]" />
    </HierarchyInfo>
  </AxisInfo>
  <AxisInfo name="Axis1">
    <HierarchyInfo name="Product">
      <UName name="[Product].[MEMBER_UNIQUE_NAME]" />
      <Caption name="[Product].[MEMBER_CAPTION]" />
      <LName name="[Product].[LEVEL_UNIQUE_NAME]" />
      <LNum name="[Product].[LEVEL_NUMBER]" />
      <DisplayInfo name="[Product].[DISPLAY_INFO]" />
    </HierarchyInfo>
    <HierarchyInfo name="Time">
      <UName name="[Time].[MEMBER_UNIQUE_NAME]" />
```

```
            <Caption name="[Time].[MEMBER_CAPTION]" />
            <LName name="[Time].[LEVEL_UNIQUE_NAME]" />
            <LNum name="[Time].[LEVEL_NUMBER]" />
            <DisplayInfo name="[Time].[DISPLAY_INFO]" />
         </HierarchyInfo>
      </AxisInfo>
      ...
```

Note that the results from the cross-join have two hierarchies, `Product` and `Time`, in the rows axis (`Axis1`).

Concluding the `OLAPInfo` section is the `CellInfo` section that enumerates the properties that will be returned for the cells. For the previous queries, this will be just the basic `Value` and `FmtValue` information:

```
<OlapInfo>
<!---the AxesInfo goes here -- >
<CellInfo>
      <Value name="VALUE" />
      <FmtValue name="FORMATTED_VALUE" />
</CellInfo>
</OlapInfo>
```

If we change the query to explicitly include property values, like so, it will return the values for the included properties in the query results.

```
select {crossjoin({[Product].children}, {[Time].children})} on rows,
{[Store].children} on columns
from Sales
CELL PROPERTIES VALUE, FORMATTED_VALUE, FORMAT_STRING, FORE_COLOR, BACK_COLOR
```

The explicitly included properties will be included in the `CellInfo` section of our `OLAPInfo` section. Note that if you explicitly list the properties to be returned, only those properties in the list will be returned. So, if you include an explicit cell property list and do not include the `Value`, it will not be returned. You can include duplicates of the same property in the list and they will appear as specified in the `CellInfo`, but they will be returned only once in the `CellData` section. The same general rules apply to member properties as they are displayed in the `HierarchyInfo` elements.

```
<CellInfo>
<Value name="VALUE" />
<FmtValue name="FORMATTED_VALUE" />
<FormatString name="FORMAT_STRING" />
```

```
<ForeColor name="FORE_COLOR" />
<BackColor name="BACK_COLOR" />
</CellInfo>
```

Axes

After the `OlapInfo`, the next section in the `MDDataSet` is the `Axes`. `Axes` contains the members returned from the query organized according to the format property specified in the `Execute` method. The XMLA provider for Analysis Server 2000 supports two formats for the `Axes: ClusterFormat` and `TupleFormat`.

To understand why there are two different formats, think of how a data set can be represented. For example, if we have three country categories (Canada, Mexico, USA) and three product categories (Drink, Food, Non-Consumable), we can represent the nine combinations of this set in two different ways. First and most simply, we can list each of them as a tuple in the set:

{(Canada, Drink), (Canada, Food), (Canada, Non-consumable),
(Mexico, Drink), (Mexico, Food), (Mexico, Non-consumable),
(USA, Drink), (USA, Food), (USA, Non-consumable)}

The advantage of representing the combinations explicitly is that it is easy to understand and manipulate. We can instantly see how many combinations there are as well as easily navigate through each one. This is the kind of set representation that is used by the `TupleFormat`.

A second way of representing the combinations of the two sets is to use a Cartesian product: {Canada, Mexico, USA} × {Drink, Food, Non-consumable}. This Cartesian product is a much more compact representation, but it does require a bit more interpretation to understand and navigate. This is the kind of representation that is used by the `ClusterFormat`.

`ClusterFormat` divides members on each axis into clusters that contain cross-products from each hierarchy. So, every `Axis` element in `Axes` has one or more `CrossProduct` elements, each with a `Size` attribute that indicates the number of tuples in the cross-product. All of the `CrossProduct` elements contain a `Members` element for each hierarchy on the axis with the corresponding `Hierarchy` attribute. So, as does the simple example just shown, `ClusterFormat` has the advantage of reducing the amount of data that is needed to express the axes at the expense of greater complexity in interpreting the results.

Unfortunately, the XML provider for Analysis Services does not truly take advantage of the capabilities of the format since it maps the results back to a tuple-like format. However, this format might become more useful in the future because it can reduce the amount of data that is needed to express a complex set of tuples. For example, using `ClusterFormat`, the query

```
select
{[Product].children} on rows,
{[Store].children} on columns
from Sales
```

returns the following `Axes` section:

```
<Axes>
<Axis name="Axis0">
<CrossProduct Size="3">
<Members Hierarchy="Store">
<Member>
  <UName>[Store].[All Stores].[Canada]</UName>
  <Caption>Canada</Caption>
  <LName>[Store].[Store Country]</LName>
  <LNum>1</LNum>
  <DisplayInfo>131073</DisplayInfo>
  </Member>
<Member>
  <UName>[Store].[All Stores].[Mexico]</UName>
  <Caption>Mexico</Caption>
  <LName>[Store].[Store Country]</LName>
  <LNum>1</LNum>
  <DisplayInfo>131078</DisplayInfo>
  </Member>
<Member>
  <UName>[Store].[All Stores].[USA]</UName>
  <Caption>USA</Caption>
  <LName>[Store].[Store Country]</LName>
  <LNum>1</LNum>
  <DisplayInfo>131075</DisplayInfo>
  </Member>
  </Members>
  </CrossProduct>
  </Axis>
<Axis name="Axis1">
<CrossProduct Size="3">
<Members Hierarchy="Product">
<Member>
  <UName>[Product].[All Products].[Drink]</UName>
  <Caption>Drink</Caption>
```

```
    <LName>[Product].[Product Family]</LName>
    <LNum>1</LNum>
    <DisplayInfo>131075</DisplayInfo>
    </Member>
  <Member>
    <UName>[Product].[All Products].[Food]</UName>
    <Caption>Food</Caption>
    <LName>[Product].[Product Family]</LName>
    <LNum>1</LNum>
    <DisplayInfo>131087</DisplayInfo>
    </Member>
  <Member>
    <UName>[Product].[All Products].[Non-Consumable]</UName>
    <Caption>Non-Consumable</Caption>
    <LName>[Product].[Product Family]</LName>
    <LNum>1</LNum>
    <DisplayInfo>131077</DisplayInfo>
    </Member>
    </Members>
    </CrossProduct>
    </Axis>
  <Axis name="SlicerAxis">
  <CrossProduct Size="1">
  <Members Hierarchy="Measures">
  ...
    </Members>
  <Members Hierarchy="Time">
  ...
    </Members>
  <Members Hierarchy="Promotion Media">
  ...
    </Members>
  <Members Hierarchy="Promotions">
  ...
    </Members>
  <Members Hierarchy="Customers">
  ...
    </Members>
  <Members Hierarchy="Education Level">
  ...
    </Members>
  <Members Hierarchy="Gender">
  ...
    </Members>
```

```
<Members Hierarchy="Marital Status">
...
  </Members>
<Members Hierarchy="Store Size in SQFT">
...
  </Members>
<Members Hierarchy="Store Type">
...
  </Members>
<Members Hierarchy="Yearly Income">
...
  </Members>
  </CrossProduct>
  </Axis>
  </Axes>
```

The more commonly used and default format for the `Axes` is the `TupleFormat`. `TupleFormat` represents an axis as a set of tuples with each tuple containing a member from each dimension included in the results. This representation is very close to the representation of `Axes` in ADOMD. The same query we just discussed will return the following results in `TupleFormat`:

```
<Axes>
<Axis name="Axis0">
<CrossProduct Size="3">
<Members Hierarchy="Store">
<Member>
  <UName>[Store].[All Stores].[Canada]</UName>
  <Caption>Canada</Caption>
  <LName>[Store].[Store Country]</LName>
  <LNum>1</LNum>
  <DisplayInfo>131073</DisplayInfo>
  </Member>
<Member>
  <UName>[Store].[All Stores].[Mexico]</UName>
  <Caption>Mexico</Caption>
  <LName>[Store].[Store Country]</LName>
  <LNum>1</LNum>
  <DisplayInfo>131078</DisplayInfo>
  </Member>
<Member>
  <UName>[Store].[All Stores].[USA]</UName>
  <Caption>USA</Caption>
  <LName>[Store].[Store Country]</LName>
```

```
<LNum>1</LNum>
<DisplayInfo>131075</DisplayInfo>
</Member>
</Members>
</CrossProduct>
</Axis>
<Axis name="Axis1">
<CrossProduct Size="3">
<Members Hierarchy="Product">
<Member>
  <UName>[Product].[All Products].[Drink]</UName>
  <Caption>Drink</Caption>
  <LName>[Product].[Product Family]</LName>
  <LNum>1</LNum>
  <DisplayInfo>131075</DisplayInfo>
  </Member>
<Member>
  <UName>[Product].[All Products].[Food]</UName>
  <Caption>Food</Caption>
  <LName>[Product].[Product Family]</LName>
  <LNum>1</LNum>
  <DisplayInfo>131087</DisplayInfo>
  </Member>
<Member>
  <UName>[Product].[All Products].[Non-Consumable]</UName>
  <Caption>Non-Consumable</Caption>
  <LName>[Product].[Product Family]</LName>
  <LNum>1</LNum>
  <DisplayInfo>131077</DisplayInfo>
  </Member>
  </Members>
  </CrossProduct>
  </Axis>
<Axis name="SlicerAxis">
<CrossProduct Size="1">
<Members Hierarchy="Measures">
...
  </Members>
<Members Hierarchy="Time">
...
  </Members>
<Members Hierarchy="Promotion Media">
...
  </Members>
```

```
<Members Hierarchy="Promotions">
...
  </Members>
<Members Hierarchy="Customers">
...
  </Members>
<Members Hierarchy="Education Level">
...
  </Members>
<Members Hierarchy="Gender">
...
  </Members>
<Members Hierarchy="Marital Status">
...
  </Members>
<Members Hierarchy="Store Size in SQFT">
...
  </Members>
<Members Hierarchy="Store Type">
...
  </Members>
<Members Hierarchy="Yearly Income">
...
  </Members>
  </CrossProduct>
  </Axis>
  </Axes>
```

Despite the organizational differences between the `ClusterFormat` and the `TupleFormat`, the `Member` elements are identical and include the unique name (`Uname`), `Caption`, level name (`Lname`), level number (`Lnum`) and display Info.

There is also one more format available according to the XMLA specification, `CustomFormat`. According to the specification, it is acceptable to return one of the other formats in place of the `CustomFormat`. The XMLA Provider for Analysis Services returns the `TupleFormat` when the `CustomFormat` is requested.

CellData

The last section in `OlapInfo` is the `CellData` section. This is the section that contains the property values for each cell. If a cell is not present and there is no default value specified in the `AxisInfo`, the value is set to null. The cells are referred to by ordinal in a zero-based array. To calculate the cell ordinal when given the tuple ordinals S_i in a p-dimensional data set, we can use the following formula for each axis k with M_k members:

$$n = \sum_{i=0}^{p-1} Si \times Ei \text{ where } Ei = \prod_{k=0}^{i-i} M_k \text{ and } E_0 = 1$$

To see an example of calculating the ordinal for a cell, consider the following sample of `CellData` that is taken from the results of an MDX query:

```
<CellData>
<Cell CellOrdinal="2">
  <Value xsi:type="xsd:double">24597</Value>
  <FmtValue>24,597.00</FmtValue>
  </Cell>
<Cell CellOrdinal="5">
  <Value xsi:type="xsd:double">191940</Value>
  <FmtValue>191,940.00</FmtValue>
  </Cell>
<Cell CellOrdinal="8">
  <Value xsi:type="xsd:double">50236</Value>
  <FmtValue>50,236.00</FmtValue>
  </Cell>
  </CellData>
```

We can imagine this being presented in a row-major 3×3 matrix. So, to figure out what value is in the top right corner of the matrix with coordinates 2,0 (third column, first row), we can use the aforementioned formula using the values $p = 2$, $S_0 = 2$, $S_1 = 0$:

$$E_0 = 1$$

$$E_1 = \prod_{k=0}^{0} M_k = 3$$

$$n = \sum_{i=0}^{1} S_i \times E_i = S_0 \times E_0 + S_1 \times E_1 = 2 \times 1 + 0 \times 3 = 2$$

So, from our calculation, we see that the value for the top right corner should be 24597.

Another thing to note about `CellData` is that the data type is of the value is specified in each `Value`. All of the data types are specified in the `MDDataSet` schema. As noted previously, no property is returned more than once in the `Cell` even if it is specified more than once in an MDX `CELL PROPERTIES` statement.

Sample Application

To show how to use XMLA in an application, we will go through an example that uses both `Discover` and `Execute`, and renders the results on a client. To use this sample on Analysis Services 2000, you must first install and configure the XML for Analysis SDK available on Microsoft's Web site at *http://www.microsoft.com/downloads/details.aspx?FamilyId=0E93B1EE-BE73-4D15-9C37-6CC2DCC2AC33&displaylang=en*. In addition to the XML for Analysis SDK, you will also need to retrieve the WSDL files that define the SOAP interface for XMLA to be able to work with it easily from Visual Studio .NET. This file is available at *http://www.microsoft.com/downloads/details.aspx?familyid=F9B689D5-CCD8-4941-AE56-E3E4D3E9A950&displaylang=en*. Installing the WSDL files is described in the XML for Analysis SDK documentation.

ON THE CD

The following code is from the XMLA sample on the CD-ROM, which uses `Discover` to find and render properties of a selected data source, and binds the results of an MDX query run through `Execute` to a grid displayed in a form. The complete code is available in the project on the CD-ROM in the Chapter 5\XMLA directory.

Discovering Metadata

The most important code in the sample implements the XMLA schema as a set of .NET classes in the file Xmla.cs. To see how `Discover` is used to get information about a data source, let's look at the constructor for the `Datasources` collection in Xmla.cs.

```
public Datasources(string xmlaUrl)
{
// create the container for the data sources
_datasources = new ArrayList();
// Create the Xml for Analysis proxy class
MsXmlAnalysis xa = new MsXmlAnalysis();
xa.Url = xmlaUrl;
// call discover on the xmla server
XmlElement xml =
 xa.Discover("DISCOVER_DATASOURCES", null, null);
// parse the xml and iterate through each row
XPathNavigator nav = xml.CreateNavigator();
XPathNodeIterator iterator =
  nav.SelectChildren("row",
  "urn:schemas-microsoft-com:xml-analysis:rowset");
while (iterator.MoveNext())
{
```

```
string name;
string description;
string url;
string info;
string providerName;
string providerType;
string authentication;

name =
  XmlaHelper.GetElements("DataSourceName", iterator);
description =
  XmlaHelper.GetElements("DataSourceDescription",
   iterator);
url = XmlaHelper.GetElements("URL", iterator);
info = XmlaHelper.GetElements("DataSourceInfo",
  iterator);
providerName = XmlaHelper.GetElements("ProviderName",
  iterator);
providerType = XmlaHelper.GetElements("ProviderType",
  iterator);
authentication =
  XmlaHelper.GetElements("AuthenticationMode",
  iterator);

Datasource source = new Datasource(name,
    description, url, info,
    providerName, providerType, authentication);

_datasources.Add(source);
}
}
```

First, we create an array list to hold the list of data sources that we retrieve. Next, we create the proxy class to be able to talk to the XMLA server. This is worth a little bit more explanation. As discussed previously in this chapter, Visual Studio .NET makes it very easy to work with SOAP and we will use that capability here.

To begin creating a proxy class for XMLA in Visual Studio .NET, select "Project . . . Add Web Reference . . . " from the main menu to display the Add Web Reference window. In the Add Web Reference window, type the address of the WSDL file for XMLA that you installed with the SDK. For example, if you want to reference the WSDL file installed on localhost, use a URL such as *http://localhost/xmla/msxmlanalysis.wsdl.* Your Add Web Reference window will display information about the contents of the WSDL file and should look something like Figure 5.2

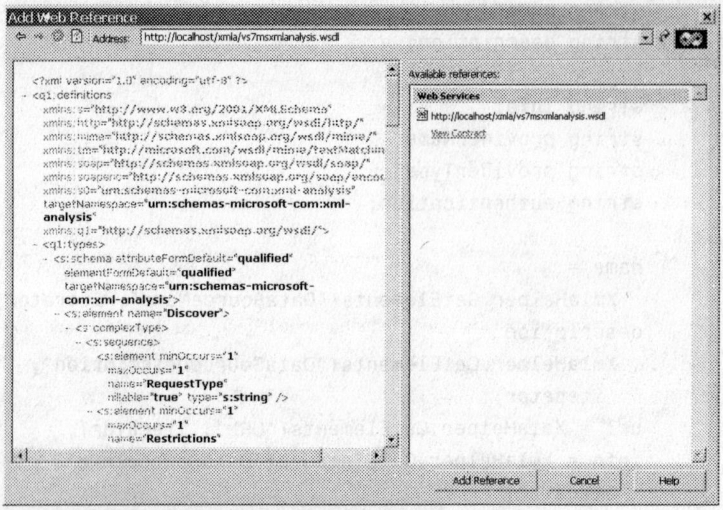

FIGURE 5.2 Ready to add Web reference.

after you have added the URL for your WSDL file. Simply clicking the Add Reference button will add the proxy class to your project. After you have added the reference to the project, you will be able to browse the methods available in the MsXmlAnalysis class in the Visual Studio .NET Object Browser.

Back to the `Datasources` constructor, we create an instance of the XMLA proxy and set the URL property to point to an XMLA provider passed into the constructor as a string argument in the form of a URL (such as *http://localhost/xmla/msxisapi.dll*). This provider can be local or on another machine.

After we have set the URL, we are ready to call `Discover` to retrieve the list of data sources that are available on the server. The line of code that does this is

```
XmlElement xml = xa.Discover("DISCOVER_DATASOURCES", null, null);
```

As we have discussed earlier in the chapter, the first argument to `Discover` is the request type, the next is the restrictions, and the third is the properties. In this case, we will accept the default values for the restrictions and properties since we want all of the available data sources in the default format, so we pass in null values for each. The results of the `Discover` call are returned to an `XmlElement` that we parse using `Xpath` to get each of the rows in the result set. For each of the rows, we get the values and use them to construct a `Datasource` object that we add to our collection. The `Datasource` object itself is a very simple container class that holds the properties for each data source.

We do something similar for each of the other types of metadata that we retrieve through `Discover`. Each subsequent layer of the metadata is dependent on the layer that came before. To retrieve the set of `Catalogs` we start with a `Datasource`, to retrieve a set of `Cubes` we start with a `Catalog`, to retrieve a set of `Dimensions` we start with a `Cube` and so on. After we have retrieved our metadata, we can run some MDX queries to get the data stored in the cubes.

Retrieving Data

As we discussed previously, the `Execute` method is used to run MDX queries against data sources and retrieve results. The key class in our sample for retrieving results from an MDX query via XMLA is `MDDataSet`. Let's take a look at the constructor for the `MDDataSet`.

```
public MDDataSet(Catalog catalog, string mdx)
    {
// Create the Xml for Analysis proxy class
MsXmlAnalysis xa = new MsXmlAnalysis();
xa.Url = catalog.Datasource.Url;
// create the properties
string ds =
 String.Format
  ("<DataSourceInfo>{0}</DataSourceInfo>
    <Catalog>{1}</Catalog>
    <Format>Multidimensional</Format>
    <AxisFormat>TupleFormat</AxisFormat>",
    catalog.Datasource.Info, catalog.Name);
XmlElement props =
  XmlaHelper.CreateXmlElement("PropertyList", ds);
XmlElement query =
  XmlaHelper.CreateXmlElement("Statement", mdx);
// call execute on the xmla server
_xml = xa.Execute(query, props);

// create the axis info
_axesInfo = new AxesInfo(_xml["OlapInfo"]["AxesInfo"]);
// create the cell info
_cellInfo = new CellInfo(_xml["OlapInfo"]["CellInfo"]);
// create the axes
_axes = new Axes(_xml["Axes"]);
// create the cell data
_cellData = new CellData(_xml["CellData"]);
```

```
// create datatable representation
_ds = new DataSet("MDData");
_tbl = _ds.Tables.Add("table");

Axis a0 = _axes["Axis0"];
Axis a1 = _axes["Axis1"];
int rowCount = a1.Tuples.Count;
int colCount = a0.Tuples.Count;

// add the tuple columns
AxisInfo ai = _axesInfo["Axis1"];
foreach(AxisInfo.HierarchyInfo hi in ai)
{
    _tbl.Columns.Add(hi.Name,
      Type.GetType("System.String"));
}

// add the data columns
foreach(Tuple t in a0.Tuples)
{
    Debug.WriteLine(String.Format
       ("{0} tuple members", t.Count));
    if (t.Count > 1)
    {
        // add all of the tuples as the column name
        string columnName = "";
        foreach(Tuple.Member tm in t)
        {
            columnName += tm.Caption + " ";
        }
        _tbl.Columns.Add(columnName,
           Type.GetType("System.Double"));
    }
    else
    {
        // just the single tuple name as a column name
        _tbl.Columns.Add(t[0].Caption,
         Type.GetType("System.Double"));
    }

}

// add the rows
for (int i = 0; i < rowCount; i++)
{
```

```
            ArrayList arr = new ArrayList();
            // include each tuple member
            foreach(Tuple.Member tm in a1.Tuples[i])
            {
                arr.Add(tm.Caption);
            }
            // add the data
            for(int j = 0; j < colCount; j++)
            {
                // calculate the indexer
                int index = i * colCount + j;
                // get the cell data
                Cell c = _cellData[index];
                if (c != null)
                    arr.Add(c.Value);
                else
                    arr.Add(null);
            }
            // create a row and add it to the table
            _tbl.Rows.Add(arr.ToArray());
        }
    }
```

As in that `Datasource` constructor, the first thing we do is create an instance of the `MsXmlAnalysis` Web Services proxy. After we have the proxy, we retrieve the URL property of the `Datasource` associated with the `Catalog` passed into the `MDDataSet` constructor and assign it to the Web Services proxy.

Next, we create a string for the properties that should be used in our call to `Execute`. We create an XML fragment that contains the `DataSourceInfo` and `Catalog` from the passed in `Catalog` object as well as specify the `Format` and `AxisFormat` of the results that will be returned. We turn both the property list and the passed in query into `XmlElements` and call `Execute`.

After we have retrieved the results from the MDX query, we parse the XML to retrieve the `AxesInfo`, `Axes`, `CellInfo` and `CellData` sections by using the `Item` indexer. We then pass the retrieved `XmlNode` into the constructor for the appropriate object. We will return to cover the constructors for `AxesInfo`, `Axes`, `CellInfo` and `CellData` later.

Next, we construct a `DataTable` representation of the query results that we can use in binding. It is important to note that this technique works only with two-dimensional data (columns and rows) because that is all that can be exposed through data binding. To envision how this works, see Figure 5.3. That figure shows the results of an MDX query bound to the .NET `DataGrid` control.

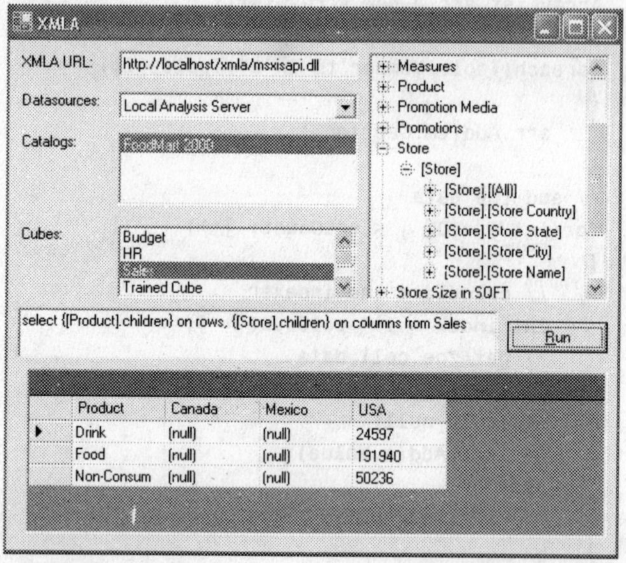

FIGURE 5.3 MDX query results bound to the .NET `DataGrid` control.

To create a flattened `DataTable` that represents the multidimensional results that are returned we first create a column for each of the tuples in `Axis1`. Our query shown in Figure 5.3 has one tuple (Product) and that becomes the first column in the flattened data set. Next we add in each of the tuples from `Axis0`. Note that multiple tuples are concatenated together to form the name of the column. For example, if we run a query that applies a `CrossJoin` on `Axis0` (columns) such as

```
SELECT
{CrossJoin({[Store].children},
{[Gender].children}) } ON COLUMNS,
{[Product].children} ON ROWS
FROM Sales
```

we will get the results shown in Figure 5.4. Concatenating the tuples is a simple way of rendering a multidimensional result set as a tabular data set. Although the `DataGrid` control works fine in a sample application, to create a better user interface in a production application, it would be appropriate to use one of the commercially available bindable grids that have much more flexibility in how they bind to and render data. Using a more advanced control would allow us to render the data set in a more user-friendly way.

After we have added the columns, we add each of the rows to the `DataTable`. First, we add the captions for each of the tuples in `Axis1` that we have added to the

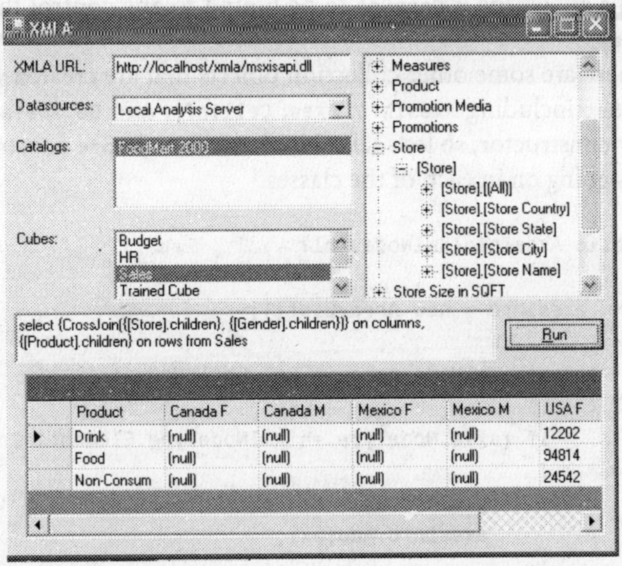

FIGURE 5.4 Multiple tuples are concatenated for each column.

columns to an `ArrayList`. After that, we get the cell value from the `CellData` for each of the cells returned from the query and add them to the `ArrayList`. Finally, we take the `ArrayList` and add a row to the `DataTable` and then repeat for each row in the result set.

The `DataTable` is exposed through the `IListSource` interface, which is implemented for the `MDDataSet` with the following code:

```
public IList GetList()
{
    return new DataView(_tbl);
}

public bool ContainsListCollection
{
    get
    {
        return false;
    }
}
```

This allows the MDDataSet to be bound to any control that can be bound to a DataView.

There are some other collection objects that are created when constructing an MDDataSet including AxesInfo, Axes, CellInfo, and CellData. Each of these has a similar constructor, so let's take a look at the AxesInfo constructor to get a feel for what is going on in each of the classes.

```
public AxesInfo(XmlNode xml)
{
    _axesInfo = new ArrayList();

    foreach(XmlNode axis in xml.ChildNodes)
    {
        if (axis.NodeType == XmlNodeType.Element)
        {
            AxisInfo ax = new AxisInfo(axis);
            _axesInfo.Add(ax);
        }
    }
}
```

We walk with the XmlNode passed in through each of the child nodes and create a new AxisInfo object with the child node. Similarly for each of the other collection objects: the XmlNode is parsed into its constituent parts and used to build the elements in the collection.

SUMMARY

In this chapter, we have covered the basics of XMLA, illustrated how it works, and created a sample application that uses XMLA in .NET. As we have seen, XMLA provides a simple way to query OLAP data using standard Internet protocols. Due to the .NET Framework's excellent support for integrating with Web Services, creating an application that uses XMLA in .NET provides an excellent platform for building business intelligence applications in .NET.

REFERENCES

XMLA specification, available online at *http://www.xmla.org/*, or at *http://msdn.microsoft.com/library/default.asp?url=/library/en-us/dnxmlspec/html/xmlanalysis.asp.*

6 ADOMD.NET

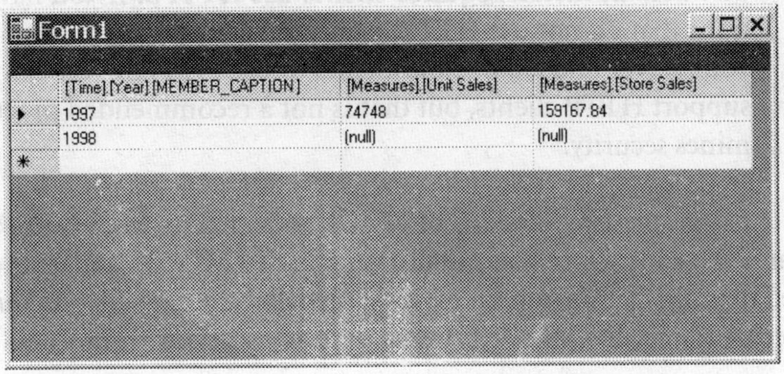

OVERVIEW

In this chapter, we will talk about one of the important new technologies that will impact business intelligence development with .NET in the near future—ADOMD.NET. Building on XMLA, ADOMD.NET is a .NET data provider that can be used to build applications that consume multidimensional data. ADOMD.NET implements an object model that wraps XMLA, and can be used in any .NET application. At the time of this writing, ADOMD.NET is in beta release, so it is still subject to change before the final release.

XMLA 1.1

ADOMD.NET requires XMLA Version 1.1, so we will briefly cover this version of XMLA first. The implementation of XMLA 1.1 provided by Microsoft is also in beta as of this writing. When it is released, this will be the version that the next version of SQL Server (code named Yukon) uses. Yukon is slated to provide native XMLA support, so you won't have to have the XMLA SDK configured in IIS to use XMLA.

It is important to know that there are breaking changes between XMLA 1.0 and XMLA 1.1. The changes between 1.0 and 1.1 are not extensive, but they are enough to break code that was written against the older schema. The specific breaking changes between Versions 1.0 and 1.1 are:

- **The namespace of the elements that are returned has changed:** You will need to make sure that any clients that are written using the old namespace are updated.
- **The properties of the `DataSourceInfo` to establish a connection are different:** If your 1.0 clients were not using Discovered `DataSourceInfo`, they will have to be updated to connect to the data source.
- **The default install requires clients use HTTPS:** If you have existing applications that do not use HTTPS-secured clients, you will need to install a key on your server and change the clients to use HTTPS. You can install the SDK to support HTTP clients, but that is not a recommended practice since it undermines security.

Lastly, the two versions of XMLA provided by Microsoft can't be run on the same machine. Once you install a version of XMLA on a machine, you are committed to using that version unless you reinstall the other version. This means that if you decide to install XMLA 1.1, the sample applications from Chapter 5 will not work.

Object Model

As we have mentioned, ADOMD.NET is an object model that wraps XMLA so that it can be used from any .NET application without having to directly write to the XMLA specification. ADOMD.NET is very similar to the older ADOMD that we discussed in Chapter 4. As we have seen, using ADOMD through COM Interop is quite feasible, but it does have some rough edges.

When released, ADOMD.NET is definitely the way to go for new .NET applications. Porting an existing application from ADOMD to ADOMD.NET should be easy, even though they aren't 100 percent compatible. ADOMD.NET is to be forward compatible with Yukon, so anything you build now using Analysis Services 2000 and ADOMD.NET should work in the new environment.

The ADOMD.NET object hierarchy is in the Microsoft.AnalysisServices.AdomdClient namespace. There are some new classes in ADOMD.NET that were not in ADOMD including Measures and Named Sets, but for the most part the object model is very similar to the ADOMD object model we discussed in Chapter 4. An illustration of the object model for ADOMD.NET is shown in Figures 6.1 and 6.2. A brief description of the more important ADOMD.NET classes is provided in Table 6.1.

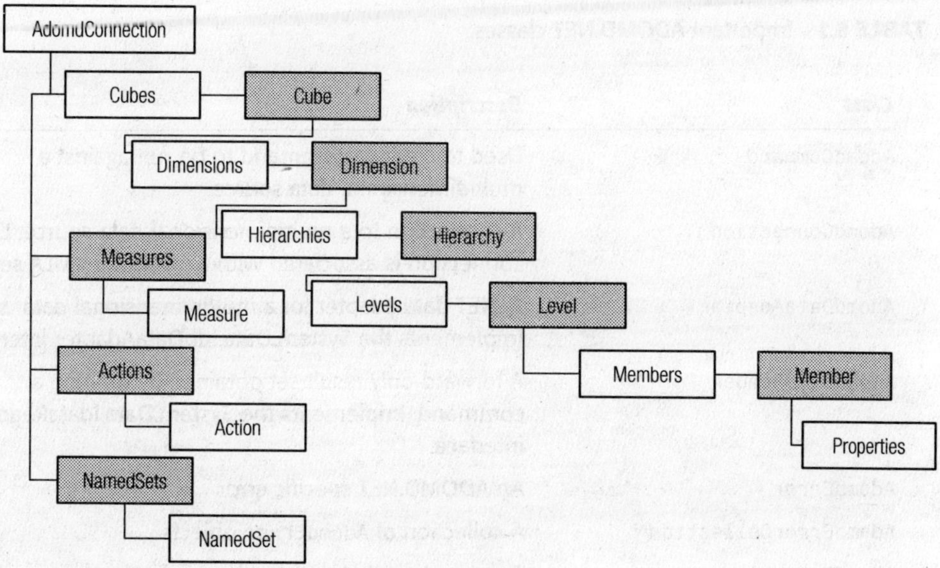

FIGURE 6.1 ADOMD.NET metadata object model.

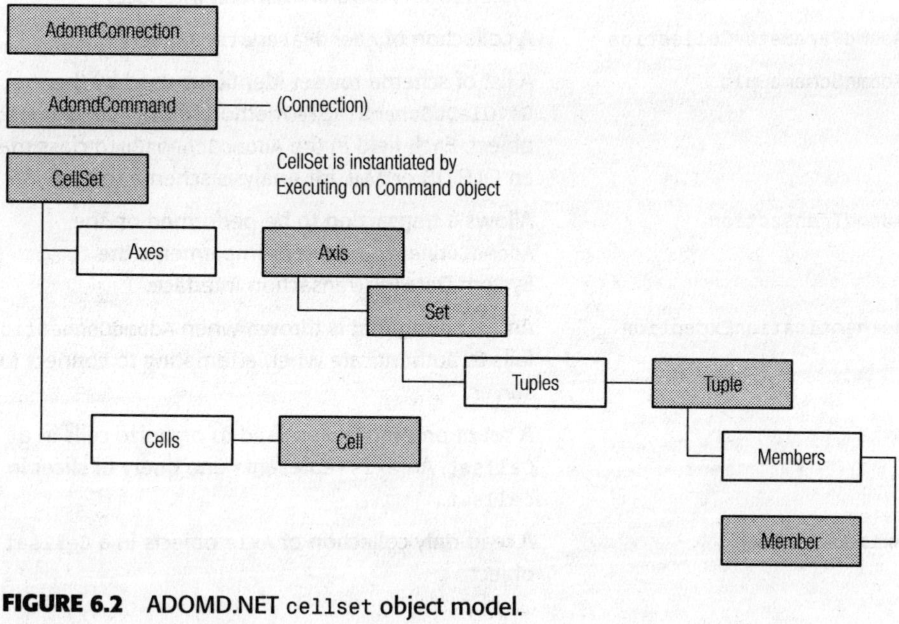

FIGURE 6.2 ADOMD.NET `cellset` object model.

TABLE 6.1 Important ADOMD.NET classes.

Class	*Description*
`AdomdCommand`	Used to create a command to be run against a multidimensional data source
`AdomdConnection`	A connection to a multidimensional data source. Each connection is associated with a particular XMLA session.
`AdomdDataAdapter`	A .NET data adapter for a multidimensional data source. Implements the System.Data.IdbDataAdapter interface.
`AdomdDataReader`	A forward-only result set obtained by running a command. Implements the System.Data.IdataReader interface.
`AdomdError`	An ADOMD.NET specific error
`AdomdErrorCollection`	A collection of `AdomdError` objects
`AdomdException`	An exception that may be thrown by the `AdomdConnection` object when the `Open` or `GetOleDbSchemaTable` method is called. The `AdomdException` object contains a collection of `AdomdError` objects.
`AdomdParameter`	An `AdomdCommand` object parameter. Implements the System.Data.IdbDataParameter interface.
`AdomdParameterCollection`	A collection of `AdomdParameter` objects
`AdomdSchemaGuid`	A list of schema rowset identifiers used by the `GetOleDbSchemaTable` method of the `AdomdConnection` object. Each field in the `AdomdSchemaGuid` class maps to an OLE DB or XML for Analysis schema rowset
`AdomdTransaction`	Allows a transaction to be performed on the `AdomdConnection` object. Implements the System.Data.IdbTransaction interface.
`AuthenticationException`	An exception that is thrown when `AdomdConnection` fails to authenticate when attempting to connect to a server
`Axis`	A set of ordered tuples used to organize cells in a `Cellset`. An `axis` represents one query or slicer in that `cellset`.
`AxisCollection`	A read-only collection of `Axis` objects in a `Cellset` object

TABLE 6.1 *(Continued)*

Class	*Description*
`Cell`	The unique logical intersection of one position from every axis in the `cellset`. Not every cell in a `cellset` will contain data.
`CellCollection`	A read-only collection of `Cell` objects in a `Cellset` object
`CellProperty`	The cell properties for a given cell. Usually used to help format the cells for display in the user interface.
`CellPropertyCollection`	A read-only collection of `CellProperty` objects in a `Cell` object
`Cellset`	The multidimensional result set returned from the `Execute` or `ExecuteCellSet` method of the `AdomdCommand`. It contains a collection of cells organized into axes.
`ConnectionException`	The exception that is thrown when an error occurs while attempting to connect to a server using the `AdomdConnection` object
`CubeCollection`	A read-only list of `CubeDef` objects in an `AdomdConnection` object `CubeDef` The metadata for a cube consisting of the collection of measures organized into dimensions
`Dimension`	A set of members organized into levels and hierarchies
`DimensionCollection`	A read-only collection of `Dimension` objects in a `CubeDef` object
`Hierarchy`	A set of members and their positions relative to each other
`HierarchyCollection`	A read-only collection of `Hierarchy` objects in a `Dimension` or `Set` object
`Level`	A set of members organized into a level within a hierarchy
`LevelCollection`	A read-only collection of `Level` objects in a `Hierarchy` object
`LevelProperty`	The properties for a given level
`LevelPropertyCollection`	A read-only collection of `LevelProperty` objects in a `Level` object

TABLE 6.1 *(Continued)*

Class	*Description*
Measure	A measure within a cube
MeasureCollection	A read-only collection of Measure objects in a CubeDef object
Member	A member, representing one or more records in the underlying database, within a hierarchy, tuple, level, or member. This is the lowest level of cell data in a cube.
MemberCollection	A read-only collection of Member objects in a Level, or Tuple object
MemberProperty	A single member property for a given member
MemberPropertyCollection	A read-only collection of MemberProperty objects in a Member object
NamedSet	A named set for a given cube
NamedSetCollection	A read-only collection of NamedSet objects in a CubeDef object Position A tuple on an axis PositionCollection A read-only collection of Position objects in an Axis object
Set	An ordered collection of zero or more tuples, organized along hierarchies that is commonly used to define axes in a multidimensional query
Tuple	An ordered collection of members from different dimensions.
TupleCollection	A read-only collection of Tuple objects contained by a Set or Axis object

Accessing Data

Accessing data with ADOMD.NET has some strong similarities to accessing data in ADO.NET. There are also many differences because of the nature of multidimensional data. For structured data from a relational database, metadata is fairly standard. You know that each rowset is going to be of two dimensions (rows and columns). With multidimensional data, you don't know the dimensionality of the data that is returned. To be able to interpret the data properly, you need to get the metadata that describes the results. The basic steps to accessing data in ADOMD.NET are:

1. Create a connection
2. Get metadata
3. Run commands
4. Get data
5. Close connection

Create a Connection

The AdomdConnection object is similar to the ADO.NET Connection object and is used in a similar fashion. When connected to a data source, the AdomdConnection object creates an internal client that communicates with the data source using XMLA. In addition to connecting to XMLA servers, the AdomdConnection can access local cubes (although this feature does not work in the beta).

The ConnectionString used by the AdomdConnection is similar to that used by an ADO.NET Connection object. An example of an ADOMD.NET ConnectionString is

```
Datasource=http://localhost/xmla/msxisapi.dll;
DataSourceInfo=Local Analysis Server;Catalog=Foodmart 2000
```

The properties that are used in the ConnectionString are shown in Table 6.2.

When the Open method is called, the connection string is evaluated. If a property is set to an unsupported value or the connection string is invalid, an exception is thrown. If the connection string is good, a session is created on the XMLA provider with the criteria specified in the connection string.

The AdomdConnection object uses sessions in XMLA with the SessionID property of the object representing the active session. An AdomdConnection object can be connected to or disconnected from a valid session. You can attach multiple AdomdConnection objects to a single session. When the Open method is called, AdomdConnection checks its SessionID value with the XMLA provider. If it matches an active session on the provider, the AdomdConnection is connected to that session. If it does not match an active session, a new session is created and the AdomdConnection is attached to that new session.

With each method call that goes through the AdomdConnection object, the SessionID is sent to the provider. If the session expires, any method calls on that object will throw an exception. You can catch the exceptions and handle them to continue processing by reconnecting the AdomdConnection to a valid session and proceeding.

TABLE 6.2 Properties used in the `ConnectionString`.

Setting name	*Description*
`Catalog`	Sets the catalog (database) to connect to
`ConnectionTimeout`	Sets the number of seconds that the `AdomdConnection` object will wait before the attempt to establish a connection to the data source is terminated and an error is thrown
`DataSource`	Sets the instance or local cube (.cub) file to which the `AdomdConnection` object establishes a connection
`DataSourceInfo`	Name of the configured XMLA datasource to connect to
`Password`	Sets the password used by the `AdomdConnection` object to establish a connection with the specified user name
`ProtectionLevel`	Sets the protection level used by the provider to sign or encrypt the connection. Valid values are `None` and `PktPrivacy`.
`Timeout`	Sets the number of seconds that the `AdomdConnection` will wait before an attempt to run a statement is terminated and an exception thrown
`UserName`	Sets the user ID used by the `AdomdConnection` object to establish a connection

Get Metadata

As we have discussed, metadata is very important to the effective use of multidimensional data. ADOMD.NET supports three ways to get metadata, each that can be used for different purposes.

The first of these is to access the `CubeDef` objects that are exposed in the `Cubes` property of the `AdomdConnection` object. The `CubeDef` exposes descriptive information as well as the dimensions and measures for a given cube. This information is very useful for constructing queries on the cube either programmatically or through a user interface.

Next, you can get metadata from the `Cellset` that is returned from the execution of an MDX query. The `Cellset` contains the organization of returned data into `Axes` and `Cells`, and can be used to display the information in an application. The `Axes` contain information about the name and position for each returned `Axis` object. The `Cells` also contain the data consisting of values and properties representing the information stored in the cube.

Lastly, ADOMD.NET can return any of the schema rowsets used for interaction with a multidimensional database. This includes the schemas included in OLE DB, OLE DB for OLAP, OLE DB for Data Mining, and XML for Analysis. These schemas can be useful when you want to view the metadata about a cube in a table and are especially useful when used with data-mining structures in the catalog.

RUN COMMANDS

The most useful thing you can do with a multidimensional database is to run queries and retrieve data. You create a command using the `AdomdCommand` class constructor and run the commands through an `AdomdConnection` object. You can also run a command directly on the `AdomdConnection` object using the `CreateCommand` method.

Either way the `AdomdCommand` is constructed, it can be used with methods on the `AdomdConnection`. There are a number of different execute methods that can be used depending on how you want to use the data that is returned.

The `ExecuteCellset` method returns a `Cellset` object that contains the complete set of multidimensional cells. The `Cellset` has more flexibility than the other return types for interacting with multidimensional data. However, this interactivity comes at the price of overhead. The `Cellset` not only contains all of the data, but, as we have discussed earlier, a large amount of metadata as well. This results in more data that needs to be processed and passed over the wire from a remote server.

The `ExecuteReader` method returns an `AdomdDataReader` object, which can be used to navigate through the data through the IDataReader interface. The data reader is a forward-only mechanism for reading the data. The `AdomdDataReader` provides methods for retrieving metadata and data for the result set. `AdomdDataReader` is a much lighter weight interface than the `Cellset`.

The `ExecuteXML` method returns an `XmlReader` that allows reading the raw XMLA information. Since this method does very little to the data, it is the fastest in terms of retrieval. However, the client will still need to parse the returned XMLA to be able to use it for meaningful actions.

Lastly, `ExecuteNonQuery` can be used to run commands that don't return any rows. Obviously, this is the best choice for queries that do not expect to return any results.[1]

Close Connection

After you are finished with an `AdomdConnection`, it should be explicitly closed. If an `AdomdConnection` is simply allowed to fall out of scope and be collected as garbage, the server resources may be tied up unnecessarily while waiting for the object to be destroyed. This can slow down server performance.

To shut down an `AdomdConnection`, you use the `Close` method which has one Boolean argument specifying whether the session is to be ended. If `Close` is called with `true` (which is the default value), then the session is ended and the `AdomdConnection` is closed. If `false` is passed in, the session remains active but the `AdomdConnection` is closed. This session can be reused later with another `AdomdConnection`.

Security

Security is an important aspect of any business intelligence application. Encrypting the HTTP communications between the client and server using Secure Sockets Layer provides security in ADOMD.NET. The default installation of XMLA requires that communications between the client and server go through HTTPS, and not HTTP, to make sure that the channel is secure. HTTPS is the only security option when using the XMLA SDK. ADOMD.NET used with Yukon will provide more security options.

Installing the Beta

First, you need to install and configure the XMLA SDK version 1.1. By default, this will limit connections to using HTTPS, so you will need to install a server certificate on your IIS server or use the `AllowUnsecuredConnection` option in the XMLA configuration file. After you have installed XMLA and created the virtual directory, you are ready to install the ADOMD.NET beta.

Installing the ADOMD.NET beta is simple. Download the install package and run the installer. If you accept the defaults, it will install the files in a convenient location and you will be ready to go.

You can access both the XMLA SDK and ADOMD.NET betas from MSDN at *http://msdn.microsoft.com/library/default.asp?url=/downloads/list/dataaccess.asp*. Note that the documentation for ADOMD.NET is a separate download. So, if you want the documentation, you will have to download and install it as well. Again, this is a beta release; so expect the details of the installation process to change with the release.

A Simple Example of ADOMD.NET

ON THE CD

As our first illustration of getting ADOMD.NET data in an application, we will create an `AdomdConnection` and an `AdomdCommand`, and then use the `AdomdDataAdapter` to create a `DataSet` that can be bound to a `DataGrid`. Although this example is trivial, it does show how to get data out of ADOMD.NET and display it in an application. The source code for this application is provided on the CD-ROM in the Chapter 6 directory.

To create this application, open up Visual Studio .NET and create a new C# Windows Application. Next, add a reference to the ADOMD.NET library by browsing to the location where you installed the library. By default, this path is C:\Program Files\Microsoft.NET\ADOMD\msadomdp.dll.

After you have added the reference, you are ready to start creating the application. Open the Toolbox and drag a `DataGrid` control onto the surface of Form1. Now switch to the Code View for Form1 and add the following code to the constructor for Form1, replacing the existing code:

```
InitializeComponent();
AdomdConnection conn = new AdomdConnection();
conn.ConnectionString ="Datasource=http://localhost/xmla/msxisapi.dll;" +
  "DataSourceInfo=Local Analysis Server; " +
  "Catalog=Foodmart 2000";
conn.Open();
AdomdCommand cmd = conn.CreateCommand();
cmd.CommandText = "SELECT " +
  "[Measures].[Unit Sales], [Measures].[Store Sales] } ON COLUMNS, " +
  "{ [Time].[1997], [Time].[1998] } ON ROWS " +
  "FROM Sales " +
  "WHERE ( [Store].[USA].[CA] )";
AdomdDataAdapter adapter = new AdomdDataAdapter(cmd);
DataSet ds = new DataSet();
adapter.Fill(ds);
dataGrid1.SetDataBinding(ds, "Table");
conn.Close();
```

Now compile and run the application. It will display the `DataGrid` populated with the results of the MDX query that was assigned to the command text as shown in Figure 6.3.

After you have run the code, let's examine what is going on. The first line initializes the components for the Windows form, as usual. Next, we create a new `AdomdConnection` object and assign the `ConnectionString`. In the example, we used localhost as the server name and a data source that is installed by default with the SDK, but you can use any server that has the XMLA 1.1 SDK installed and any data source that you have defined in the XMLA configuration.

After initializing the `ConnectionString`, we open the connection to the XMLA provider and create an `AdomdCommand` object. Next, we assign an MDX statement to the `CommandText` property of the `AdomdCommand` object. After we have created the `AdomdCommand`, we are ready to create our `AdomdDataAdapter`. This data adapter works very much as any other data adapter and can be used to fill `DataSet` objects with data from the `CommandText`.

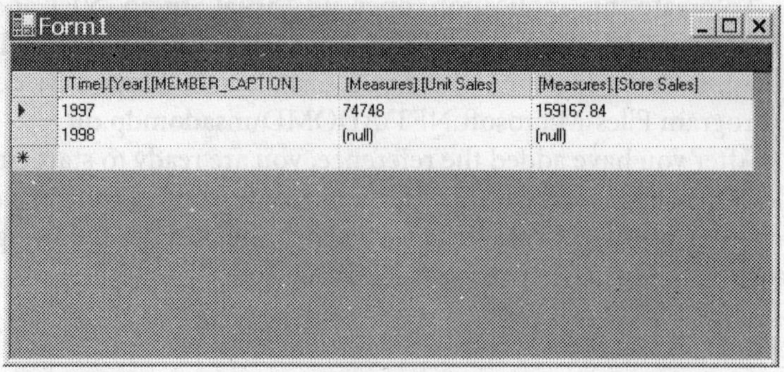

FIGURE 6.3 ADOMD.NET data bound to a `DataGrid`.

We next create a `DataSet` that we will use to bind to the `DataGrid`. After creating the `DataSet`, we call the `Fill` method on the `AdomdDataAdapter` to populate the `DataSet`. This creates a `DataTable` in the `DataSet` called "`Table`" that we then use in the call to the `DataGrid`'s `SetDataBinding` method. Lastly, we call `Close` on the `AdomdConnection` to clean up. That's all there is to it. If you are familiar with ADO.NET programming, this will seem very familiar.

SUMMARY

As we have seen in this chapter, ADOMD.NET is a .NET data provider that can be used with multidimensional data without the inconvenience of using COM Interop. ADOMD.NET is a wrapper around XMLA 1.1 and allows you to use a service-based architecture without having to manipulate XML manually. The object model for ADOMD.NET is similar to that of other .NET data providers and will be familiar to anyone that has done ADO.NET development. Although it is currently in beta, ADOMD.NET will be the standard technology for creating multidimensional applications using .NET.

ENDNOTES AND REFERENCES

1. `ExecuteScalar` is also defined in the object model and is designed to support queries that return only a single value, but it is not supported in the beta release. To return a scalar value, you can just use the other `Execute` methods and get the returned value from the structure that is returned. ADOMD.NET help files, available by opening the Help menu from within the program.

The ADOMD.NET beta with documentation can be downloaded from *http://www.microsoft.com/downloads/details.aspx?FamilyId=49737737-681E-465E-83C5-51B7223B1585&displaylang=en.*

7 Reporting

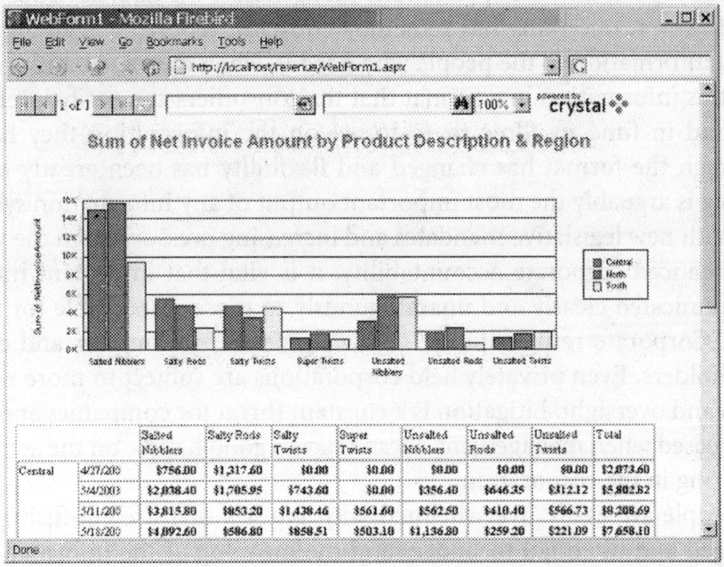

OVERVIEW

As discussed in the previous chapters, OLAP provides a way to access and analyze data that is contained in your data warehouse. However, the tools we have used for querying data in the data warehouse are not suitable for broad distribution to a wide population of non-technical users. In addition to providing the ability to query the data, in a successful business intelligence platform, you need to publish the data and share the results of any analysis that has been performed in a way that is easy for the audience to access and comprehend. As we discussed in Chapter 1, the value of business intelligence is subject to strong network effects: the more people in the organization know about it the more valuable it is. So, how do we share the information we have gathered? The best answer is often with reports.

Although it is sometimes associated with the ugly, static "green-bar" reports that were printed out from mainframe applications years ago and delivered by a guy walking around the office with a cart full of accordion paper, reporting has evolved considerably in the last twenty years. When the laser printer became commonplace, reports migrated from the mainframe to the PC and started to be distributed by LAN and e-mail. This evolution has continued with modern reports coming in all kinds of formats—Web pages, PDFs, PDA screens, and voice mail. Today, it is very difficult to even determine exactly what we mean by reporting since the lines between reports and the applications that generate the data have been blurred.

However, one thing has remained constant: reporting is all about providing useful information to the people who need it, when they need it. Good reports deliver this information in a format that the consumers can easily interpret and understand in time to allow them to act on the information they have received. Although the format has changed and flexibility has been greatly enhanced, reporting is arguably the most important output of any information system.

With new legislative mandates and increasing pressure from the world at large for enhanced corporate accountability, it is vital that important information be communicated clearly and unambiguously to those responsible for making decisions. Corporate responsibility is now legislated by Congress and demanded by shareholders. Even privately held corporations are subject to more rigorous regulation and oversight. Litigation is a constant threat for companies and the problem is increased when management doesn't have a good handle on the activities that are occurring in the corporation.

People are easily overwhelmed with reports that are confusingly labeled or arranged and often fail to understand the meaning of the information they have been given. So it is vital to be able to provide well-designed reports that are highly usable and understandable. This means more than just a series of tables and columns of figures, it means meaningful graphics and appropriate summaries. It also means being able to drill through the information on a report to view the granular information that went into creating the report.

In addition to the challenge of providing understandable information, business is a dynamic game and the reporting requirements change as often as the business does. The increased competitive climate and rapid pace of change present in most businesses require that new views of corporate activity are created on a regular basis. It is important that a business intelligence solution be capable of responding quickly to these changes and not requiring a custom development effort to respond to routine changes in reporting.

In this chapter we will focus on how .NET can provide flexible reporting services that support business intelligence and good decision-making. Our focus will be on traditional reporting techniques involving both printed and screen output. We will not cover reports that are delivered via PDA or other technologies in detail.

Many of the same general principles apply, and adapting the approaches shown in this chapter to include alternate display devices should be reasonably straightforward. We will build on the topics we have covered in data warehousing and OLAP to show how we can use .NET to deliver information to decision makers.

Designing Reports

Regardless of the technology used, there are some important issues to consider before creating a report. The first thing that should be done is to discover the requirements for the report. Much as creating requirements for a software project, figuring out the basic requirements that go into a report is essential for it to meet the user's needs. The basic steps for creating a report follow:

1. Understand the intention of the report.
2. Understand the users and uses of the report.
3. Collect the data fields and sources for the report.
4. Create a layout for the report.

Understand the Intention

In order to create a successful report, the first thing you need is to understand the high-level intention of the report. Understanding intention is crucial to creating a report that meets the needs of the users. As in software development, shortcomings in understanding the requirements are often fatal to the success of the product. It is an excellent idea to formulate a short description of the use and intent of the report so that you can use that to establish a starting point and create further requirements for the report. For example, the intention of the report might be to create a top-level revenue report for the whole corporation broken down by division and product line. Another example would be to create a view of slow-moving inventory broken down by region and SKU. Whatever the specific intention of the report, writing a brief one- or two-sentence description will help to make sure that the intention of the report is clear in the minds of both the developers of the report and the consumers.

Understand the Users

In addition to understanding the purpose of the report, you need to understand who is going to be using the report and the context in which they will be using it. In many cases, this will be a large and diverse group of people, each with different areas of concern. For example, a top-level revenue report for the entire company might be used by almost everyone in the company from the CEO on down, and by analysts and investors outside the company. Regardless of the number and type of users, it is important to consider what they are going to consider important in the report. The CEO would use the report to evaluate the revenue-generating performance of the divisions and might want to coordinate the numbers with other reports showing the costs associated with each division and the bottom-line contribution for each. A divisional general manager might be concerned with the same things that the CEO is, but on a divisional basis. A divisional sales manager might be concerned with the detailed breakdown of revenue generated by salesperson and product line. A salesperson or product manager would be chiefly concerned with the performance of their particular domain.

Understanding who is using the report and how they will be using it can help refine the purpose. If the uses of the report and the purpose don't line up, it might be a good idea to investigate whether this report is indeed appropriate for the intended use and can be modified to suit other required purposes, or whether another report is needed. As long as the numbers gathered from the data warehouse provide a single version of the truth, creating different reports for different uses is not a problem. When it becomes a problem is when different reports give different answers.

Collect the Data Fields

Based on understanding the intention and use of the report, we next determine the data that should be contained in the report. In many cases, it might require considerable effort to track down a reliable source for the data. In any event, you will need data that will allow the intention of the report to be fulfilled. Sometimes, at this point, you will discover that the report cannot be created without considerable investment in time and resources to collect the data. This is where the effort to collect the metadata for your data warehouse really pays off.

As we discussed in Chapter 2, the metadata in a data warehouse describes the data much as a card catalog describes the books in a library. Being able to determine if the appropriate data exists in the data warehouse and find it easily considerably shortens the time and effort required to create a report. If the metadata is not kept up to date, finding the data scattered throughout the organization becomes a tedious process of trial and error.

In addition to providing the data fields that will be present in the report, you will need to consider the organization of the report. In what order should the data be sorted? How should the data be filtered? At what level should the data be summarized? In some cases, the answers to these questions will be obvious. In others, it might be quite difficult to determine. Again, answering these questions becomes much easier with accurate metadata that describes the grain and source for the data.

Create the Layout

While setting the data fields for the report, you'll want to begin to create the report layout. One of the first things to consider when creating a report layout is the title of the report. It should be indicative of its purpose to those who will be reading the report. In the best cases, the title can be easily derived from the purpose statement that was written when the process of creating the report was started. For example, the top-level revenue report described earlier might be called "Corporate Revenue Report." In other cases, creating a title can be very difficult. It is, however, a vital step in maximizing the value of the report. In most cases, you'll want to avoid cryptic naming for a report. Titles like "R101A" are not very useful. Cryptic titles inhibit sharing of the information in the report because people who might benefit from the contents of a report will have no idea from the title of the report what it is about and might never discover it unless someone who is "in the know" points them to it.

Another important element in the layout is how to highlight exceptional data. Most people tend to manage by exception, so the rules for determining what an exception is and how it is to be indicated on the report are important. There are many possible conditions that can be used to determine which elements are exceptions. Using a formula different than the one expected by the users of the report can lead to fairly serious consequences if conditions that should be addressed are not because they are not flagged as exceptional on a report. Or the opposite can happen and a report can flag too many elements as exceptional even though they are not beyond the normal range of expected operations. In this case, the report can "cry wolf" and cause real exceptions to be ignored when they do occur. When possible, the formula used to determine the exceptions should be shown on the screen or page along with the data. This way, the viewer of a report understands how the exceptions were generated and can take that into account as the information is digested.

It is difficult to overestimate the significance of the formatting and presentation of data in a report. In his seminal book, *Visual Explanations*, Edward Tufte, a noted expert on information design, presents some very compelling examples of both good and bad information presentation impacting important decisions. In the tragic case of the space shuttle Challenger accident in 1986, an engineering report that showed the relationship between cold temperatures and failed O-rings was displayed to management before the fateful decision to launch on a very cold January day. This report failed to sway their decision because it was very difficult to disentangle the true meaning of the data that was displayed. Poorly designed charts and graphs made discerning the true story behind the data difficult. In this case, it is possible that a better-designed report would have averted a disaster.[1]

Although most business reports don't have the same criticality as the Challenger example, it is still important to pay careful intention to the layout of the report and the impact it has on the understanding of the data conveyed by the report. A well-crafted report will enable the reader to comprehend the situation being described quickly and unambiguously.

Layout considerations for a report to be delivered on-line are different from those that are delivered on paper. The greater interactivity allowed by on-line reports is counterbalanced by the lower resolution that is generally available on computer monitors vs. the printed page. Understanding who will be using the report and how they will be using it can be very useful in optimizing a report for either printed output or viewing on a screen. In addition to the standard print and computer screen outputs, modern reports are sometimes viewed on PDAs or other devices without full screen capabilities. Designing reports for these devices can be difficult, but basically the less screen resolution and real estate you have to work with, the more carefully designed the report needs to be to make sure the information is understandable.

Strongly consider creating a prototype to show to the report consumers after gathering some initial requirements. It is often much easier to critique and improve upon something that is more concrete than a list of fields. An iterative process is the best way to generate refined and useful reports. A good first step is to create a mock-up in a word processor or spreadsheet that can be used to elicit feedback from the users of the report. Any tool you are comfortable and efficient with can be used for a mock-up: a word processor, spreadsheet, or even pencil and paper.

A mock-up is easy to do and is extremely useful in reducing miscommunication between the stakeholders and the report designer. It is frustrating to go to great lengths to secure a particular piece of information for a report just to find out that it really isn't useful to the intended users and could just as easily be omitted. Or conversely, sometimes the crucial data is readily accessible but isn't included in the report because it is simply overlooked. In any case, the point is that consumers of a report will be much more likely to notice discrepancies in a mockup that is closer to the real thing than in a list of fields to be included in the report. In addition, prototyping will help identify what information might be required in the future. This will help to future-proof the report as much as possible by allowing you to anticipate user requirements. You can use this input in your next iteration of your data warehouse to be sure that the required information is captured and that you can readily build reports that more fully meet user needs.

One caveat about prototypes is to avoid spending too much time on them. You could easily spend as much time creating an elaborate prototype as creating the actual report itself, which isn't the best use of time. Instead, concentrate on providing a prototype that is good enough for users to understand and give feedback on. The key to the successful use of prototypes is iteration and feedback; overly elaborate efforts just get in the way.

After we have gone to all of the trouble to understand the requirements for the report and produce a design, we need a means to create the report and distribute it to our users. One technology that we can use for this purpose in a .NET business intelligence application is Crystal Reports®.

Crystal Reports for Visual Studio .NET

Crystal Reports for Visual Studio .NET comes with every copy of Visual Studio .NET. Crystal Reports has long provided flexible and powerful reporting based on many different kinds of data.

Flexible Presentation

One of the best things about using Crystal Reports is that it provides an attractive and flexible presentation for data. In rare cases, it is necessary to write your own report layout code that displays specialized data. However, in the many cases that are covered by the capabilities built into Crystal Reports, you will save yourself a lot of code and effort by reusing the polished interface presented by Crystal Reports. Right out of the box, Crystal Reports provides you with the ability to deliver both Web- and Windows-based reports, export report contents to many different file formats (including PDF, HTML, Excel and Word formats), and interact with other Windows and Web controls.

Web Distribution

For sharing information in a business intelligence application, it makes sense to use the Web distribution model for our reports. The Web support in Crystal Reports is built on ASP.NET and is fully integrated into Visual Studio .NET. For those of you that aren't familiar with ASP.NET, a bit of background information will help you understand how it works.

Developing programs that work over the Web is more complicated than writing Windows applications. Since the Web was originally designed for the distribution of static HTML documents, it has some characteristics that don't lend themselves well to developing applications with dynamic data. For one, the Web is stateless, that is, each request to a Web page is independent of any previous request. It is all based on a very simple request and response model—the browser requests a specific URL and the Web server responds with the content at that location. This is in stark contrast to the environment in a single PC or even a networked application in which the application state is maintained and easily accessible inside of the running program.

Another characteristic is the spare common components built into HTML. Basically, HTML supports a very primitive set of common components such as text boxes, buttons, and images. To create an intricate interface in HTML requires either a lot of HTML or the inclusion of non-standard elements such as Java applets or ActiveX controls. Working around these characteristics is what leads to the greater complexity of Web applications.

The first way that people began to work around the limitations of the static content model was with the Common Gateway Interface (CGI). CGI establishes a convention that allows programs to interact with Web servers and produce dynamic content on the fly in response to requests. One of the most common uses for CGI programs was to handle forms that are submitted from a Web page. Another very common use is to provide access to databases. CGI is a very stable technology and has been around for a long time. There are many options for developing CGI applications, but many are developed using scripting languages such as PERL that can be easily changed without recompiling. However, CGI has some performance liabilities. Each request to a CGI application spawns a new process. The creation of a process is very intensive in terms of both memory and processor cycles that are used. Also, the creation of an entirely new process for each request makes database optimizations such as connection pooling impossible, increasing the number of times the database must create and destroy connections. The combination of heavy process creation and inefficient resource usage can be a performance killer for CGI applications.

To help the performance issues that surrounded creating a process to support each Web request, Web server vendors introduced low-level APIs that enabled the same kind of interaction provided by CGI programs, but that ran in the process space of the Web server. Internet Server API (ISAPI) is the API that is provided by Microsoft Internet Information Server (IIS). ISAPI is very fast and flexible. ISAPI works by loading a DLL into the Web server that accesses the same memory space as the Web server itself and has a lifetime that is concurrent with the server. So, when requests come into the Web server, they can be served by the ISAPI DLL with a minimum of delay. However, that speed and versatility come at the price of a more complex development effort. ISAPI applications must be written in a compiled language (typically C++) and can be difficult to design, construct, and test. In addition, any change to an ISAPI DLL requires that the Web server be shut down and restarted to use the new code. This makes management and deployment of updates to the Web application more complicated.

In the late 1990s, Microsoft introduced a technology called Active Server Pages (ASP). In ASP, you write the application logic in an interpreted script, usually VBScript, instead of creating a compiled application. But, the interpreter is run in-process on the IIS server (the ASP interpreter is actually an ISAPI DLL), so ASP doesn't have to create a new process for each request.

In ASP, the script is incorporated with the HTML so that you have a single file that represents the entire dynamic page. This integration between the script and

HTML was very intuitive and became quite popular. However, the combination of the application logic and the HTML is a double-edged sword; although the combined files are easy to understand and create for simple applications, it also made it very difficult to maintain complex applications. In addition, interpreted script is not very fast and was difficult to debug.

One technique that is widely used to build complex applications with ASP is encapsulating complex business logic inside compiled COM objects. These COM objects are used inside of the script and allow the script to become much simpler. Although this design overcomes many of the shortcomings of a pure script solution, the cure is sometimes worse than the disease. Adding compiled COM code to an ASP application makes the structure of the application more complex. Although COM components can be created quite easily using tools such as Microsoft Visual Basic, high performance COM components require a solid understanding of COM internals. Also, you have the same management problems as ISAPI in that updating the COM components requires that the Web server be stopped. Putting logic into separate COM components broke the nice simple structure of all of the code in one file, and introduced all of the complexities of COM into an otherwise straightforward technology.

To remedy the issues in ASP, Microsoft released ASP.NET as part of the .NET Framework. ASP.NET does for the Web what the very successful and popular Visual Basic environment did for Windows in the early 1990s. Basically, ASP.NET enables a container- and controls-based approach to building Web applications. The containers in the case of both Visual Basic and ASP.NET are called forms. As in Visual Basic, the Web controls used by ASP.NET have properties and methods and raise events. Instead of the heavy emphasis on custom scripting used by ASP, ASP.NET development is done in terms of adding controls to Web Forms, setting properties, calling methods, and handling and raising events.

Each Web Forms page consists of two files: the .aspx file that contains the controls and layout information, and a separate class file that contains the logic behind the page (sometimes called the "code-behind" file). When a Web Forms page is requested from a Web browser, the layout file is dynamically compiled and combined with the logic from the code-behind page with the resulting HTML output returned to the browser. This clean separation between layout and logic allows for a much more intuitive programming model. You can use controls placed on the Web Forms page as if they are client controls, without having to concern yourself with state management, low-level event handling, and special coding to provide support for different Web browsers. This allows you to focus on the functionality you are trying to build, not on the infrastructure.

As does ASP, ASP.NET runs on an IIS server. However, ASP.NET is part of the overall .NET Framework. You can access any of the features provided by the framework. This means that you can create ASP.NET applications in the same languages that you can create any .NET Framework application, as well as access all of the various pieces of the framework in a similar way. A diagram of how ASP.NET fits in with the rest of the .NET framework is presented in Figure 7.1. For more information on ASP.NET, see End Notes and References at the end of the chapter.

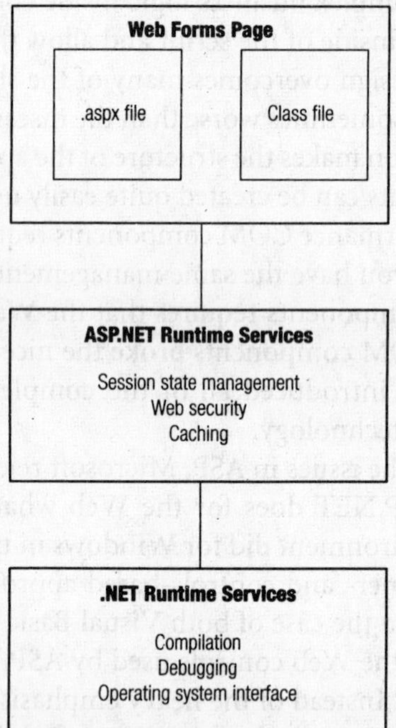

FIGURE 7.1 ASP.NET in context with the .NET Framework.

Although it is not necessary to use Visual Studio .NET to create ASP.NET applications, the powerful project management and visual editing capabilities provided by Visual Studio .NET make Web application development very efficient. These features include designers that allow drag-and-drop construction of Web pages, automatic deployment of updated files to Web servers, and integrated Web application debugging. In addition, and particularly relevant to this chapter, Visual Studio .NET includes a copy of Crystal Reports for Visual Studio .NET.

Creating a Report

Now that we understand a little bit about the fundamental technology used to distribute Web-based Crystal Reports, let's go through a scenario in which we will create a Web-based report for the Chocolate Pretzel Company. Suppose we have been assigned the task of creating a revenue report for the company. Doing our best to understand the intention of the report, we learn that it should be a company-wide report that can be used by both corporate management and regional sales managers to analyze sales broken down by product line and region. The report will be generally accessible to anyone in the company and should contain all of the revenue data for the last full month broken down by product line for each week in the month. Now that we understand a little bit more about the intention of the report, we make a simple mock-up of the report to show to the stakeholders to solicit feedback. The first prototype appears in Figure 7.2.

Net Invoices by Product

Product	Week 1	Week 2	Week 3	Week 4	Total
Pro quid pro	$1000	$900	$890	$1000	$2790
Ipso facto	$770	$890	$770	$890	$1150
E plurubus	$770	$1000	$1000	$890	$2500
Deus ex	$1000	$890	$1000	$770	$2250
Causus belli	$1000	$1000	$890	$1000	$1785
Sonorous ab	$890	$1000	$770	$1000	$1450
Veni vechi	$1000	$770	$1000	$1000	$3200
Total	$2790	$3570	$3240	$4510	$11560

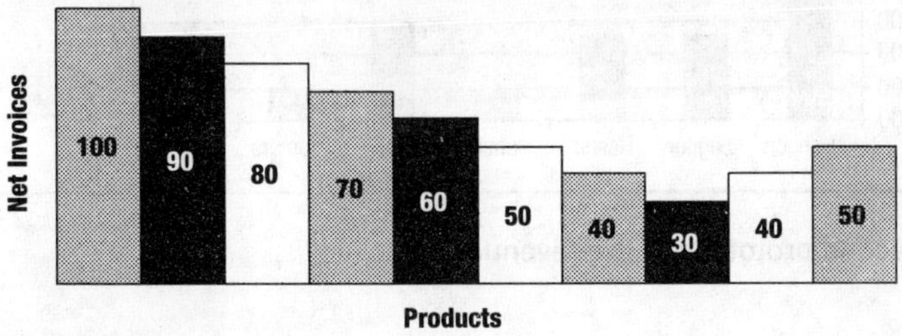

FIGURE 7.2 The first prototype of the revenue report.

After showing the prototype to the relevant stakeholders, we learn that an additional requirement is to break the sales down by sales region, as well as by product. The earlier changes are spotted the easier it is to make them. In this sense, creating reports is like creating software with the cost of change increasing exponentially as we get further along in the development cycle. Although it is difficult to see in this very simple example, it is easy to imagine a case in which a large effort is made to get data that turns out is not very important to the final report; a better decision would have been to not expend the effort to capture the data. Applying the modification, we have the final prototype shown in Figure 7.3.

Net Invoices by Product and Sales Region

		Fluvengon	Abegnor	Hastar	Flumilla	Itarson	Promera	Umleto	Total
Central	Week 1	$756.00	$1,317.60	$0.00	$0.00	$0.00	$0.00	$0.00	$2,073.60
	Week 2		$1,705.95	$743.60	$0.00	$356.40	$646.35	$312.12	$5,802.82
	Week 3	$3,815.80	$853.20	$1,438.46	$561.60	$562.50	$410.40	$566.73	$8,208.69
	Week 4	$4,092.60	$586.80	$858.51	$503.10	$1,136.80	$259.20	$221.09	$7,658.10
North	Week 1	$4,296.90	$986.70	$1,657.33	$269.10	$1,075.50	$483.30	$172.13	$8,940.96
	Week 2	$1,764.00	$108.00	$856.08	$0.00	$1,576.20	$638.40	$0.00	$4,942.68
	Week 3	$3,477.70	$794.40	$482.85	$257.40	$1,120.30	$0.00	$1,211.27	$7,343.92
	Week 4	$2,512.80	$1,850.55	$715.46	$865.80	$2,444.40	$518.40	$532.20	$9,439.61
South	Week 1	$4,448.20	$1,449.60	$570.24	$725.40	$674.00	$518.40	$0.00	$8,385.84
	Week 2	$3,542.00	$594.00	$862.88	$0.00	$0.00	$741.15	$0.00	$5,740.03
	Week 3	$0.00	$0.00	$469.85	$0.00	$571.00	$0.00	$474.12	$1,514.97
	Week 4	$2,378.70	$539.70	$2,084.62	$0.00	$1,665.00	$510.30	$338.13	$7,516.45
Total		$40,112.90	$12,691.50	$12,666.83	$4,290.00	$14,630.70	$4,928.40	$4,943.76	$94,264.09

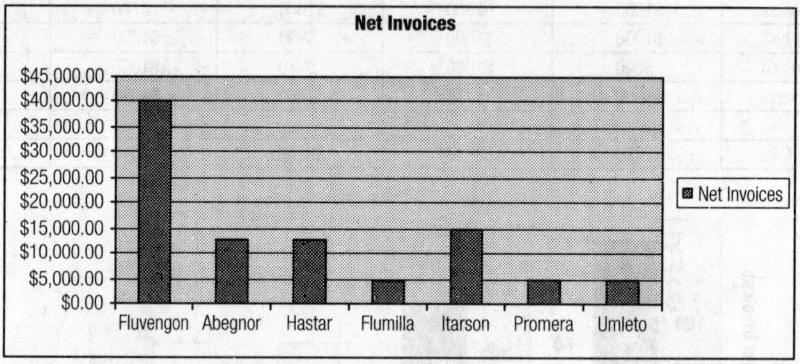

FIGURE 7.3 The second prototype of the revenue report.

ASP.NET Reporting Applications

After we have designed the prototype for the report, we are ready to start building our ASP.NET reporting application. The goal of this sample is to take you through the steps of creating a Web application in .NET that displays a Crystal Report while explaining what is going on along the way. After we are done, you should have a good idea of how to build your own reports with Crystal Reports and ASP.NET to support business intelligence needs. If you want to learn more about Crystal Reports, please consult the End Notes and References section at the end of the chapter.

Crystal Reports has three separate object models that can be used to display reports. A basic understanding of the different object models is helpful in getting the most out of Crystal Reports. The object models are contained in the following namespaces:

- CrystalDecisions.CrystalReports.Engine
- CrystalDecisions.Windows.Forms
- CrystalDecisions.Web

Engine Namespace

The CrystalDecisions.CrystalReports.Engine namespace contains the Engine object model. The most important object in the Engine object model is the `ReportDocument` object. The `ReportDocument` object has a very flexible interface to manipulate a report that has been loaded into the object. It does not have a user interface, but either a Windows or Web Forms Viewer can use a `ReportDocument` as a `ReportSource` for displaying a report.

Windows.Forms Namespace

The CrystalDecisions.Windows.Forms namespace contains the Windows Forms Viewer control. With the Windows Forms Viewer, you can view Crystal Reports in a Windows Forms application. The Windows Forms Viewer inherits from the Control class and can interact with other controls on a Windows Form with properties, methods, and events. The Windows Forms Viewer supports high-fidelity printing and exporting to different file formats. The Windows Forms Viewer's `ReportSource` property can be bound to a file path, a `ReportDocument` object, or a URL that references a Report Web Service. A limitation of the Windows Forms Viewer is that, unlike the `ReportDocument`, it does not have access to the complete set of report properties. The Windows Forms Viewer is limited to setting logon information, selection formulas, and report parameters.

Web Namespace

The CrystalDecisions.Web namespace contains the Web Forms Viewer and necessary supporting classes. The Web Forms Viewer allows you to view Crystal Reports in a Web Forms application by rendering HTML for display on the Web browser. The Web Forms Viewer inherits from the Web Control class and can interact with other Web Controls on the Web Form. The Web Forms Viewer `ReportSource` property can be set to a file, a `ReportDocument` on the Web server or a Report Web Service. Although the Web Forms Viewer can do all this in addition to what was mentioned in the previous paragraph, it renders the results in HTML. Printing capabilities are limited to what is available in the Web browser.

To decide which object model is appropriate for a given situation, it is important to consider the capabilities and limitations of each. For example, if you want to use Report Web Services, you cannot use the `ReportDocument` object. If you want to use an ADO.NET data source, you have to use `ReportDocument`. A comparison of the capabilities of the three object models is presented in Table 7.1.

TABLE 7.1 Comparison of the three object models.

Feature	*ReportDocument*	*Windows Forms Viewer*	*Web Forms Viewer*
Selection Formula	X	X	X
Parameters	X	X	X
Formula Fields	X		
Format Report Objects	X		
Group	X		
Print Options	X		
Sorting	X		
View Reports		X	X
Use Report Web Services		X	X
Printing	X	X	
Exporting	X	X	
ADO and ADO.NET Support	X		

A quick note before we get started building our application: to be able to create ASP.NET applications you will need to make sure that your installation of Visual Studio .NET has been properly configured to be able to create and run Web applications. For more information on configuring Visual Studio .NET, see the on-line help topic "Visual Studio .NET Software Requirements."

Reporting Example

We first create an ASP.NET Web project. To do this, open up Visual Studio .NET and select New Project from the Start Page, or File . . . New . . . Project from the menu, depending on how you have Visual Studio .NET configured. Select "Visual C# Projects" from the Project Types folder list and select the "ASP.NET Web Application" item from the Templates list. After you have selected the template, update the location so that the Web site will be called "revenue." After you have made your selections, the New Project dialog will appear as in Figure 7.4 and you can click OK.

At this point, Visual Studio .NET will start to create the basic structure of the application. When it is finished creating the Web application, Visual Studio .NET will display the Design view of a file called WebForm1.aspx. On the Design view, you can add controls by dragging and dropping from the Toolbox, which can be

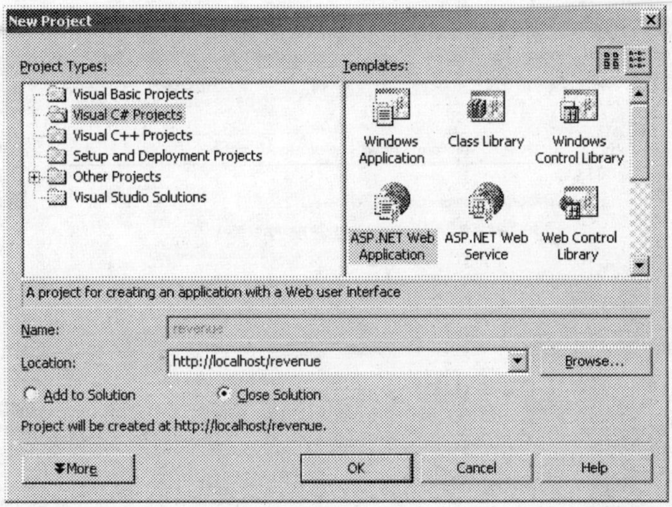

FIGURE 7.4 The New Project dialog.

displayed by selecting View . . . Toolbox (or Ctrl+Alt+X). Adding components to the Design view creates an instance of that component on your page, ready for you to use in your aspx page. Let's add a CrystalReportViewer onto our page by selecting it from the Toolbox (it should be in the Web Forms section) and dragging it onto our Design view. You should have a screen that looks like Figure 7.5. Notice that adding the CrystalReportViewer to the Web Form has automatically added the references needed to support the viewer.

Creating a Report

After we have added the CrystalReportViewer, we are ready to create a report to view in it. To do this, we will create a new Crystal Report by selecting Project . . . Add New Item from the menu and choosing Crystal Report from the list of templates that appears in the Add New Item dialog.[2] Name the new report RevenueReport.rpt. At this point, the Add New Item dialog should look like Figure 7.6. Click Open to dismiss the dialog window and begin working on the revenue report.

When your new report is added, Crystal Reports shows the Crystal Report Gallery (see Figure 7.7) so that you can choose the method you will use to create the report. We can work from a Blank Report, which creates a shell report that contains the basic sections (report header, page header, details, page footer, and report footer) that we can populate with the fields we select from a database. Or, if we already have a report that we would like to modify in some way, we can start with an Existing Report, which will create a copy of it for us to change for the application.

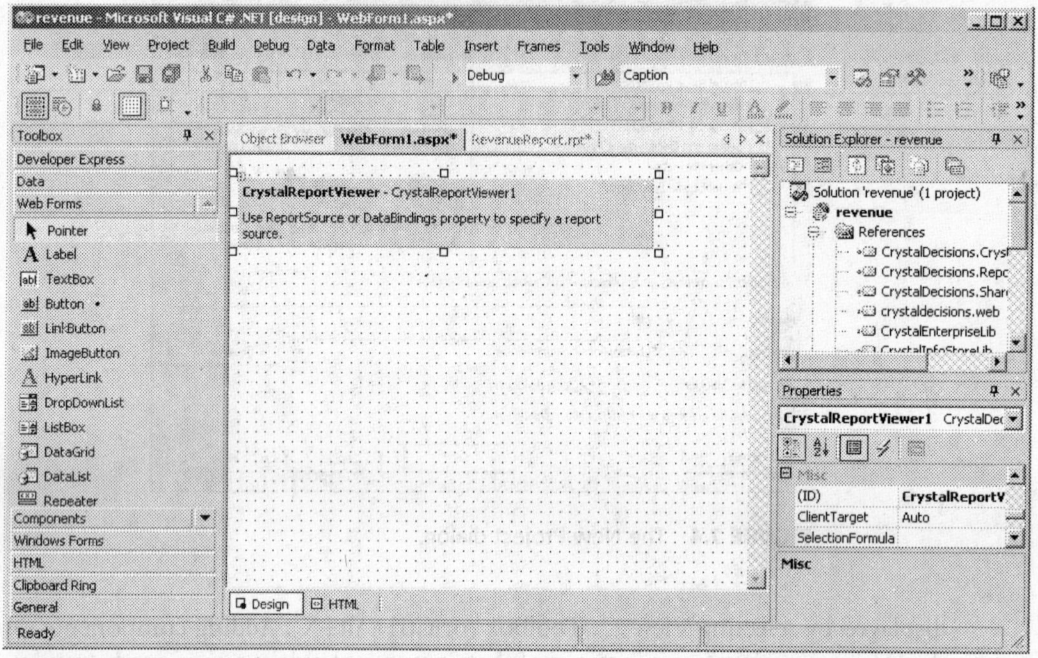

FIGURE 7.5 CrystalReportViewer in the Design view.

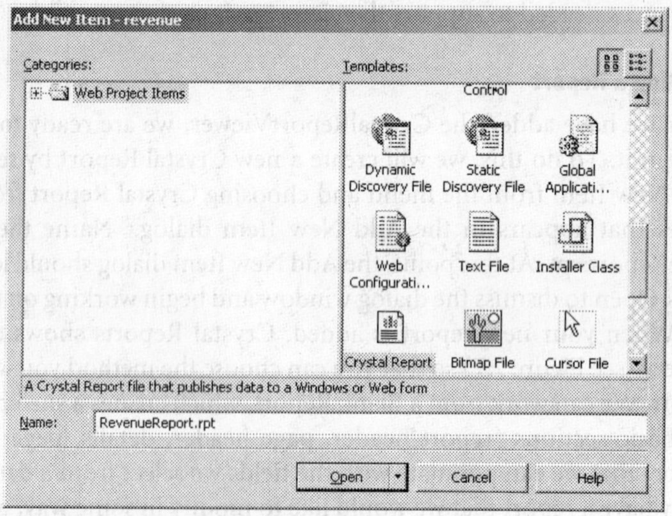

FIGURE 7.6 The Add New Item dialog with Crystal Report selected.

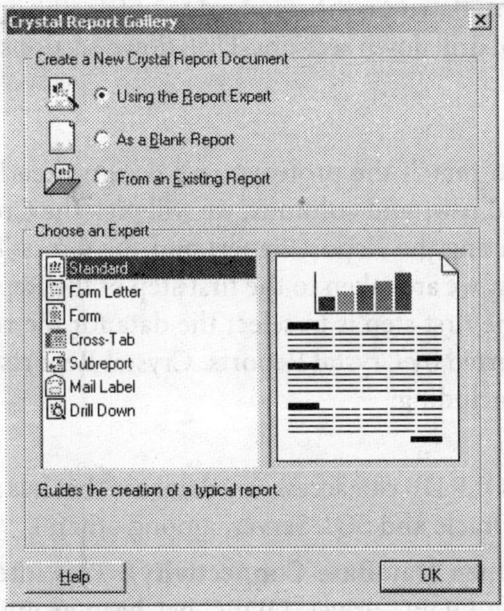

FIGURE 7.7 The Crystal Report Gallery.

If we choose the Report Expert, we are guided through a series of steps in a wizard to create the basic format of our report. For the most part, unless you have a very specific report in mind or are working from an existing report, the Report Expert is the way to go. This is because it uses your answers to simple questions to create the basic skeleton of many different types of reports. Each report template produces a different type of report and is built with slightly different steps. The templates available in the Report Expert are:

Standard: This template creates a standard banded report, with sections for headers, details, and footers.

Form-letter: This template creates a text-based report that can be populated with information from a database to create form letters.

Form: This template is similar to the Standard template, but is designed to make it easy to create forms such as invoices and customer statements.

Cross-tab: The cross-tab template creates a report with a cross-tab set up according to specified row, column, and summary fields.

Subreport: The Subreport template allows you to create a main report that contains a subreport. The subreport can be an existing report or you can create a new one.

Mail label: This template creates a report that is formatted to fit on standard commercial mailing labels.

Drill down: Based on the standard template, the drill down template allows the creation of drill down sections. Drill down sections are hidden until they are selected.

In this case, to match the prototype we designed earlier, which breaks summary data down into rows and columns, we will pick the Cross Join report template.

After selecting the Report Expert and the Cross-Tab report from the Crystal Report Gallery, we are taken to the first step of the Report Expert to begin creating our report. The first step is to select the data for the report from the data sources that are supported by Crystal Reports. Crystal Reports can access a wide variety of data sources including:

OLE DB: OLE DB can access any database that has an OLE DB Provider (which includes Oracle and SQL Server, among others).

ODBC (Open DataBase Connectivity): This interface can use any database that has an ODBC driver. ODBC has been around a very long time and just about every mainstream database has an ODBC driver.

Microsoft Access and Excel files: These can be accessed by selecting the file in the file system.

ADO.NET Datasets: These can be used to connect to any database with a managed provider.

In our case, we use the Database Files option and locate the sales.mdb database containing the data for our sales data mart. Once we have selected the database, we can choose individual tables in it to use in the report. For this report, we select the Date, Invoice, Product, and SalesRep tables as illustrated in Figure 7.8.

After we have selected the data, we create links among the tables in our report. As all products that rely on relational data, Crystal Reports needs to link different tables together to produce correct results. If the tables aren't linked, Crystal Reports will create a report based on the Cartesian product of all of the tables involved. In many cases, Crystal Reports will be able to automatically link the tables together based on the foreign key relationships among the tables. Since the sales database we selected previously was designed using a star schema, the foreign key relationships are very straightforward, with each dimension table being joined to our central fact table (invoices). This simplicity of design makes it easy for the Report Expert to pick the links we want to have among the tables. If we were adding in another data source that wasn't linked in by foreign key, we might have to add new links in to retrieve the data properly for our report. The results of Crystal Reports automatically linking the tables together are shown in Figure 7.9 and we don't have to make any modifications.

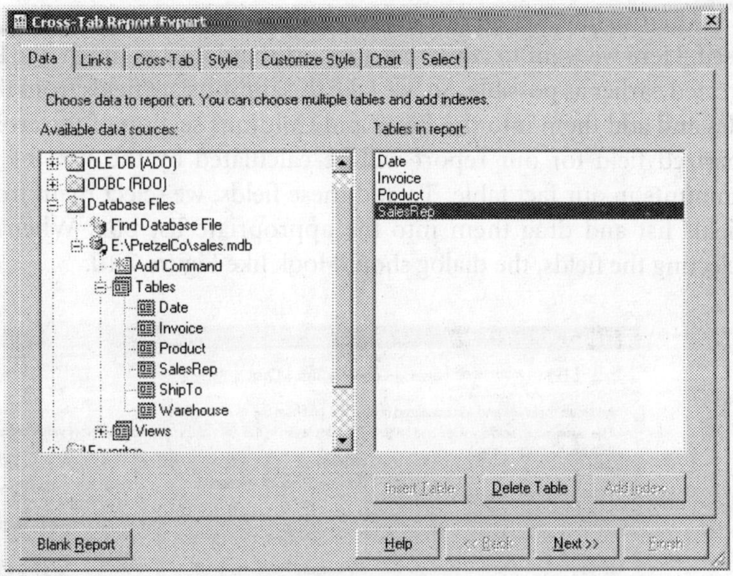

FIGURE 7.8 Selecting Data in the Report Expert.

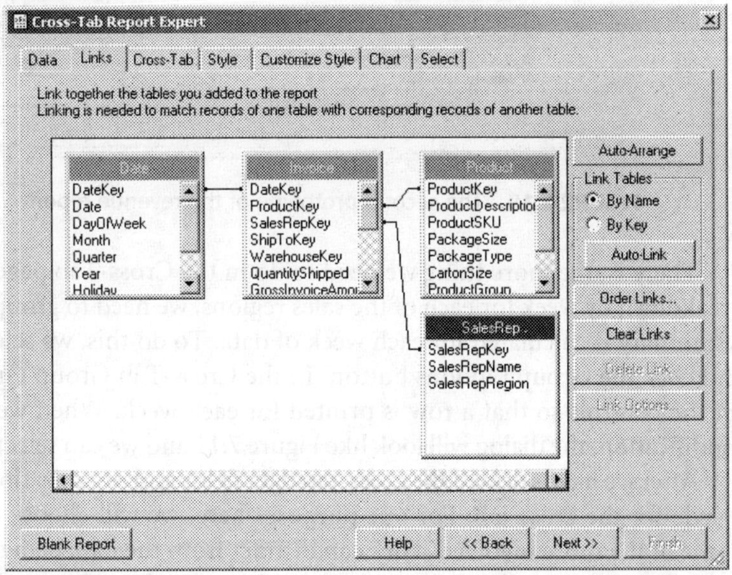

FIGURE 7.9 Linking the tables in the Report Expert.

After we have set up our data and links, the next step is to design the cross-tab itself. Here we want to construct a report that looks as much like the prototype we created earlier as possible. So, we take the appropriate fields from the dimension tables and add them into the Rows and Columns section of the cross tab. The summarized field for our report will be calculated by the sum of the Net Invoice Amounts in our fact table. To add these fields, we select them from the Available Fields list and drag them into the appropriate list box. When we are finished selecting the fields, the dialog should look like Figure 7.10.

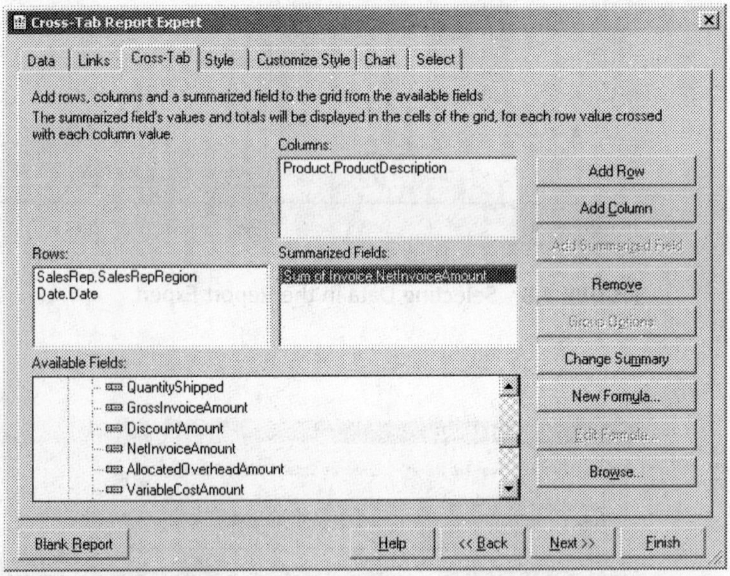

FIGURE 7.10 The second prototype of the revenue report.

There is one more thing we need to do in the Cross-Tab page. To provide the breakdown by week for each of the sales regions, we need to group the data so that a summary is calculated for each week of data. To do this, we select the Date field and click the Group Options button. In the Cross-Tab Group Options dialog, we set the controls so that a row is printed for each week. When we have made that modification, the dialog will look like Figure 7.11 and we can select OK to move on.

After we have selected the cross-tab data fields and organization, we can choose a style for the cross-tab. For our purposes here, we will choose the default style. Some of the more involved styles can distract from the data being displayed. Similarly, the next page allows you to further customize the style to reflect different display requirements. We will leave this page alone as well and click Next.

Many people absorb quantitative information more readily in a graphical format. The next step of the Report Expert allows us to configure a chart of the data to

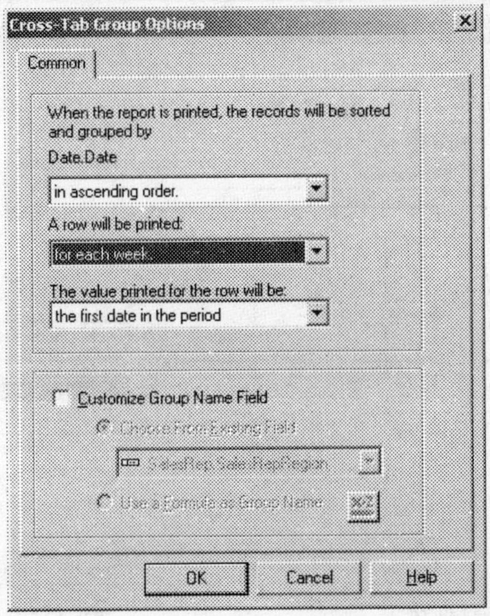

FIGURE 7.11 The second prototype of the revenue report.

be displayed in our report. The Chart page of the Report Expert has three sub-tabs within it. On the first, we select the Chart type to be displayed. For our example, we will leave this at the default setting of a vertical 2D bar chart since that matches what we described in the prototype. The Data tab allows us to decide where the chart is placed and which data ranges should be displayed on the chart. We will place the chart in the header of the report by leaving the default Header option button selected. For the data, we will break down the chart first by Product Description then by the Sales Rep Region and show the value of the summation of the Net Invoices. When we are finished making our changes to the Chart tab, it will look like Figure 7.12, and we are ready to move on to the final tab in the Report Expert.

The final step in constructing our report with the Report Expert is to set the selection criteria for the information to be displayed in the cross tab. For now, let's just display the data for the last full month based on today's date. To do this, choose Date from the Report Fields and add it to the Select Fields list box. Then, with Date selected in the list box, change the first drop down below the Select Fields list to read "is in the period" and the second drop down to "LastFullMonth." After making the selections, the screen will look like Figure 7.13. This will limit our results to only those dates in the last full month before today. For example, if today is June 5, the data for the month of May will be selected.

We then click Finish. The Report Expert will now create the report and display it in a Design view in the main window of Visual Studio .NET as shown in Figure

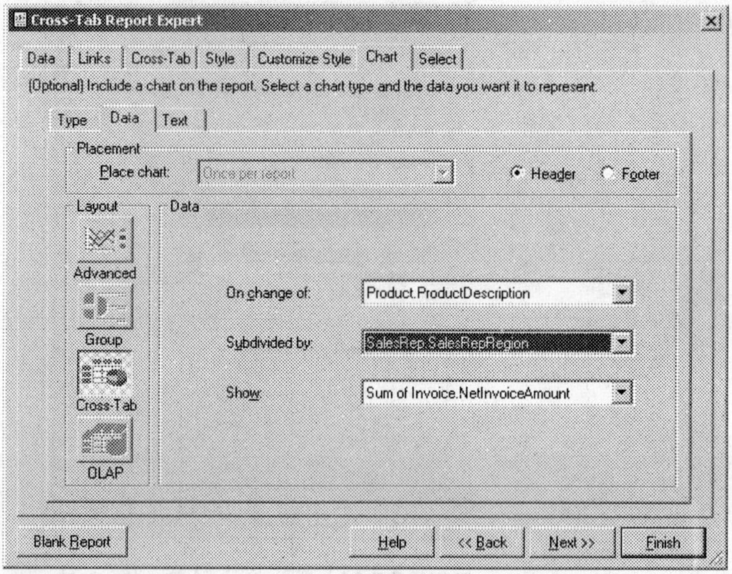

FIGURE 7.12 Selecting fields for the chart in the Report Expert.

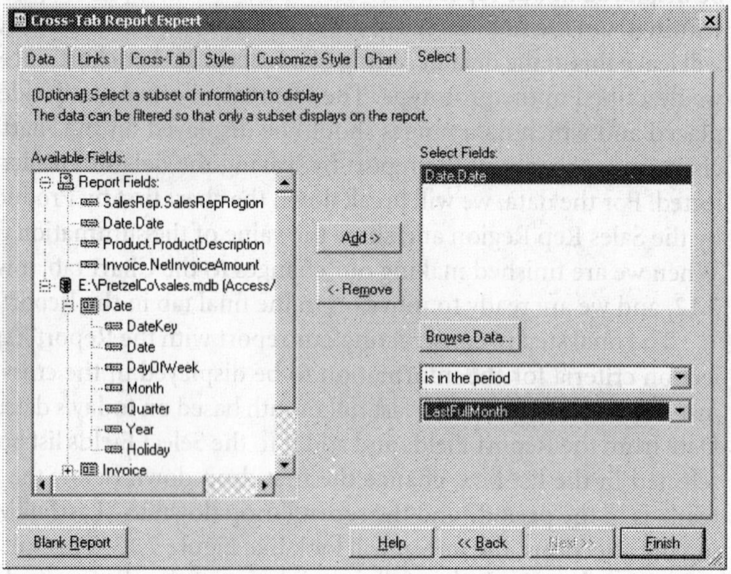

FIGURE 7.13 Configuring the data selection in the Report Expert.

7.14. On the report Design view, we can modify the chart layout and content in a WYSIWYG fashion by selecting the elements and moving them around on the screen. In addition, selecting an element and displaying the Properties window (View . . . Show Properties, or F4) allows us to modify any of the properties applicable to the element displayed. Right clicking on the elements in the report allows us to bring up the Expert that applies to the specific item selected and change properties though a guided procedure. For example, try right clicking on the chart and selecting the Chart Expert from the context menu. If we want to add more elements to the report, we can drag them from the Field Explorer to the surface of the report and modify their layout and properties. To find out more about designing reports, consult the "Designing Reports" topic in the online Visual Studio .NET help.

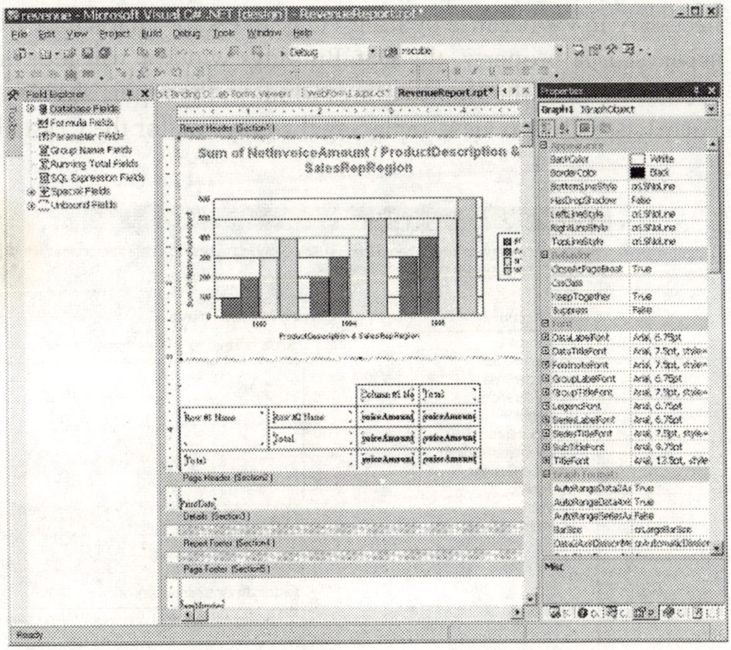

FIGURE 7.14 Preview of our report in the Design view.

Binding the Report

After we have completed our report, we need to "bind" the revenue report we just created to the CrystalReportViewer we added to the Web page so that we can view the report via the Web. Binding is the process of attaching a report to a viewer. There are two basic options for binding the report to the control: design time and run time, which we will discuss further later. Here, we will go through the steps of binding the report to the viewer.

To bind a report at design time, we set the DataBindings through the properties of the CrystalReportsViewer. We can bind to the report file directly by setting the path of the report to the `ReportSource` property. To do this, select the CrystalReportViewer control and view the Properties by selecting View . . . Properties (or using the keyboard shortcut F4). In the Properties window, find the DataBindings property and open the DataBindings dialog by clicking the ellipsis button in the Value field. In the DataBindings dialog, select `ReportSource` from the Bindable Properties list and select the Custom binding expression option button. In the text box for the binding expression, enter the full path to the report file we just created. For example, if it is stored in the Web folder, we would set the `ReportSource` to be "C:\\Inetpub\\wwwroot\\revenue\\RevenueReport.rpt" (the extra backslashes are necessary in C# because by itself "\" is an escape character). After we have set the `ReportSource` property, the DataBindings window will look like Figure 7.15. As soon as we close the DataBindings window, the report should appear in the WebForm1.aspx Design view, replacing the gray box for the CrystalReportViewer.

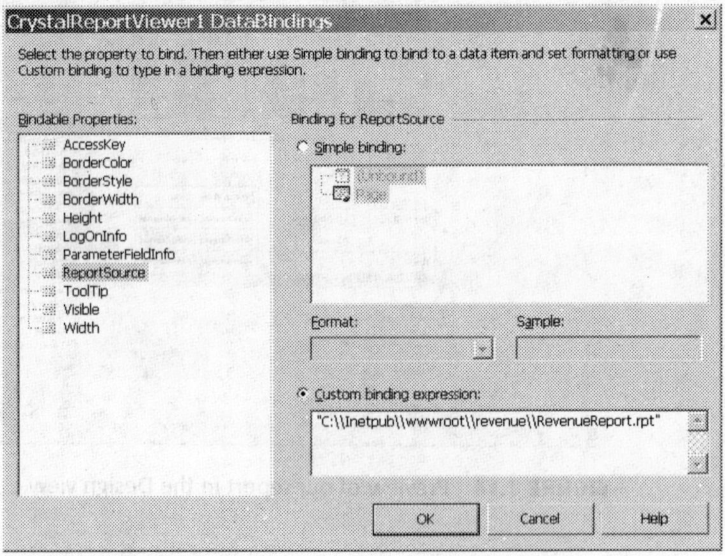

FIGURE 7.15 Setting a custom binding expression.

Putting the Pieces Together

Before we can view the report in the Web browser, we have one more change to make to the Web form. Open up the Web Form code by selecting the Web-

Form1.aspx and choosing View . . . Code (or the shortcut key F7). This will open an editor window with the code for WebForm1.aspx.cs (which is the code-behind for WebForm1.aspx). Find the `Page_Load` method and add the following line to it·

```
CrystalReportViewer1.DataBind();
```

This line of code tells the CrystalReportViewer control to get the data for the report that we bound to it when the page loads. Now we are ready to view the application. To do this, choose Debug . . . Start without Debugging (or the shortcut Ctrl+F5). After a few moments, we will see the report rendered in Internet Explorer. Without a whole lot of work on our part (adding a control to a page, creating a report, binding a report to the control, and writing one line of code) we have rendered a high-fidelity report in a Web browser.

Tweaking the Output

You will notice that there are a few things that require some tweaking in the report as it appears on the Web page. For example, there is a large block of white space on the left of the report, the table is broken into two parts, and the chart has some text overlapping. To fix the white space, go to the WebForm1.aspx Design view, select the CrystalReportViewer control, and show the Properties page (either View . . . Properties or F4). The block of white space on the left is intended to display the Group Tree, which is a way to navigate through long reports. In this case, since we have only one page of data, we can set the `DisplayGroupTree` property to false. This will get rid of the unused space in the control.

To fix the table layout issues, we first open the RevenueReport.rpt window in Visual Studio .NET. In the revenue report, select the cross-tab element and reduce the size of the Row #1 Name, Row #2 Name and Column #1 Name fields. You can do this either by dragging the control handles on the fields to make them smaller or by typing a lower number into the Width property. The Width property displays the size in twips, a unit of screen measure that is 1/1440 of an inch). A width that will work well for the rows is 800 twips and 900 twips for the column. Next, choose the Column #1 Name field and change the height to 420 twips so that the names can wrap across two rows.

Finally, to fix the chart display, select the Graph element on the revenue report and set the property values as shown in Table 7.2.

After changing the properties and recompiling the application by choosing Build . . . Build Solution (keyboard shortcut Ctrl+Shift+B), you can refresh the Web browser and view the final report as shown in Figure 7.13. To prove the earlier point about the ASP.NET rendering cross-browser-compatible results, notice that the screenshot in Figure 7.16 is from the Mozilla Firebird browser.

TABLE 7.2 Property values.

Property	***Value***
Height	4500
Width	10500
Title	Sum of Net Invoice Amount by Product, Description, & Region
XaxisTitle	<empty>

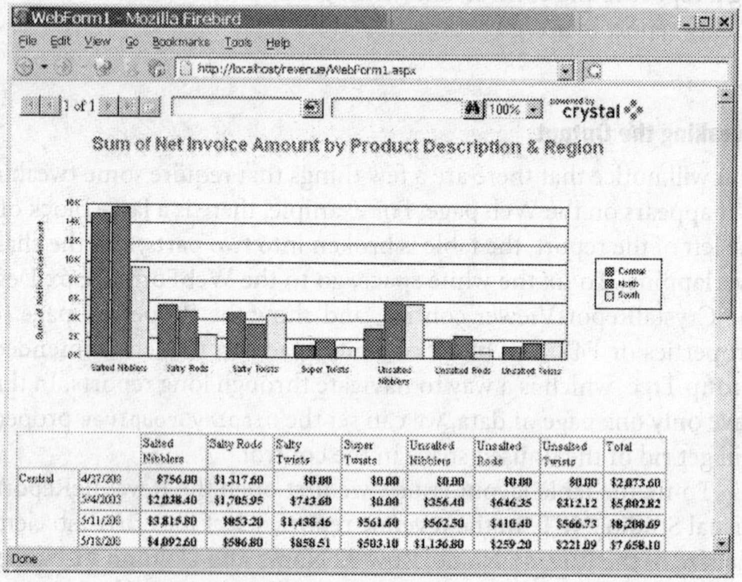

FIGURE 7.16 Viewing the revenue report in a Web browser.

Through this example, you have seen how to create a report and display it in a Web Forms application. As we have seen, building a basic application and making it look presentable is not verv difficult, but it does require some planning and iteration. From here, we will discuss some more details about using Crystal Reports for .NET.

Report Binding

Now that we have a sample report created and showed how we can statically bind the report to a CrystalReportsViewer at design time, we can explore some of the other ways to bind a report to a Web viewer.

Run-time Binding

Another very simple technique is to bind the `ReportSource` to the report file at run time. This gives us the flexibility to determine at run time which report should be bound to the control. To modify our sample to show this, we need to make two changes. First, we want to clear the static binding to the report. So we open up the WebForm1.aspx window and select the CrystalReportViewer1 object. Open the Properties page for CrystalReportViewer1 and open the Data Bindings dialog by clicking the ellipsis button in the Value field. In the Data Bindings dialog, select `ReportSource` from the Bindable Properties list. Then remove the `CustomBinding` property we added previously by changing the `ReportSource` binding to SimpleBinding and making sure that Unbound is selected in the SimpleBinding list box.

Second, we need to modify the code to bind to the report at run time. To do this, open the code for the WebForm1 and replace the line we added previously in the Page_Load event handler with the line:

```
CrystalReportViewer1.ReportSource =
"C:\\Inetpub\\wwwroot\\revenue\\RevenueReport.rpt";
```

This will bind the specified report into the `ReportSource` when the page is loaded and display it on the browser. Try it by compiling the application and viewing it. You should see the same report as before.

In addition to binding the `ReportSource` to the path of the report, we can bind it to an object dynamically at run time. Every Crystal Report that is added to a project has a report class behind it (much as every .aspx page has a code-behind class).[3] We can bind to this class by replacing the line in the Page_Load event handler with:

```
CrystalReportViewer1.ReportSource = new RevenueReport();
```

This will create an instance of the `RevenueReport` class and assign it to the `ReportSource`. Again, if you compile the application and view it, you get the same results as when you bind to a file.

Typed Report Objects

The last technique we will discuss is using a typed report object. Typed reports come in two flavors: strongly typed and weakly typed. A strongly typed report object is a `ReportDocument` that has been added to the Web Form and set to bind to a Crystal Report that is in your project. To create a strongly typed `ReportDocument`, open the Toolbox and find the `ReportDocument` in the Components section of the toolbox and drag it onto the surface of the Web Forms designer. After you have dragged the component over, the "Choose a Report Document" dialog will open

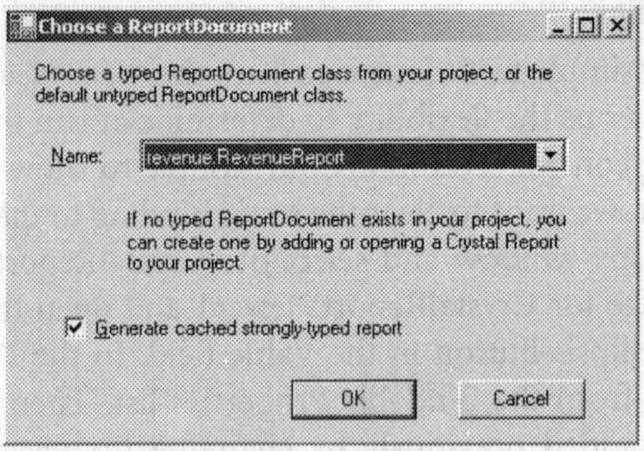

FIGURE 7.17 Selecting a report for the `ReportDocument`.

(shown in Figure 7.17). Here you can choose which report in your project you would like to display. You can also choose whether or not you want to cache the report. Caching a report makes it load faster when accessed by multiple users, so caching might be a good idea for reports that contain relatively static data that is accessed by many users at the same time.

After you have added the `ReportDocument`, select the CrystalReportViewer1 object on the Web Forms designer and open the DataBinding properties as we did before. This time, instead of making a custom binding, you can use the Simple Binding tree-view to bind the `ReportDocument` we just created to the viewer, as shown in Figure 7.18. After we have bound the `ReportDocument`, the contents of the report in CrystalReportViewer in the Design view (as shown in Figure 7.14).

A weakly typed report is very similar to a strongly typed one, except that it is bound to a specific report at run time. To create a weakly typed report object, you create an instance of the `ReportDocument` and then bind a report to it in code. For example, adding the following code to the Page_Load event handler will create a weakly typed report:

```
ReportDocument doc = new ReportDocument();
doc.Load
   ("C:\\Inetpub\\wwwroot\\revenue\\RevenueReport.rpt");
CrystalReportViewer1.ReportSource = doc;
```

This will accomplish the same end result as the strongly typed example with the added flexibility of being able to choose a report to load at run time in code.

Report Web Services

Lastly, you can bind to a report that is published as a Web Service. We covered the basics of Web Services in Chapter 5, so refer to that chapter if you have questions

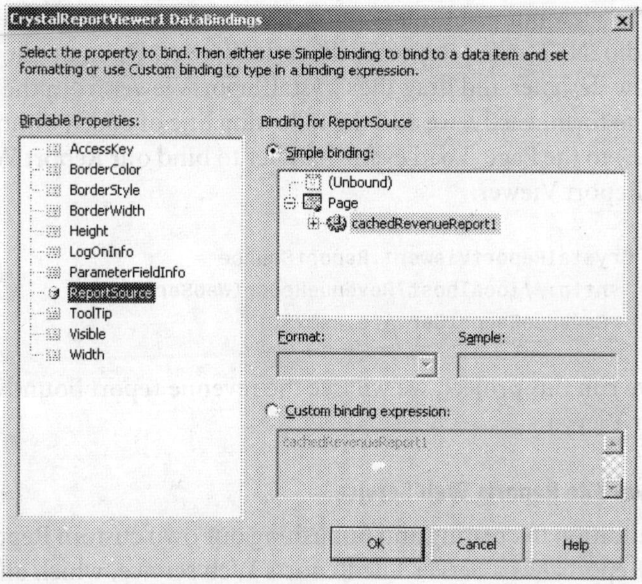

FIGURE 7.18 Binding the `ReportDocument` to the Crystal Report Viewer.

on the fundamentals of Web Services. As with all Web Services, Report Web Services offer many benefits including the capability to integrate disparate systems and distribute information across the Internet or an intranet. Distributing reports via Web Services is very powerful and easy to accomplish.

ON THE CD

Publishing a Crystal Report as a Report Web Service is very simple. Let's walk through the steps of publishing our revenue report as a Web Service. First, let's create a new Web Service project in Visual Studio .NET called RevenueReportWebService. Do this by clicking File . . . New . . . Project or pressing Ctrl+Shift+N, and selecting Visual C# from the Project Types list and ASP.NET Web Service from the Templates list. The project template for Web Services projects creates a default Web Service file that we don't want. We will remove it by selecting the Service1.asmx file in the Solution Explorer and deleting it. Next, we add our existing RevenueReport.rpt file to the project by choosing Project . . . Add Existing Item (Shift+Alt+A) and finding the .rpt file in the Reports folder on the CD-ROM shipped with the book. This will add the revenue report to our project as well as the References required to create a Report Web Service. Last, we enable the Report Web Service by right-clicking on the RevenueReport.rpt file in the Solution Explorer and selecting Publish as Web Service from the context menu. That's all there is to it.

Consuming a Report Web Service is just as easy—we can use the published Web Service as the `ReportSource`. Let's create an ASP.NET application that we can use to view our published report. First, we create a new ASP.NET project in Visual Studio .NET called ReportWebServiceViewer. Open up the WebForms1.aspx page in the designer and drag the CrystalReportViewer from the Toolbox to the surface of the form. Lastly, we add the following line of code (without the line break in the URL) to the Page_Load event-handler to bind our Report Web Service to the Crystal Report Viewer:

```
CrystalReportViewer1.ReportSource =
  "http://localhost/RevenueReportWebService/
  RevenueReportService.asmx";
```

If we run this project, we will see the revenue report bound to the Web Crystal Report Viewer.

Server File Reports Web Service

In addition to creating and publishing our own custom Report Web Services, Crystal Reports has a Server File Reports Web service, which allows the publication of any reports stored in a folder hierarchy as a Web Service. Using the Server File Reports Web service, you can publish a report as a Web Service just by saving it to a particular folder specified in a configuration file and then dragging and dropping the report from the Server Explorer to the Solution Explorer.

Before we get started with the sample application, please note that the Server File Reports Web service is not a part of the default installation of Visual Studio .NET. To check if you have installed this feature, open the Server Explorer (either with View . . . Server Explorer from the menu or the keyboard shortcut Ctrl+Alt+S). Below your machine name, you should see a Crystal Services entry in the tree-view. Open it up and then open up the Server Files entry beneath it. If you have a list of folders and reports as shown in Figure 7.19, then you have installed the Server File Reports.

If you do not see the list of folders, you will need to run the Visual Studio .NET installer to add it in. Run the Visual Studio .NET installer and choose Add or Remove Features. You'll want to add Crystal Web Services under Crystal Reports for Visual Studio .NET in the Items to Install tree-view. After selecting the Crystal Web Services check box, finish the install by selecting Update Now. After you have done that, you should be able to open up the Server Files as discussed earlier.

If you are still having problems, see the Crystal Decisions Knowledge Base articles on problems with Crystal Web Services: *http://support.crystaldecisions.com/library/kbase/articles/c2010774.asphttp://support.crystaldecisions.com/library/kbase/articles/c2010984.asp*. To see the Report Web Service in action, let's add our revenue report to the Report Web Service folder. The folder that the Report Web Service uses for publishing reports is configured in the crystalserverfile.config file which, by

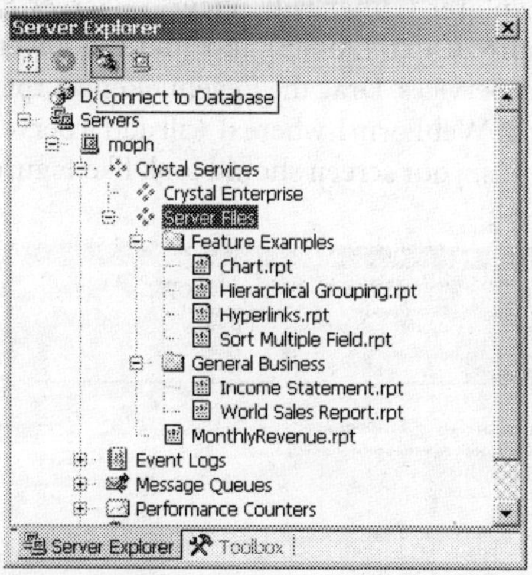

FIGURE 7.19 Crystal Server Files in the Server Explorer.

default, is in the C:\Program Files\Microsoft Visual Studio .NET\Crystal Reports\Config folder. The contents of the crystalserverfile.config will look something like:

```
<?xml version="1.0" encoding="utf-8"?>
<ServerFileConfig
    xmlns:xsd=http://www.w3.org/2001/XMLSchema
    xmlns:xsi="http://www.w3.org/2001/XMLSchema-instance">
    <RootDirectory>
        C:\Program Files\Microsoft Visual Studio .NET\
        Crystal Reports\Samples\Reports
    </RootDirectory>
</ServerFileConfig>
```

ON THE CD

The location of the reports published by the Report Web Service is determined by the value in the RootDirectory tag. Adding a report for publication is as easy as adding it to the folder hierarchy under the root. By default, you will have the sample reports that ship with Crystal Reports in the folders. Let's add the RevenueReport.rpt to the Report Web Service by copying it from the Reports directory on the CD-ROM that comes with the book to the RootDirectory specified in the crystalserverfile.config.

Next, let's create a new ASP.NET Web application called "rws_revenue" and add a CrystalReportViewer to WebForm1, as we have done before. Next, open up the Server Explorer (either with View . . . Server Explorer from the menu or the keyboard shortcut Ctrl+Alt+S) and find the RevenueReport.rpt in the tree-view under Crystal Services. Drag the RevenueReport.rpt from the Server Explorer to the Design view of WebForm1 where it will add a Server File Report to the Web Form. After doing this, your screen should look like Figure 7.20.

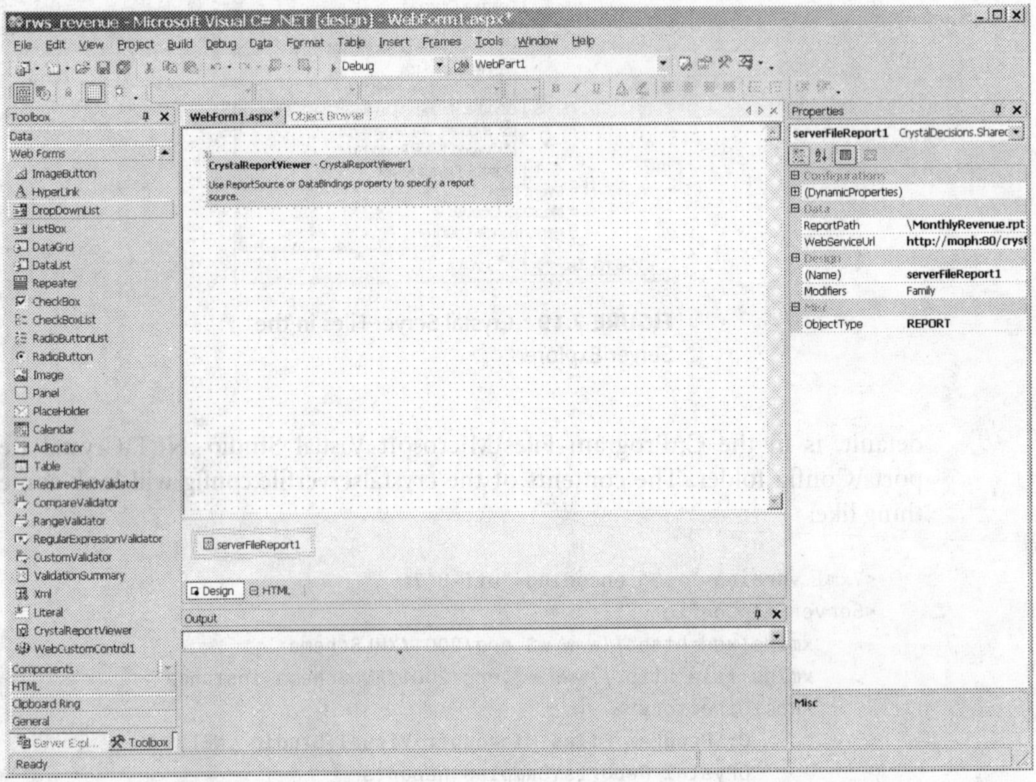

FIGURE 7.20 Drag and drop the RevenueReport.rpt from the Server Explorer to the Design view.

To bind the Server File Report to the Crystal Report Viewer, open up the properties page for CrystalReportViewer1 and choose the DataBindings property. As we did with the strongly-typed report, we use the Simple Binding tree-view to bind the serverReport1 to the `ReportSource` property (shown in Figure 7.21).

As you can see, using the Report Web Service makes creating applications with published reports very simple. Report Web Service is a good way to create a centralized repository of reports that can be shared across business intelligence applications and complements a well-constructed metadata repository.

In addition to simply using Report Web Services to make construction of applications easier, we can use it directly to distribute reports. As another illustration

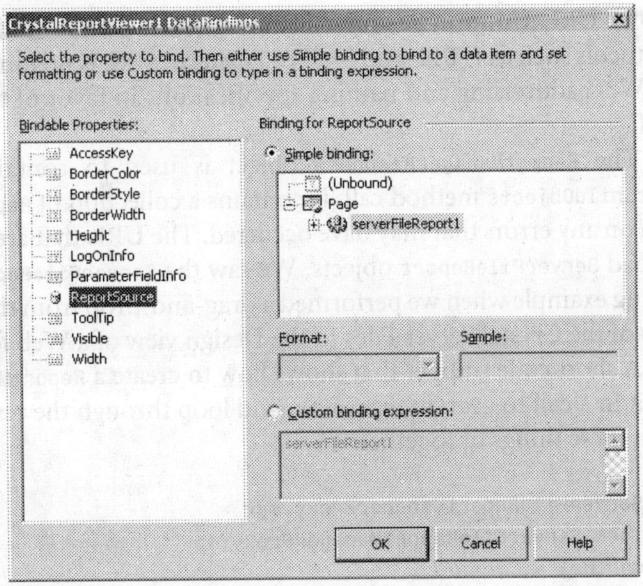

FIGURE 7.21 Bind the Server Report to the Crystal Report Viewer `ReportSource`.

of using the Report Web Service, we will build a simple report distribution system that uses it. The example we walk through will use a Windows Forms-based solution to allow browsing and accessing reports that are stored in a centralized location on a Web Server via Web Services. The example is called ReportSvcViewer and it is available on the CD-ROM included with the book in the Chapter 7\ReportSvcViewer directory.

ON THE CD

The most important object to understand in accessing Report Web Services is the ServerFileReportManagerProxy. This class provides a SOAP interface to the ServerFileReportManager.asmx web service and allows a client to access the reports that are published by the service. To formulate a query and retrieve the results of queries against the service, the ReportManagerRequest and ReportManagerResponse objects are used in calling the `ListChildObjects` method of the ServerFileReportManager.

The `ReportManagerRequest` object is used to specify what is returned in the call to `ListChildObjects`. It has two properties that must be populated before calling the method. The properties are `ExtraData` and `ParentUri`. `ExtraData` is used principally to set name-value pairs of information that are used to locate the Web Service. The name-value pairs are provided in the form of a `NameValuePairs` class that is part of the CrystalDecisions.Shared namespace. The `ParentUri` sets the root level folder where `ListChildObjects` should begin. A *URI* is a Uniform Resource Identifier that is used to identify resources on the Web. A URI is the same as the more commonly known URL, Uniform Resource Locator, which is associated with popular Internet protocols such as HTTP and SMTP. The term URL is no longer used in the technical W3C addressing and naming specifications in favor of the more precise term, URI.

The `ReportManagerResponse` object is used to contain the results of the `ListChildObjects` method call. It contains a collection of `ReportUris` and information on any errors that may have occurred. The URIs that are retrieved can be used to load `ServerFileReport` objects. We saw the `ServerFileReport` object in the preceding example when we performed a drag-and-drop from the Server Explorer display of the Crystal Server Files to the Design view of a Web form.

A short code snippet that shows how to create a `ReportManagerRequest` object, use it in a call to `ListChildObjects`, and loop through the response illustrates how all of these things fit together:

```
ServerFileReportManagerProxy mgr =
 new ServerFileReportManagerProxy();
mgr.Url =
 "http://localhost:80/CrystalReportWebFormViewer/
 ServerFileReportManager.asmx";
ReportManagerRequest req = new ReportManagerRequest();
NameValuePairs nvp = new NameValuePairs();
nvp.Add("WEBSERVICEURL",
 "http://localhost:80/crystalreportwebformviewer/
 ServerFileReportService.asmx");
req.ExtraData = nvp;
req.ParentUri = "crnet-sfr://loopback/?OBJECTTYPE=FOLDER";
ReportManagerResponse res = mgr.ListChildObjects(req);
ServerFileReport rpt = null;
foreach (Object obj in res.ReportUris)
{
  string childUri = obj.ToString();
  rpt = ServerFileReport.FromUri(childUri);
  Debug.WriteLine(rpt.ObjectType + ":" + rpt.ReportPath);
}
```

In this code we create an instance of the `ServerFileReportManagerProxy` that points to the service installed on our local machine. Next, we create the `ReportManagerReqest` object and populate the `ExtraData` and `ParentUri` properties with some values that will cause the `ListChildObjects` method to list the root of our local Server Files. After calling `ListChildObjects`, we loop through the returned collection of `ReportUris` that is contained in the `ReportManagerResponse` object and create an instance of a `ServerFileReport` from each one. In the `ReportSvcViewer` sample application we use this same basic code in a recursive function called `GetChildObjects`, which retrieves all of the levels of the Server Files recursively. The code looks very similar to the previous snippet:

```
protected void GetChildObjects
(string uri, TreeNodeCollection nodes)
{
    // create the request object
    ReportManagerRequest req = new ReportManagerRequest();
    NameValuePairs nvp = new NameValuePairs();
    nvp.Add("WEBSERVICEURL", _serverFileReportUrl)    ;
    req.ExtraData = nvp;
    req.ParentUri = uri;
    // get the list of uris
    ReportManagerResponse res = _mgr.ListChildObjects(req);
    ServerFileReport rpt = null;
    // loop through the uris adding each to the tree
    foreach (Object obj in res.ReportUris)
    {
        // load a report from the uri
        string childUri = obj.ToString();
        rpt = ServerFileReport.FromUri(childUri);

        // if we have a report, add a node
        if (rpt.ObjectType == EnumServerFileType.REPORT)
        {
            TreeNode node = new TreeNode
              (rpt.ReportPath, 1, 1);
            node.Tag = rpt;
            nodes.Add(node);
        }
        // if we have a folder, start another recursion
        else if
           (rpt.ObjectType == EnumServerFileType.FOLDER)
        {
            TreeNode node = new TreeNode(rpt.ReportPath);
            nodes.Add(node);
            GetChildObjects(rpt.ToUri(), node.Nodes);
        }
        else
        {
            throw new Exception("Unknown URI type");
        }
    }
}
```

The `GetChildObjects` method is the core of the `ReportSvcViewer` application. The main form of the application is `ReportListForm`, which populates a tree-view of the reports contained in the server referenced by the `ManagerServerUrl` configured in the ReportSvcViewer.exe.config file using `GetChildObjects`. Double-clicking on a report loaded in the tree-view retrieves the report and loads it into the `ReportViewForm`. The `ReportViewForm` is simple and contains a Windows Crystal Report Viewer and one line of code in the constructor:

```
crystalReportViewer1.ReportSource = rpt;
```

This line probably looks familiar by now. In this case, we take the report passed into the constructor and assign it to the `ReportSource` of our report viewer.

Although this is a very simple example, we can see how easy it is to use Server File Reports as a basis for report distribution. We can retrieve the list of reports using the Server File Report Manager service and then display them in a viewer with a minimal amount of code.

Crystal Enterprise

For a more robust solution for delivering reports on the Web, you might consider using Crystal Enterprise. Crystal Enterprise is a multi-tiered report management and distribution system that provides security, automated report publication, and other services that make report distribution much easier. For more information on this product, see the Crystal Decisions Website at *http://www.crystaldecisions.com*.

Printing Reports on the Web

After we have published the report and displayed it on the Web, we will want to consider how we will handle printed output. Although the Web is ubiquitous in business today, printed output is very important to business users. It is much easier to discuss a report printed on a piece of paper around a conference room table or in a hallway than to share thoughts about a report displayed on a laptop. Paper still has a vital place in business today so we need to provide quality printed output.

Printing from the Browser

The easiest thing to do is to print straight from the browser. Although this will work and is extremely easy to implement (you don't have to do anything additional), this can yield unsatisfactory printed output. Although Web browsers have become much better at producing printed output in the past few years, they still have a tendency to clip the output at the wrong places and generally produce sub par printed output. After all, they are designed primarily to render good-looking output on a screen, not on a printer. Also, the way that Crystal Reports renders multi-page reports by default would require the user to go to each page and print it, which is very tedious if there are more than a very few pages. In addition, the group tree-view that is displayed on the right of the reports by default, although very handy for navigation, detracts from printed output.

There are some simple modifications that can be made to the default report display provided by the Crystal Report Viewer to improve browser-based printing. The first is to get rid of the Toolbar on the displayed page. This is very simple to do; simply set the `DisplayToolbar` property to false. To have all of the pages on a multi-page report render on the same HTML page, set the `SeparatePages` property to false. To get rid of the group tree-view, you can set the `DisplayGroupTree` property to false. Although these features are good for online reports, they are not very useful on printed output. One idea is to follow the example set by many Internet sites and create a way to display a more printer-friendly HTML page for use as printed output.

To do this, let's create a new ASP.NET project called "print_report" following the steps outlined in the "Building an ASP.NET Reporting Application" earlier. After you have created the project, open the Toolbox (Ctrl+Alt+X) and drag a Button control onto the top of the WebForm1 designer. Open up the Properties of the Button and change the Text property to "Printable View." Next, drag a CrystalReportViewer from the Toolbox and put it underneath the Button.

ON THE CD

After we have designed our Web Form, let's add the revenue report to our project. Do this by selecting Project . . . Add Existing Item (shortcut key Shift+Alt+A) and locating a copy of the Detailed Revenue Report in the Add Existing Item dialog. This is a multi-page report that shows order details over the past month. There is a copy on the CD-ROM accompanying the book in the Reports folder.

Now we are ready to add some code to WebForm1.aspx.cs. First, we add some code to bind the report to the ReportViewer by adding the line:

```
CrystalReportViewer1.ReportSource =
  new RevenueDetailReport();
```

in the `Page_Load` event handler, just as we did before.

After the report has been bound to the `CrystalReportViewer` object, we will insert the following code into the Button control we added, which will display a more printable report in the browser:

```
private void Button1_Click
  (object sender, System.EventArgs e)
{
```

```
        CrystalReportViewer1.DisplayToolbar = false;
        CrystalReportViewer1.DisplayGroupTree = false;
        CrystalReportViewer1.SeparatePages = false;
        Button1.Visible = false;
    }
```

Now we are ready to run the project by selecting Debug . . . Start (shortcut key F5). We will see an initial page that displays our report. Click the "Printable View" button and the Web browser will reload the page with a view of the report that we can print out. While this printed page is better than the default page, we still have some problems with headers, footers, and page breaks.

High-fidelity Formats

A better solution is to take advantage of the capability of Crystal Reports to export to other files formats such as Excel, Word, and PDF and print from the resulting high-fidelity output. However, using this functionality means that you cannot use Web Services to bind to your reports because of the limitations in the `ReportDocument` object, as we discussed in the beginning of the section of Crystal Reports. This problem can limit the usefulness of Web report distribution. However, the alternative design of using a Windows Forms Viewer combined with a Report Web Service, as demonstrated by our earlier Report Web Service example, can offer a reasonable solution to this shortcoming. The combination of the rich functionality provided by the Windows Forms Viewer and the ease of distribution provided by the Report Web Service offer a powerful combination for providing reporting solutions in .NET.

Caveats

A limitation of Crystal Reports for .NET that is particularly binding for Business Intelligence applications is it does not support accessing OLAP data through OLE DB for OLAP. However, if you want to create reports on your OLAP cubes, you can upgrade Crystal Reports for .NET to Crystal Reports 9 Professional or later, which does support OLAP reporting. Crystal Reports 9 has other features that you may find useful as well. For more information on Crystal Reports 9, see the Crystal Decisions Web site at *http://www.crystaldecisions.com*.

SUMMARY

In this chapter, we covered the evolution of reporting in the continuing quest to deliver useful and timely information with a focus on how .NET can provide flexible reporting services. We addressed the basic process for designing a report with an emphasis on gathering requirements and understanding the intention behind the reports. We also talked about the significance of formatting and presentation, and the utility of creating prototypes to evolve report design. We then dove into some technical details of Web development using ASP.NET and creating reports in this environment with examples that illustrate various techniques for distributing reports in Crystal Reports for .NET including Report Web Services and Server File Reports.

ENDNOTES AND REFERENCES

1. Tufte, Edward R., *Visual Explanations Visual Explanations: Images and Quantities,* Graphics Press, Cheshire, Connecticut, 1997, pp. 38–53.
2. If this is the first time you have used Crystal Reports, it will prompt you to register the product on the Crystal Decisions Web site. You either register the product now or choose Register Later.
3. The code-behind files created for Crystal Reports files are not visible by default in the Solution Explorer. If you would like to see this file, select Show All Files in the Solution Explorer.

Onion, Fritz, *Essential ASP.NET With Examples in C#,* Addison Wesley Professional, 2003.

Liberty, Jesse, and Hurwitz, Dan, *Programming ASP.NET,* O'Reilly & Associates, 2002.

Tufte, Edward, *The Visual Display of Quantitative Information,* Graphics Press, 2001.

Tufte, Edward, *Envisioning Information,* Graphics Press, 1990.

Norman, Donald, *The Design of Everyday Things,* Basic Books, 2002.

Peck, George; Wald, Lyssa; and Mueller, Michael; *Crystal Reports 9: The Complete Reference,* McGraw-Hill Osbourne Media, 2002.

8 Data Mining

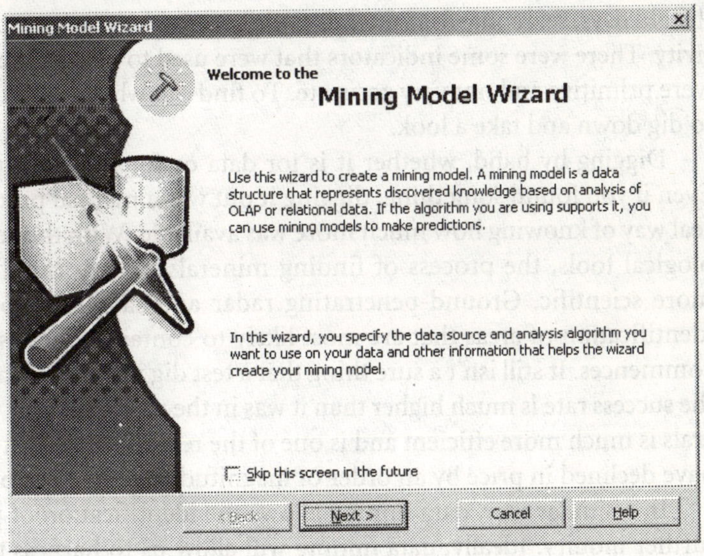

In this chapter, we will discuss data mining and where it fits into your business intelligence platform. We will cover the definition and utility of data mining; and discuss some of the mainstream techniques and the importance of the source data. We will then discuss the data mining support built into Analysis Services, and close with an example of using data mining in XMLA.

WHAT IS DATA MINING?

Data mining is a process of looking at your data to find patterns that you didn't know were present. The explosion of data that is being stored contributes to the problem. With the declining prices of disk space and the increasing capabilities of database management systems, the amount that businesses store is growing at a very fast pace. The cost of data storage has plummeted from $11,540 per gigabyte in 1988 to about $3 per gigabyte in 2002, with the result that the world's total information production is about 250 megabytes for every person on earth.[1]

The common tools used for analyzing data, such as spreadsheets, reports, and ad hoc query tools have improved over the same period of time, but they have not improved as quickly as the amount of data being stored. Similarly, our human brains have not evolved any additional analysis capacity in the past thirty years. The exponential growth in the quantity of data and the linear growth in our abilities to handle it is why we feel as if we are drowning in information.

Information extraction has followed the same pattern as mineral extraction. In the old days, searching for minerals underground was pretty much a hit-or-miss activity. There were some indicators that were used to help locate minerals, but these were primitive and not very accurate. To find out what was in the ground, you had to dig down and take a look.

Digging by hand, whether it is for data or for minerals, is always expensive. Even if you found something, digging it out was a manual process and you had no real way of knowing how much more was available. With the advent of modern geological tools, the process of finding minerals underground has become much more scientific. Ground-penetrating radar and satellite photography allow the identification of areas that are most likely to contain minerals before any digging commences. It still isn't a sure thing that a test dig will find what was indicated, but the success rate is much higher than it was in the past. This new way of finding minerals is much more efficient and is one of the reasons that most extracted resources have declined in price by an order of magnitude over the last one hundred years.

In a similar way, data mining allows the identification of promising areas for further inquiry. Ideally, data mining will allow us to harness the prodigious processing power of computers to identify points of interest. Data mining is a combination of statistics data warehousing, machine learning, and several distinct areas of inquiry being applied to solving business problems. In very simple terms, data mining filters a large amount of data in a search for useful information—patterns and trends—that are contained in the data. Patterns and trends are how people make sense of the world.

This doesn't mean that you can simply turn data mining algorithms loose on your data and expect to gain anything—data mining needs to have questions and answers that can be framed in the terms of the business. Using the tools without thinking about the business implications will reveal useless results such as people with call waiting also have phone service and people with dogs tend to buy dog leashes.

Data mining begins by selecting an area of interest and a goal. You might not know exactly what you are looking for, but setting a goal at the beginning, say identifying cross-selling opportunities, is very important. If you don't set a goal, it is possible that you will invest considerable time and effort that yields results that are not usable, or are trivial or incorrect. What data mining will help you do is weed through all of the possible factors to find patterns, saving a tremendous amount of trial and error.

Data mining is also known as *knowledge discovery*, in that you discover knowledge that is hidden in the data. In a business environment, the end result of this newfound knowledge is some kind of policy or action that improves profits. The mechanism by which the action improves profits is not necessarily as simple as the impact a price increase has on the top line. Instead, it may be a better retention of existing customers that allows steady growth or at least stops sales erosion. There is an element of process that is essential to being able to get the most out of data mining. Just finding a bunch of patterns in your data does you little good unless you can use that newfound knowledge to improve business processes and decision making.

Data mining is an excellent complement to OLAP analysis. Although OLAP makes it possible, even easy, to view data in all kinds of new ways and learn a great deal about the underlying business processes, it is still bound by the basic limitation that it will return no more than exactly what you ask of it. Data mining breaks that barrier by applying techniques that can create a new model of the data that might not have been considered before. So, OLAP is a user-directed activity, while algorithms control data mining.

Data mining as a discipline is relatively new, having emerged into the mainstream in the 1990s. Despite its recent vintage, many large companies use data mining. According to a Forrester Research study conducted in 2001, 24 percent of the Global 3500 use data mining, and another third were piloting data mining programs.[2]

Data mining can be used to take advantage of many different types of business opportunities. For example, data mining has been used to do the following:

- Increase sales by aligning customer profiles with product promotions.
- Improve advertising effectiveness by identifying target audiences that respond to different types of advertising.
- Identify baskets of goods that are sold together to improve product placement and promotion.
- Improve customer satisfaction by analyzing warranty repair and return information to make product and service improvements.
- Reduce credit defaults by analyzing customer profiles and payment histories.
- Reduce fraud by examining transactional patterns.
- Analyze Web sites to improve functionality and usability.

Data mining is inherently a back-office activity because it requires data cleansing and manipulation to produce useful results. Data mining is dependent on a solid data-warehousing effort to be as successful as possible. The results from data mining can be integrated into line-of-business applications to improve performance and profitability.

Data Mining vs. Statistical Analysis

Data mining is different from traditional statistical analysis. Data mining starts with a general goal that you want to learn more about. This is in contrast to statistical analysis, in which you form a formal hypothesis and conduct various statistical tests to determine whether the hypothesis can be rejected. In fact, the term "data mining" used to have a very pejorative meaning in the statistics field: looking through piles of data for interesting results without any theoretical guidance.

Traditional statistics and data mining can be complementary, with data mining identifying areas where it might be useful to conduct a statistical analysis, and statistical analysis helping to verify the results of data mining. For example, data mining might help you discover a grouping of customers that share a characteristic, say boat ownership, and tend to spend more than other customers. You can then follow up on that initial analysis with a statistical analysis of the data to confirm that, indeed, the boat owners spend more money. If your business involves boats, this analysis would be trivial to the point of absurdity. However, if your business is not related to boating, then identifying the characteristic, understanding the causes, and changing your promotion and sales strategies might help you target this audience more effectively.

Do More With Less

It is important to note that data mining will not replace your skilled analysts and subject matter experts. Instead, data mining will help these knowledge workers to be more efficient in their roles. Data mining offers a whole new set of tools that analysts can use to find and focus on the interesting parts of the data. In conjunction with the other facets of business intelligence, data mining can be a very effective way to do more with less.

DATA MINING TECHNIQUES

There are many different kinds of analysis techniques that can be called "data mining." Many books have been written on the different techniques used for data mining. For our purposes, we will stick to the mainstream data mining techniques, the ones most likely to be of use in a business intelligence platform. The techniques we will discuss in this chapter are:

- Decision trees
- Clustering
- Neural networks

Although they all work, each of these has different strengths and weaknesses, and are not mutually exclusive. It is a good idea to try different techniques on the same data to see which one works best for your situation. In many cases, the process of applying multiple data mining techniques will help you gain a much better understanding of your data. In any event, by applying multiple techniques to your data set you will be able to see which ones work the best.

Decision Trees

Decision trees separate data into subsets by a series of rules. Decision trees have been around since the 1960s and are one of the most widely used techniques because they are easy to understand and display. In addition, decision trees make very few assumptions about the underlying data and can model many different relationships among predictors. In general, decision tree algorithms build a series of split conditions that classify cases from the training set. This summary of what we know about the training set can be used to predict the values of unknown cases. A complete discussion of decision tree algorithms is beyond the scope of this chapter, but we will introduce and briefly describe some of the most common algorithms.

There are two kinds of decision trees: classification trees and regression trees. *Classification trees* produce a set of logical splits that can be used to classify discrete cases. For example, you might want to classify a dog into a particular breed by evaluating various continuous (such as weight) and discrete (such as color) variables. *Regression trees* produce a prediction of a continuous variable from continuous and categorical predictor variables. For example, you might want to predict the value of a piece of land depending on both continuous variables (such as acreage) and discrete variables (such as zip code).

Simple Example

As a simple example of the classification performed by a decision tree, take a look at Table 8.1. This table presents data about the decision to issue vehicle insurance.

This data can be rendered as the decision tree shown in Figure 8.1. Interpreting the results of a decision tree is simple. You start with an individual case and trace it down to each level to determine the resultant decision. The structure is readily apparent to everyone who looks at the tree and it is easy to determine where a case took one branch or another. For example, in the decision tree data in Table 8.1 if we were trying to decide whether to issue insurance to a 22-year-old truck

TABLE 8.1 Motor vehicle insurance issuance.

Vehicle Type	Prior Accidents	Age > 25	Issue Insurance
Car	No	Yes	Yes
Car	No	No	Yes
Car	Yes	Yes	No
Car	Yes	No	No
Motorcycle	No	Yes	Yes
Motorcycle	No	No	Yes
Motorcycle	Yes	Yes	Yes
Motorcycle	Yes	No	Yes
Truck	No	No	No
Truck	No	Yes	Yes
Truck	Yes	Yes	No
Truck	Yes	No	No

driver with a clean driving record, we could follow the tree by first taking the truck branch of the tree, then the no prior accidents branch, and then the age less than 25 branch to determine that we would not issue insurance.

Due to their simplicity, decision trees also tend to be blunt tools. Each layer of a decision tree represents a question about a certain variable. Is the customer's income greater than $50,000? Is the customer male or female? The leaf level of the tree represents the culmination of the series of questions and represents a grouping of data with the same characteristics. There is no room for grey areas in a decision tree.

Decision Tree Algorithms

There are a number of algorithms commonly used for creating decision trees. Three of the most prevalent algorithms for producing decision trees are CART (Classification and Regression Trees), CHAID (Chi-squared Automatic Interaction Detection), and C4.5.

CART produces binary trees that can be used to predict both continuous and discrete variables from continuous or discrete predictors. CART splits the node on the basis of how well the split separates the members of the parent node, continuing recursively until the tree is completed. CART is non-parametric and does not require the specification or assumption of a particular function. CART uses a step-

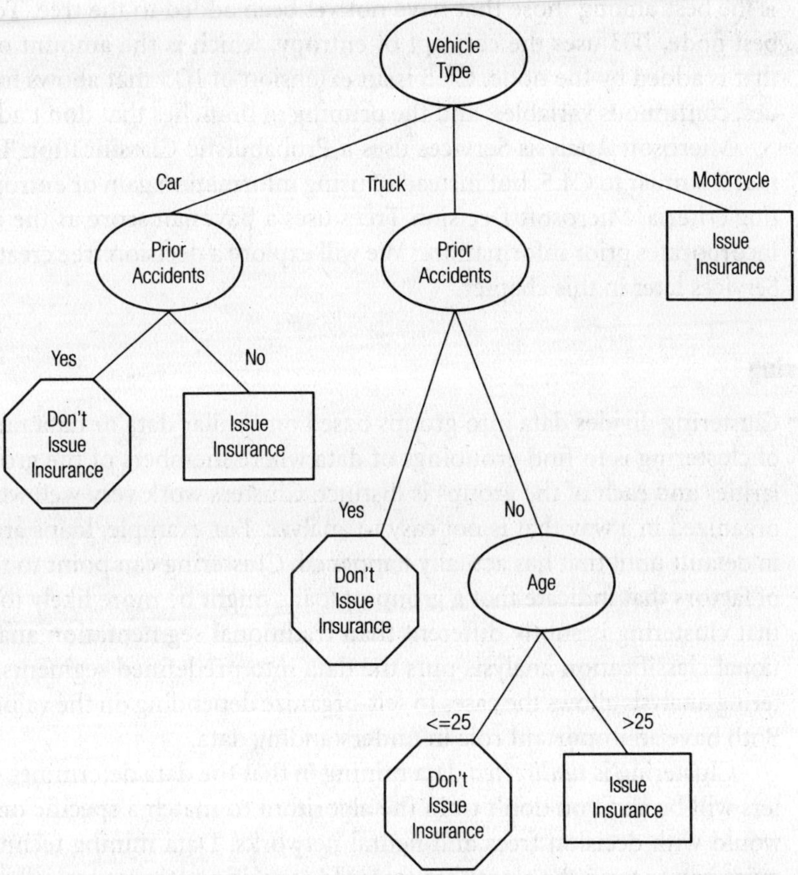

FIGURE 8.1 A decision tree.

wise technique so you do not have to order variables in advance. CART is very robust with respect to noisy data and outliers.

CHAID is one of the oldest tree classification techniques and is particularly popular in marketing research applications because of its flexibility and capability of handling continuous variables well. Instead of the binary trees produced by CART, CHAID produces trees that can have more than one split per level. Although it would seem to be an advantage to have multiple splits, that is not always the case. Any tree that can be represented by a multiple split can also be represented by a binary tree, and having a deeper tree may aid in understanding of the underlying phenomena.

C4.5 is an extension of an older algorithm called ID3 invented by J. Ross Quinlan. ID3 is a simple algorithm that builds a decision tree on the basis of which node is the best among those that have not yet been added to the tree. To calculate the best node, ID3 uses the concept of entropy, which is the amount of information that is added by the node. C4.5 is an extension of ID3 that allows for missing values, continuous variables, and the pruning of branches that don't add value.

Microsoft Analysis Services uses a Probabilistic Classification Tree algorithm that is similar to C4.5, but instead of using information gain or entropy as the splitting criteria, Microsoft Decision Trees uses a Bayesian score as the default, which incorporates prior information.[3] We will explore a decision tree created in Analysis Services later in this chapter.

Clustering

Clustering divides data into groups based on similar data or data ranges. The goal of clustering is to find groupings of data where members of the group have similarities and each of the groups is distinct. Clusters work very well when the data is organized in a way that is not easy to analyze. For example, loans aren't labeled as in default until that has actually happened. Clustering can point to the confluence of factors that indicate that a group of loans might be more likely to default. Note that clustering is subtly different than traditional segmentation analysis. A traditional classification analysis puts the data into predefined segments, while a clustering analysis allows the cases to self-organize depending on the values in the cases. Both have an important role in understanding data.

Clustering is *undirected* data mining in that the data determines what the clusters will be and you don't train the algorithm to match a specific outcome as you would with decision trees and neural networks. Data mining techniques that require you to train the algorithm towards a specific outcome are called *directed* data mining techniques.

Although an undirected approach allows the data to self-organize, you still need to have a strong understanding of the business to be able to make sense of clusters. Developing clusters is an iterative process. In many cases, the initial run at clustering will produce groupings that don't have much relevance to the business. After a few iterations, you can fine tune the number and data elements included in the clusters to discover a grouping that really helps you understand your data. Additional data that is gathered can be run through the clustering model to see what clusters it will belong to.

One of the most common algorithms for creating a clustering model is the *k-means* algorithm. The steps in constructing a k-means cluster are the following:

1. Choose a number of clusters for k.
2. Pick initial values for the center point of each cluster.
3. Figure out which data points are associated with each cluster center point.

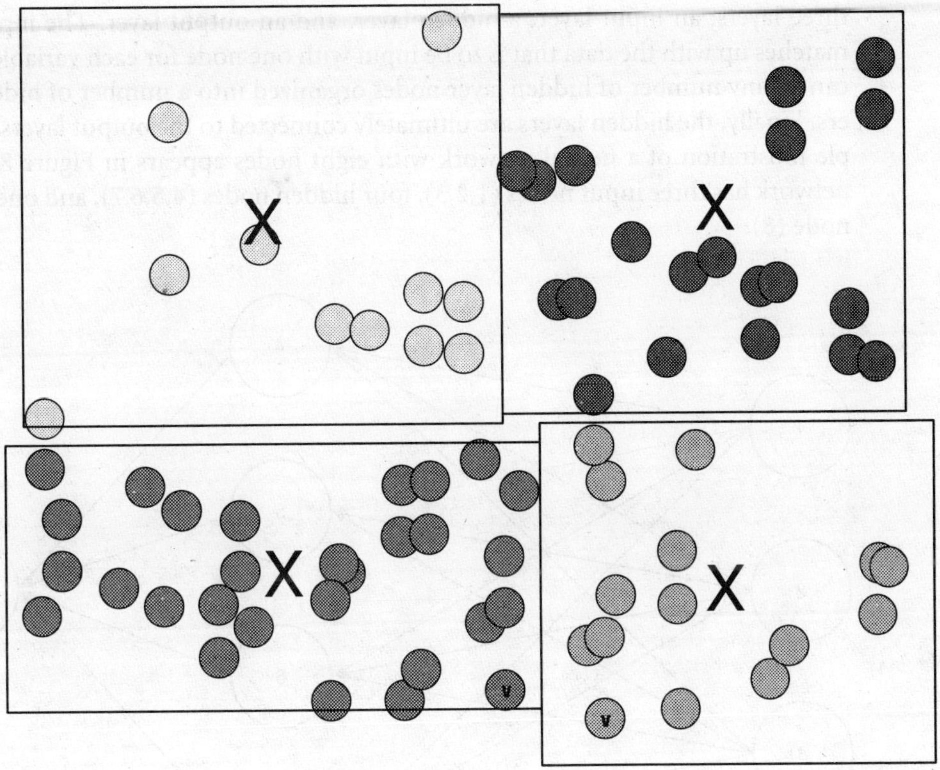

FIGURE 8.2 The k-means clustering process.

4. Using the results from Step 3, recalculate the center point for each cluster.
5. Move the center points and repeat Steps 3 through 5 until satisfied.

A graphical illustration of the first two steps of the k-means process is shown in Figure 8.2 with the number of clusters chosen as four.

There are many other clustering algorithms in widespread use. Analysis Services uses an Expectation-Maximization algorithm. Unlike k-means, which simply measures some kind of distance between points, Expectation-Maximization creates a more complex statistical model of the data and is able to handle both continuous and discrete data effectively.[4]

Neural Networks

Neural networks have been around for a very long time with some of the initial research being done in the 1940s. Basically, a neural network is a complex set of nonlinear equations that works much as a brain does. A neural network consists of three layers: an input layer, a hidden layer, and an output layer. The input layer matches up with the data that is to be input with one node for each variable. There can be any number of hidden layer nodes organized into a number of hidden layers. Finally, the hidden layers are ultimately connected to the output layers. A simple illustration of a neural network with eight nodes appears in Figure 8.3. This network has three input nodes (1,2,3), four hidden nodes (4,5,6,7), and one output node (8).

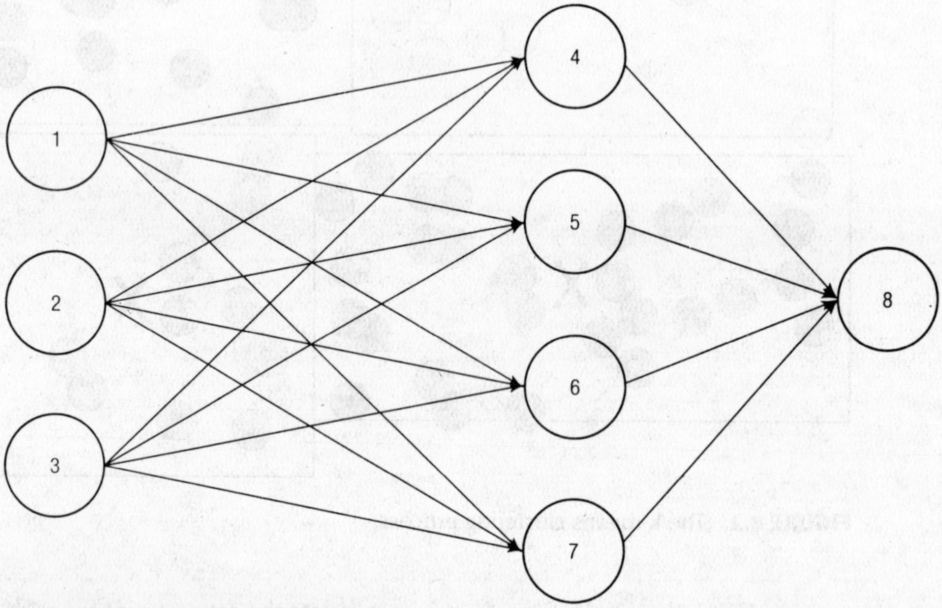

FIGURE 8.3 A simple neural network.

As data is fed through the neural network, associations between layers are formed. This is called training the network. As the network is trained, weights are assigned to the connections between the nodes. These weights represent the strength of the connection in the network. An illustration of a trained model is presented in Figure 8.4, where weight from node *i* to node *j* is shown as W*ij*.

The most common technique for training a neural network is called *backpropagation.* With backpropagation we run through the entire training set repeatedly, each time trying to minimize the error between the generated output layer and the training cases. With each pass through the training set, we should be getting closer and closer to matching the training set exactly. One pitfall to avoid is overfitting the model. Since there are so many variables in a neural network, it can be trained to fit a specific set of data perfectly. Although this might sound like a good thing, what it really does is reduce the robustness of the network to fit only that specific data.

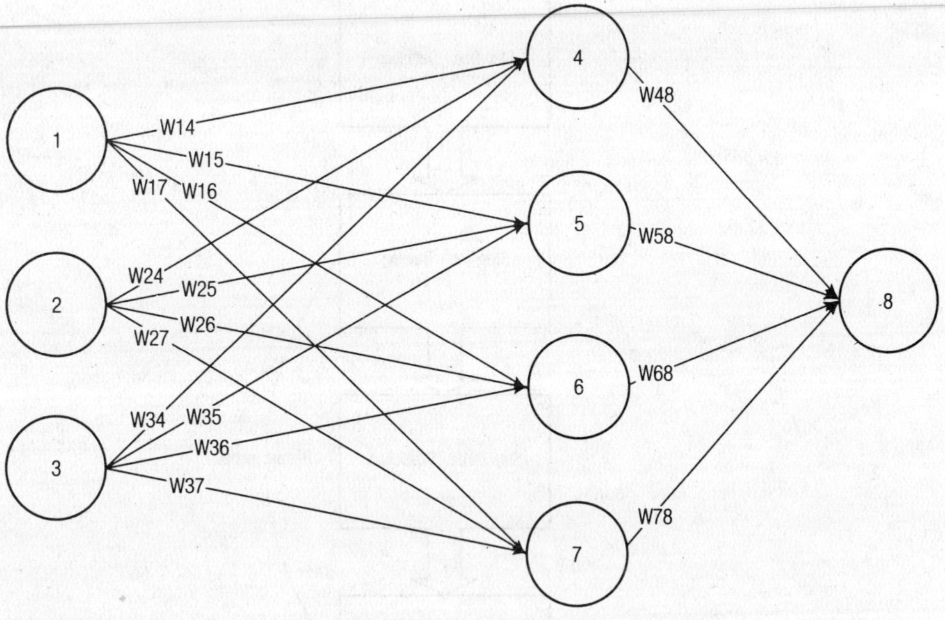

FIGURE 8.4 A trained neural network.

Instead of shooting for an exact fit of the training data, you should be concerned with creating a model that fits the entire population of data.

Once the network is trained, data from the same problem domain can be fed through the network to make predictions. Neural networks are especially good with predicting numerical values from a series of inputs, and can handle very large models. However, a neural network does not explain how that output was reached—the network is very difficult to interpret in terms of the data.

Analysis Services does not contain a neural network implementation. The architecture of Analysis Services allows the addition of custom data mining algorithms that comply with the OLE DB for Data Mining specification. The implementation of a custom data mining algorithm is beyond the scope of this chapter. There are a number of tools available to perform neural network analysis and you should be able to locate a tool suitable to your task by searching the Internet.

STEPS FOR DATA MINING

Regardless of the specific software and algorithm used to process the data, data mining involves four basic steps: model definition, training, prediction, and querying and retrieval of a model, as shown in Figure 8.5.

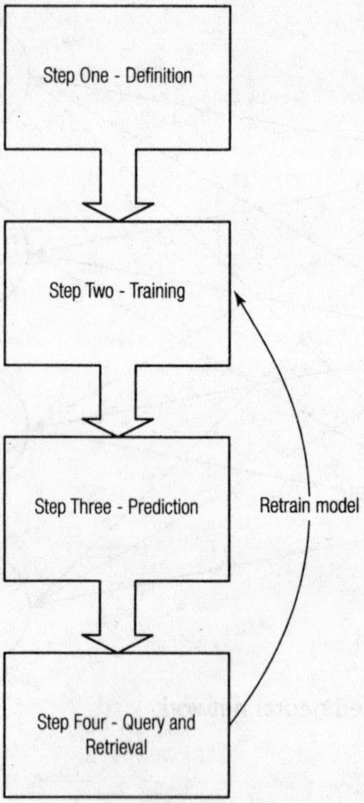

FIGURE 8.5 The four steps of data mining.

Step One: Definition

The first step is to create the basic structure of the model itself. But even before you can do that you have to make sure you understand the business problem that you are trying to solve. Just simply attacking a pile of data with data mining tools will not do much good unless you have some distinct goal in mind. These goals should be concrete enough that you know when you have made some progress. A goal such as "identify factors that determine the best store placements" or "improve customer profitability by understanding our best customer characteristics" are reasonable. Whatever the goal is, it needs to be something that you can hope to solve with data mining on the data you already have or can reasonably get. It doesn't do any good to make goals that will not be attainable with your available resources.

After you understand the business goal and have a basic understanding of the data that is available, you will want to define the data-mining model. This involves choosing an algorithm that is most suited to the type of knowledge you want to gain from mining as well as the type of data to be mined. As we noted in the previous discussion, some algorithms do very well with continuous data while others require discrete data. Choosing the proper algorithm is an important first step in achieving your data-mining goals.

Step Two: Training

After defining the model, you train the model against a set of data. In data-mining parlance, each instance of interest is called a *case*. So, we would call a set of data with cases a *case set*. The *training case set* is a set of data that will be run through the selected data-mining algorithm to build a model that can later be used for prediction. The selection of a training case set is important. After training the model, you will want to evaluate it against a set of cases to determine how accurate it is. The case set used for evaluation must be different from the case set used to train the model. If you evaluate the trained model against the training case set, you will see that the model is very accurate, but you will have no idea how the model will perform against other case sets.

Choosing Cases

In general, you want to have as many cases as possible with which to train the data model. These cases should be representative of the population or anticipated population of cases as a whole. If you train with data that is not representative, predictions on the population will not be as accurate. One of the best ways to ensure you get representative cases is to select a random sample of data. Random sampling ensures that the cases selected are distributed throughout the overall population of cases.

There are times when a random sample won't work very well. Sometimes the events that are being predicted in the cases are very rare and a random sample simply won't produce enough cases with the desired events. For example, if you are producing a mining model to help predict production equipment failures and you have only one failure out of every hundred-thousand units produced, a random sample will produce only one case with a failure for every 100,000 cases. This would produce a model that was extremely accurate in predicting non-failures, but not very accurate in identifying failures.

Instead of using a random sample in cases where the events are very sparse, you might consider using *oversampling*. Oversampling is a data enhancement technique in which you amplify the rare events you are looking for in the data. For example, if you have records for five million units produced with 57 failures, you could create a training set with 300 cases including the 57 failures and 243 cases that were randomly selected from the rest of the data. Instead of a population failure rate of 0.0000114, the training set failure rate would be 19 percent. This over sampling of the cases of interest makes the model more accurate in identifying rare events by giving the model more rare events to evaluate. A pitfall of oversampling is that you will need to be careful take account of the bias towards the rare event when you are evaluating the accuracy of the predictions given by the mining model.

Evaluating Effectiveness

Evaluating the effectiveness of a data-mining model is an important step in the process. One method of measuring the effectiveness of a model is to look at lift. *Lift* is measure of the effectiveness of a predictive model. Lift is calculated by the ratio of the results that would be obtained with the predictive model against the results obtained without the predictive model. Lift can be very effectively communicated in a graphical format that compares the lift curve to the baseline. Lift is a concept that can be well understood with a simple example. Let's suppose we are conducting a marketing campaign for a company. We know from past experience that our response rate from sending direct mail to our 10,000 customers is 5.5%. So, if we send a mailing out to the whole customer list, we should expect to get 550 responses. Creating a mining model that predicts which customers are most likely to respond, and ordering our customer list in decreasing likelihood of response, we can make predictions about the different response rates of our customers. These are shown in Table 8.2.

This table can be plotted into a chart, shown in Figure 8.6, which shows the percentage of responses with the predicted model and baseline response rate with random sampling. The amount of the "bow" above the baseline is an indication of

TABLE 8.2 Mass mailing mining model predictions.

Cumulative Mailings	*Responses*
1000	100
2000	190
3000	270
4000	340
5000	400
6000	450
7000	490
8000	520
9000	540
10000	550

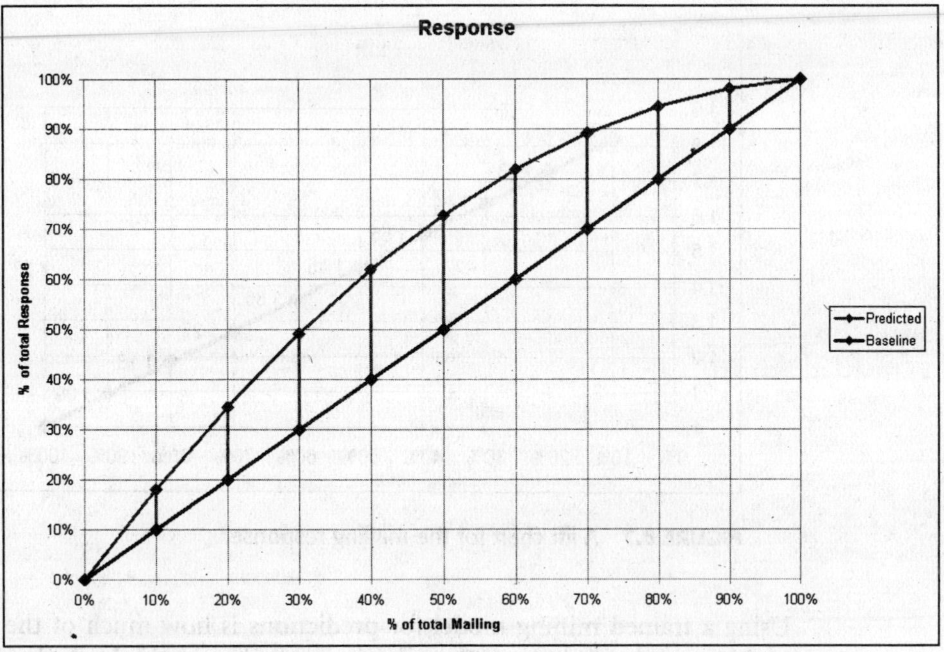

FIGURE 8.6 Responses using mining model vs. baseline response rate.

the lift provided by the mining model. The steeper slope of the lift curve in the region nearest the origin indicates the area where the mining model is achieving a much higher response rate than the baseline model. As we get out to the customers that are only marginally likely to respond, the lift curve begins to flatten out.

Another view of the lift is seen in Figure 8.7, which is commonly called a lift chart. This chart is created by plotting the ratio of responses predicted by the mining model to the ratio expected by the baseline response rate. So for example, if we send out 1000 mailings, the mining model predicts a response of 100, while we would expect only 55 with a random sample, so we have a lift of 100/55=1.82.

Step Three: Prediction

After you have constructed the model, trained it, and are satisfied with the results, the model can be used for predictions. Some types of data mining don't produce predictions because they are more focused on developing an understanding of the data (such as those types that perform clustering), but for those mining models that create predictions, this is where the rubber meets the road. Models that don't make predictions are still very useful in understanding your data. This greater understanding might lead to a new data-mining model that can produce predictions.

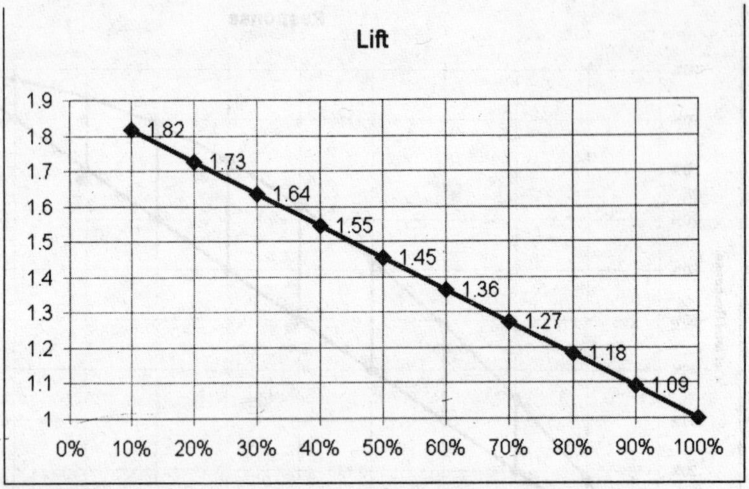

FIGURE 8.7 A lift chart for the mailing response.

Using a trained mining model for predictions is how much of the business value of data mining is derived. To make the predictions usable by the business, the mining models should be published in some way so that they can be used to make informed decisions; otherwise, building the models would be a waste of time.

It is important to note that models should be retrained from time to time to allow them to keep pace with changes in the underlying data. To adapt your models, you have to continuously evaluate model accuracy and make sure it is achieving the desired goals. Retesting your models with new data will make sure that they are performing as well as they should over time.

Finally, you need to understand that your best data mining efforts are limited to discovering patterns. These patterns may or may not have anything to do with the causes of the business events being analyzed. If you discover that owners of boats are more likely to buy your products, that doesn't necessarily explain why they are purchasing them. Maybe your products are available only in areas with large populations of boat owners. Maybe there is some other factor that offers an even better explanation. Only a firm understanding of the underlying business and the processes that go into it will enable you to understand the causes of the patterns observed. Data mining will reveal the patterns, but not the cause.

THE IMPORTANCE OF QUALITY DATA

Although each of these techniques may require different kinds of data (discrete versus continuous, aggregated versus granular), the basic requirement that they have in common is that they need good data. As with any analysis involving data, the "garbage-in, garbage-out" principle is very strong with data mining. If the data that we feed into the analysis is somehow misleading or biased, the results will be, at best, irrelevant and, at worst, harmful. To make sure we have the best possible data, it is strongly advisable to use either data directly from the data warehouse, which has already been cleansed and verified through our ETL process. Although it is possible to do data mining directly from OLTP source data, in general, this is not advisable.

Most data mining techniques work better with a large number of discrete factors. If you have years of historical data on only a few fields or on records that contain large text fields, it won't be very useful to mine using the algorithms we have discussed in this chapter. There are some interesting techniques emerging for the analysis of textual data, but these are not quite in the mainstream yet. Although these techniques have great promise for the analysis of the large amount of unformatted data that is collected today, we will not cover them here.

Sometimes, it is useful to combine internal company data with data gathered from outside sources. Because data mining performs quite well when cases have a large number of fields, adding relevant external data can be a good way of enhancing your mining results. For example, if you have data stored by zip code, you can get demographic information about that zip code to provide more insight.

Legalities of Data Use

Other important considerations for your data might revolve around making sure it is legal for you to construct mining models with that data and use the results of the analysis. If your organization rents a mailing list, for example, it may go beyond your licensed use of the data to do anything with it beyond sending a mailing. There may be other legal constraints around mining with different types of data that vary from jurisdiction to jurisdiction. The European Union has much tighter privacy rules than the United States, so doing some types of customer analysis that is perfectly legal in the US might run you afoul of the authorities in the EU. In addition, creating a mining model that causes discrimination against protected classes in any country could cause legal trouble down the road. In short, be careful about using data that might be illegal or unethical, and if in doubt, seek legal counsel before doing something that could cause great long-term damage to your company and career.

SHOULD YOU DO DATA MINING?

In order to be successful with data mining, you need to make sure that you can benefit from the effort. First and foremost, you need to be sure that you have the right kinds of data for data mining. If you are doing data mining on customer behavior, then you need to have detailed records on the traits and activities of those customers. If your data is of poor quality, you will not gain much value or even worse, you may obtain misleading results.

Next, you need to make sure that you can actually use the results of data mining in a productive manner. Discovering new information does you no good unless you can act on it. For example, if you find that pricing for customers is not optimal but you are constrained by regulatory or contractual issues, it does you little good. It is much better to understand how the results of data mining will be used before you begin the activity.

In a similar vein, you need to make sure you understand what you hope to gain from data mining. The most appropriate questions for data mining are questions about the patterns of behavior in a business process. Data mining is about improving business process, not about reporting on current process. It can help you learn about the process, but the end results are typically fed directly back into the process, not consumed directly by decision makers. If business users are complaining about the timeliness and accuracy of reports that are being delivered to them, data mining will do you no good. Don't treat data mining as a one-size-fits-all-solution. It is not a silver bullet for data analysis needs.

DATA MINING WITH ANALYSIS SERVICES

One of the key additions to Microsoft Analysis Services in the upgrade from version 7.0 to 2000 is the addition of data-mining capabilities. The data-mining capabilities included in Microsoft Analysis Services 2000 are based on the OLE DB for Data Mining standard.

OLE DB for Data Mining

OLE DB for Data Mining (DM) is an extension to the OLE DB standard to provide convenient access to data-mining functionality in a standardized way through an API. OLE DB for DM builds on the increasing need to analyze large amounts of data in a corporate environment. The overall goal of OLE DB for DM is to make the creation and use of data-mining applications much easier in a corporate environment.

Prior to the introduction of OLE DB for DM in 1999, data mining was not very well suited for deployment in many corporate environments. Although there were many excellent data mining applications on the market, they were oriented towards specialist researchers. The specialized knowledge of statistics and pattern recognition required to create the mining models are not very widespread in typical corporate information technology departments. More importantly, most of the tools assumed that the data to be mined would be stored in memory or in large flat files extracted specifically for the purpose of data mining.

While this is a reasonable assumption for a data-mining specialist, it is not as good for a corporate database environment. Creating a series of export and transformation scripts as well as potentially large export files creates, in effect, a parallel data management system. The additional overhead of maintaining the data sources for data mining and keeping them in synch with the rest of the data warehouse adds considerably to the cost and complexity of data-mining applications.

In addition to the difficulties of maintaining data consistency, there was not much attention paid to how the trained models could be deployed in an organization to create predictions and help improve understanding of corporate data. In a sense, the state of data-mining software was similar to that of database software before the emergence of SQL as a standard for data management. Before SQL became the standard, each database had its own query languages and required specialized knowledge to use effectively. Now, although the various flavors of SQL vary from vendor to vendor, the basic language is portable from database to database.

To improve on these shortcomings with traditional data-mining tools and make it easier for non-specialists to create and use data-mining models, OLE DB for DM is based on a concept that corporate developers understand well: the relational database. Since OLE DB is the de facto standard for data access in the enterprise, it made sense to create the data-mining API on the basis of that standard.

OLE DB for DM is independent of any specific software or data-mining algorithm. Third parties can also build applications based on the specification. The API is not specialized to any particular model of data mining. It seeks to find a common ground among all of the well-known algorithms, and specific algorithms can be implemented as an OLE DB for DM provider to create new types of analysis. The two data-mining algorithms provided by Microsoft in Analysis Services are built on the same OLE DB for DM specification that is available to everyone.

One of the central concepts of OLE DB is support for SQL to create database structures and to query them. Supporting data-mining models in a database-like environment means that the same concept should apply: SQL can be used to support the creation and use of data mining models. To make this work, the four basic steps for data mining need to be available through SQL syntax:

1. Definition of a model
2. Training of the model
3. Prediction using the model
4. Querying and retrieval of the model

With these four operations supported in an SQL-like environment, it is possible to manage the lifecycle of a data-mining model in terms that are very understandable to corporate developers.

To make this translation from data mining to SQL work, OLE DB for DM treats important elements of data mining as tables. So cases that are used to train the model or make predictions are treated as a table. Traditional data mining algorithms work with flattened tables in which the entire relational structure has been unrolled into one table.

For some types of data, flattening the structure is not a problem. However, there are many types of data that are hierarchical in nature. In this case, creating a flattened view involves duplicating a large portion of the data. For example, the schema depicted in Figure 8.8 has a very common hierarchical organization. In this schema, the customer is related to both products purchased and publications subscribed to. To read this schema, we say "A customer has purchased zero or more products" and "A customer subscribes to zero or more publications." The terminology describing the relationships implies a hierarchy. If we want to analyze the data with one case per customer, we will need to flatten this hierarchy.

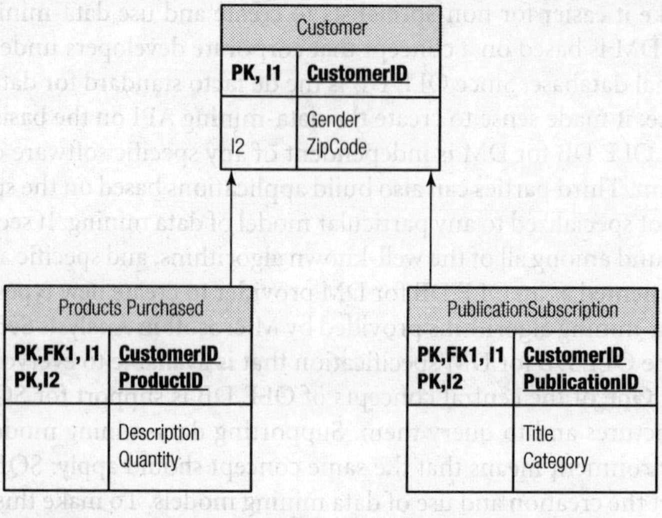

FIGURE 8.8 A common schema design for customer data.

To understand the problem that can face us when we try to flatten records for data mining, consider the single customer record shown in Figure 8.9. This particular customer has purchased five products and subscribes to three magazines.

To capture this hierarchy in a flattened rowset, we have to query against the three tables and retrieve each individual record. This means there will be 10 records returned in our flattened data set for data mining, as shown in Table 8.3.

Instead of relying on flattened records, OLE DB for DM allows you to work with nested tables by using Data Shaping. Data Shaping is part of OLE DB and makes it possible to create rowset hierarchies with data that is retrieved from the

CustomerID	Gender	ZipCode
1	M	22903

CustomerID	ProductID	Description	Quantity
1	1	Beer	6
1	2	Bread	1
1	3	Socks	2
1	4	Coffee	1
1	5	Gum	3

CustomerID	PublicationID	Title	Category
1	1	Fishing	Sports
1	2	Sense	News

FIGURE 8.9 A single customer record.

TABLE 8.3 A flattened rowset from a single customer record.

CustomerID	*Gender*	*ZipCode*	*ProductID*	*Description*	*Quantity*	*PublicationID*	*Title*	*Category*
1	M	22903	1	Beer	6	1	Fishing	Sports
1	M	22903	1	Beer	6	2	Sense	News
1	M	22903	2	Bread	1	1	Fishing	Sports
1	M	22903	2	Bread	1	2	Sense	News
1	M	22903	3	Socks	2	1	Fishing	Sports
1	M	22903	3	Socks	2	2	Sense	News
1	M	22903	4	Coffee	1	1	Fishing	Sports
1	M	22903	4	Coffee	1	2	Sense	News
1	M	22903	5	Gum	3	1	Fishing	Sports
1	M	22903	5	Gum	3	2	Sense	News

data source. This means that the cases can be created in a compact format from a relational database without going through the intervening step of creating a flattened table. In this case we would get a record set that looked like Figure 8.8 with each customer row having a set of product and publication records related directly to it. Once we have created a set of cases in a hierarchical record set, we can train a mining model with it or use it for creating predictions.

Defining a Model

To create a data-mining model in OLE DB for DM, we need to define it. As we discussed earlier, the definition of a mining model in OLE DB for DM is parallel to the definition of a table in SQL, although a mining model is more complex than a table. To define a table in SQL, you specify the name of the table, the fields that it contains and their data types, as well as keys and constraints. Similarly, in OLE DB for DM, to define a data model you specify the name of the mining model, the algorithm and parameters used to build the model and the fields. data types, and relationships of the cases.

Defining a Relational Mining Model

The basic syntax of defining a relational mining model looks like the following:

```
CREATE MINING MODEL «mining_model»
(
    «column_definition_list»
) USING «dmm_algorithm»
```

where `mining_model` specifies the name of the mining model (enclosed in square brackets if there is a space in the name), `column_definition_list` defines the columns that are to be used in the model, and `dmm_algorithm` specifies the mining algorithm to be used to create the model (currently, the only values supported are `Microsoft_Decision_Trees` and `Microsoft_Clustering`). A concrete example of creating a mining model from a relational data source follows:

```
CREATE MINING MODEL [Gender Prediction]
(
[Customer ID] LONG KEY,
[Gender] TEXT DISCRETE PREDICT,
[Zip Code] TEXT DISCRETE,
[Products] TABLE (
[Product ID] LONG KEY,
[Description] TEXT DISCRETE ))
USING Microsoft_Decision_Trees
```

Creating an OLAP Mining Model

In addition to creating a relational mining model, you can create a mining model based on an OLAP cube. To create a mining model based on an OLAP cube, you use the following syntax:

```
CREATE OLAP MINING MODEL «mining_model» FROM «cube»
(
    «olap_def»
) USING «dmm_algorithm»
```

where, as earlier, `mining_model` specifies the name of the mining model (enclosed in square brackets if there is a space in the name), `olap_def` defines the values that are used in the model by dimension and level. Finally, `dmm_algorithm` specifies the mining algorithm to be used to create the model. For example,

```
CREATE OLAP MINING MODEL [MyOlapModel] FROM [Sales]
  (
    CASE
      DIMENSION [Customers]
      LEVEL [Name]
        PROPERTY [Marital Status],
        PROPERTY [Education],
        PROPERTY [Gender] PREDICT
  )
USING Microsoft_Decision_Trees
```

Predictive Model Markup Language

Lastly, you can create a mining model using Predictive Model Markup Language. PMML is an XML schema that is backed by the Data Mining Group, a consortium of data-mining vendors. PMML is used to describe statistical and data mining models that define the models and transformations used to create the model. For more information on PMML, see the Data Mining Group's Web site at *http://www.dmg.org*. The syntax for creating a mining model with PMML is simple, as follows:

```
CREATE MINING MODEL «mining_model»
FROM PMML «string»
```

where `mining_model` specifies the name of the mining model and the `«string»` specifies the PMML that defines the model. In the following example, much of the detail of the PMML describing the model has been deleted for brevity. If you want to see the PMML file in its entirety, open the pmml.xml file on the CD-ROM.

ON THE CD

```
CREATE MINING MODEL [Customer Pattern Discovery] FROM PMML
'<pmml name="Customer Pattern Discovery" GUID="{7BE42428-AF08-484D-
BF60-6D690FDE7007}" creation-time="2003-08-20T02:01:00" modified-
time="2003-08-20T02:01:03">
    <statements>
      <statement type="CREATE" value="CREATE OLAP MINING MODEL
       [Customer  Pattern Discovery'S] FROM [Sales] (CASE DIMENSION
       [Customers] LEVEL [Name]  PROPERTY [Gender] ,
       PROPERTY [Marital Status] , PROPERTY [Education] ,
       PROPERTY [Yearly Income] , PROPERTY [Member Card] PREDICT)
```

```
            USING Microsoft_Decision_Trees"/>
         </statements>
         <OLAP-schema database="FoodMart 2000" cube="Sales">

    <!--schema details elided for brevity →

    </OLAP-schema>
         <data-dictionary column-ordering="ORDINAL" column-count="6">
            <key name="Customers.Name" datatype="TEXT"
              isinput="true" column-ordinal="0"/>
            <categorical name="Customers.Name.Gender"
              isinput="true" datatype="TEXT" column-ordinal="1">
                <category missing="true"/>
                <category value="F"/>
                <category value="M"/>
            </categorical>
            <categorical name="Customers.Name.Marital Status"
              isinput="true" datatype="TEXT" column-ordinal="2">
                <category missing="true"/>
                <category value="M"/>
                <category value="S"/>
            </categorical>
            <categorical name="Customers.Name.Education"
              isinput="true" datatype="TEXT" column-ordinal="3">
                <category missing="true"/>
                <category value="Partial College"/>
                <category value="Graduate Degree"/>
                <category value="Partial High School"/>
                <category value="Bachelors Degree"/>
                <category value="High School Degree"/>
            </categorical>
            <categorical name="Customers.Name.Yearly Income"
              isinput="true" datatype="TEXT" column-ordinal="4">
                <category missing="true"/>
                <category value="$30K - $50K"/>
                <category value="$110K - $130K"/>
                <category value="$130K - $150K"/>
                <category value="$10K - $30K"/>
                <category value="$70K - $90K"/>
                <category value="$50K - $70K"/>
                <category value="$150K +"/>
                <category value="$90K - $110K"/>
            </categorical>
            <categorical name="Customers.Name.Member Card" isinput="true"
```

```
ispredict="true" datatype="TEXT" column-ordinal="5">
    <category missing="true"/>
    <category value="Bronze"/>
    <category value="Golden"/>
    <category value="Normal"/>
    <category value="Silver"/>
  </categorical>
 </data-dictionary>
 <global-statistics>
<!--global statistics elided for brevity →
 </global-statistics>
 <tree-model>
<!--tree model elided for brevity →
 </tree-model>
</pmml>'
```

Mining Location

An important consideration when using the `CREATE MINING MODEL` statements is where the models will be created. Whenever you create a model using `CREATE MINING MODEL`, you are creating a local mining model using PivotTable Services. If you do not specify a `Mining Location` property in the connection string to the database, the mining models will exist only for the duration of the connection to the database. If a `Mining Location` is specified in the connection, then the mining model will be created in the specified directory.

If you want to create models that will be saved in Analysis Services, you will need to use either the Mining Model Wizard in the Analysis Manager application or script them directly in DSO. We cover an example of using the Mining Model Wizard later in this chapter in the section Using Analysis Server Tools. See the Books Online or one of the references at the end of the chapter for details on creating mining models in DSO.

Content Types

To understand the model that is created using `CREATE MINING MODEL`, you need to understand the content types for the columns. The content type allows the mining model to use the column properly by specifying the columns role in the mining model. Note that the content type is different from the data type of the column—the data type is independent of the role of the column in the mining model. There are six different column content types: Key, Attribute, Qualifier, Relation, Table, and Prediction.

Key Columns

One or more key columns are used to uniquely identify a case. The key column in a mining model is analogous to the key in a relational database table. In the previous example, we are using `[Customer ID]` as our key column.

Attribute Columns

Attribute columns are the most numerous columns in most mining models. They contain the attributes of the case that is to be used in constructing the model. In addition to the specification of the column name, attribute columns also include domain information about the range and type of possible values for the attribute. In the earlier example, Gender and Zip Code are attribute columns with discrete domains. There are six possible domain types, as follows:

`CONTINUOUS`: These values are ordered and have a set way of measuring distance and magnitude. A continuous variable can be characterized further by a description of the statistical distribution that it follows, either normal or uniform. A normal distribution is distributed in a bell curve, with the most common of values occurring in the middle of the range. A uniform distribution has values that are equally likely to occur anywhere in the range. For more information on statistical distributions, see Appendix F.

`CYCLICAL`: These values form an ordered cyclical set. As an example, consider the numbered months of the year with the values 1 for January, 2 for February and so on.

`DISCRETE`: These values are categorical, with each distinct value representing something separate from every other. They do not imply any kind of order or distance. An example of discrete data is gender or zip code.

`DISCRETIZED`: These have continuous data values, but are transformed into ordered data for the analysis. This is to help data-mining algorithms that cannot handle continuous data.

`ORDERED`: These values form an ordered set that can be ranked. For example, a skill level can be an ordered set of low, medium, and high.

`SEQUENCE_TIME`: These values indicate a time measurement range. This can be a number that indicates any kind of time interval.

In addition to the basic attributes, there are some provider-specific attributes that can be used to help the data-mining algorithm build better models using the attributes. These include the following:

`MODEL_EXISTENCE_ONLY`: Tells the algorithm that the value of the column is less important than the fact that it is present.

`NOT NULL`: Tells the algorithm that there should never be a null value in this column and it is an error if a null is present.

`IGNORE NULL`: Tells the algorithm to ignore any null values.

`NULL INFORMATIVE`: Means that the null information implies a missing state that is meaningful to the mining model.

Qualifier Columns

Qualifier columns can be used to provide information about other attribute columns. OLE DB for DM supports the following qualifier columns:

`PROBABILITY`: Gives the probability of the associated value.

`VARIANCE`: The variance of the associated value.

`STDEV`: The standard deviation of the associated value.

`SUPPORT`: The weight of the associated value.

`PROBABILITY_VARIANCE`: The variance of the probability of the associated value.

`PROBABLILITY_STDEV`: The standard deviation of the probability of the associated value.

`ORDER`: The ordering of the associated value.

RELATION Columns

`RELATION` columns are used to further classify an attribute by establishing a relationship between two columns. This allows a simple mapping from a relational database to a data-mining model.

TABLE Columns

`TABLE` columns contain a nested table. As we discussed earlier, this nested table is built by using Data Shaping and contains other columns. For each case, the value of a TABLE column is the entire contents of the associated nested table. In the earlier example, each customer has all of their products included in the case.

PREDICTION Columns

`PREDICTION` columns are used as the output of a mining model. Not only do the predictions carry a simple estimate, but they can also contain more information about the predicted value, such as the confidence level or standard deviation. Extracting all of the information out of a prediction is done with transformation functions that can return either scalar data about the predicted value such as the probability, or nested tables that contain data such as histograms and the like.

Training a Model

Following the SQL-like structure in OLE DB for DM, to train a model, we use the `INSERT` statement. Instead of adding records to a table as `INSERT` does in SQL, `INSERT` on a data-mining model adds the inserted cases to the body of cases used to train the model. The basic syntax for inserting cases into a model follows:

```
INSERT INTO «mining_model»
(
    «column_ list»
) «data»
```

For example, consider the following `INSERT` statement:

```
INSERT INTO [Gender Prediction]
(
[Customer ID],
[Gender],
[Zip Code],
/* Define the nested table */
[Products] (
[Product ID],
[Description])
)
SHAPE
{
OPENROWSET('SQLOLEDB', 'INITIAL CATALOG=FoodMart 2000;',
'SELECT [Customer ID], [Gender], [Zip Code]
FROM Sales
ORDER BY [Customer ID]'
}
APPEND
(
(OPENROWSET('SQLOLEDB', 'INITIAL CATALOG=FoodMart 2000;',
'SELECT [Customer ID], [Gender], [Zip Code]
FROM Sales
ORDER BY [Customer ID]')
)RELATE [Customer ID] To [Customer ID]
AS [Products]
}
```

There are few things to note in this INSERT statement. First, to get to the training data, you use the OPENROWSET statement. This allows you to open up any OLE DB data source and run a query. The syntax for OPENROWSET is as follows:

```
OPENROWSET('<<Provider>>',
'<<Connection String>>',
'<<Query>>')
```

where Provider specifies any OLE DB data provider, Connection String specifies the connection string to be used to open the data source, and Query specifies the data that should be returned from the data source.

The second point of interest is the use of the SHAPE command to return the nested records for the case. The first OPENROWSET retrieves the parent rows, followed by the APPEND statement that creates the nested table relationship, and another OPENROWSET statement to retrieve the child rows. It is important to make sure that you order the records in the parent and child rows so that all of the records in the nested table can be properly joined and returned. In this case, we have ordered both the parent and child rows using the Customer ID field.

Making Predictions

After defining and training our data-mining model, we use it for creating predictions. Making predictions in OLE DB for DM uses the SELECT statement. Generically, the SELECT statement for prediction is as follows:

```
SELECT [FLATTENED] <Fields> FROM <mining model>
PREDICTION JOIN <source data query> ON <join condition>
[WHERE <WHERE-expression>]
```

As an example of a prediction query, consider the following:

```
SELECT t.[Customer ID], [Age Prediction].[Age]
FROM [Age Prediction]
PREDICTION JOIN
(
  SHAPE
  {
  SELECT [Customer ID], [Gender], FROM Customers ORDER BY [Customer ID]
}
APPEND
  (
  {SELECT [CustID], [Product Name], [Quantity] FROM Sales ORDER BY [CustID]}
```

```
RELATE [Customer ID] To [CustID]
  )
  AS [Product Purchases]
) as t
ON [Age Prediction] .Gender = t.Gender
  and
  [Age Prediction].[Product Purchases].[Product Name] =
  t.[Product Purchases].[Product Name] and
  [Age Prediction] .[Product Purchases].[Quantity] =
  t.[Product Purchases].[Quantity]
```

Note the similarity between the training query and the prediction query. They both use the same structures to insert the cases that are used in the model, the differences being that the cases for prediction don't include the variable to be predicted. The source query returns the cases to be used for prediction and the `JOIN` describes the way in which the cases are to be used in the prediction model.

Browsing Content

In addition to creating predictions, you can also browse the data-mining model using the `SELECT` statement. Browsing the content of the model is important in understanding the structure of the data that was used to create it, and might suggest additional ways of analyzing the data.

The simplest way to browse a mining mode is simply to return the contents of the model in a query:

```
SELECT * FROM MyOlapModel.CONTENT
```

This query will return all of the content of the mining model in the `MINING_MODEL_CONTENT` schema. We discuss this schema later in the context of the XMLA. In addition to simply selecting all of the elements in the model, you can create queries that look at distinct parts of the mining model. For example,

```
SELECT Age
FROM HairColorPredictDMM.Content
WHERE Gender = 'Male' and HairColor = 'Black'
```

will return the content of the mining model only for elements in the model specified by the query.

Using Analysis Server Tools

The application we will construct for the Chocolate Pretzel Company looks at the existing stores that sell their products to analyze the likelihood of stores selling their products based on demographic information on their locations.

Clustering

To investigate the stores' data, let's use Analysis Services to create a clustering model based on the data in the Chocolate Pretzel Company's data warehouse. In this walk-through, we will show how to create a mining model from data that is extracted into an Excel spreadsheet and manipulate the model to understand the results.

From our data warehouse, we can create an extract of data that we want to analyze in Excel. Fields that might be interesting for analysis with respect to stores are shown in Table 8.4.

TABLE 8.4 Chocolate Pretzel Company's retail store data fields.

Field	*Description*
ShipToID	Identifier for the store
StoreType	Type of store: Gourmet or Market
CustomerCredit	Credit history of customer: Poor, Fair, Good, or Excellent
TotalPopulation	Population of store Zip Code Tabulation Area (ZCTA), bracketed into Low, Medium, and High
ProportionMale	Proportion of males in ZCTA, bracketed into Low, Medium, and High
PerCapitaIncome	Per capita income of ZCTA
MedianHomeValue	Median home value in ZCTA
SalesRepName	The assigned sales representative
SalesRepRegion	The assigned sales region
SumOfContribution	The total contribution from that store in dollars

ON THE CD You can see the extracted Excel file on the CD-ROM saved as StoreMining.xls in the Chapter 8 directory.

To create our clustering model, we open up our PretzelCo database in the Analysis Manager and select Action . . . New Mining Model from the menu. This will open up the Mining Model Wizard shown in Figure 8.10. We then click Next.

The next page in the Mining Model Wizard asks us to choose the type of data to base our model on. Our choice is either relational data or an OLAP cube. Relational data can use any kind of data that is accessible through an OLE DB provider supported by Analysis Manager, while OLAP data will create the model from exist-

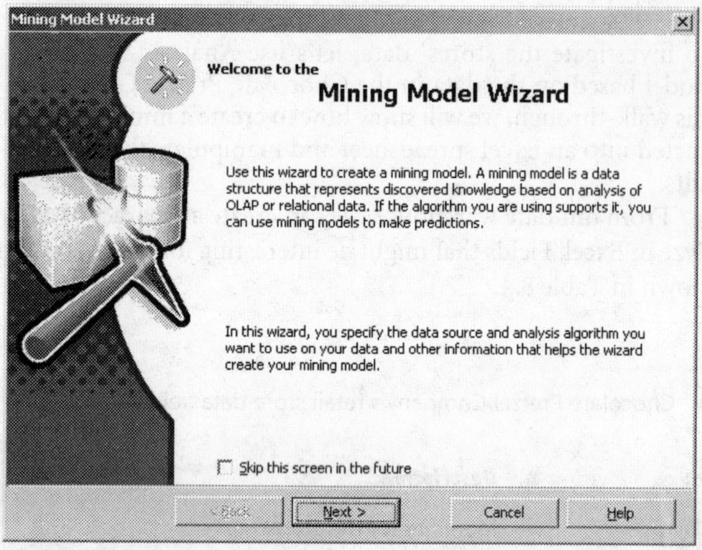

FIGURE 8.10 The Mining Model Wizard.

ing OLAP data. For this example, we will select Relational data as shown in Figure 8.11, and then click Next.

The next page in the Wizard allows us to select our case tables. Since we want to use the StoreMining.xls file, we will need to create a data source for it by clicking the New Data Source button. This will show the Provider page of the Data Link Properties dialog where we select the "Microsoft OLE DB Provider for ODBC" entry from the OLE DB Providers list and click the Next button, which shows the Connection tab of the same dialog (Figure 8.12).

Here we select the Use connection string option button and click the Build button. The Build button will open up the Select Data Source dialog, where we choose the Machine Data Source tab and click the New button. On the Create New Data Source dialog, we select the System Data Source option button and click Next. We then choose the Microsoft Excel Driver from the list of ODBC drivers and click Next. After selecting the driver, we are finished with the Create New Data Source dialog, so we click Finish. Next, the Microsoft Excel Driver prompts us to provide a name and a description for the Data source and a location of the Excel file.

ON THE CD

Click Select Workbook and navigate to the location where the StoreMining.xls file is located. Since this is read-only data, you can leave it on the CD-ROM, but it might be best to copy it to your local hard disk and point the data source to that location so you can refresh the data without having the CD-ROM in the drive. After you have specified the location, click OK to close the ODBC Microsoft Excel Setup dialog. Make sure the Store Mining data source is selected in the Select Data Source dialog and click OK to close the dialog. You will then see the Select Workbook dialog with the location of the StoreMining.xls file chosen. Click OK to finish build-

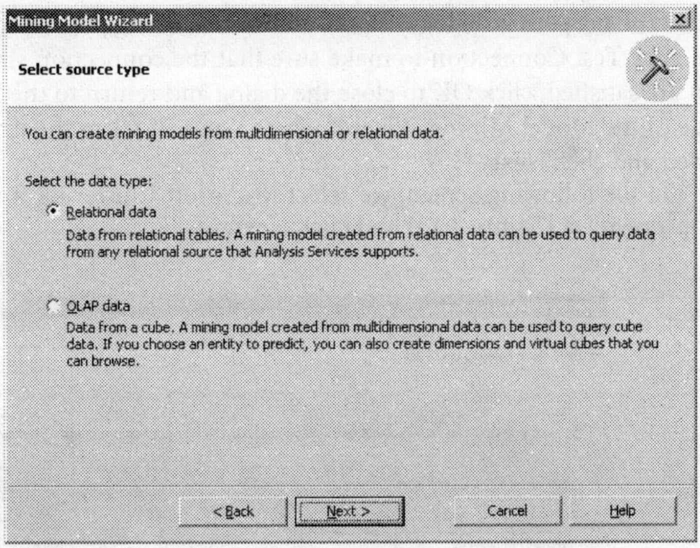

FIGURE 8.11 Selecting Relational data.

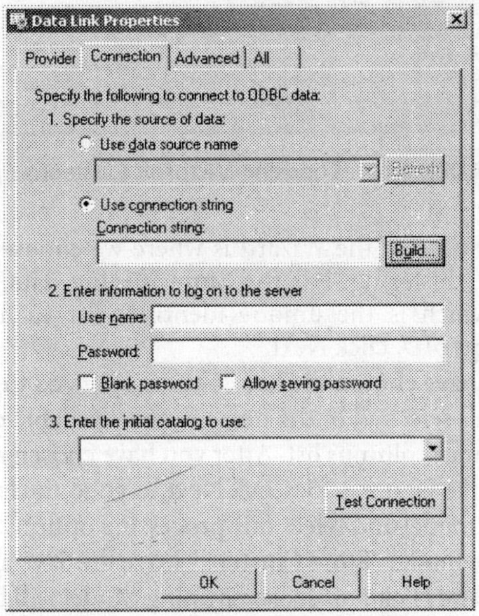

FIGURE 8.12 The Connection tab of the New Data Source dialog.

ing the connection string. Now you should be back at the Connection tab of the Data Link Properties dialog with the connection string populated. If you want, you can click Test Connection to make sure that the connection string is valid. Once you are satisfied, click OK to close the dialog and return to the Select Case Tables page of the Model Mining Wizard, where you will select the data source you just added and click Next.

On the following screen, we select Microsoft Clustering from the Technique drop-down list (Figure 8.13) and click Next.

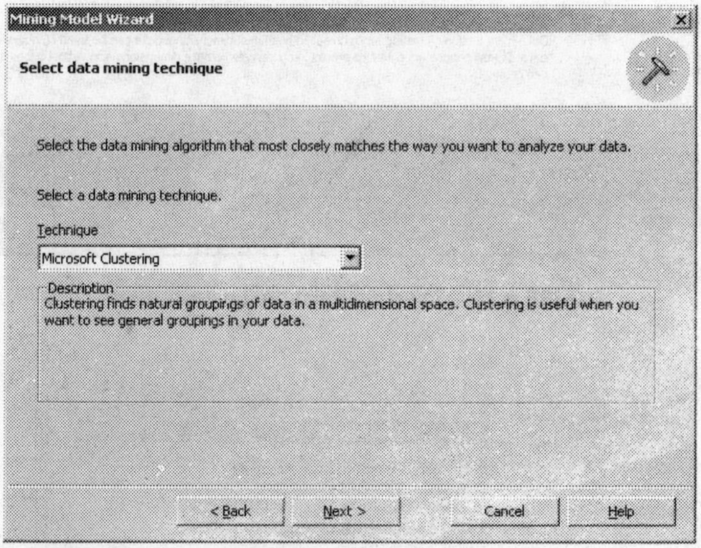

FIGURE 8.13 Choosing Microsoft Clustering.

The next page of the Wizard is where we choose our key column to identify the cases for clustering. For the Store Mining data, the key column should be ShipToID, which is the unique identifier for each store (Figure 8.14). After choosing ShipToID, click Next.

After we have chosen the key column, we need to pick our input columns. To start with, let's select all of the items in the Available columns list and move them over to the Input columns list. After you have chosen all of the columns, the dialog should look like Figure 8.15. Click Next to go to the last page of the Wizard where we name the model and select our processing options.

Name the model "Store Clusters," leave the Save and Process Now option button selected, and click Finish. The Mining Model will be processed and you will see the Schema tab of your clustering model in the Relational Mining Model Editor (Figure 8.16).

The Schema tab is where you can view the tables that make up the data-mining model. In this case, we only have one table, so it isn't very interesting. What is

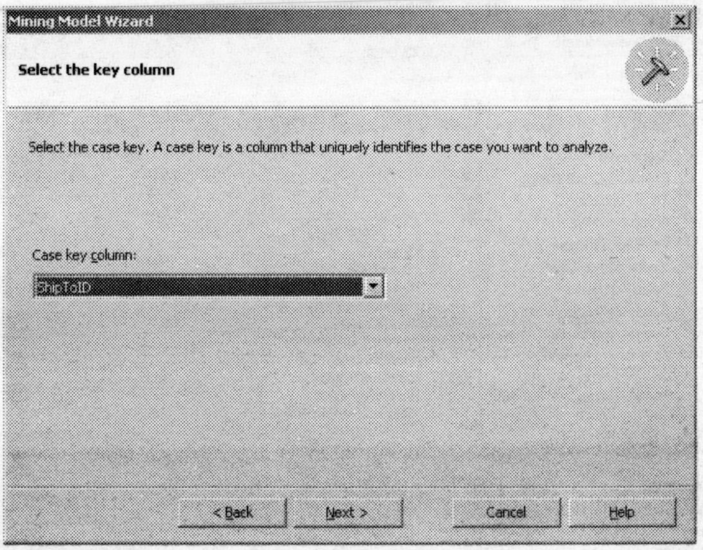

FIGURE 8.14 Selecting the key column.

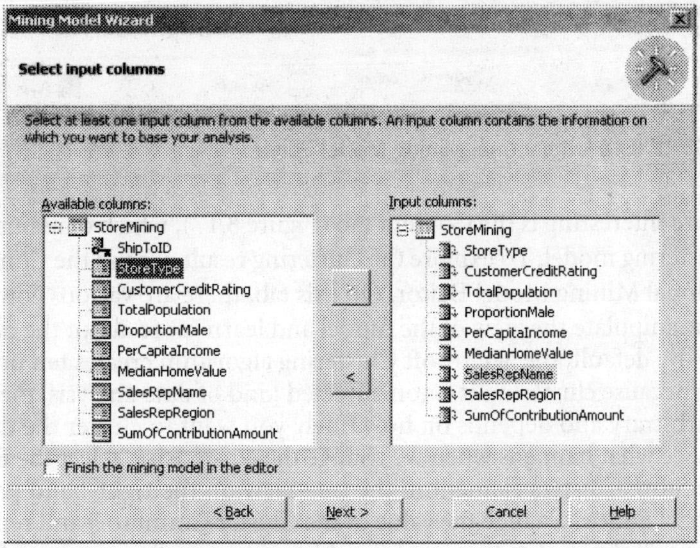

FIGURE 8.15 Choosing input columns.

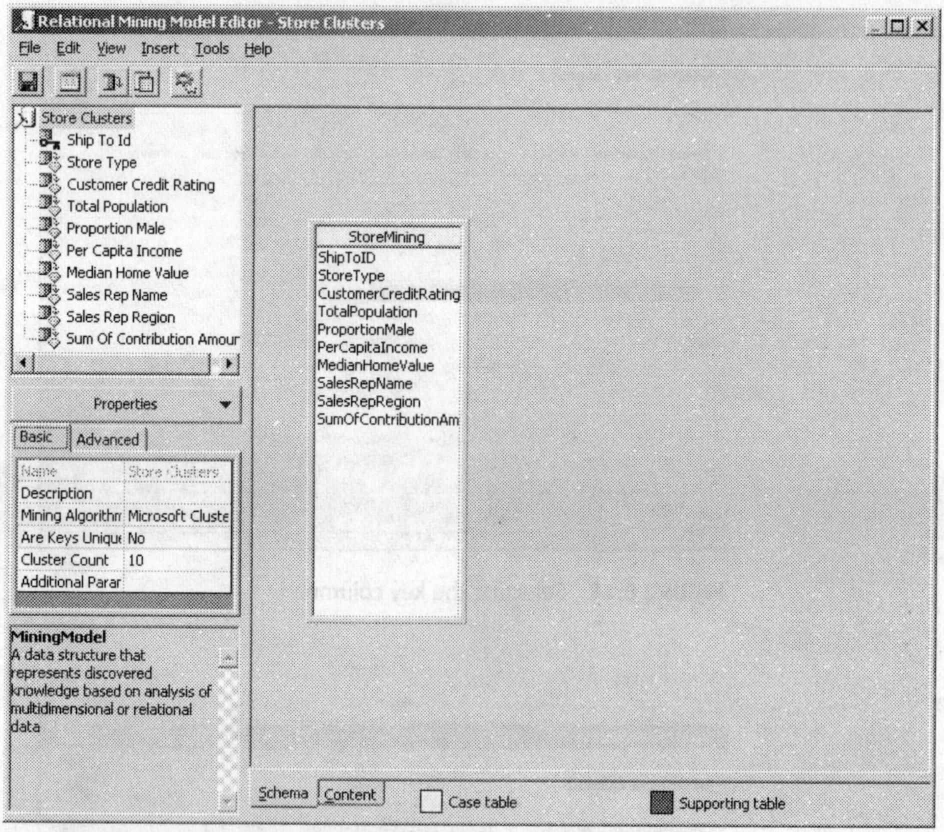

FIGURE 8.16 Relational Mining Model Editor.

more interesting is the Content tab (Figure 8.17), which contains the results of our clustering model. To explore the clustering result, we use the Content tab of the Relational Mining Model Editor. On this tab, there are various controls that allow us to manipulate the view of the model and learn more about the data.

By default, the Microsoft Clustering algorithm creates ten nodes for the analysis. Because clustering is a non-directed kind of data analysis, the number of nodes is arbitrary and depends on how finely you want to cluster the data that you have. To see what happens when we change the cluster size, select the Basic Properties of the Store Clusters element in the tree-view on the right-hand pane of the Mining Model Editor. Change the value of the Cluster Count to 5 and reprocess the model. This will show what the data looks like with a smaller number of clusters.

You can continue to refine the model in the Mining Model Editor until you are satisfied with the results. While the Mining Model Editor is a nice tool, you might also want to construct a more specialized application for managing your data mining models.

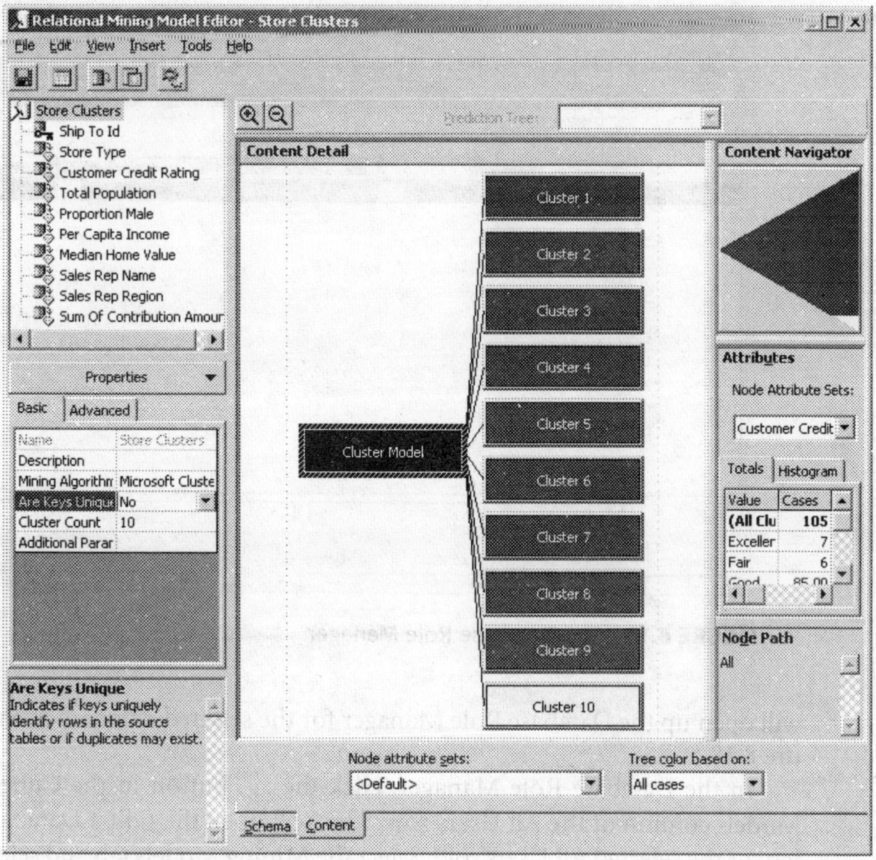

FIGURE 8.17 The Content of the Mining model.

Example

The sample application for this chapter will use XMLA to work with data-mining models in Analysis Services. The application is built on the same structure we saw in Chapter 5, but with a different interface designed to allow manipulation of mining models instead of OLAP objects. Many of the same principles apply and we won't rehash the general discussion of XMLA, but we will cover the areas of the code that are different or specialized for data mining.

Before running the application, you will need to make sure that you have permissions properly configured in Analysis Services to allow access to mining models via XMLA. To manage the security settings for the mining models, go into the Analysis Manager and select the database that you would like to work with. After selecting the database, select Action . . . Manage Roles from the main menu. This

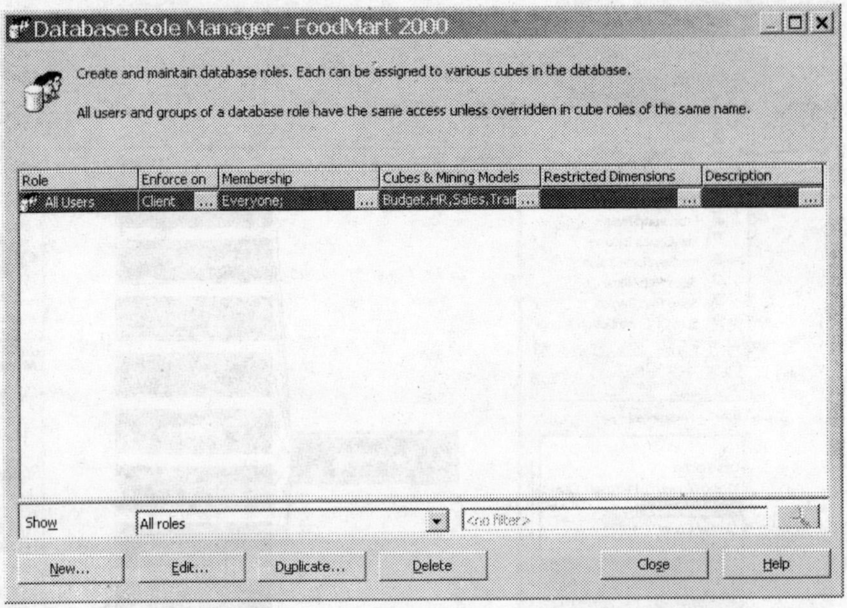

FIGURE 8.18 The Database Role Manager.

will open up the Database Role Manager for the selected database as shown in Figure 8.18.

In the Database Role Manager, click the . . . button in the Cubes & Mining Models column of the All Users row. This will open the Edit a Database Role dialog for the selected All Users role. Select the Mining Models tab and select the check boxes next to the mining models that you want to use via XMLA, as shown in Figure 8.19. Close the Edit a Database Role dialog and the Database Role Manager and you are ready to run the sample DMXMLA application.

Before we cover the code involved in accessing data mining models via XMLA, let's examine the XML results that are returned from a data-mining query via XMLA. We will run a data-mining `SELECT` query from the FoodMart 2000 sample database:

```
SELECT *
FROM [Customer Pattern Discovery].CONTENT
```

This query will return all columns from the `MINING_MODEL_CONTENT` schema. `MINING_MODEL_CONTENT` contains all of the information you would need to browse the mining model. If you want to query for specific columns in the schema, you can specify them in the query. For example, the following code returns the display caption for each node in the model:

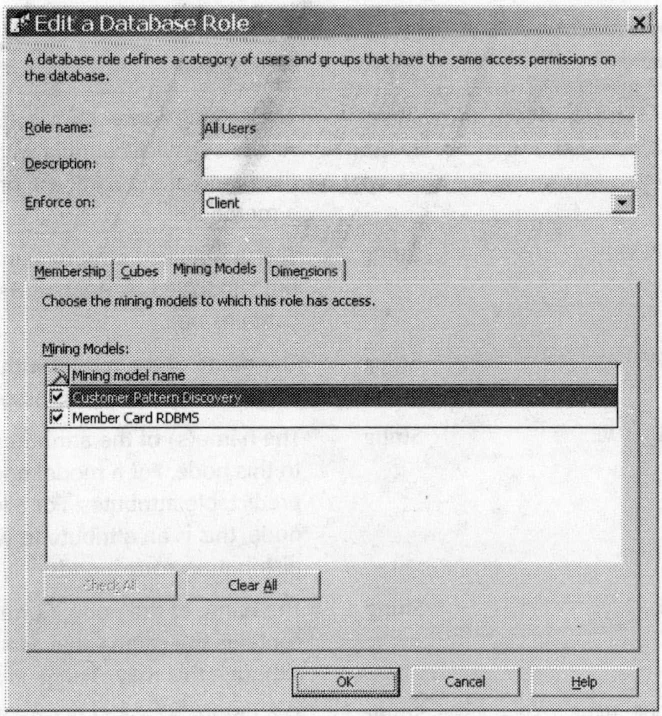

FIGURE 8.19 The Edit a Database Role dialog.

```
SELECT MSOLAP_NODE_SHORT_CAPTION
FROM [Customer Pattern Discovery].CONTENT
```

You can run SELECT on any of the elements in the MINING_MODEL_CONTENT schema. The entire MINING_MODEL_CONTENT schema appears in Table 8.5.

In addition to returning MINING_MODEL_CONTENT data, a query can return data from other schemas as well to get different information about the mining model. To return information from the MINING_MODEL_CONTENT_PMML structure, you can use a query such as the following:

```
SELECT *
FROM [Customer Pattern Discovery].PMML
```

As we discussed previously, Predictive Model Markup Language (PMML) is an XML-based markup language used to describe statistical and data-mining models. The columns returned by a query on the MINING_MODEL_CONTENT_PMML structure appear in Table 8.6.

TABLE 8.5 MINING_MODEL_CONTENT schema.

Column name	***Type***	***Description***
MODEL_CATALOG	String	The catalog name. Microsoft SQL Server2000 Analysis Services populates this column with the name of the database of which the model is a member.
MODEL_SCHEMA	String	The unqualified schema name. This column is not supported by Analysis Services; it always contains null.
MODEL_NAME	String	The name of the model with which the content described by this row is associated
ATTRIBUTE_NAME	String	The name(s) of the attribute(s) corresponding to this node. For a model node, this is a list of predictable attributes. For a leaf distribution node, this is an attribute to which the distribution corresponds.
NODE_NAME	String	The name of the node. Currently, this column contains the same value as NODE_UNIQUE_NAME, although this may change in future releases.
NODE_UNIQUE_NAME	String	The unique name of the node
NODE_TYPE	Integer	The type of the node. It can be one of the following values: • DM_NODE_TYPE_MODEL • DM_NODE_TYPE_TREE • DM_NODE_TYPE_INTERIOR • DM_NODE_TYPE_DISTRIBUTION • DM_NODE_TYPE_CLUSTER • DM_NODE_TYPE_UNKNOWN
NODE_GUID	GUID	The node GUID. This column is not supported by Analysis Services; it always contains null.
NODE_CAPTION	String	A label or a caption associated with the node. This property is used primarily for display purposes. If a caption does not exist, the contents of the NODE_NAME column is returned.
CHILDREN_CARDINALITY	Integer	An estimate of the number of children that the node has
PARENT_UNIQUE_NAME	String	The unique name of the node's parent. Null is returned for any nodes at the root level.

TABLE 8.5 *(Continued)*

Column name	Type	Description
NODE_DESCRIPTION	String	A user-friendly description of the node
NODE_RULE	String	An XML description of the rule that is embedded in the node
MARGINAL_RULE	String	An XML description of the rule that is moving to the node from the parent node
NODE_PROBABILITY	Float	The probability associated with this node
MARGINAL_PROBABILITY	Float	The probability of reaching the node from the parent node
NODE_DISTRIBUTION	Table	A table that contains the probability histogram of the node
NODE_SUPPORT	Float	The number of cases that support this node
MSOLAP_MODEL_COLUMN	String	The name of the column from the model definition that this node pertains to
MSOLAP_NODE_SCORE	Float	The score that was computed for this node
MSOLAP_NODE_SHORT_CAPTION	String	A short caption for the node that can be used for display purposes to improve readability

TABLE 8.6 Columns returned by a query on MINING_MODEL_CONTENT_PMML.

Column name	Type	Description
MODEL_CATALOG	String	The catalog name. Microsoft SQL Server 2000 Analysis Services populates this column with the name of the database of which the model is a member.
MODEL_SCHEMA	String	The unqualified schema name. This column is not supported by Analysis Services; it always contains null.
MODEL_NAME	String	Model name. This column cannot contain null.
MODEL_TYPE	String	The model type. It is a provider-specific string. It can be null.
MODEL_GUID	Guid	The GUID that identifies the model. Providers that do not use GUIDs to identify tables return null.
MODEL_PMML	String	An XML representation of the model's content in PMML format
SIZE	Integer	Number of bytes in the XML string

ON THE CD

As with OLAP queries, the results from a data-mining query are returned from the XMLA Web service in an XML format. In the case of a `SELECT` from the content of a mining model, the results contain the `MINING_MODEL_CONTENT` schema in an XML format. The first section of the XML query results contains the root element and the schema that defines the document. For brevity, we have omitted the details of the schema that is returned. If you want to see the entire result set, view the DMXMLA.xml file on the CD-ROM in the Chapter 8 directory.

In general, the results are returned as a series of row elements that specify the contents of the mining model. The next section contains the each of the rows of the results that are returned. We will go through a few of them to illustrate the data returned and the format.

This first section returned contains the name of the catalog and is a header row for the results. As specified earlier in the `MINING_MODEL_CONTENT` schema, the `NODE_TYPE` for this element is a `DM_NODE_TYPE_MODEL` or the root of the mining model.

```
<row>
  <MODEL_CATALOG>FoodMart 2000</MODEL_CATALOG>
  <MODEL_NAME>Customer Pattern Discovery</MODEL_NAME>
  <ATTRIBUTE_NAME />
  <NODE_NAME>0</NODE_NAME>
  <NODE_UNIQUE_NAME>0</NODE_UNIQUE_NAME>
  <NODE_TYPE>1</NODE_TYPE>
  <NODE_CAPTION />
  <CHILDREN_CARDINALITY>1</CHILDREN_CARDINALITY>
  <PARENT_UNIQUE_NAME />
  <NODE_DESCRIPTION />
  <NODE_RULE />
  <MARGINAL_RULE />
  <NODE_SUPPORT>0</NODE_SUPPORT>
  <MSOLAP_MODEL_COLUMN />
  <MSOLAP_NODE_SCORE>0</MSOLAP_NODE_SCORE>
  <MSOLAP_NODE_SHORT_CAPTION />
</row>
```

The next section is representative of the `DM_NODE_TYPE_TREE` rows that are returned. This row contains the results for the top level of the tree with nested distribution elements for the probability distribution of each of the results. This is the same information that is shown in the Attributes window of the Mining Model Editor when you select the root node of the decision tree (shown in Figure 8.20).

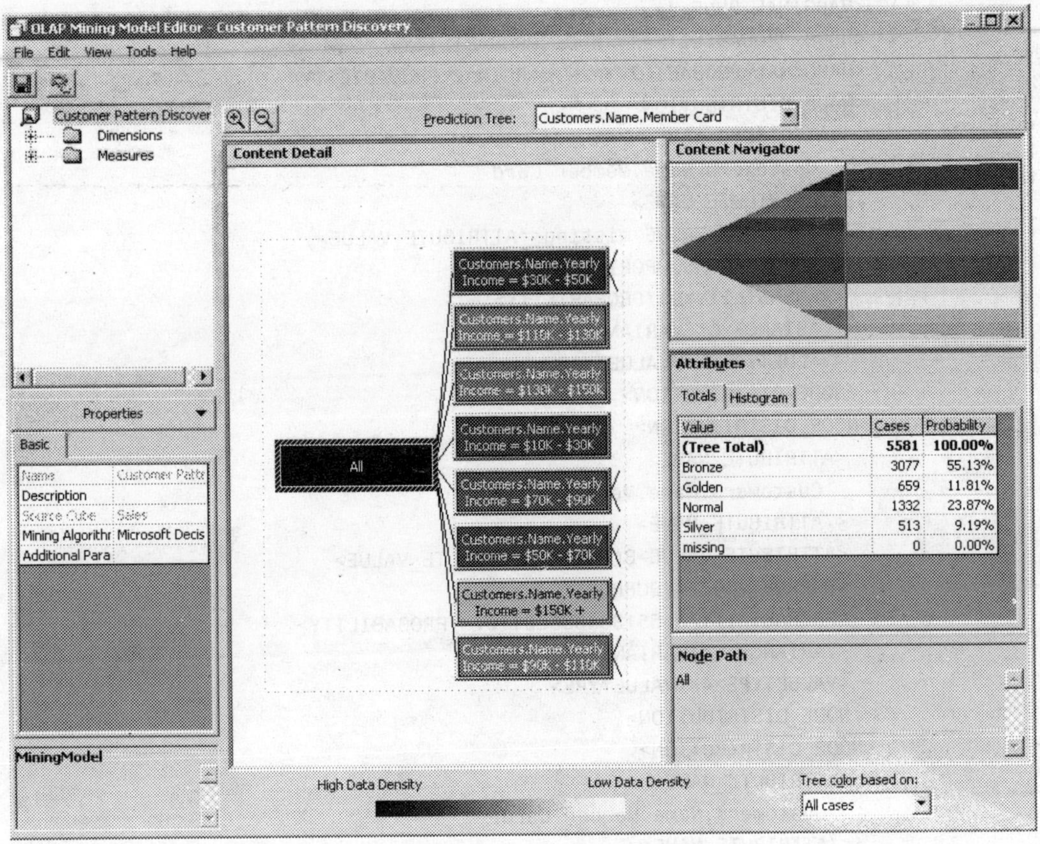

FIGURE 8.20 Root node.

```
<row>
 <MODEL_CATALOG>FoodMart 2000</MODEL_CATALOG>
 <MODEL_NAME>Customer Pattern Discovery</MODEL_NAME>
 <ATTRIBUTE_NAME>
   Customers.Name.Member Card
 </ATTRIBUTE_NAME>
 <NODE_NAME>2147483652</NODE_NAME>
 <NODE_UNIQUE_NAME>2147483652</NODE_UNIQUE_NAME>
 <NODE_TYPE>2</NODE_TYPE>
 <NODE_CAPTION>All</NODE_CAPTION>
 <CHILDREN_CARDINALITY>8</CHILDREN_CARDINALITY>
 <PARENT_UNIQUE_NAME>0</PARENT_UNIQUE_NAME>
 <NODE_DESCRIPTION>All</NODE_DESCRIPTION>
 <NODE_RULE />
```

```
<MARGINAL_RULE />
<NODE_PROBABILITY>1</NODE_PROBABILITY>
<MARGINAL_PROBABILITY>1</MARGINAL_PROBABILITY>
<NODE_DISTRIBUTION>
  <ATTRIBUTE_NAME>
    Customers.Name.Member Card
  </ATTRIBUTE_NAME>
  <ATTRIBUTE_VALUE>missing</ATTRIBUTE_VALUE>
  <SUPPORT>0</SUPPORT>
  <PROBABILITY>0</PROBABILITY>
  <VARIANCE>0</VARIANCE>
  <VALUETYPE>1</VALUETYPE>
</NODE_DISTRIBUTION>
<NODE_DISTRIBUTION>
  <ATTRIBUTE_NAME>
    Customers.Name.Member Card
  </ATTRIBUTE_NAME>
  <ATTRIBUTE_VALUE>Bronze</ATTRIBUTE_VALUE>
  <SUPPORT>3077</SUPPORT>
  <PROBABILITY>0.551334886221107</PROBABILITY>
  <VARIANCE>0</VARIANCE>
  <VALUETYPE>4</VALUETYPE>
</NODE_DISTRIBUTION>
<NODE_DISTRIBUTION>
  <ATTRIBUTE_NAME>
    Customers.Name.Member Card
  </ATTRIBUTE_NAME>
  <ATTRIBUTE_VALUE>Golden</ATTRIBUTE_VALUE>
  <SUPPORT>659</SUPPORT>
  <PROBABILITY>0.118079197276474</PROBABILITY>
  <VARIANCE>0</VARIANCE>
  <VALUETYPE>4</VALUETYPE>
  </NODE_DISTRIBUTION>
<NODE_DISTRIBUTION>
  <ATTRIBUTE_NAME>Customers.Name.Member Card</ATTRIBUTE_NAME>
  <ATTRIBUTE_VALUE>Normal</ATTRIBUTE_VALUE>
  <SUPPORT>1332</SUPPORT>
  <PROBABILITY>0.238666905572478</PROBABILITY>
  <VARIANCE>0</VARIANCE>
  <VALUETYPE>4</VALUETYPE>
</NODE_DISTRIBUTION>
<NODE_DISTRIBUTION>
  <ATTRIBUTE_NAME>
    Customers.Name.Member Card
```

```
    </ATTRIBUTE_NAME>
    <ATTRIBUTE_VALUE>Silver</ATTRIBUTE_VALUE>
    <SUPPORT>513</SUPPORT>
    <PROBABILITY>9.19190109299409E-02</PROBABILITY>
    <VARIANCE>0</VARIANCE>
    <VALUETYPE>4</VALUETYPE>
  </NODE_DISTRIBUTION>
  <NODE_SUPPORT>5581</NODE_SUPPORT>
  <MSOLAP_MODEL_COLUMN>
    Customers.Name.Member Card
  </MSOLAP_MODEL_COLUMN>
  <MSOLAP_NODE_SCORE>1948.401692055</MSOLAP_NODE_SCORE>
  <MSOLAP_NODE_SHORT_CAPTION>All</MSOLAP_NODE_SHORT_CAPTION>
</row>
```

The next section contains the row for a tree element directly under the root node for customers with yearly income between $30 and $50K. Like the last element, this node has five child NODE_DISTRIBUTION elements (one for each state of the Member Card attribute). In addition, there is node rule specified that shows how the path of the tree was chosen. The data contained in this section is the same as that presented in the Mining Model Editor in the Attributes section when the "Customers.Name.Yearly Income = $30K– $50K" node is selected in the Content Detail pane, as shown in Figure 8.21.

```
<row>
  <MODEL_CATALOG>FoodMart 2000</MODEL_CATALOG>
  <MODEL_NAME>Customer Pattern Discovery</MODEL_NAME>
  <ATTRIBUTE_NAME>
    Customers.Name.Member Card
  </ATTRIBUTE_NAME>
  <NODE_NAME>002147483652</NODE_NAME>
  <NODE_UNIQUE_NAME>002147483652</NODE_UNIQUE_NAME>
  <NODE_TYPE>3</NODE_TYPE>
  <NODE_CAPTION>
    Customers.Name.Yearly Income = $30K - $50K
  </NODE_CAPTION>
  <CHILDREN_CARDINALITY>2</CHILDREN_CARDINALITY>
  <PARENT_UNIQUE_NAME>2147483652</PARENT_UNIQUE_NAME>
  <NODE_DESCRIPTION>
    Customers.Name.Yearly Income = $30K - $50K
  </NODE_DESCRIPTION>
  <NODE_RULE>
    <predicate op = "eq" value = "$30K - $50K">
```

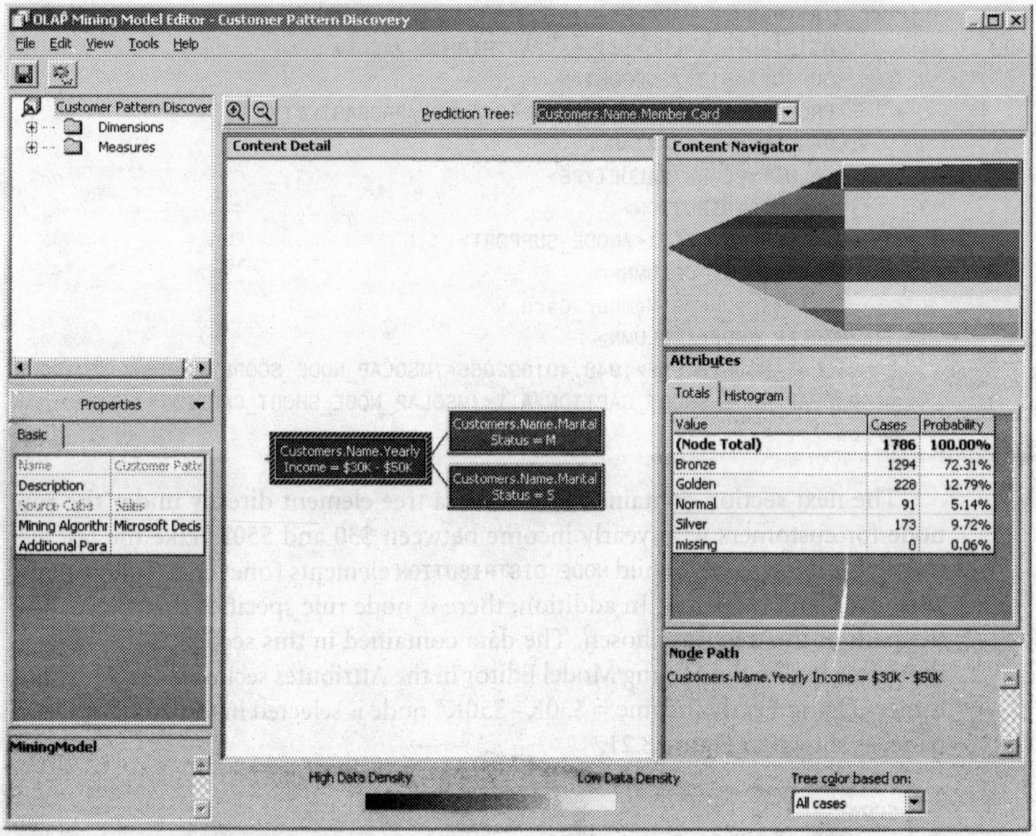

FIGURE 8.21 Content Detail.

```
      <simple-attribute
        name = "Customers.Name.Yearly Income"/>
      </predicate>
    </NODE_RULE>
    <MARGINAL_RULE>
      <predicate op = "eq" value = "$30K - $50K">
      <simple-attribute
        name = "Customers.Name.Yearly Income"/>
      </predicate>
    </MARGINAL_RULE>
    <NODE_PROBABILITY>
      0.320014334348683
    </NODE_PROBABILITY>
    <MARGINAL_PROBABILITY>
     0.320014334348683
```

```
</MARGINAL_PROBABILITY>
<NODE_DISTRIBUTION>
  <ATTRIBUTE_NAME>
    Customers.Name.Member Card
  </ATTRIBUTE_NAME>
  <ATTRIBUTE_VALUE>missing</ATTRIBUTE_VALUE>
  <SUPPORT>0</SUPPORT>
  <PROBABILITY>5.58347292015634E-04</PROBABILITY>
  <VARIANCE>0</VARIANCE>
  <VALUETYPE>1</VALUETYPE>
</NODE_DISTRIBUTION>
<NODE_DISTRIBUTION>
  <ATTRIBUTE_NAME>
    Customers.Name.Member Card
  </ATTRIBUTE_NAME>
  <ATTRIBUTE_VALUE>Bronze</ATTRIBUTE_VALUE>
  <SUPPORT>1294</SUPPORT>
  <PROBABILITY>0.723059743160246</PROBABILITY>
  <VARIANCE>0</VARIANCE>
  <VALUETYPE>4</VALUETYPE>
</NODE_DISTRIBUTION>
<NODE_DISTRIBUTION>
  <ATTRIBUTE_NAME>
    Customers.Name.Member Card
  </ATTRIBUTE_NAME>
  <ATTRIBUTE_VALUE>Golden</ATTRIBUTE_VALUE>
  <SUPPORT>228</SUPPORT>
  <PROBABILITY>0.12786152987158</PROBABILITY>
  <VARIANCE>0</VARIANCE>
  <VALUETYPE>4</VALUETYPE>
</NODE_DISTRIBUTION>
<NODE_DISTRIBUTION>
  <ATTRIBUTE_NAME>
    Customers.Name.Member Card
  </ATTRIBUTE_NAME>
  <ATTRIBUTE_VALUE>Normal</ATTRIBUTE_VALUE>
  <SUPPORT>91</SUPPORT>
  <PROBABILITY>5.13679508654383E-02</PROBABILITY>
  <VARIANCE>0</VARIANCE>
  <VALUETYPE>4</VALUETYPE>
</NODE_DISTRIBUTION>
<NODE_DISTRIBUTION>
  <ATTRIBUTE_NAME>
    Customers.Name.Member Card
```

```
      </ATTRIBUTE_NAME>
      <ATTRIBUTE_VALUE>Silver</ATTRIBUTE_VALUE>
      <SUPPORT>173</SUPPORT>
      <PROBABILITY>9.71524288107203E-02</PROBABILITY>
      <VARIANCE>0</VARIANCE>
      <VALUETYPE>4</VALUETYPE>
    </NODE_DISTRIBUTION>
    <NODE_SUPPORT>1786</NODE_SUPPORT>
    <MSOLAP_MODEL_COLUMN>
      Customers.Name.Member Card
    </MSOLAP_MODEL_COLUMN>
    <MSOLAP_NODE_SCORE>62.3358100489147</MSOLAP_NODE_SCORE>
    <MSOLAP_NODE_SHORT_CAPTION>
      Customers.Name.Yearly Income = $30K - $50K
    </MSOLAP_NODE_SHORT_CAPTION>
  </row>
```

This pattern is repeated for the remaining nodes in the decision tree hierarchy. The following node shows what a two-layer-deep node looks like. Note the use of a compound predicate to get to the node in the tree. The XML is shown with the distribution details removed for brevity.

```
<row>
  <MODEL_CATALOG>FoodMart 2000</MODEL_CATALOG>
  <MODEL_NAME>Customer Pattern Discovery</MODEL_NAME>
  <ATTRIBUTE_NAME>
    Customers.Name.Member Card
  </ATTRIBUTE_NAME>
  <NODE_NAME>00002147483652</NODE_NAME>
  <NODE_UNIQUE_NAME>00002147483652</NODE_UNIQUE_NAME>
  <NODE_TYPE>4</NODE_TYPE>
  <NODE_CAPTION>
    Customers.Name.Marital Status = M
  </NODE_CAPTION>
  <CHILDREN_CARDINALITY>0</CHILDREN_CARDINALITY>
  <PARENT_UNIQUE_NAME>002147483652</PARENT_UNIQUE_NAME>
  <NODE_DESCRIPTION>
    Customers.Name.Marital Status = M and
    Customers.Name.Yearly Income = $30K - $50K
  </NODE_DESCRIPTION>
  <NODE_RULE>
    <compound-predicate op = "and">
    <predicate op = "eq" value = "$30K - $50K">
      <simple-attribute
```

```
        name = "Customers.Name.Yearly Income"/>
    </predicate>
    <predicate op = "eq" value = "M">
      <simple-attribute
        name = "Customers.Name.Marital Status"/>
    </predicate>
    </compound-predicate></NODE_RULE>
  <MARGINAL_RULE>
    <predicate op = "eq" value = "M">
      <simple-attribute
        name = "Customers.Name.Marital Status"/>
    </predicate></MARGINAL_RULE>
  <NODE_PROBABILITY>0.154810965776743</NODE_PROBABILITY>
  <MARGINAL_PROBABILITY>
    0.483762597984323
  </MARGINAL_PROBABILITY>

  <! – Distribution details removed -- >
  ...
   </row>
```

After this node, the pattern repeats itself for all of the remaining nodes in the decision tree. As you can see, the structure of the mining model is reflected in the results returned.

Most of the code used to access data-mining models is similar to the code used in Chapter 5 to access OLAP data via XMLA. The following code shows the `MiningModels` class that contains the collection of mining models in a catalog. Retrieving the collection of mining models is very similar to retrieving the list of OLAP cubes with a few exceptions. To get the OLAP cubes, we have only to specify the `DataSourceInfo` element in the properties for the call to Discover. To retrieve the list, as with Cubes, we call `Discover` and parse the results to create a collection. Also, as with Cubes, we implement an enumerator in the class to make it easier to navigate the collection of models.

```
public class MiningModels : IEnumerable
{
    private ArrayList _miningModels;

    public MiningModels(string xmlaUrl, Catalog catalog)
    {
        // create the container for the catalogs
        _miningModels = new ArrayList();
        // Create the Xml for Analysis proxy class
```

```
MsXmlAnalysis xa = new MsXmlAnalysis();
xa.Url = xmlaUrl;
// create the properties
XmlDocument doc = new XmlDocument();
doc.LoadXml("<PropertyList></PropertyList>");
XmlElement props = doc.DocumentElement;
// need the data source
XmlElement ds = doc.CreateElement("DataSourceInfo");
ds.InnerText = catalog.Datasource.Info;
props.AppendChild(ds);
// and the catalog (which is not required for OLAP)
XmlElement cat = doc.CreateElement("Catalog");
cat.InnerText = catalog.Name;
props.AppendChild(cat);

// create the restrictions
string restrictString =
 String.Format("<MODEL_CATALOG>{0}</MODEL_CATALOG>",
 catalog.Name);
XmlElement restrict =
 XmlaHelper.CreateXmlElement("RestrictionList",
 restrictString);
// call discover on the xmla server
XmlElement xml =
 xa.Discover("DMSCHEMA_MINING_MODELS", restrict,
 props);
// parse the xml and iterate through each row
XPathNavigator nav =
 xml.CreateNavigator();
XPathNodeIterator iterator =
 nav.SelectChildren("row",
 "urn:schemas-microsoft-com:xml-analysis:rowset");
while (iterator.MoveNext())
{
    string name;
    string description;
    string serviceName;

    name = XmlaHelper.GetElements("MODEL_NAME",
     iterator);
    description =
     XmlaHelper.GetElements("DESCRIPTION",
     iterator);
    serviceName =
     XmlaHelper.GetElements("SERVICE_NAME",
```

```
            iterator);

            Model model = new Model(name, description,
             serviceName, catalog);
            _miningModels.Add(model);

        }
    }

    public IEnumerator GetEnumerator()
    {
        return new ModelsEnumerator(this);
    }

    private class ModelsEnumerator : IEnumerator
    {
        private int _position = -1;
        private MiningModels _cs;

        public ModelsEnumerator(MiningModels cs)
        {
            this._cs = cs;
        }

        public bool MoveNext()
        {
            if (_position < _cs._miningModels.Count - 1)
            {
                _position++;
                return true;
            }
            else
            {
                return false;
            }
        }

        public void Reset()
        {
            _position = -1;
        }

        public object Current
        {
```

```
                get
                {
                    return _cs._miningModels[_position];
                }
            }
        }
    }
```

The `Model` class is very similar to the `Cube` class in that it is in the top-level collection of elements. However, it is very different in that it is also the bottom layer of the hierarchy. Mining models are much flatter than OLAP cubes.

```
public class Model
    {
        private string _name;
        private string _description;
        private Catalog _catalog;
        private string _serviceName;

        public Model(string name,
          string description,
          string serviceName,
          Catalog catalog)
        {
            _name = name;
            _description = description;
            _serviceName = serviceName;
            _catalog = catalog;
        }

        public override string ToString()
        {
            return Name;
        }

        public string Name
        {
        get
            {
                return _name;
            }
        }
```

```
        public string Description
        {
            get
            {
                return _description;
            }
        }

        public string ServiceName
        {
            get
            {
                return _serviceName;
            }
        }

        public Catalog Catalog
        {
            get
            {
                return _catalog;
            }
        }

    }
```

The last distinct element of XMLA code that deals specifically with mining models is the `DMDataSet`. This class is analogous to the `MDDataSet` class that contains the results of an OLAP query. The biggest difference is in the way the much flatter `DMDataSet` is constructed from the XML returned by the call to `Execute`. In the `MDDataSet`, the returned XML is traversed and parsed into the proper hierarchical structure. For `DMDataSet`, the XML is simply translated into a flattened `DataSet`. A note about the schema used for XMLA results is that, even for the flat results returned by data mining queries, it is not compatible with the ADO.NET `DataSet`. However, we can still read the XML data into a `DataSet` by using the `XmlReadMode.InferSchema` read mode. This flag lets the `DataSet` infer the schema from the structure of the data that is provided and ignore the incompatible schema that is provided with the query results via XMLA. As with `MDDataSet`, the exposed `DataSet` property in `DMDataSet` can be used to bind to controls for display.

```
public class DMDataSet
{
    XmlElement _xml;
```

```
DataSet _ds;

public DMDataSet(Catalog catalog, String sql)
{
    // Create the Xml for Analysis proxy class
    MsXmlAnalysis xa = new MsXmlAnalysis();
    xa.Url = catalog.Datasource.Url;
    // create the properties
    string propList =
     String.Format("<DataSourceInfo>{0}</DataSourceInfo>
     <Catalog>{1}</Catalog><Format>Tabular</Format>",
     catalog.Datasource.Info, catalog.Name);
    XmlElement props =
     XmlaHelper.CreateXmlElement("PropertyList",
     propList);
    XmlElement query =
     XmlaHelper.CreateXmlElement("Statement", sql);
    // call execute on the xmla server
    _xml = xa.Execute(query, props);

    // check if we have results
    if (_xml == null) return;

    // put the xml into a string reader
    System.IO.StringReader sr =
     new System.IO.StringReader(_xml.OuterXml);
    _ds = new DataSet();
    // read the xml and infer the schema
    _ds.ReadXml(sr, XmlReadMode.InferSchema);
}

public DataSet DataSet
{
    get
    {
        return _ds;
    }
}
}
```

ON THE CD

The sample application shows how we use XMLA to browse and access data-mining models. You can extend this application to do any number of things with mining models via XMLA. The complete code for the application is provided on the CD-ROM in the Chapter 8\DMXMLA directory and you can examine and compile all of the code or modify it to better suit your data-mining requirements.

SUMMARY

As we have seen in this chapter, data mining is a process that can be used to discover patterns and relationships in data. We began with some general coverage of data mining, establishing the utility and importance of data mining in today's business conditions. With the explosion in the amount of data generated and stored by today's businesses, data mining is an important part of a complete business intelligence platform. Data mining can be used to identify areas that can be more fully explored with traditional reporting and with OLAP tools by your business analysts.

Some data-mining models can also generate predictive models that can be used directly to forecast business events. We discussed three data mining techniques: decision trees, clustering, and neural networks. Each of these methods has its strengths and weaknesses. It can be very useful to try a few different models to see which one works best in the given situation. Regardless of the technique applied, there are four essential steps in producing a mining model: understand the business problem, define the model, train and evaluate the model, and use the model for predictions.

We discussed the importance of having clean data, some of the characteristics of good data for mining, and whether or not data mining is a good solution for you.

After our general discussion of data mining, we turned to cover data mining with Microsoft Analysis Services including a discussion of OLE DB for Data Mining and its role in bringing data mining into the mainstream. We covered the specifics of how to create a mining model using Analysis Services and went through some examples of using the Analysis Server tools.

END NOTES AND REFERENCES

1. Lyman, P., and Varian, H. R., 2000, "How Much Information?" Available online at *http://www.sims.berkeley.edu/how-much-info/* (7/7/2003).
2. Callinan, Patrick, "Data Mining Thrives in eCommerce," Forrester Research, July 24, 2001. Available online at *http://www.forrester.com* (7/15/2003).
3. Soni, Sanjayi; Tang, Zhaohui; and Yang, Jim, "Performance Study of Microsoft Data Mining Algorithms," Microsoft Corporation, 2001. Available online at *www.microsoft.com/sql/evaluation/ compare/AnalysisDM.doc* (7/19/2003).

4. Tang, Zhaohui, and Kim, Pyungchul, "Building Data Mining Solutions with SQL Server 2000," Microsoft Corporation. Available online at *http://www.dmreview.com/whitepaper/wid292.pdf* (7/19/2003)

Deidman, Claude, *Data Mining with Microsoft SQL Server 2000 Technical Reference*, MS Press, 2001.

deVille, Barry, *Microsoft Data Mining: Integrated Business Intelligence for e-Commerce and Knowledge Management*, Butterworth-Heinemann, 2001.

Han, Jiawei, and Kamber, Micheline, *Data Mining: Concepts and Techniques*, Morgan Kaufmann Publishers, 2000.

9 Analytic Applications

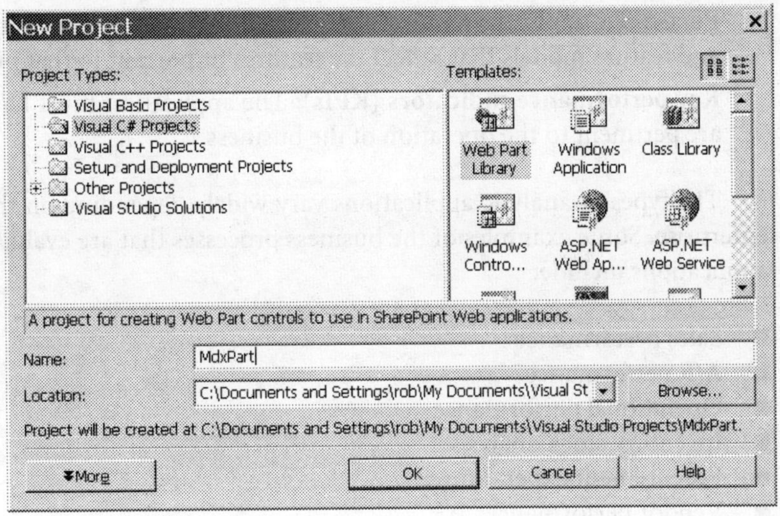

In today's fast-changing business environment, receiving reports is just not enough. Even with the sophisticated analyses made possible with OLAP and data mining, it is critical to be able to take the next step and convert the information into action. There is vast potential in the terabytes of information that are stored in the enterprise today. Using all of this data effectively is where *analytic applications* come in. Built on a more generic business intelligence platform, an analytic application is targeted at a specific business process such as accounts receivable or inventory management. An analytic application, based on the Data Warehousing Institute's definition, is a customized program that provides for the access and analysis of data pertinent to a business process, and enables that information to be acted upon.[1]

The analytics being referred to in the name analytic applications is a very broad term, with almost as many definitions as there are vendors selling analytic applications. Analytics encompass everything from simple summarization and exploration of OLAP data to complex data-mining algorithms. For our purposes, we will assume the definition of analytics to mean mathematical or statistical operations on data to facilitate business action.

An analytic application must be more than just a collection of related reports. An analytic application is focused on the application of analytics to improve a business process, not merely reporting the facts. Most analytic applications meet the following requirements:

Analysis: The capability to apply techniques that extend beyond simple summaries and OLAP drill downs.

Focus: The application must be organized around a specific business problem and feature models that reflect the features important to that problem.

Key performance indicators (KPIs): The application must have metrics that are pertinent to the operation of the business.

The types of analytic applications vary widely depending on the needs of the enterprise. Some examples of the business processes that are evaluated by analytic applications include:

- Sales performance
- A/R performance
- Operational performance
- Inventory stock analysis
- Procurement expenditure
- Vendor performance
- Production time-to-delivery analysis

Analytic applications are different from run-of-the-mill business applications. To develop an analytic application successfully, you need to adhere to some design rules that account for these differences and maximize your chances of success. The three areas that must be covered are:

- Analytic domain characterization
- Integration with multidimensional databases
- Report organization and development

It is possible to build analytic applications for a variety of analytical domains. In general we can classify the domains into the following categories:

- Process
- Issue
- Function

An example of a business process domain application would be a sales force automation application. A business issue application might address vendor performance. What these two have in common is that their scope extends across traditional functional business departments. The main difference is that a process application is intended to facilitate a certain business process while an issue application is usually built in response to a pressing business issue that needs to be managed in a specific way. A functional analytic application addresses a more traditional line of business such as finance or marketing. These categories aren't necessarily mutually exclusive, but to keep the application understandable to users, most analytical applications tend to limit their focus.

There are a few critical success factors that can be observed in analytical applications. Integration with the multidimensional architecture in the data warehouse is an essential element of successful analytic application architecture. Ideally, the application should be designed to be robust in the face of missing data elements. A modular architecture can be a huge asset in making an analytic application flexible in the face of business changes. Simple relationships among the data further reduce the brittleness of an analytical application by reducing the dependence on a very specific data structure. Of course, making the application as independent as possible from a physical database schema is important. If you are building analytical applications that might be used across different branches or operating units of a business, a focus on horizontal business areas makes the application much more useful as a starting point for applications developed later. Lastly, the best analytical applications are designed to be very user friendly.

As we discussed in Chapter 7, reporting is a vital part of any business intelligence framework, and it is no less important in an analytic application. Although an analytic application will consist of more than a set of interrelated reports, it is crucial for the reports to be well conceived and implemented. An analytic application should provide an organized report library that groups the reports into different areas of analysis and limits the overlap among reports. These reports should be customizable by the user to allow flexibility from the standard baseline reporting.

Although some analytics are focused on understanding the past, much of the activity involved in analytics is centered on creating predictions. For example, what would happen if you raised prices by 5% across the board? How many customers would you be likely to lose? What would the revenue impact be? What is the current rate of customer churn, the rate at which customers come and go? Although it is very useful to use analytics to better understand the past, the real value comes when you can use the data that you have gathered to predict the future and act on it. One reason people don't use analytics as well as they could is that they don't have systems that can respond to predictions by changing business activities dynamically. To use a phrase coined by Bill Gates, you need a Digital Nervous System in order to respond to the stimulus provided by analytic applications and flex your business muscles.

Analytic applications have become increasingly important in recent years and will continue to be a growing part of the information technology landscape. Now that a substantial portion of firms have already deployed operational systems, implementations of business intelligence software and analytic applications are outpacing deployments of traditional software packages such as ERP and CRM. Over 44 percent of firms surveyed reported that they are considering a purchase of an analytical application in 2003 according to Forrester Research.[2] Successful companies have been deploying analytic applications to use their information to the fullest and give them a competitive edge. In effect, many of these companies are run with an experimental mindset. The management will make a business hypothesis followed by execution of a pilot program, and then analyze the results to see how well the program has worked. Turning ideas into profits is what business analytics is all about.

STEPS FOR ANALYTIC APPLICATIONS

One of the first decisions to be made with respect to creating an analytic application is whether you should build your own or buy one off the shelf. To make an intelligent decision on this, you need to understand the requirements very well. The focus in this book is on building your own analytic applications, but you would be remiss if you simply assumed that this is the proper path for you and your business. Make a careful assessment of what you are trying to accomplish with your analytic application and evaluate what vendors have to offer that will meet your needs. Even if you decide that building is a better option for your situation, evaluating vendors will encourage you to understand the requirements better before you start to build.

One of the biggest difficulties of an analytic application is getting the data. This should sound familiar by now, since getting solid data is at the core of the entire business intelligence platform. Also unsurprising is that one of the best places to retrieve the data is from your data warehouse. Because the data in the data warehouse has already undergone ETL and data cleansing, it should be in very good shape to use in an analytic application. However, you might still need to do more transformation on the data in the data warehouse to use it effectively in an analytic application. For example, transforming sales data using a logarithm will yield results in terms of growth percentages. Also, data may need to be deseasonalized before using a regression technique.

You need to form a team of the right players to succeed with an analytic application. You need to have people with analytic expertise, business expertise, and database knowledge, as well as application development skills. Of these, strong business understanding is the most important. If you create the most technically adept analytic application in the history of the world and it doesn't solve a real business problem, you have failed. But, the other skills are necessary as well. If you are using advanced statistical techniques, you need to be sure that they are being applied properly, otherwise you might get misleading results. If you don't have database knowledge and an understanding of what information is available in your data warehouse, you might end up doing a lot of work that has already been done or using data in an incorrect context. Lastly, if you don't have strong development skills on your team, you will probably not end up with a flexible and reliable application.

Getting a Return

A big pitfall to analytic applications is measuring the return on investment (ROI) and making sure that you are getting the highest possible. The application has to be used in order to save money, so one of the keys to a successful project is to make sure that users are actively involved in the success of the application. Only in rare cases will the application be able to save money without being fully utilized.

One problem is that applications are rolled out without user involvement. If users are not involved in an analytic application from the beginning, it might be difficult to get them interested after it is deployed. In most companies today, people are very busy and won't make the time to learn a new application that doesn't impact them directly. Getting executive support is vital in getting users to actually use the applications that are deployed.

Training is also vital to the success of an analytic application. The new application will represent a new way of doing things, and if users are not equipped with the knowledge on how to use the application they will not be able to get the most out of it. In some cases, they may even push back against the application if they perceive it as a threat to "the way we do things around here." In addition, training will help users understand the application and may turn them from skeptics into supporters.

To maximize the appeal of your analytic application to its users, you will need to pay careful attention to usability concerns. Although usability is vital for any application, the complexity of analytic applications can be daunting to even sophisticated users. Making sure that presentation of information and options is as clear as possible is paramount to the acceptance and success of your analytic application.

To maximize the ROI, you should also make sure that you have the right number of software licenses available for your audience. Many companies buy too many seat licenses in anticipation of a peak usage that rarely, if ever, occurs. On the other end of the spectrum, you want to avoid potential liabilities from being short of valid software licenses. For an analytic application that has broad distribution through a company, especially using intranet technologies, you want to consider other licensing models, such as per CPU or concurrent user, that will allow you to make sure that you have your bases covered without buying too much capacity.

Despite your best efforts to maximize ROI, it is still difficult to measure the benefits of an application. A part of your requirements-gathering effort should be devoted towards discovering the success criteria for the application and designing a mechanism to be used to collect and report this information. Unless you have very specific KPIs and goals that can be directly attributed to use of the analytic application, disentangling the benefits from an analytic application from background noise can be impossible. Measures such as usage levels, user satisfaction, and productivity should be included in your evaluation of an analytic application in addition to the purely financial payback of better decision making.

The team responsible for implementing an analytic application should have a direct relationship with the business unit it is assisting. A close tie helps make sure that the analytic application is tightly focused on providing real value to the business unit. Without that bond, there is a chance that the application will not be viewed within the business unit as "theirs," and acceptance may suffer. On the other side of the relationship, if the analytic group is perceived to be on the same team as the business people, they will be able to gather requirements more effectively and get more cooperation throughout the project lifecycle.

Digital Dashboards

An excellent way to present analytic applications to users is through a digital dashboard. A *digital dashboard* is a presentation of information that functions much as the dashboard of an automobile. An automobile dashboard presents just the data most pertinent to operating an automobile, such as speed, fuel level, and engine temperature. Like an automobile dashboard, a digital dashboard is designed to be easy to read and understand. However, unlike an automobile dashboard, a digital dashboard can be modified for particular needs.

A digital dashboard is a collection of reports and performance indicators. Usually delivered in a browser-based interface, a dashboard allows users to navigate from a high level KPI metric to the underlying causes to understand the origins and meaning of the KPI. Decision makers often want to focus on exceptions and be able to identify and understand causes of the exceptions. In addition, definitions and relationships between KPIs should be available to help decision makers understand the total impact of a deviation in expected performance.

However, dashboards go only so deep. The display of top-level KPIs provides only a superficial view of the state of the enterprise. The real power of a dashboard is that it can be connected to an analytical application to allow drilling down into the data. It is only through understanding the underlying data and processes that the true state of the business process can be seen.

MICROSOFT SHAREPOINT

A .NET technology for presenting digital dashboards is incorporated into Microsoft SharePoint technologies. As the name implies, SharePoint is designed to create a collaborative workspace. There are two components of SharePoint: Windows® SharePoint™ Services and SharePoint Portal Server. Our focus in this chapter is on SharePoint Services. We will cover the capabilities of SharePoint Portal Server only briefly.

Windows SharePoint Services

Windows SharePoint Services, a component of Microsoft Windows Server 2003, offers the capability of creating sites for team collaboration. SharePoint Services is designed to create a shared file system that can be used to work together on documents, tasks, and other sorts of information. You can put event calendars, contacts, links, discussions, issues lists, and other pertinent team material in a SharePoint site. Users can configure alerts to send them an e-mail notification when changes to files or folders they are interested in occur. The basic idea is to create a collaboration space, not simply a shared file repository. SharePoint Services provides document storage with versioning, check-in and check-out, custom metadata, and personalized views.

It is designed to be easy to deploy and administer. You can grant users the privilege to control site membership, monitor usage, and moderate content. Templates can be created, allowing users to share solutions developed by others, which reduces duplication of effort. Even though SharePoint services delegates control of site content to users, an administrator can still set limitations on the quantity of information stored and how long it will be stored, and limit the types of files that can be posted to a site.

SharePoint Services is also a platform for application development. SharePoint Sites are based on ASP.NET and can be extended using the .NET Framework. The SharePoint Services object model can be used to create custom applications that take advantage of the SharePoint platform. Users can add Web parts to their pages to customize the sites to their needs, and developers can build new Web parts that can be added as content to a site. Web parts are building blocks for creating modular Web sites and are one of the key features of SharePoint. Web parts enable non-programmers to create personalized interfaces that contain information that they want to see, and configure it in the way they want to see it. So, for example, a user should be able to assemble a personal interface that contains stock quotes of interest, the local weather report, and their daily calendar, as well as KPIs of interest to them. We will discuss Web parts in more detail in a later section.

SharePoint Portal Server 2003

SharePoint Portal Server builds on the capabilities of Windows SharePoint Services by connecting these sites together to facilitate more efficient information sharing across the enterprise. While Windows SharePoint Services is targeted at creating places for teams to collaborate, SharePoint Portal Server is designed to connect things together to create a smarter organization.

Microsoft designed SharePoint Portal Server with three goals at the forefront: personalization, integration, and collaboration. Personalization allows information workers and site managers to create personal sites with a search function, audience targeting, and, of course, categorization of subject matter. The audience-targeting feature can be based on virtually any criteria, including the audience's role in the organization, or membership in teams, security groups, or other entities.

SharePoint Portal Server uses SharePoint sites to create customized pages for individuals, information, and organizations. These features are specific to SharePoint Portal, but they reuse Web parts and document libraries from the SharePoint Services platform.

The integration of Windows SharePoint Services sites provides a seamless view of information that may have been scattered across multiple intranet sites. This organization provides a much easier way to discover and reuse information across a business. The collaboration components of SharePoint Portal allow people to connect and communicate with each other. Microsoft SharePoint Portal Server 2003 allows the integration of information from various systems into one location—a portal. This portal can be integrated with other applications through single sign-on and application integration capabilities. SharePoint provides deployment and management tools to keep operational costs to a minimum.

ASP.NET CONTROLS

To build Web parts, you need to understand ASP.NET controls. We discussed ASP.NET in Chapter 7, so you might want to refer back to that chapter or one of the ASP.NET references listed at the end of that chapter for background information.

There are two kinds of controls available in ASP.NET: HTML controls and Web controls. The classes for HTML controls are in the System.Web.UI.HtmlControls namespace. An HTML control derives from the System.Web.UI.HtmlControls.HtmlControl class.

HTML Controls

An HTML control is created by adding a `RunAt="server"` property to HTML tags. For example,

```
<button id="myButton" runat="server">
```

creates an instance of the `HtmlButton` class. You could then access the button in the ASP.NET code-behind page by using the `id`. So, for example, if you wanted to change the button programmatically, you could use the following C# code in the code-behind page:

```
myButton.InnerHTML = "Please press this button";
```

The hierarchy of the System.Web.UI.HtmlControls namespace is presented in Figure 9.1, and a mapping of HTML tags to their corresponding HTML controls is listed in Table 9.1.

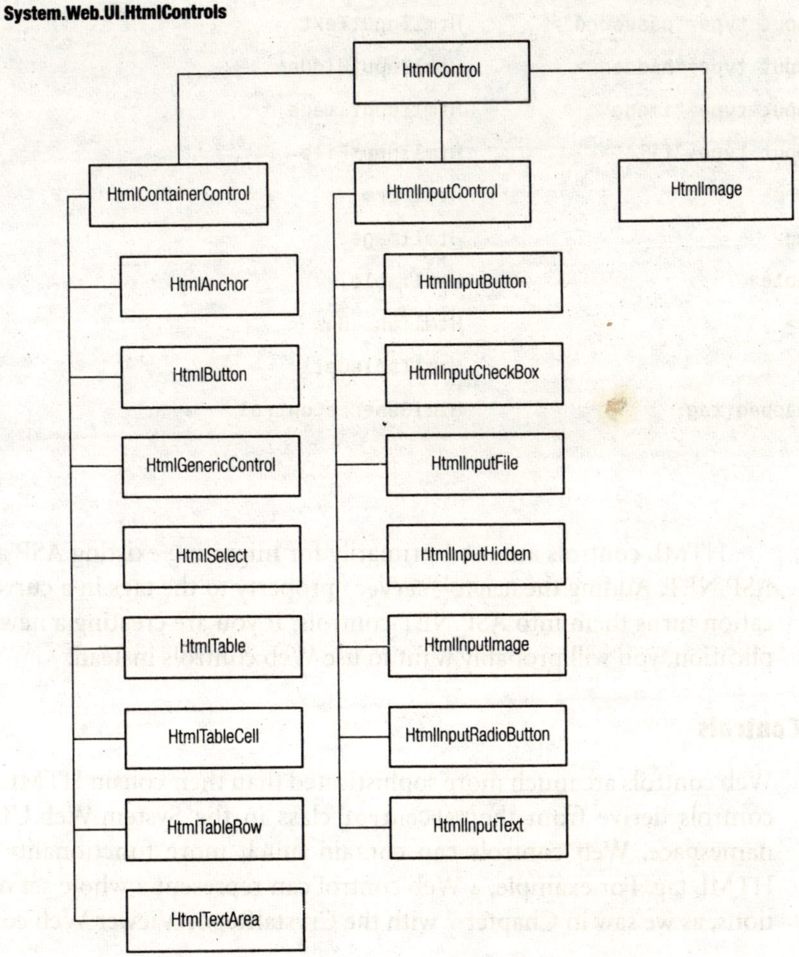

FIGURE 9.1 The System.Web.UI.HtmlControls hierarchy.

TABLE 9.1 HTML tags and their corresponding HTML controls.

HTML Tag	*HTML Control*
<a>	HtmlAnchor
<button>	HtmlButton
<select>	HtmlSelect
<textarea>	HtmlTextArea
<input type="button">	HtmlInputButton
<input type="check">	HtmlInputCheckBox
<input type="radio">	HtmlInputRadioButton
<input type="text">	HtmlInputText
<input type="password">	HtmlInputText
<input type="hidden">	HtmlInputHidden
<input type="image">	HtmlInputImage
<input type="file">	HtmlInputFile
<form>	HtmlForm
<img>	HtmlImage
<table>	HtmlTable
<tr>	HtmlTableRow
<td>	HtmlTableCell
Unmapped tag	HtmlGenericControl

HTML controls are used primarily for migrating existing ASP applications to ASP.NET. Adding the `RunAt="server"` property to the tags in a current ASP application turns them into ASP.NET controls. If you are creating a new ASP.NET application, you will probably want to use Web controls instead.

Web Controls

Web controls are much more sophisticated than their cousin HTML controls. Web controls derive from the `WebControl` class in the System.Web.UI.WebControls namespace. Web controls can contain much more functionality than a single HTML tag. For example, a Web control can represent a whole set of user interactions, as we saw in Chapter 7 with the CrystalReportViewer Web control. In addition to encapsulating an entire set of interactions, Web controls can render themselves to adapt to the capabilities of the Web browser that is currently displaying them. For example, if a control that requires client-side script is rendered on a browser that does not support script, the control will adapt itself to use server processing via roundtrips. The class hierarchy of the System.Web.UI.WebControls namespace is presented in Figure 9.2.

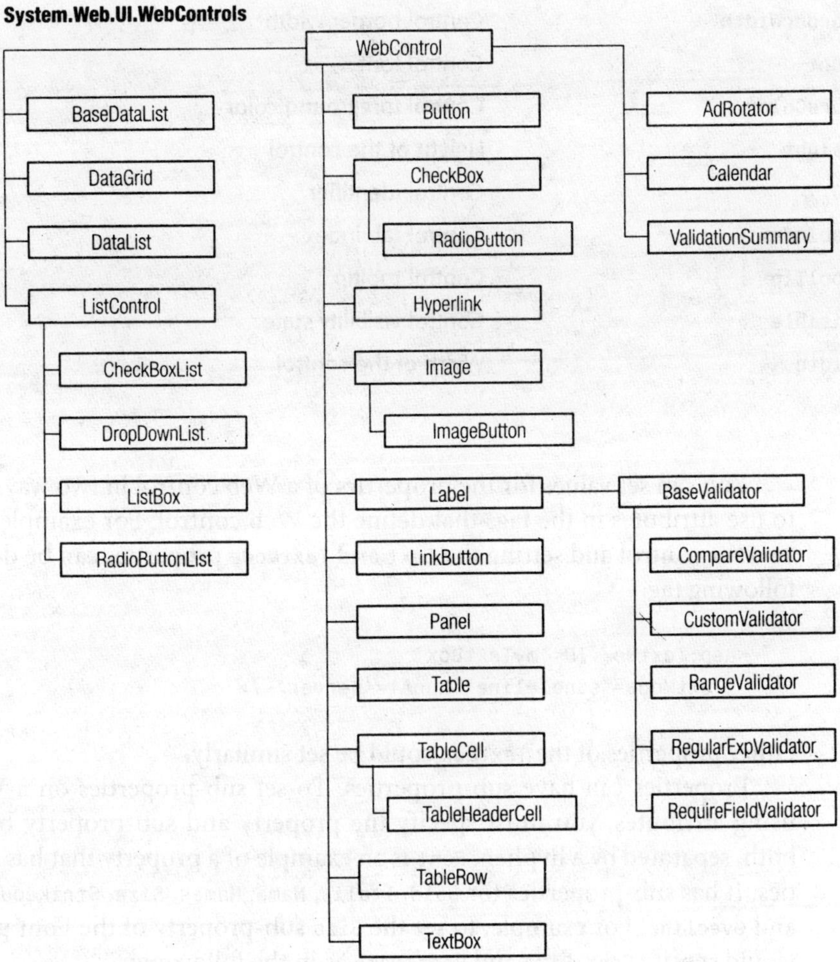

FIGURE 9.2 The System.Web.UI.WebControls hierarchy.

Each Web control implements a set of common properties and can implement custom properties needed to implement specific functionality. The common properties from the `WebControl` base class are shown in the Table 9.2.

TABLE 9.2 Common properties from the `WebControl` base class.

Property	*Description*
`BackColor`	Control background color
`BorderColor`	Control border color
`BorderStyle`	Control border style
`BorderWidth`	Control border width
`Font`	Control font
`ForeColor`	Control foreground color
`Height`	Height of the control
`ID`	Control identifier
`TabIndex`	Control tab index
`ToolTip`	Control tooltip
`Visible`	Control visibility state
`Width`	Width of the control

You can set values for the properties of a Web control in two ways. The first is to use attributes in the tags that define the Web control. For example, declaring a `TextBox` control and setting the `Text` and `TextMode` properties can be done with the following tag:

```
<asp:TextBox ID="myTextBox"
  TextMode="singleline" RunAt="server" />
```

Other properties of the `TextBox` could be set similarly.

Properties can have sub-properties. To set sub-properties on a Web control using attributes, you must specify the property and sub-property by specifying both, separated by a hyphen. `Font` is an example of a property that has sub-properties. It has sub-properties for `Bold`, `Italic`, `Name`, `Names`, `Size`, `Strikeout`, `Underline` and `Overline`. For example, to set the `Size` sub-property of the Font property you would specify `Font-Size` and `Font-Name` as in the following:

```
<asp:TextBox ID="myTextBox"
  Font-Size="12pt" RunAt="server" />
```

The syntax used to specify `Height`, `Width` and `BorderWidth` is straightforward. By default, these values are set in pixels, but you can also specify them in points or percentages:

```
<asp:TextBox ID="myTextBox" Width="100px" RunAt="server" />
<asp:TextBox ID="myTextBox" Width="220pt" RunAt="server" />
<asp:TextBox ID="myTextBox" Width="50%" RunAt="server" />
```

You can specify the color attributes using the HTML color names or the hexadecimal RGB color values:

```
<asp:TextBox ID="myTextBox"
  BackColor="Yellow" RunAt="server" />
<asp:TextBox ID="myTextBox"
  BackColor="#ffff00" RunAt="server" />
```

Also note that custom properties (such as `Text` in the case of a `TextBox`) can be specified with the tag attributes. To see what custom properties are available for each control, look in the .NET Framework Developer's Guide for more information.

In addition to setting properties with the tag attributes, you can set them programmatically in the code-behind page. All of the objects specified in tags are first-class .NET objects and can be manipulated in code, just as other objects. For example, to change the contents of the text box specified in the tags just shown, you could use the following line of C# code:

```
myTextBox.Text = "Hello World"
```

Events

Both HTML controls and Web controls have an event model that allows you to hook events on the page to server-side event handlers. A Web request communicates a client-side action (such as a click) to the server. The server then handles the event and sends a response back to the client. The overall programming model is similar to that of a desktop application, but developers must be aware that only the postback event sent explicitly by the control is sent back to the server. Events such as mouse movement on the browser or key presses are not communicated back to the server. For more information on event raising and handling in Server controls, see the .NET Framework Developer's Guide.

Web Parts

Microsoft has had Web parts technology available for quite some time. In its initial version, Web parts were incorporated into Microsoft Outlook. As the Web browser emerged as the ubiquitous interface, the Web parts technology was migrated into that environment. These early implementations of Web parts were very interesting, but difficult to develop, deploy, secure, and maintain. So, although the early Web parts technologies had promise, these difficulties curtailed its widespread adoption.

The latest version of SharePoint breaks down many of those barriers to using Web parts and makes them much more usable than previous versions. In SharePoint 2003, Web parts have been implemented to take advantage of all of the capabilities of the .NET Framework. Extending the ASP.NET server control object model, Web parts now offer advanced and sophisticated development, deployment, security, and maintenance options.

Development of Web parts is done in a very similar way as the development of ASP.NET server controls. The big difference between Web parts and ASP.NET controls lies in how they are added to pages for display. Web parts are designed to be added by users to their individualized pages, while ASP.NET controls are used by developers in a development environment to a Web forms page. This involvement of end users as the consumers of the Web parts is one of their great strengths. Instead of needing to involve developers to create sophisticated interfaces, they can handle many of the tasks on their own.

Web parts inherit from the `WebPart` class in the Microsoft.SharePoint.WebPartPages namespace. The `WebPart` class inherits from the System.Web.UI.Control class. A view of the class hierarchy is presented in Figure 9.3.

One difference between a `WebControl` and a `WebPart` is that you cannot override the `Render` method in a `WebPart` because the method is locked from being overridden by child classes. This makes sense because the `WebPart` needs to have a known rendering mechanism if it is going to be able to be placed in the SharePoint framework. A `WebPart` with arbitrary rendering would be difficult to place in a structured interface like the SharePoint framework.

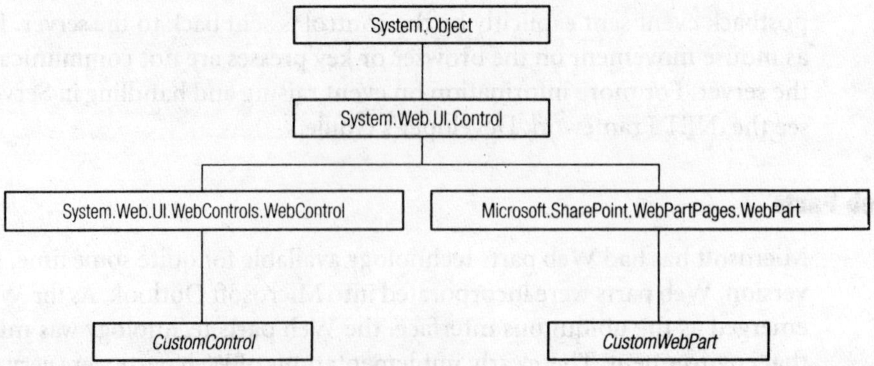

FIGURE 9.3 Web parts in the class hierarchy.

Example of a Web Part

To illustrate the concepts we have discussed in this chapter, we will construct a Web part that facilitates the display of cube data. To construct this Web part, we will first build a Web control and then wrap it into a Web part that exposes the properties necessary to configure the display of data This example will also use the ADOMD.NET library to give another illustration of how to work with it. We will not cover the setup and configuration of SharePoint Services. If you need help with those steps, please consult the documentation that comes with the product. All of the source code for this project is available on the CD-ROM in the Chapter 9 directory.

ON THE CD

For the first part of the sample, we will create a Web control that renders an ADOMD.NET `CellSet` as an HTML table. Create a new project in Visual Studio .NET using the C# Web Control Template and name it MdxReport as shown in Figure 9.4.

After you have created the MdxReport project, replace the `WebCustomControl` class that is created by default with the following code that will render a `CellSet` as an HTML table:

```
[ToolboxData("<{0}:MdxReportControl
  runat=server></{0}:MdxReportControl>")]
public class MdxReportControl : System.Web.UI.WebControls.WebControl
{
    private CellSet _cs;
```

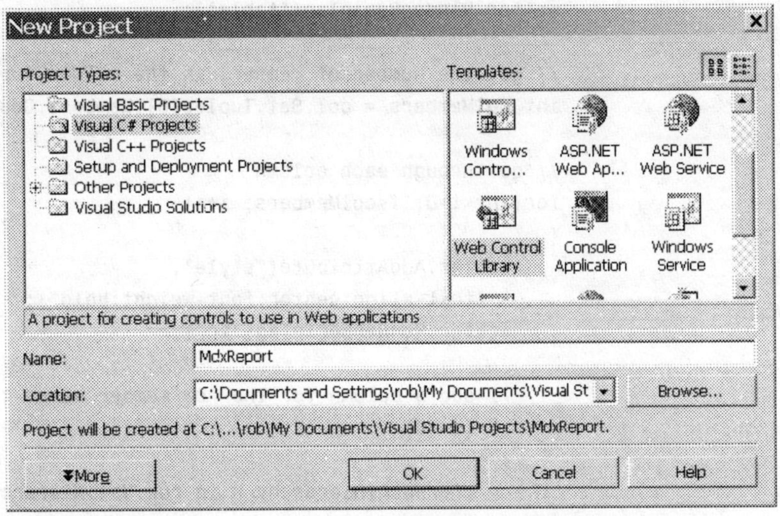

FIGURE 9.4 Create a new Web Control Template project.

```
public CellSet CellSet
{
    get
    {
        return _cs;
    }
    set
    {
        _cs = value;
    }
}

/// <summary>
/// Renders the CellSet as an HTML table
/// </summary>
/// <param name="writer">HtmlTextWriter for HTML output</param>
protected override void Render(System.Web.UI.HtmlTextWriter writer)
{
    if (_cs != null)
    {
        //GetCubeData();
        int rowCount = _cs.Axes["Axis1"].Positions.Count;
        int colCount = _cs.Axes["Axis0"].Positions.Count;
        Axis col = _cs.Axes["Axis0"];
        Axis row = _cs.Axes["Axis1"];

        writer.AddAttribute("border", "1");
        writer.RenderBeginTag("table");

        // get the number of members in the column tuple
        int colMembers = col.Set.Tuples[0].Members.Count;

        // go through each column
        for(int i=0; i<colMembers; i++)
        {
            writer.AddAttribute("style",
              "text-align:center;font-weight:bold");
            writer.RenderBeginTag("tr");

            // add a column for the row member names through
            if (i==0)
            {
                foreach(Hierarchy h in row.Set.Hierarchies)
                {
```

```
                writer.AddAttribute("rowspan",
                  colMembers.ToString());
                writer.RenderBeginTag("td");
                writer.Write(h.Name);
                writer.RenderEndTag();
            }
        }

        // add the correct column span for repeated members
        int tupleCount = col.Set.Tuples.Count;
        foreach(Tuple t in col.Set.Tuples)
        {
            if (t.TupleOrdinal == 0 ||
              col.Set.Tuples[t.TupleOrdinal-1].Members[i].Caption
                != t.Members[i].Caption)
            {
                int match = 0;
                for(int j=t.TupleOrdinal; j<tupleCount; j++)
                {
                    if (col.Set.Tuples[j].Members[i].Caption ==
                      t.Members[i].Caption)
                        match++;
                    else
                        break;
                }
                if (match > 0)
                    writer.AddAttribute("colspan",
                      match.ToString());
                writer.RenderBeginTag("td");
                writer.Write(t.Members[i].Caption);
                writer.RenderEndTag();
            }
        }
        writer.RenderEndTag();
    }

    // render  the row member names and the data in the cell set
    for(int i=0; i < rowCount; i++)
    {
        // render the headers
        writer.RenderBeginTag("tr");
        int memCount = row.Positions[i].Members.Count;
        for(int k=0; k < memCount; k++)
```

```
                {
                    string currentMember =
                        row.Positions[i].Members[k].Caption;
                    // check to see if we need a new row
                    if (!RepeatedMember(i, k))
                    {
                        // add the row span
                        writer.AddAttribute("style",
                          "text-align:center;font-weight:bold");
                        writer.AddAttribute("rowspan",
                         Convert.ToString(MatchingMembersBelow(i, k)+1));
                        writer.RenderBeginTag("td");
                        writer.Write(currentMember);
                        writer.RenderEndTag();
                    }
                }
                // get the data
                for(int j=0; j < colCount; j++)
                {
                    writer.AddAttribute("align", "right");
                    writer.RenderBeginTag("td");
                    writer.Write(_cs.Cells[j, i].FormattedValue);
                    writer.RenderEndTag();
                }
                // end the row
                writer.RenderEndTag();
            }
            //end the table
            writer.RenderEndTag();
        }
    }

    private bool RepeatedMember(int row, int m)
    {
        // first row is never a repeat
        if (row - 1 < 0)
            return false;
        // check if the row is the same as the one above
        return _cs.Axes["Axis1"].Positions[row-1].Members[m].Caption
            == _cs.Axes["Axis1"].Positions[row].Members[m].Caption;
    }

    private int MatchingMembersBelow(int row, int m)
    {
```

```
        int count = 0;
        if (row == _cs.Axes["Axis1"].Positions.Count)
            return count;
        while (row < _cs.Axes["Axis1"].Positions.Count-1)
        {
            if(_cs.Axes["Axis1"].Positions[row].Members[m].Caption
                == _cs.Axes["Axis1"].Positions[++row].Members[m].Caption)
                count++;
            else
                break;
        }
        return count;
    }
}
```

Before you compile the project, be sure to add a reference to the project to the ADOMD.NET library and add the following line to the top of the file:

```
using Microsoft.AnalysisServices.AdomdClient;
```

After you have finished with the Web control, you are ready to create a Web part that displays the control in SharePoint. However, before beginning the Web part, you will need to download the Web Part Templates for Visual Studio .NET. The Web Part Templates make it much easier to build Web parts in Visual Studio .NET by creating the necessary supporting files and a class with the basic interfaces necessary to create a Web part. These are available from Microsoft at *http://msdn.microsoft.com/library/default.asp?url=/library/en-us/dnspts/html/sharepoint_CreatingCustomWPPTemplates.asp*. This page gives instructions for installing and using the Web Part Templates.

After you have installed the Web Part Templates, open up the MdxReport project you had created earlier and add a new project. Use the C# Web Part Template to make a new Web part and name it MdxPart, as shown in Figure 9.5.

After you have created the new project, you will need to add the code to the Web part to configure and display the Web part we just created. In this example, we will use the stock controls available in SharePoint to create two properties: one for the `Datasource` and the other for the `Command` that will be used in creating the `Cellset` to be shown. To do this, we need to edit the code that is created by the template. In the MdxPart project, change the name of the WebPart1.cs file to MdxReportPart.cs and then edit the `MdxReportPart` so that it has the following contents:

```
/// <summary>
/// MdxReportPart displays the MdxReportControl in SharePoint.
```

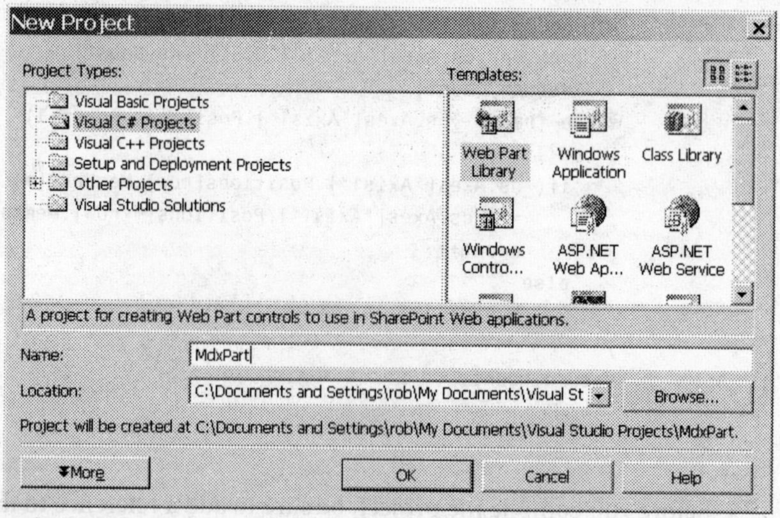

FIGURE 9.5 Create a new Web Part Template project.

```
/// </summary>
[DefaultProperty("Text"),
    ToolboxData("<{0}:MdxReportPart runat=server></{0}:MdxReportPart>"),
    XmlRoot(Namespace="MdxPart")]
public class MdxReportPart : Microsoft.SharePoint.WebPartPages.WebPart
{
    private string _command;
    private string _datasource;
    protected MdxReport.MdxReportControl _mdxReportControl;

    [Browsable(true),Category("Miscellaneous"),
        DefaultValue(""),
        WebPartStorage(Storage.Personal),
        FriendlyName("Command"),Description("Command Property")]
    public string Command
    {
        get
        {
            return _command;
        }

        set
        {
            _command = value;
        }
    }
```

```
[Browsable(true),Category("Miscellaneous"),
DefaultValue(""),
WebPartStorage(Storage.Personal),
FriendlyName("Datasource"),Description("Datasource Property")]
public string Datasource
{
    get
    {
        return _datasource;
    }

    set
    {
        _datasource = value;
    }
}

/// <summary>
/// Create the child controls in the WebPart.
/// </summary>
protected override void CreateChildControls()
{
    _mdxReportControl = new MdxReport.MdxReportControl();
}

/// <summary>
/// Render this Web part***QUERY: Is this edit OK?******Yes.
Microsoft does capitalize the term "Web Part" in many cases.*** to the
output parameter specified.
/// </summary>
/// <param name="output"> The HTML writer to write out to </param>
protected override void RenderWebPart(HtmlTextWriter output)
{
    try
    {
        AdomdConnection conn = new AdomdConnection();
        conn.ConnectionString = _datasource;
        conn.Open();
        AdomdCommand cmd = conn.CreateCommand();
        cmd.CommandText = _command;
        CellSet cs = cmd.ExecuteCellSet();
        _mdxReportControl.CellSet = cs;
        _mdxReportControl.DataBind();
        EnsureChildControls();
        _mdxReportControl.RenderControl(output);
```

```
            }
            catch(Exception ex)
            {
                output.Write(SPEncode.HtmlEncode(ex.Message));
            }
        }
    }
```

As in the MdxReport, you will need to add a reference to ADOMD.NET to the project and edit the MdxReportPart.cs file to use the reference by adding this line:

```
using Microsoft.AnalysisServices.AdomdClient;
```

The next change that needs to be made is to the dwp file that configures the assemblies and classes that are used in each Web part. To configure this Web part, rename the WebPart1.dwp file to MdxReportPart.dwp and edit the contents so that you have the following:

```
<?xml version="1.0" encoding="utf-8"?>
<WebPart xmlns="http://schemas.microsoft.com/WebPart/v2" >
    <Title>MdxReportPart</Title>
    <Description>Displays MDX query results in a grid.</Description>
    <Assembly>MdxPart</Assembly>
    <TypeName>MdxPart.MdxReportPart</TypeName>
</WebPart>
```

Next, we need to specify the configuration for installing the Web part. This is done in the Manifest.xml file, which contains a list of the controls that are to be allowed for use in the Web part, and which references the dwp file. For the MdxReportPart, the Manifest.xml file should be edited to look like this:

```
<?xml version="1.0"?>
<WebPartManifest
  xmlns="http://schemas.microsoft.com/WebPart/v2/Manifest">
  <Assemblies>
    <Assembly FileName="MdxPart.dll">
      <ClassResources/>
      <SafeControls>
        <SafeControl
          Namespace="MdxPart"
          TypeName="*"
        />
      </SafeControls>
    </Assembly>
```

```
      <Assembly FileName="MdxReport.dll">
        <ClassResources/>
        <SafeControls>
          <SafeControl
            Namespace="MdxReport"
            TypeName="*"
          />
        </SafeControls>
      </Assembly>
    </Assemblies>
    <DwpFiles>
      <DwpFile FileName="MdxReportPart.dwp"/>
    </DwpFiles>
  </WebPartManifest>
```

The last step in creating the Web part is to create a cab file that contains all of the compiled assemblies and configuration information so that it can be installed on the SharePoint server. Add a new project to the MdxReport project by selecting File . . . Add Project . . . New Project from the menu. Use the Cab Project template and name the project MdxReportCab, as shown in Figure 9.6.

FIGURE 9.6 Create a new Cab project.

To create the cab file, we need to add items to it. First, select the MdxPartCab project in the Solution Explorer and add the Manifest.xml and MdxReportParts.dwp files to the MdxPartCab project by using Project . . . Add . . . File from the menu. After you have added the files, choose Project . . . Add . . . Project Output to display the Add Project Output Group dialog. Select the MdxReport project from

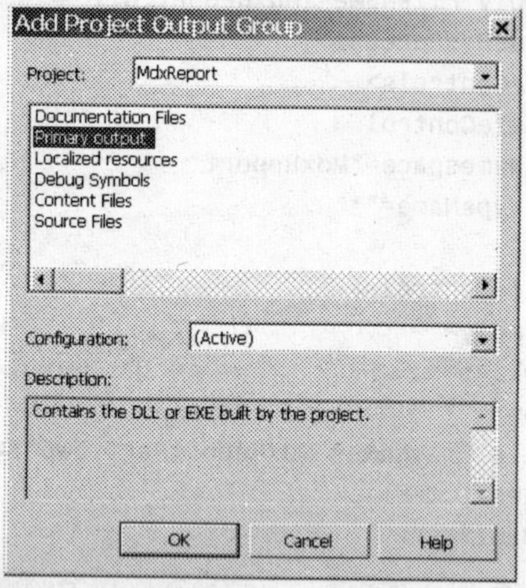

FIGURE 9.7 Add MdxReport Output to the cab.

the Project drop-down list, and Primary Output as shown in Figure 9.7 and click OK. Next, add the Project Output for the MdxPart by following the same steps.

Now you are ready to build the whole project. After it has been built, you are ready to install the Web part and see it in action. To install the MdxPartCab.cab, we use stsadm.exe. This program is located in the C:\Program Files\Common Files\Microsoft Shared\Web server extensions\60\BIN directory on your SharePoint server. The syntax to install the cab file is:

```
stsadm.exe -o addwppack –filename <path to file>mdxpartcab.cab
```

After the Web part has been installed, you are ready to add it to a portal page and configure it for viewing. These steps assume you are starting with a default portal configuration and have appropriate permissions to add Web parts to pages. The first step is to open up the portal home page in your Web browser and select Edit Page from the Select Action section (by default, this will be on the left pane of the home page). After you have selected Edit Page, you then select the Modify Shared Page menu on the upper right of the page and choose Add Web Parts . . . Browse as shown in Figure 9.8.

Choosing Browse will display a list of Web part libraries that are accessible from the server. The `MdxReportPart` has been installed into the Virtual Server library, so choose that entry from the list to get a listing of the Web parts available on that virtual server. To add the `MdxReportPart` to the page, simple drag and drop the icon of the Web part where you want it to display on the page.

When you first display the `MdxReportPart` on the page, it will show an error (probably something like "Value cannot be null") because it has not been config-

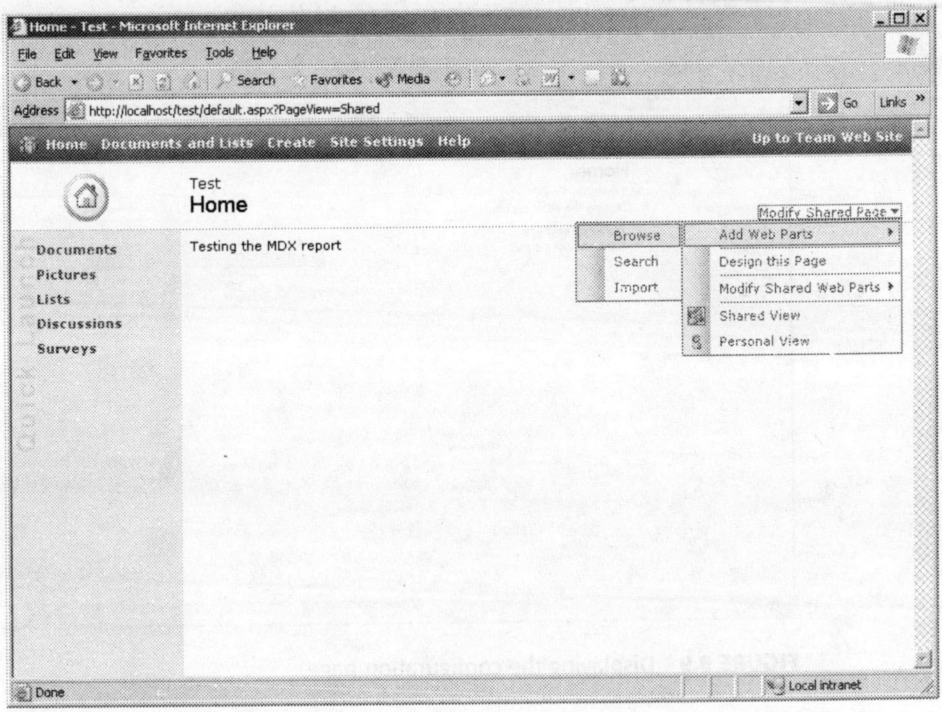

FIGURE 9.8 Adding a Web part.

ured to connect to an XMLA server and run a query. To configure the part, select the Modify Shared Part item from the drop-down menu on the part, as shown in Figure 9.9.

In the properties page that is displayed for the `MdxReportPart`, expand the Miscellaneous section and populate the `Command` and `Datasource` fields with information that will allow the Web part to connect to an XMLA server and run the command that you choose. For example, your `Datasource` field might be set to (without the line breaks):

```
Datasource=http://<machine name>/xmla/msxisapi.dll;
DataSourceInfo=<server name>;Catalog=PretzelCo;
```

The command can be any valid MDX command that can be executed on the configured data source. In Figure 9.10 you can see the results of the following MDX query on the Pretzel Co. data source:

```
with member [Measures].[Delta] as
'[Measures].[Gross Invoice Amount]-[Measures].[Gross Sales Planned]'
select {DrilldownLevel({[Time].[All Time].[2003]})} on columns,
```

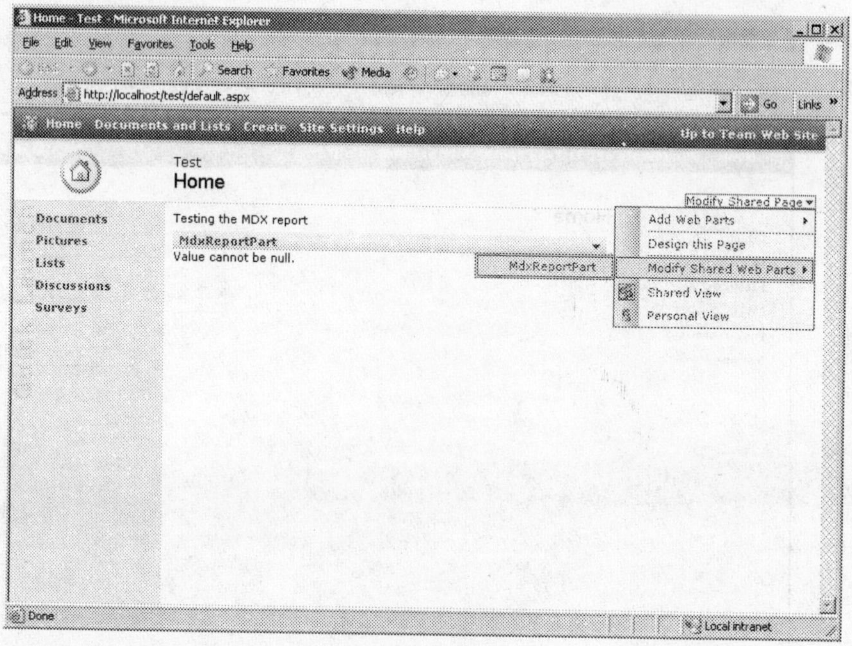

FIGURE 9.9 Displaying the configuration page.

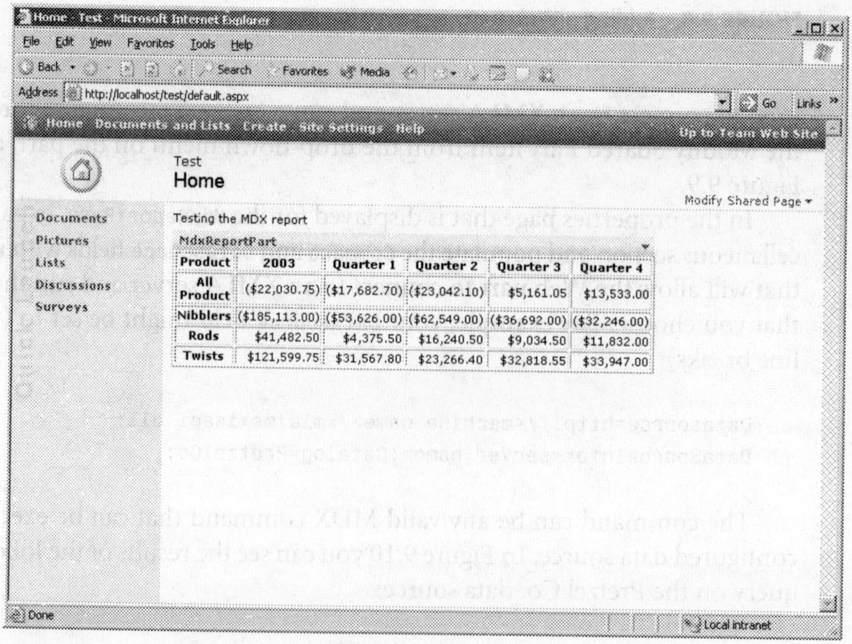

FIGURE 9.10 Displaying the properties page.

```
{DrilldownLevel({[Product].[All Product]})} on rows
from InvoicePlan
where ([Measures].[Delta])
```

As you can see from this example, creating a Web part to wrap an existing Web control and provide customizable functionality is simple. Although this simple example doesn't really meet the criteria of being an analytical application, since the analysis provided would only be as deep as that allowed by a single MDX statement, it would be possible to extend the Web part to provide an easily accessed application that is customized to support a given business process.

SUMMARY

In this chapter, we discussed the definition and need for analytical applications. An analytical application should be more than just a simple summary of data; it should provide a focused look at the KPIs that are important to the operation of the business. There are three main categories of analytical application. The first are applications that address a specific process, such as sales automation. The second type address business issues, such as vendor performance, and the third type focus on a line-of-business function such as finance. Some critical success factors for an analytical application were identified with tight integration with the data warehouse, flexible architecture, and ease of use leading the way. We then enumerated some steps to building analytical applications that echo some common themes throughout this book: identify the requirements, make a well-informed build vs. buy decision, determine how to get the data, get the right team, and focus on application ROI.

We then moved on to discuss dashboards with a specific discussion of Microsoft SharePoint technologies. SharePoint refers to two interrelated technologies: SharePoint Services, which is a platform for developing collaborative applications, and SharePoint Portal Server, which provides a means to organize information for personal presentation. We then moved on to discuss the technical details behind Web controls and Web parts, two of the fundamental building blocks for SharePoint applications, and concluded with an example that illustrated the use of these technologies.

CONCLUSION

Business intelligence is a broad and rapidly changing subject. In this book, we have explored using .NET technologies to collect, analyze, and communicate information. We discussed the many ways that business intelligence can play a crucial role in making an organization more effective in their day-to-day and strategic activities.

We began with a discussion of the data warehouse and how to use Microsoft SQL Server at the core of your data warehouse. Next, we moved on to cover the role of OLAP and Microsoft Analysis Services in your business intelligence platform, using both Excel and MDX to extract multidimensional data for analysis. After that, we moved on to discuss ways of accessing and manipulating OLAP cubes programmatically, using technologies such as ADOMD, DSO, and XMLA. Of the three, XMLA is the most forward looking technology, since it is Web Services-based and provides the basis for ADOMD.NET, the next generation of programmatic interface for OLAP. After our discussion of OLAP, we moved to an issue of fundamental importance in business intelligence: reporting. Here, we covered some of the details of building a reporting environment based on ASP.NET and Crystal Reports. After exploring reporting, we moved on to cover data mining and its role in discovering patterns and relationships in the ever-increasing amount of business data. Lastly, we moved on to a discussion of analytical applications and presenting business intelligence information using Web Parts in a SharePoint environment.

Even after all of the coverage of these specific .NET technologies, we barely scratched the surface of using .NET to provide business intelligence solutions. As reflected in the increasing sales and utilization of business intelligence applications, mastery of business intelligence technologies is essential, both for information technology professionals and business users alike. The risks of not knowing are simply too great.

ENDNOTES AND REFERENCES

1. Eckerson, Wayne, "Analytic Applications: Build or Buy?," The Data Warehousing Institute, 2002, pp 3.
2. Orlov, Laurie, "Using Business Intelligence to Manage Velocity," Forrester Research, 2003. Available online at *http://www.forrester.com/ER/Research/Report/0,1338,15780,FF.htm* (7/22/2003).

A MDX Functions

This appendix lists all of the built-in MDX functions. We will describe each of the functions in alphabetical order and provide examples of how they might be used from the sample Food Mart 2000 cube that comes with Analysis Services. For more information on the MDX functions, see the Analysis Services online help topic "MDX Function Reference" and the OLE DB for OLAP specification.

AddCalculatedMembers (Set)

In a typical case, when a set of members is returned from a set function, only the non-calculated members are returned. `AddCalculatedMembers` adds the calculated members that are siblings to the members in the set if the set is from a single dimension. For example, the following MDX statement returns all of the base (non-calculated) measures from the Sales cube:

```
select
{[Measures].members} on columns,
{[Time].[1997].[Q1]:[Time].[1997].[Q4]} on rows
from Sales
```

Using AddCalculatedMembers returns all of the members in the columns axis:

```
select
AddCalculatedMembers({[Measures].members}) on columns,
{[Time].[1997].[Q1]:[Time].[1997].[Q4]} on rows
from Sales
```

Aggregate (Set [, Numeric Expression])

`Aggregate` returns a numeric calculated value across the set. The `Numeric Expression` argument is summed over the set. If no `Numeric Expression` is provided, then the default aggregation is used. For example, the following MDX statement uses

`Aggregate` to create a new member that shows the total calculation for the year and uses it in the same set as each quarterly value.

```
with
member [Time].[1997Totals] as
'Aggregate([Time].[1997].[Q1]:[Time].[1997].[Q4])'
select
{[Measures].[Unit Sales]} on columns,
{[Time].[1997].[Q1]:[Time].[1997].[Q4],
  [Time].[1997Totals]} on rows
from Sales
```

AllMembers

By default, calculated members are not enumerated when dimensions members are retrieved. The `AllMembers` function is similar to `AddCalculatedMembers` in that it adds the calculated members to the members in the set. `AllMembers` is used in reference to a dimension or level. For example,

```
select
{[Measures].AllMembers} on columns,
{[Time].[1997].[Q1]:[Time].[1997].[Q4]} on rows
from Sales
```

returns the same results as our example in `AddCalculatedMembers`. The distinction between `AddCalculatedMembers` and `AllMembers` is that if there are no members, as in the `Measures` dimension, the `AllMembers` function will still return the calculated members.

Ancestor (Member, Level)

This function returns the member ancestor of the given member at the specified level of the member hierarchy. If the level given is the same as the member, then the member itself is returned. For example,

```
select
{Ancestor([Store].[All Stores].[USA].[WA].[Seattle],
  [Store State])} on columns,
{[Time].[1997].[Q1]:[Time].[1997].[Q4]} on rows
from Sales
```

returns the results shown in Table A.1.

Ancestor (Member, Numeric Expression)

This function returns the member ancestor of the given member at the given numeric expression steps up in the member hierarchy. If the numeric expression given is zero, then the member itself is returned. For example, the MDX query

```
select
{Ancestor([Store].[All Stores].[USA].[WA].[Seattle],1)}
```

TABLE A.1 Quarterly sales results for WA.

	WA
Q1	30, 114.00
Q2	29, 479.00
Q3	30, 538.00
Q4	34,235.00

```
 on columns,
{[Time].[1997].[Q1]:[Time].[1997].[Q4]} on rows
 from Sales
```

returns the same results as the example in `Ancestor` (Member, Level).

`Ancestors` (Member, Level)

This function returns the set of ancestors of the given member at the specified level of the member hierarchy. If the level given is the same as the member, then the member itself is returned in the set. Note that the difference between this and the `Ancestor` function with the same arguments is that `Ancestors` returns a set and `Ancestor` returns a member.

`Ancestors` (Member, Numeric Expression)

This function returns the member ancestor of the given member at the given numeric expression steps up in the member hierarchy. If the numeric expression given is zero, then the member itself is returned in a set. Note that the difference between this and the `Ancestor` function with the same arguments is that `Ancestors` returns a set and Ancestor returns a member.

`Ascendants` (Member)

The `Ascendants` function returns the complete set of ancestors from the given member all the way up to the root of the hierarchy, including the given member. This function can be useful to compare a member to its parent levels. For example,

```
select
{Ascendants([Store].[All Stores].[USA].[WA].[Seattle])}
 on columns,
{[Time].[1997].[Q1]:[Time].[1997].[Q4]} on rows
from Sales
```

returns the result set shown in Table A.2.

TABLE A.2 Quarterly results for the Ascendants of `[Store].[All Stores].[USA].[WA].[Seattle]`.

	Seattle	*WA*	*USA*	*All Stores*
Q1	6,098.00	30,115.00	66,291.00	66,291.00
Q2	5,922.00	29,479.00	62,610.00	62,610.00
Q3	6,322.00	30,358.00	65,848.00	65,848.00
Q4	6,669.00	34,235.00	72,024.00	72,024.00

`Avg` (Set [, Numeric Expression])

`Avg` returns the average value of the numeric expression over the set. The average is calculated by the sum of the cells divided by the count of the non-empty cells. For example,

```
with member [Measures].[QtrAverage] as
  'Avg([Time].[1997].[Q1]:[Time].[1997].[Q4],
  [Measures].[Profit])'
select
{[Measures].[QtrAverage]} on columns,
{[Product].[Product Family].members} on rows
from Sales
```

returns the average of profit over the quarters in 1997 for each of the product family members.

`Axis` (Numeric Expression)

`Axis` returns the set of members from the given axis index. `Axis(0)` returns columns and `Axis(1)` returns rows. Higher numeric expressions return higher axes.

`BottomCount` (Set, Count [, Numeric Expression])

`BottomCount` returns the bottom count number of members in the set. If a numeric expression is provided, the set is sorted by the expression. If it is not provided, the elements are ordered by the default. Like the other `Count` and `Percent` functions, `BottomCount` treats the results as being at the same level in the hierarchy. If there are tied elements in the sort order, some may be arbitrarily left out of the results. For example,

```
select
BottomCount([Product].[All Products].[Food].children,
  3, Profit)
on columns,
```

```
{[Time].[1997]} on rows
from Sales
```

returns the three least profitable food elements.

`BottomPercent` (Set, Percentage, Numeric Expression)

`BottomPercent` returns the bottom percentage members of the members in the set sorted by the numeric expression. The percentage is specified with a number between 0 and 100 (although using a number greater than 100 does not cause an error). Unlike the `BottomCount` function, the numeric expression is not optional. Like the other `Count` and `Percent` functions `BottomPercent` treats the results as being at the same level in the hierarchy. If there are tied elements in the sort order, some may be arbitrarily left out of the results.

`BottomSum` (Set, Value, Numeric Expression)

`BottomSum` returns the bottom members of the set sorted by the numeric expression such that the sum of the members is at least the given value. Unlike the `BottomCount` function, the numeric expression is not optional. Like the other `Count` and `Percent` functions, `BottomSum` treats the results as being at the same level in the hierarchy. For example,

```
select
BottomSum([Product].[All Products].[Food].children,
  5000, Profit)
on columns,
{[Time].[1997]} on rows
from Sales
```

returns the data shown in Table A.3.

TABLE A.3 The BottomSum of the profit of `[Product].[All Products].[Food].children`.

	Canned Products	*Meat*	*Seafood*
1997	1,812.00	1,714.00	1,764.00

`CalculationCurrentPass()`

This function returns the current calculation pass count for the query being calculated. This is a zero-based count and the first pass will return 0.

`CalculationPassValue` (Expression, Pass Value [, Access Flag])

This function returns the value of the given expression at the given pass value. The expression can be either a numeric expression or a string expression. The access flag can be used to modify the behavior of the pass value argument. The possible flags and their descriptions are listed in Table A.4 with the default value being ABSOLUTE.

TABLE A.4 Possible flags and their descriptions.

Flag	*Description*
ABSOLUTE	The pass value contains the zero-based index for a calculation pass. Using a number higher than the current pass will cause the higher passes to run for cell values referenced in the expression.
RELATIVE	The pass value contains a relative offset from the current calculation pass. If the offset resolves into a calculation pass less than 0, calculation pass 0 is used.

The following MDX statement is an example of how to use `CalculationPassValue` to set the cell font to Bold (`font_flags = '1'`) if the value of the cell is less than 10000 in a calculated cell:

```
with cell calculation [Sales Exceptions] for
 '([Store].[Store City].Members)'
as 'CalculationPassValue(([Store].CurrentMember,
   [Store Sales]), 0)',
condition =
   'CalculationPassValue(([Store].CurrentMember,
   [Store Sales]), 0) < 10000',
font_flags = '1'
select
   {[Store].[All Stores].[USA].[WA].Children}
     on columns,
   {[Time].[1997].children} on rows
from Sales
where ([Measures].[Store Sales])
cell properties value, formatted_value, font_flags
```

`Call` UDF Name

The `Call` function invokes the registered user-defined function specified by UDF Name. `Call` can be used only to execute functions that return void values and arguments can be passed as part of the specified UDF. For example, Call MyFunction("Hello") would pass the string "Hello" to the UDF. `Call` returns an empty cell value and cannot be combined with other functions.

`Children`

This function is used in reference to a member and returns the set of children from that member. A simple example is:

```
select
{[Product].Children}
on columns,
{[Time].[1997]} on rows
from Sales
```

ClosingPeriod ([Level [, Member]])

Returns the last descendant of a member at the specified level. If no level is provided, the `Time` dimension is used. If no level or member is provided, then the default is `Time.CurrentMember`. This function is very similar to `OpeningPeriod`, except that it returns the last member instead of the first. An example is:

```
select
{[Product].Children}
on columns,
{ClosingPeriod()} on rows
from Sales
```

CoalesceEmpty (Expression [, Expression]...)

This function returns the first expression listed that is not null. If all given expressions evaluate to null, it returns null. `CoaleseEmpty` can either use all numeric expressions or all string expressions. All expressions listed must evaluate to the same data type or to an empty cell value. For example,

```
with member [Measures].[NonEmptyProfit] as
 'CoalesceEmpty(Measures.[Profit], 0)'
select [Product].children on columns,
{crossjoin([Store].[All Stores].[USA].[CA]:[WA],
[Time].[Year].Members)} on rows
from [Sales]
where [Measures].[NonEmptyProfit]
```

returns a result set with 0 for all of the cells that do not have a value.

Correlation (Set, Numeric Expression [,Numeric Expression])

This function returns the coefficient of correlation between two series in a set. This function evaluates the set against the first numeric expression to get the values for the *y*-axis. The set is evaluated against the second numeric expression, if present, to get the values for the *x*-axis. The second numeric expression is optional. If the second numeric expression is not supplied, the current context values are used for the *x*-axis. Empty cells or cells containing text or logical values are ignored. As an example,

```
with member [Measures].[Correlation] as
 'Correlation({[Time].[1997].[Q1].Children},
 Measures.[Profit], Measures.[Sales Average])'
select
```

```
{[Store].[USA].Children} on columns,
{[Measures].[Correlation]} on rows
from [Sales]
```

would give us the correlation between the Profit and Sales Average for 1997 Q1.

Count

`Count` returns the number of items in a specific set or tuple. There are two variations on syntax for using `Count` with sets. The first is `Count` (Set [, ExcludeEmpty | IncludeEmpty]). The flags for `IncludeEmpty` or `ExcludeEmpty` determine whether or not empty are included in the resulting count. The second variation is Set.`Count`, which returns the number of tuples in the set and behaves as if the `IncludeEmpty` flag were set.

Cousin (Child, Ancestor)

The `Cousin` function returns the member that has the same relative position to its ancestor member as the child member. This is most useful with dimensions that will have the same structure repeatedly, such as time. For example,

```
select
{[Store].[USA].Children} on columns,
{Cousin([1998].[Q1], [1997])} on rows
from [Sales]
```

will return the results for Q1 1997.

Covariance (Set, Numeric Expression [, Numeric Expression])

This function returns the population covariance between two series in a set. `Covariance` measures the tendency of two values to vary together. The covariance is calculated by the average of the product of the deviations of each value from their means where *n* is the number of pairs $\bar{x}$ and $\bar{y}$ and are the mean of *x* and *y*, respectively.

$$c(x, y) = \frac{\sum_{i=1}^{n} (\bar{x} - x_i)(\bar{y} - y_i)}{n}$$

If *x* and *y* tend to vary together, then $c(x,y) > 0$. If *x* tends to decrease when *y* increases then $c(x,y) < 0$. If *x* and *y* are independent, then $c(x, y) = 0$. The Covariance function evaluates the set against the first numeric expression to get the values for the *y*-axis. The set is evaluated against the second numeric expression, if present, to get the values for the *x*-axis. The second numeric expression is optional. If the second numeric expression is not supplied, the current context values are used for the *x*-axis. Empty cells or cells containing text or logical values are ignored. For example,

```
with member [Measures].[Covar] as
'Covariance([Product].children,[Measures].[Profit],
 [Measures].[Store Sales])'
select
    {[Measures].[Covar]} on columns,
    {[Time].children} on rows
from Sales
```

CovarianceN (Set, Numeric Expression [, Numeric Expression])

This function returns the sample covariance between two series in a set. CovarianceN measures the tendency of two values to vary together. The sample covariance is calculated by the average of the product of the deviations of each value from their means where n is the number of pairs $\bar{x}$ and $\bar{y}$ and are the mean of x and y, respectively.

$$c(x, y) = \frac{\sum_{i=1}^{n} (\bar{x} - x_i)(\bar{y} - y_i)}{n - 1}$$

If x and y tend to vary together, then $c(x,y) > 0$. If x tends to decrease when y increases then $c(x,y) < 0$. If x and y are independent, then $c(x, y) = 0$. This function evaluates the set against the first numeric expression to get the values for the y-axis. The set is evaluated against the second numeric expression, if present, to get the values for the x-axis. The second numeric expression is optional. If the second numeric expression is not supplied, the current context values are used for the x-axis. Empty cells or cells containing text or logical values are ignored. For example,

```
with member [Measures].[CovarN] as
'CovarianceN([Product].children,[Measures].[Profit],
  [Measures].[Store Sales])'
select
    {[Measures].[CovarN]} on columns,
    {[Time].children} on rows
from Sales
```

Crossjoin (Set1, Set2)

This function returns the Cartesian product of two sets. There is an alternate syntax in which a cross-join may be specified with *Set1 * Set2*. The expression *Set1 * Set2 * Set3* is syntactically the equivalent of Crossjoin(Set1, Crossjoin(Set2, Set3)). Note that each set must be from a different dimension or an error will result. The order of the resulting set is dependent on the order of Set1 and Set2. For example,

```
select
{Crossjoin([Store].[USA].Children,[Product].Children) }
  on columns,
{[1997].Children} on rows
from [Sales]
```

Current

`Current` is used in reference to a set and returns the current tuple during iteration. It is valid only when iteration is being processed over a set.

CurrentMember

Used in context of a dimension, `CurrentMember` returns the current member for that dimension during an iteration. See `Generate` for an example of how `CurrentMember` is used.

DataMember

Used in the context of a member, `DataMember` returns the system-generated data input member that is associated with the context member. When you are using an updatable cube, `DataMember` allows you to write data to the actual member.

DefaultMember

Used in context of a dimension, `DefaultMember` returns the default member of the dimension. Used in context of a hierarchy, `DefaultMember` returns the default member of the hierarchy. If the property is empty, `DefaultMember` returns the member for the (All) level for the dimension or hierarchy. If there is no (All) level, `DefaultMember` returns an arbitrary member of the highest level.

Descendants (Member, [Level [,Flags]])

`Descendants` returns the set of descendants for a given member at a given level. If no level or descendant flags are specified, then the member and all of its descendants are returned. The descendant flags that are supported are shown in Table A.5.

An example follows:

```
select
{Descendants([Store].[USA], [Store City]) } on columns,
{[1997].Children} on rows
from [Sales]
```

Descendants (Member, Distance [, Flags])

Returns the set of descendants for the given member at a specified distance. Specifying a distance of zero returns the specified member. The same descendant flags apply as in the `Descendants` (Member, [Level [,Flags]]) function. For example,

```
select
{Descendants([Store].[USA], 2) } on columns,
{[1997].Children} on rows
from [Sales]
```

TABLE A.5 Supported descendant flags.

Flag	*Description*
`SELF`	This is the default value if no value is specified. It returns descendant members from `Level` only. `SELF` includes `Member`, if and only if `Level` specified is the level of `Member`.
`AFTER`	Returns descendant members from all levels below to `Level`
`BEFORE`	Returns descendant members from all levels between `Member` and `Level`, not including members from `Level`
`BEFORE_AND_AFTER`	Returns descendant members from all levels below the level of `Member` except members from `Level`
`SELF_AND_AFTER`	Returns descendant members from `Level` and all levels below `Level`
`SELF_AND_BEFORE`	Returns descendant members from `Level` and all levels between `Member` and `Level`
`SELF_BEFORE_AFTER`	Returns descendant members from all levels below the level of `Member`
`LEAVES`	Returns leaf descendant members between `Member` and `Level` or `Distance`

`Dimension`

Used in the context of a `Hierarchy`, `Level` or `Member`, `Dimension` returns the dimension that contains the specified context. Because of the way Analysis Serivces handles hierarchies as different dimensions, `Hierarchy.Dimension` returns the given `Hierarchy`.

`Dimensions` (Numeric Expression)

Returns the dimension that is in the position of the numeric expression index in the cube. The array of dimensions is zero-based and the `Measures` dimension is always dimension 0. So

```
select
{[Store].Children}  on columns,
{[Measures].Members} on rows
from [Sales]
```

is equivalent to

```
select
{[Store].Children}  on columns,
```

```
{Dimensions(0).Members} on rows
from [Sales]
```

`Dimensions` (String Expression)

Returns the dimension named by the string expression. So

```
select
{[Store].Children}  on columns,
{[Measures].Members} on rows
from [Sales]
```

is equivalent to

```
select
{[Store].Children}  on columns,
{Dimensions("Measures").Members} on rows
from [Sales]
```

`Distinct` (Set)

`Distinct` removes duplicate members from the given set. The first instance of each duplicate is retained in the returned set.

`DistinctCount` (Set)

`DistinctCount` returns the count of distinct, non-empty tuples in a set of `Measures`. It is equivalent to the statement `Count(Distinct`(Set), `ExcludeEmpty`). For example,

```
with member [Measures].[Product Count] as
'DistinctCount({[Product Name].Members})'
select
{[Measures].[Product Count]}  on columns,
{[Store].[USA].[WA].children} on rows
from [Sales]
```

returns the number of distinct products sold in each store in WA.

`DrilldownLevel` (Set [, {Level |, Index}])

`DrilldownLevel` returns a set from a drill-down on the given set to the one level below the specified level. If no level is specified, the set from one level down from the current level is returned. `Index` is used to specify which dimension should be drilled-down as a zero-based collection. The drilled-down members that are returned are placed underneath their parent members in the returned set and the parents are maintained in order. For example,

```
select
{[Measures].[Unit Sales]}  on columns,
{DrilldownLevel({[Store].[USA].[OR].children})} on rows
from [Sales]
```

returns what is shown in Table A.6.

TABLE A.6 The `DrillDownLevel` on unit sales from `[Store].[USA].[OR].children`.

	Unit Sales
Portland	26,079.00
Store 11	26,079.00
Salem	41,580.00
Store 13	41,580.00

`DrilldownLevelBottom` (Set, Count[, [Level][, Numeric Expression]])

This function is similar to the `DrilldownLevel` function, but returns only the bottom count number of children, instead of all children at the specified level. If a numeric expression is included, it is used to sort the children. If a numeric expression is not included, the default context is used. For example,

```
select
{[Measures].[Profit]} on columns,
{DrilldownLevelBottom({[Store].[Store State].[CA]},
  3, , [Profit])} on rows
from Sales
```

returns a set with CA and the three least profitable stores in CA.

`DrilldownLevelTop` (Set, Count[, [Level][, Numeric Expression]])

This function is similar to the `DrilldownLevel` function, but returns only the top count number of children, instead of all children at the specified level. If a numeric expression is included, it is used to sort the children. If a numeric expression is not included, the default context is used.

```
select
{[Measures].[Profit]} on columns,
{DrilldownLevelTop({[Store].[Store State].[CA]},
  3, , [Profit])} on rows
from Sales
```

returns a set with CA and the three most profitable stores in CA.

`DrilldownMember` (Set1, Set2 [, Flag])

`DrilldownMember` returns a set by drilling down on each member in Set1 that is in Set2. If `RECURSIVE` is set, the drilldown continues by comparing the resulting set against Set2 until there are no further matches. `DrilldownMember` can also be used with tuples. If Set1 contains tuples, the function will return the set of each member of Set1 that has a matching member of Set2. For example,

```
select
{[Measures].[Profit]} on columns,
{DrilldownMember({[Store].[All Stores].[USA]},
  {[USA],[CA]}, RECURSIVE) } on rows
from Sales
```

will return the set of USA, CA, and all of the members in CA, OR, and WA.

DrilldownMemberBottom (Set1, Set2, Count [, [Numeric Expression][,Flag]]

`DrilldownMemberBottom` works much as `DrilldownMember` and returns a set that consists of the members of Set1 matched against Set2. Instead of returning all of the members in that set, it returns the bottom count members as ordered by the numeric expression. If a numeric expression is not provided, the members are ordered by the context. For example,

```
select
{[Measures].[Profit]} on columns,
{DrilldownMemberBottom({[Store].[All Stores].[USA]},
  {[USA],[CA]}, 3, [Profit], RECURSIVE ) } on rows
from Sales
```

will return the set of USA, CA, and the three least profitable members in CA, OR, and WA.

DrilldownMemberTop (Set1, Set2, Count [, [Numeric Expression][, Flag]]

`DrilldownMemberTop` works much as `DrilldownMember` and returns a set that consists of the members of Set1 matched against Set2. Instead of returning all of the members in that set, it returns the top count members as ordered by a numeric expression. If a numeric expression is not provided, the members are ordered by the context. For example,

```
select
{[Measures].[Profit]} on columns,
{DrilldownMemberTop({[Store].[All Stores].[USA]},
  {[USA],[CA]}, 3, [Profit], RECURSIVE ) } on rows
from Sales
```

will return the set of USA, CA, and the three most profitable members in CA, OR, and WA.

DrillupLevel (Set [, Level])

This function removes members from the set that are below the given level. If level is not specified, then the level is set to one level above the lowest level members of the set.

`DrillupMember` (Set1, Set2)

`DrillupMember` returns a set by drilling up on each member in Set1 that is in Set2. That is, it removes the members in Set1 that are descendants of Set2.

`Except` (Set1, Set2 [, Flag])

`Except` returns a set that is the difference between Set1 and Set2. The `ALL` flag retains duplicates.

`Extract` (Set, Dimension [, Dimension ...])

`Extract` does the opposite of `Crossjoin`. It returns a set of tuples extracted from a given set for the specified dimensions. Duplicates are always removed.

`Filter` (Set, Condition)

`Filter` returns a set from the given set that matches the search condition. Each member of the set is evaluated against the search condition, which must be a Boolean expression. If the result of the expression is true, the member is added to the return set. If the result is false, the member not returned. If no members match the search conditions, an empty set is returned. For example,

```
select
{[Time].[1997].[Q1],[Time].[1997].[Q2] } on columns,
{Filter([Store].Members,
  ([Time].[1997].[Q1], [Profit]) > ([Time].[1997].[Q2],
  [Profit]))} on rows
from Sales
where [Measures].[Profit]
```

will return all store members that have declining profits from Q1 1997 to Q2 1997.

`FirstChild`

`FirstChild` is used in context of a member and returns the first child member of that member.

`FirstSibling`

`FirstSibling` is used in context of a member and returns the first child of the parent of a member. The `FirstChild` of a parent is its own `FirstSibling`.

`Generate` (Set1, Set2 [, Flag])

`Generate` creates a set by applying each member of Set2 to Set1 and joining them with a union. When Set2 is static, the results are similar to a `Crossjoin`. When combined with the `CurrentMember` function, `Generate` can create some very useful results. If the `ALL` flag is set, the duplicates in the set are retained. For example,

```
select {Generate({[Time].[Year].[1997]},
{[Time].Currentmember,
[Time].CurrentMember.Children})} on columns,
[Product].[Product Family].Members on rows
from [Sales]
where (Measures.[Profit])
```

returns the result set shown in Table A.7.

TABLE A.7 Results of using `Generate`.

	1997	*Q1*	*Q2*	*Q3*	*Q4*
Drink	29,358.98	6,964.30	7,186.11	7,203.34	8,005.22
Food	245,764.87	60,814.47	57,323.37	61,262.55	66,364.47
Non-Consumable	64,487.05	16,097.34	15,192.56	15,901.13	17,296.02

From the results, you can see how `Generate` is used to create a set of members that includes both the year and the child quarters that make up the year.

`Generate` (Set, String Expression [, Delimiter])

This generates a concatenated string by evaluating an expression over a set. The resulting string can be delimited between each result by the optional supplied delimiter.

`Head` (Set [, Numeric expression])

`Head` returns the first numeric expression elements from the given set as a set. The order of the elements is preserved. If the numeric expression evaluates to less than 1, an empty set is returned. If the numeric expression is greater than *Set*.`Count`, then the entire set is returned.

`Hiearchize` (Set [, Flag])

This function returns the set given after ordering the members into hierarchical order according to the natural ordering in the database. `POST` orders them in a child-first manner with children preceding parents.

`Hierarchy`

This function is used in context of a `Member` or `Level` and returns the hierarchy containing the specified `Member` or `Level`.

`Ignore`

`Ignore` is used in context of a dimension and will fix the member of a dimension at the current context to prevent further recursion along that dimension.

`Iif` (Logical Expression, Expression1, Expression2)

This function evaluates the logical expression and returns the value in Expression1 if true and Expression2 if false. Expression1 and Expression2 are of either string or numeric type and both have to be of the same type. Note that since null is treated as zero, there is no way to do `Iif(logical expression, "string," null)` since those would be two different types. For example,

```
with member [Measures].[Profit Growth Indicator] as
'Iif([Measures].[Profit] - ([Time].PrevMember
[Measures].[Profit]) > 0, "+","-")'
select
{[Time].[1997].[Q2].children } on columns,
{[Store].[All Stores].[USA].[CA].children } on rows
from Sales
where [Measures].[Profit Growth Indicator]
```

shows a "+" if profits this period are greater than last and a "–" if profits are lower.

`Intersect` (Set1, Set2 [, Flag])

`Intersect` returns a set that is the intersection of Set1 and Set2. By default, duplicates are eliminated. If the `ALL` flag is set, all tuples, including duplicates, are returned.

`Is`

The `Is` operator is used to compare two objects in the form of Object1 `Is` Object2 and returns true if they are equivalent, false otherwise. Objects can be compared to `NULL`.

`IsAncestor` (Member1, Member2)

This is used to determine if Member1 is an ancestor of Member2. If Member1 is an ancestor of Member2, true is returned. If not, false is returned.

`IsEmpty` (Expression)

This is used to determine if the given expression is empty. and it returns true if the expression is empty.

`IsGeneration` (Member, Numeric Expression)

This function tests if a given member is in the numeric expression generation. True is returned if the member is of the given numeric expression generation, otherwise false is returned. Leaf members are in generation 0. A leaf member is a dimension member without any descendants. Non-leaf member generations (that is those dimension members with descendants) are calculated by adding the generation numbers of all the children of the member's parent plus one. In a ragged hierarchy this means that a member may belong to more than one generation. So, the statement `IsGeneration`(member, 1) will return true if the given member is the parent of a leaf member.

IsLeaf (Member)

`IsLeaf` returns true if the given member is a leaf member, otherwise it returns false. A leaf member is a dimension member without any descendants.

IsSibling (Member1, Member2)

`IsSibling` returns true if Member1 is a sibling of Member2 and false otherwise.

Item

`Item` can be used in the context of a set. There are two variations in the way it can be used. In the first variation, `Item` is used as a numeric accessor to the array of members in the set: Set.Item(Index). This returns the member specified in the index from the zero-based array of tuples in the set. In the second variation, a string expression is used to match the first tuple in the set by name: Set.Item(String Expression [, String Expression . . .]). If more than one string is used, strings must match the number and order of dimensions in the set. `Item` is the default operator on a set so that the expressions Set.Item(index) and Set(index) are equivalent.

Lag (Numeric Expression)

Used in context of a member, `Lag` returns the member that is the specified numeric expression position's prior member along the member dimension's natural order. `Member.Lag(0)` returns the given `Member`. If the numeric expression is less than 0, a subsequent member is returned so that `Lag(-n)` is equivalent to `Lead(n)`.

LastChild

Used in context of a member, `LastChild` returns the last child of the given member.

LastPeriods (Index [, Member])

This function returns a set of periods from the given member lagging back index periods. If a member is not specified, `Time.CurrentMember` is used. If index is greater than zero, then index number of periods are returned in the set, starting with the given member. If index is less than zero, then –index number of leading periods are returned in the set, starting with the current member. If index is zero, then an empty set is returned. For example,

```
select
{[Measures].[Unit Sales]} on columns,
{LastPeriods(3, [Time].[1997].[Q1].[3])} on rows
from Sales
```

returns Quarters 1, 2 and 3 from 1997 on the rows.

LastSibling

`LastSibling` is used in context of a member and returns the last child of the parent of a member. The `LastChild` of a parent is its own `LastSibling`.

Lead

Used in context of a member, `Lead` returns the member that is the specified numeric expression position's subsequent member along the member dimension's natural order. `Member.Lead(0)` returns the given member. If the numeric expression is less than 0, a prior member is returned so that `Lead(-n)` is equivalent to `Lag(n)`.

Level

Used in context of a member, `Level` returns the level of the given member.

Levels (Numeric Expression)

Used in context of a dimension, `Levels` returns the dimension level specified by the numeric expression from a zero-based array of levels starting at the root. An error is returned if the numeric expression is larger than the number of levels. For example,

```
select
{[Measures].[Unit Sales]} on columns,
{[Time].Levels(2).Members} on rows
from Sales
```

returns all of the members of the month level on rows.

Levels (String Expression)

`Levels` returns the level specified by the string expression. For example,

```
select
{[Measures].[Unit Sales]} on columns,
{Levels("Month").Members} on rows
from Sales
```

LinkMember (Member, Hierarchy)

`LinkMember` is used to reference one hierarchy from another. `LinkMember` returns the member corresponding to the given member from the given hierarchy.

LinRegIntercept (Set, Numeric Expression[, Numeric Expression])

`LinRegIntercept` returns the intercept for a least-squares linear regression on a set. The first numeric expression is used to calculate the *y*-axis and the second numeric expression is used for the *x*-axis. If the second expression is not provided, the context values of the set are used. Empty cells and cells with non-numeric data are excluded from the calculation. For example,

```
with member [Measures].[Intercept] as
'
  LinRegIntercept(LastPeriods(10,
  [Time].[1997].[Q4].[12]),
  [Measures].[Profit], [Measures].[Store Sales])
'
select
{[Measures].[Intercept]} on columns,
{[Product].children} on rows
from Sales
```

returns the intercept for the linear regression of store sales on profit over the last ten periods for each of the product families.

LinRegPoint (Numeric Expression1, Set, Numeric Expression2[, Numeric Expression3])

`LinRegPoint` calculates the value for the linear regression line $y = mx + b$ as the other `LinRegXXX` functions and then uses numeric expression 1 to extrapolate the *y* value and return it. Numeric expression 2 represents the *y*-values and numeric expression 3 contains the *x*-values. If numeric expression 3 is not supplied, the context values for the set are used. For example,

```
with member [Measures].[Point] as
'
  LinRegPoint(10,
  LastPeriods(9,  ,[Time].[1997].[Q4].[12]),
  [Measures].[Profit], [Measures].[Store Sales])
'
select
{[Measures].[Point]} on columns,
{[Product].children} on rows
from Sales
```

returns the estimate of profit for the 10th period based on a regression of store sales on profit for the previous nine periods.

LinRegR2 (Set, Numeric Expression[, Numeric Expression])

This function returns the calculated coefficient of determination, R^2, for a least-squares linear regression on a set. The first numeric expression is used to calculate the *y*-axis and the second numeric expression is used for the *x*-axis. If the second expression is not provided, the context values of the set are used. Empty cells and cells with non-numeric data are excluded from the calculation. For example,

```
with member [Measures].[R2] as
'
LinRegR2(LastPeriods(10, ,[Time].[1997].[Q4].[12]),
[Measures].[Profit], [Measures].[Store Sales])
'
select
{[Measures].[R2]} on columns,
{[Product].children} on rows
from Sales
```

returns the R^2 for the linear regression of store sales on profit over the last 10 periods for each of the product families.

LinRegSlope (Set, Numeric Expression[, Numeric Expression])

This function returns the calculated slope for a least-squares linear regression on a set. The first numeric expression is used to calculate the *y*-axis and the second numeric expression is used for the *x*-axis. If the second expression is not provided, the context values of the set are used. Empty cells and cells with non-numeric data are excluded from the calculation. For example,

```
with member [Measures].[Slope] as
'
LinRegSlope(LastPeriods(10,[Time].[1997].[Q4].[12]),
[Measures].[Profit], [Measures].[Store Sales])
'
select
{[Measures].[Slope]} on columns,
{[Product].children} on rows
from Sales
```

returns the slope for the linear regression of store sales on profit over the last 10 periods for each of the product families.

LinRegVariance (Set, Numeric Expression[, Numeric Expression])

This function returns the calculated variance for a least-squares linear regression on a set. The first numeric expression is used to calculate the *y*-axis and the second numeric expression is used for the *x*-axis. If the second expression is not provided, the context values of the set are used. Empty cells and cells with non-numeric data are excluded from the calculation. For example,

```
with member [Measures].[Variance] as
'
LinRegVariance(LastPeriods(10),[Measures].[Profit],
[Measures].[Store Sales])
'
select
{[Measures].[Variance]} on columns,
{[Product].children} on rows
from Sales
```

returns the variance for the linear regression of store sales on profit over the last 10 periods for each of the product families.

LookupCube (String, Expression)

This function is used to retrieve a single value from another cube in the same database. The function will return the results of the given expression, which can be of numeric or string value. For example,

```
with member
Measures.[Store Budget]
as
'LookupCube(
"Budget",
"(" + MemberToStr([Store].CurrentMember)
+", [Measures].[Amount])"
)'
select
{Measures.[Store Sales], Measures.[Store Budget]}
on columns,
[Store].[USA].children on rows
from Sales
```

returns the store sales next to the store budget amount for each of the states.

Max (Set [, Numeric Expression])

`Max` returns the maximum value of the numeric expression evaluated over the given set. If no numeric expression is provided, then the context values of the cells are used. For example,

```
with member [Measures].[Max] as
'Max({[Time].[Month].members},
[Measures].[Unit Sales])'
select
{[Measures].[Max] } on columns,
{[Product].[Product Family].members} on rows
from Sales
```

returns the maximum monthly sales for each of the product family members.

Median (Set [, Numeric Expression])

`Median` returns the median value of the numeric expression evaluated over the given set. If no numeric expression is provided, then the context values of the cells are used. For example,

```
with member [Measures].[Median] as
'Median({[Time].[Month].members},
[Measures].[Unit Sales])'
```

```
select
{[Measures].[Median] } on columns,
{[Product].[Product Family].members} on rows
from Sales
```

returns the median monthly sales for the product family members.

Members

This returns the set of members in a dimension, level, or hierarchy depending on the context it is used in. Used in the context of a dimension, Members will return all of the members, including the All member. Used with a hierarchy, `Members` returns all of the members in the hierarchy. Used with a level, `Members` returns all of the members in the level.

Members (String Expression)

This syntax returns a single member with the name matching the string expression. This syntax is most commonly used with user-defined functions to retrieve the member matching a given string.

MemberToStr (Member)

`MemberToStr` returns the unique name of the member as a string. Calling `MemberToStr` results in the same string returned by `UniqueName`.

Min (Set [, Numeric Expression])

`Min` returns the minium value of the numeric expression evaluated over the given set. If no numeric expression is provided, then the context values of the cells are used. For example,

```
with member [Measures].[Min] as
'Min({[Time].[Month].members},
[Measures].[Unit Sales])'
select
{[Measures].[Min] } on columns,
{[Product].[Product Family].members} on rows
from Sales
```

returns the minimum monthly sales for the product family members.

Mtd ([Member])

`Mtd` returns the set of members from the month level in a `Time` dimension up to and including the given member. If no member is supplied, the default value is `Time.CurrentMember`. This function is the equivalent of `PeriodsToDate`(Month, member).

Name

Used in the context of a dimension, level, member, or hierarchy, this function returns the name of the context element.

NameToSet (Member Name)

`NameToSet` returns a set with the single member specified by member name. If no member matches the given member name, an empty set is returned.

NextMember

Used in context of a member, `NextMember` returns the subsequent member in the same level as the given member.

NonEmptyCrossjoin (Set1, Set2 [, Set3...][, Count])

This function returns the non-empty Cartesian product of two or more sets. Any tuples that are empty or do not contain data in the underlying fact tables are excluded. This means that calculated members are not included in the results. Set count determines the number of sets that will be included in the cross-join for the result set. If set count is not specified, all sets are included. This function is particularly useful in creating sets with sparse data. For example,

```
select
{NonEmptyCrossjoin([Store].[WA].Children,
[Promotions].[All Promotions].Children) } on columns,
{[1997]} on rows
from [Sales]
```

returns only those tuples that contain sales data for promotions in WA. Promotions that yielded no sales in WA are not included in the results.

OpeningPeriod ([Level [, Member]])

This function returns the first descendant of a member at the specified level. If no level is provided, the `Time` dimension is used. If no level or member is provided, then the default is `Time.CurrentMember`. This function is very similar to `ClosingPeriod`, except that it returns the first member instead of the last. An example follows:

```
select
{[Product].Children}
on columns,
{OpeningPeriod()} on rows
from Sales
```

Order (Set, {String Expression | Numeric Expression} [,Flag])

`Order` sorts the members of the specified set according to the options that have been provided. If a numeric or string expression is provided, that is used as the basis for the sort. If it is not provided, the context values of the cells are used. Sorts can be done in two different orders depending on the selected flag: ascending (ASC) or descending (DESC). In addition to the order, sorts can specify whether they break the hierarchy. The B in front of BASC and BDESC break the hierarchy. When the hierarchy is broken, the members are sorted without any attention to their position in the hierarchy. ASC and DESC sorts preserve the hierarchy in the set. The hierarchical sort first positions the members according to their level in the hierarchy. Next, it orders within each level. The default sort order is ASC (that is, ascending and hierarchical). For example, the following MDX

```
select
{[1997]} on columns,
{Order({[Store].[USA],
[Store].[USA].Children }, [Profit], ASC) } on rows
from [Sales]
```

returns the data presented in Table A.8.

TABLE A.8 Results of `Order` function using ASC.

	1997
USA	266,773.00
OR	67,659.00
CA	74,748.00
WA	124,366.00

while the following query

```
select
{[1997]} on columns,
{Order({[Store].[USA], [Store].[USA].Children},
[Profit], BASC) } on rows
from [Sales]
```

returns the data presented in Table A.9.

TABLE A.9 Results of `Order` function using BASC.

	1997
OR	67,659.00
CA	74,748.00
WA	124,366.00
USA	266,773.00

`Ordinal`

Used in context of a level, `Ordinal` returns the level index for the given level. The root level of a cube is 0.

`ParallelPeriod` ([Level [, Numeric Expression [, Member]]])

`ParallelPeriod` returns a member from the prior time period in the same relative position as the given member. If no level is specified, the default is the parent level of the given member. If no numeric expression is specified, the default is 1. If no member is specified, the default is `Time.CurrentMember`. For example,

```
select
{[Time].[1998].[Q1], ParallelPeriod([Quarter],
4,[Time].[1998].[Q1]) } on columns,
{[Store].[USA].Children } on rows
from [Sales]
```

returns columns with Q1 1998 and Q1 1997.

`Parent`

Used in context of a member, `Parent` returns the given member's parent.

`PeriodsToDate` ([Level [, Member]])

`PeriodsToDate` returns the set of members from the given level starting with the first member and ending with a specified member. If no level is specified, the default is to the parent level of the given member. If no member is specified, then the default member is `Time.CurrentMember`. For example,

```
select
{[Store].[USA] } on columns,
{PeriodsToDate([Year],[Time].[1997].[Q3] ) } on rows
from [Sales]
```

returns the data presented in Table A.10.

TABLE A.10 Results of `PeriodToDate` function.

	USA
Q1	66,291.00
Q2	62,610.00
Q3	65,848.00

`Predict` (Model Name, Expression)

`Predict` evaluates the numeric expression in the data mining model given by the mining model name. The syntax and use of the data mining expression is covered in Chapter 8.

`PrevMember`

Used in context of a member, `PrevMember` returns the prior member in the same level as the given member.

`Properties` (String Expression)

The `Properties` function is used in context of a member and returns the property member specified by the string expression. The string expression can specify one of the standard properties such as `CAPTION`, `NAME`, `ID` or `KEY` or a user-defined property. All properties are returned as strings.

`Qtd`

`Qtd` returns the set of members from the `Quarter` level in a `Time` dimension up to and including the given member. If no member is supplied, the default value is `Time.CurrentMember`. This function is the equivalent of `PeriodsToDate`(Quarter, member).

`Rank` (Tuple, Set [, Expression])

`Rank` returns the index of the tuple in set. If the tuple is in the first ordinal position, `Rank` returns 1. If the tuple is not found, `Rank` returns 0. If a calculated expression is specified, it is used as the basis for sorting the set. If no calculated expression is specified, then the context value is used. If tuples are tied, then the same rank is returned.

`RollupChildren` (Member , String Expression)

The `RollupChildren` rolls-up the values of the children of the given member using the unary operator specified by the string expression. The possible operators are `+`, `–`, `*`, `/`, `%` and `~`. For example,

```
with cell calculation  [First Quarter] for
'([Time].[Quarter].Members)'
as    'RollupChildren([Time].CurrentMember,
iif([Time].CurrentMember is [Time].FirstSibling,
   "+", "~"))'
select
   {[Product].children} on columns,
   {[Store].[USA].Children} on rows
from Sales
where ([Time].[1997])
```

returns cells that consist of the rollup of only the first month of each quarter.

SetToArray (Set [, Set...][, Numeric Expression])

SetToArray converts the given set into a variant of type VT_ARRAY to be used as input to a user-defined function. The number of dimensions of the resulting array is determined by the number of sets passed in. The numeric expression provides values for the array elements. If a numeric expression is not provided, the default value of the set members are used. The resulting array contains values of only one type, which is determined by the first element to be passed into the array.

SetToStr (Set)

SetToStr returns a string that has been constructed from the unique name of each member of the set.

Siblings

Used in context of a member, Siblings returns the siblings of the given member including the member itself but excluding calculated members.

Stddev

This is an alias for Stdev.

StddevP

This is an alias for StdevP.

Stdev (Set [, Numeric Expression])

Stdev returns the sample standard deviation of the numeric expression over the set. If a numeric expression is not provided, the default context values are used. The sample standard deviation is calculated by the following equation where *n* is the number of non-empty cells and is the mean of numeric expression:

$$\sqrt{\frac{\sum_{i=1}^{n}(\bar{x}-x)^2}{n-1}}$$

```
with member [Measures].[QtrStdev] as
'Stdev([Time].[1997].[Q1]:[Time].[1997].[Q4].,
[Measures].[Profit])'
select
{[Measures].[QtrStdev]} on columns,
{[Product].[Product Family].members} on rows
from Sales
```

returns the sample standard deviation of profit over the quarters in 1997 for each of the product family members.

StdevP (Set [, Numeric Expression])

StdevP returns the population standard deviation of the numeric expression over the set. If a numeric expression is not provided, the default context values are used. The population standard deviation is calculated by the following equation where n is the number of non-empty cells and is the mean of numeric expression:

$$\sqrt{\frac{\sum_{i=1}^{n}(\bar{x}-x)^2}{n}}$$

For example,

```
with member [Measures].[QtrStdevP] as
'StdevP([Time].[1997].[Q1]:[Time].[1997].[Q4],
[Measures].[Profit])'
select
{[Measures].[QtrStdevP]} on columns,
{[Product].[Product Family].members} on rows
from Sales
```

returns the population standard deviation of profit over the quarters in 1997 for each of the product family members.

StripCalculatedMembers (Set)

This function returns the given set after stripping all of the calculated members from the set. So

```
select
{StripCalculatedMembers([Measures].AllMembers)}
on columns,
{[1997]}
on rows
from Sales
```

and

```
select
{[Measures].Members} on columns,
{[1997]} on rows
from Sales
```

return the same set of columns.

StrToMember (String Expression)

This function returns the member that is specified in the string expression and is most often used in conjunction with user-defined functions.

StrToSet (String Expression)

This function returns a set that is specified by the string expression. It is most commonly used with user-defined functions.

StrToTuple (String Expression)

This function returns a tuple that is specified by the string expression. It is most commonly used with user-defined functions.

StrToValue (String Expression)

This function returns a string expression and evaluates it in the current context to return a value. This is most commonly used with a user-defined function.

Subset (Set, Start [, Count])

This function returns a subset of the given set of count tuples beginning at the index defined by start. The set is considered to be a zero-based array of tuples and start must be between 0 and the one less than the number of tuples in the array. If count is not specified, or is greater than the number of elements in the array from the start position, all of the tuples from start to the end are returned.

Sum (Set [, Numeric Expression])

Sum returns the sum of the values of the numeric expression over the set. If a numeric expression is not given, then the context is used for the values. For example,

```
with member [Measures].[QtrSum] as
'Sum([Time].[1997].[Q2]:[Time].[1997].[Q3],
[Measures].[Profit])'
select
{[Measures].[QtrSum]} on columns,
{[Product].[Product Family].members} on rows
from Sales
```

returns the sum of Q2 and Q3 profits over each member of the product family.

Tail (Set [, Count])

`Tail` returns the last numeric expression elements from the given set as a set. The order of the elements is preserved. If the numeric expression evaluates to less than 1, an empty set is returned. If the numeric expression is greater than Set.`Count`, then the entire set is returned.

ToggleDrillState (Set1, Set2 [, Flag])

This function toggles the drill state of each member of Set2 that is in the set. In effect, it is like a combination of `DrillupMember` and `DrilldownMember`. If a member in Set1 is drilled down, it is drilled up by using `DrillupMember`(set1, member). To be drilled down, a member of Set1 must have descendants immediately following it. Otherwise, it is considered drilled up. If a member in Set1 is drilled up, it is drilled down using `DrilldownMember(set1, m)`. If RECURSIVE is set in `ToggleDrillState`, it is used on the call to `DrilldownMember`.

`TopCount` (Set, Count [, Numeric Expression])

`TopCount` returns the top count number of members in the set. If a numeric expression is provided, the set is sorted by the expression. If it is not provided, the elements are ordered by the default. As do the other `Count` and `Percent` functions, `TopCount` treats the results as being at the same level in the hierarchy. If there are tied elements in the sort order, some may be arbitrarily left out of the results. For example,

```
select
TopCount([Product].[All Products].[Food].children,
3, Profit)
on columns,
{[Time].[1997]} on rows
from Sales
```

returns the three most profitable food elements.

`TopPercent` (Set, Percentage, Numeric Expression)

`TopPercent` returns the top percentage members of the members in the set sorted by the numeric expression. The percentage is specified with a number between 0 and 100 (although using a number greater than 100 does not cause an error). Unlike in the `TopCount` function, the numeric expression is not optional. Like the other `Count` and `Percent` functions, `TopPercent` treats the results as being at the same level in the hierarchy. If there are tied elements in the sort order, some may be arbitrarily left out of the results.

`TopSum` (Set, Value, Numeric Expression)

`TopSum` returns the minimum number of members of the set sorted by the numeric expression such that the sum of the members is at least the given value. Unlike in the `TopCount` function, the numeric expression is not optional. As do the other `Count` and `Percent` functions, `TopSum` treats the results as being at the same level in the hierarchy. For example,

```
select
TopSum([Product].[All Products].[Food].children,
50000, Profit)
on columns,
{[Time].[1997]} on rows
from Sales
```

returns the data presented in Table A.11.

TABLE A.11 Results of TopSum function.

	Produce	*Snacks*
1997	37,792.00	30,545.00

TupleToStr (Tuple)

This function returns a string constructed from the given tuple. The unique name of each member in the tuple is returned. If the tuple has only one member, just the unique name is returned. If there are more than one member in the tuple, the resulting string begins with an open parenthesis and ends with a close parenthesis, and each member unique name is separated by a comma and a space.

Union (Set1, Set2 [, Flag])

This function returns the union of two sets. If the ALL flag is specified, duplicates are retained. If not, duplicate members are eliminated. As an alternate syntax, you can join sets by using {Set1 , Set2} or Set1 + Set2. Both of these syntaxes result in the duplicates being retained.

UniqueName

Used in context of a dimension, level, member, or hierarchy, UniqueName returns the unique name of the context object. For a hierarchy, the unique name will be [Dimension].[Hierarchy]. For a level, the unique name will be [Dimension].[Level] or [Dimension].[Hierarchy].[Level] depending on whether the dimension has hierarchies. For a member, the name will be [Dimension].[Level].[Member].

UserName

This function returns the domain and user name of the user executing the function as domain_name\user_name.

ValidMeasure (Tuple)

This function returns a measure from the given tuple projected to a valid intersection in a virtual cube. In a virtual cube, dimensions that are not common between the underlying cubes have values only in the All level. Instead of specifying each of the dimensions to specify the measure, ValidMeasure will do that automatically. For example,

```
with member [Measures].[SWCost] as
'ValidMeasure(Measures.[Store Cost]) –
ValidMeasure(Measures.[Warehouse Cost])'
select
```

```
{[Warehouse].[USA].children} on columns,
{[Promotion Media].Children} on rows
from [Warehouse and Sales]
where [Measures].[SWCost]
```

uses `ValidMeasure` to get the store and warehouse cost since the row dimension is not in both the Warehouse and Sales cubes.

`Value`

`Value` is the default operator on a measure and returns the value of the given measure.

`Var` (Set[, Numeric Expression])

`Var` returns the sample variance of the numeric expression over the set. If a numeric expression is not provided, the default context values are used. The sample variance is calculated by the following equation where n is the number of non-empty cells and is the mean of numeric expression:

$$\frac{\sum_{i=1}^{n} (\bar{x} - x)^2}{n - 1}$$

For example,

```
with member [Measures].[QtrVar] as
'Var([Time].[1997].[Q1]:[Time].[1997].[Q4],
[Measures].[Profit])'
select
{[Measures].[QtrVar]} on columns,
{[Product].[Product Family].members} on rows
from Sales
```

returns the sample variance of profit over the quarters in 1997 for each of the product family members.

`Variance` (Set [, Numeric Expression])

`Variance` is an alias for `Var` and they can be used interchangeably.

`VarianceP` (Set [, Numeric Expression])

`VarianceP` is an alias for `VarP` and they can be used interchangeably.

`VarP` (Set [, Numeric Expression])

`VarP` returns the population variance of the numeric expression over the set. If a numeric expression is not provided, the default context values are used. The sample variance is calculated by the following equation where n is the number of non-empty cells and is the mean of numeric expression:

$$\frac{\sum_{i=1}^{n}(\bar{x}-x)^2}{n}$$

For example,

```
with member [Measures].[QtrVarP] as
'VarP([Time].[1997].[Q1]:[Time].[1997].[Q4],
[Measures].[Profit])'
select
{[Measures].[QtrVarP]} on columns,
{[Product].[Product Family].members} on rows
from Sales
```

returns the population variance of profit over the quarters in 1997 for each of the Product Family members.

VisualTotals (Set, Pattern)

`VisualTotals` returns a set that is dynamically calculated from the child members specified in the given set that consists of parent and child members. For each parent followed by one or more descendants, `VisualTotals` replaces the parent member with a calculated member that is the sum of the given descendants. Note that the order of the set is important and the descendants must appear immediately after the parent member. The pattern specifies the label for the calculated total with an asterisk (*) indicating where the name of the parent is in the specified set. Two asterisks (**) will display an asterisk in the label. For example,

```
select
{[Measures].[Profit]} on columns,
{VisualTotals({[Store].[All Stores].[USA],
[Store].[All Stores].[USA].[CA],
[Store].[All Stores].[USA].[OR]},
    "CA and OR - *")
} on rows
from Sales
```

returns the results presented in Table A.12.

TABLE A.12 Results of the `VisualTotals` function.

	Profit
CA and OR	181,141.98
CA	95,637.41
OR	85,504.57

Note that the results presented by `VisualTotals` include only those children that are explicitly included in the set. Compare these results with the results from the following:

```
select
{[Measures].[Profit]} on columns,
{[Store].[All Stores].[USA],
[Store].[All Stores].[USA].[CA],
[Store].[All Stores].[USA].[OR]} on rows
from Sales
```

which returns the data presented in Table A.13.

TABLE A.13 Results of a `select` without using `VisualTotals` show all children.

	Profit
USA	339,610.90
CA	95,637.41
OR	85,504.57

The total presented for USA includes the profit from WA, even though that is not explicitly included in the set.

Wtd

`Wtd` returns the set of members from the Week level in a Time dimension up to and including the given member. If no member is supplied, the default value is `Time.CurrentMember`. This function is the equivalent of `PeriodsToDate`(Week, member).

Ytd

`Ytd` returns the set of members from the month level in a Time dimension up to and including the given member. If no member is supplied, the default value is `Time.CurrentMember`. This function is the equivalent of `PeriodsToDate`(Year, member).

B MDX Properties

Table B.1 contains the intrinsic properties for MDX members.

TABLE B.1 Intrinsic properties for MDX members.

Name	*Type*	*Description*
CATALOG_NAME	DBTYPE_WSTR	The name of the catalog to which this member belongs
SCHEMA_NAME	DBTYPE_WSTR	The name of the schema to which this member belongs
CUBE_NAME	DBTYPE_WSTR	Name of the cube to which this member belongs
DIMENSION_UNIQUE_NAME	DBTYPE_WSTR	Unique name of the dimension to which this member belongs
HIERARCHY_UNIQUE_NAME	DBTYPE_WSTR	Unique name of the hierarchy. If the member belongs to more than one hierarchy, there is one row for each hierarchy to which it belongs.
LEVEL_UNIQUE_NAME	DBTYPE_WSTR	Unique name of the level to which the member belongs

TABLE B.1 *(Continued)*

Name	*Type*	*Description*
LEVEL_NUMBER	DBTYPE_UI4	The distance of the member from the root of the hierarchy. The root level is zero.
MEMBER_ORDINAL	DBTYPE_UI4	Ordinal number of the member. It stands for the sort rank of the member when members of this dimension are sorted in their natural sort order.
MEMBER_NAME	DBTYPE_WSTR	Name of the member
MEMBER_UNIQUE_NAME	DBTYPE_WSTR	Unique name of the member
MEMBER_TYPE	DBTYPE_I4	Type of the member. It can be one of the following values: MDMEMBER_TYPE_REGULAR MDMEMBER_TYPE_ALL MDMEMBER_TYPE_FORMULA MDMEMBER_TYPE_MEASURE MDMEMBER_TYPE_UNKNOWN MDMEMBER_TYPE_FORMULA takes precedence over MDMEMBER_TYPE_MEASURE. Therefore, if there is a formula (calculated) member on the Measures dimension, it is listed as MDMEMBER_TYPE_FORMULA.
MEMBER_GUID	DBTYPE_GUID	Member GUID
MEMBER_CAPTION	DBTYPE_WSTR	A label or caption associated with the member. It is used primarily for display purposes. If a caption does not exist, MEMBER_NAME is returned.

TABLE B.1 *(Continued)*

Name	*Type*	*Description*
CHILDREN_CARDINALITY	DBTYPE_UI4	Number of children that the member has. This can be an estimate, so consumers should not rely on this to be the exact count. Providers should return the best estimate possible.
PARENT_LEVEL	DBTYPE_UI4	The distance of the member's parent from the root level of the hierarchy. The root level is zero.
PARENT_UNIQUE_NAME	DBTYPE_WSTR	Unique name of the member's parent. NULL is returned for any members at the root level.
PARENT_COUNT	DBTYPE_UI4	Number of parents that this member has
DESCRIPTION	DBTYPE_WSTR	Description associated with the member

Table B.2 contains the intrinsic properties for cells.

TABLE B.2 Intrinsic properties for cells.

Name	*Type*	*Description*
VALUE	DBTYPE_VARIANT	Actual data value
FORMATTED_VALUE	DBTYPE_WSTR	Character string that represents a formatted display of VALUE
CELL_ORDINAL	DBTYPE_UI4	Ordinal number of the cell in the dataset
FORMAT_STRING	DBTYPE_WSTR	Format string used to create FORMATTED_VALUE

TABLE B.2 *(Continued)*

FORE_COLOR	DBTYPE_UI4	Foreground color for displaying VALUE
BACK_COLOR	DBTYPE_UI4	Background color for displaying VALUE
FONT_NAME	DBTYPE_WSTR	Font to be used to display VALUE
FONT_SIZE	DBTYPE_UI2	Font size to be used to display VALUE
FONT_FLAGS	DBTYPE_I4	Bitmask detailing effects on the font. This can be the result of a bitwise OR operation of one or more of the following: MDFF_BOLD MDFF_ITALIC MDFF_UNDERLINE MDFF_STRIKEOUT
NON_EMPTY_BEHAVIOR	DBTYPE_WSTR	Specifies the measure used to determine the behavior of calculated members when resolving empty cells.Used to set a calculated measure to null when a base measure is null.
SOLVE_ORDER	DBTYPE_I4	Sets the solve order for the cell with the cells with a lower SOLVE_ORDER being resolved first. The default SOLVE_ORDER is 0.

C Standard MDX Operators

MDX provides many standard arithmetic, comparison, and logical operators. Table C.1 has a complete list of these operators. Arithmetic operators are addition (+), subtraction (-), multiplication (*) and division (/). Per standard rules of arithmetic precedence, multiplication and division operators are processed before addition and subtraction operators. The specific precedence levels are shown in the following list. Operators on higher levels are evaluated before operators on a lower level:

- + (positive), – (negative)
- * (multiply), / (divide)
- + (add), +(concatenate), – (subtract)
- =, >, <, >=, <=, <> (Comparison operators)
- NOT
- AND
- OR, XOR

If operators have the same level of precedence, the operators are processed in a left-to-right order. Note that the addition operator (+) can also be used to concatenate strings. Comparison operators compare two values and return a logical true (1) or false (0) based on the outcome of the comparison. Supported comparison operators are less than (<), greater than (>), less than or equal to (<=), greater than or equal to (>=), not equal to (<>) and equal to (=). Special rules apply to the handling of null values. For the purposes of the comparison operators, null values are treated as zero. You can use the IS operator to check for equality between objects. IS can be used to compare against null to see if an object exists. For example, [Product].[All Products].Parent IS null returns true if the expression refers to a nonexistent object. Logical operators evaluate relationships between Boolean values. Any operation that returns a numeric value is implicitly converted into a Boolean before comparison. If the numeric value is 0 or null, it is converted to false. Any other value is converted to true. This implicit conversion can lead to some unexpected results if you are not careful, so in most instances it is best to do an explicit conversion before using logical operators on non-Boolean values. Also, string expressions are not converted to a Boolean, and using them with a logical operator will result in an error. The logical operators are AND (returns true if both expressions are true, false otherwise), OR (returns true if either expression is true, false if both are false), NOT (returns true if expression is false and false if expression is true), and XOR (returns true if one expression if true, false if both are false or both are true).

TABLE C.1 MDX operators.

Operator	***Description***
NumericExpr1 + NumericExpr2	Sum of the two numeric arguments
NumericExpr1 – NumericExpr2	Difference between numeric arguments
NumericExpr1 * NumericExpr2	Product of numeric arguments
NumericExpr1 / NumericExpr2	Division of NumericExpr1 by NumericExpr2
NumericExpr1 < NumericExpr2	True if NumericExpr1 is less than NumericExpr2, false otherwise
NumericExpr1 > NumericExpr2	True if NumericExpr1 is greater than NumericExpr2, false otherwise
NumericExpr1 <= NumericExpr2	True if NumericExpr1 is less than or equal to NumericExpr2, false otherwise
NumericExpr1 >= NumericExpr2	True if NumericExpr1 is greater than or equal to NumericExpr2, false otherwise
NumericExpr1 <> NumericExpr2	True if NumericExpr1 is not equal to NumericExpr2, false otherwise
NumericExpr1 = NumericExpr2	True if NumericExpr1 is equal to NumericExpr2, false otherwise
ObjectExpr1 IS ObjectExpr2	True if ObjectExpr1 refers to ObjectExpr2. false otherwise. Null can be used to test for non-existent objects.
BooleanExpr1 AND BooleanExpr2	True if both expressions are true, false otherwise
BooleanExpr1 OR BooleanExpr2	True if either expression is true, false if both are false
NOT BooleanExpr	True if BooleanExpr is false and false if BooleanExpr is true
BooleanExpr1 XOR BooleanExpr2	True if one expression is true, false if both are false or both are true

D XMLA Rowsets

The information returned in the Result parameter of the Discover method is in the form of one of eight rowsets. This information is a condensation of the values presented in the XML for Analysis specification focusing on those values that will be most frequently used when you are working with the Microsoft XML for Analysis Provider. We have omitted the details of the DISCOVER_ENUMERATORS, DISCOVER_PROPERTIES, DISCOVER_KEYWORDS, and DISCOVER_LITERALS because these are not likely to be used against a known provider. Full details of all of the rowsets can be found in the specification.

Each of the columns in the rowset must be present and in the order presented, although the values may be null for elements that do not apply. Additional columns can be added to the end of the rowset to contain optional provider-specific information. Each of the required columns is described in the tables in this appendix. "Column name" indicates the name of the column in the rowset, "Type" indicates the data type returned, "Description" has a brief explanation of the column, "Restriction" indicates whether or not passing in a value in Discover filters the resulting rowset to match that value, and "null" indicates whether or not the returned value can have a null value.

DISCOVER_DATASOURCES

A DISCOVER_DATASOURCES request returns the rowset described in Table D.1, which is populated with a list of data sources available on the application Web server.

TABLE D.1 Data sources available on the Web server.

Column name	*Type*	*Description*	*Restriction*	*Null?*
DataSourceName	string	Data source name such as FoodMart 2000	Yes	No
DataSourceDescription	string	Data source description	No	Yes
URL	string	Location of data source	Yes	Yes
DataSourceInfo	string	Additional connection information such as "Provider=MSOLAP; Data Source=Local;"	No	Yes
ProviderName	string	Provider supplying the data source such as "MSDASQL"	Yes	Yes
ProviderType	array	Type of provider. The ProviderType array has an element for each type that the provider supports and includes one or more of the following values: **TDP:** Tabular data provider **MDP:** Multidimensional data provider **DMP:** Data mining provider	Yes	No
AuthenticationMode	EnumString	Indicates security mode required by the data source with one of the following values: **Unauthenticated:** No user ID or password is required. **Authenticated:** User ID and Password must be included in connection information. **Integrated:** The data source uses a built-in security mechanism.	Yes	No

DISCOVER_SCHEMA_ROWSETS

A DISCOVER_SCHEMA_ROWSETS request returns the rowset described in Table D.2, which contains a list of all the request types supported by the provider.

TABLE D.2 List of request types.

Column name	*Type*	*Description*	*Restriction*	*Null?*
`SchemaName`	`String array`	Name of the schema. The possible values appear in Table D.3.	Yes	No
`Restrictions`	`array`	An array of the restrictions supported by the provider	No	Yes
`Description`	`string`	Description of the schema	No	Yes

Table D.3 contains a list of the `SchemaNames` that can be returned with a brief description.

TABLE D.3 `SchemaNames` with descriptions.

SchemaName	*Description*
`DBSCHEMA_CATALOGS`	Catalogs available through the provider
`DBSCHEMA_COLUMNS`	Listing of the columns in tables
`DBSCHEMA_PROVIDER_TYPES`	Data types supported by the provider
`DBSCHEMA_TABLES`	Tables available in the catalog
`DBSCHEMA_TABLES_INFO`	List of information about tables in catalog
`MDSCHEMA_ACTIONS`	Actions available in the catalog
`MDSCHEMA_CUBES`	Cubes available in the catalog
`MDSCHEMA_DIMENSIONS`	Dimensions in the cubes in the catalog
`MDSCHEMA_FUNCTIONS`	List of MDX functions supported by provider
`MDSCHEMA_HIERARCHIES`	Hierarchies in all dimensions in the catalog
`MDSCHEMA_MEASURES`	Measures of all cubes in the catalog
`MDSCHEMA_MEMBERS`	All members in all dimensions of all cubes
`MDSCHEMA_PROPERTIES`	User-specified properties available for cells and members
`MDSCHEMA_SETS`	Sets available in a catalog

E OLE DB for OLAP Schemas

These are the possible schema values for use when retrieving schemas via ADOMD or XMLA. Each of the columns listed is a member of the rowset that is returned. Columns that are in bold can be used to filter the resultant rowset.

TABLE E.1 Schemas for ADOMD and XMLA.

Constant and Description	*Rowset Name and Columns*
AdSchemaAsserts	**ASSERTIONS Rowset**
Returns the assertions specified in the catalog that are owned by a given user	CONSTRAINT_CATALOG CONSTRAINT_SCHEMA CONSTRAINT_NAME IS_DEFERRABLE INITIALLY_DEFERRED DESCRIPTION
AdSchemaCatalogs	
Returns the physical attributes associated with catalogs that are accessible from the DataBase Management System (DBMS)	**CATALOGS Rowset**
	CATALOG_NAME DESCRIPTION
AdSchemaCharacterSets	CHARACTER_SETS Rowset
Returns the character sets specified in the catalog that are accessible to a given user	CHARACTER_SET_CATALOG CHARACTER_SET_SCHEMA CHARACTER_SET_NAME

	FORM_OF_USE NUMBER_OF_CHARACTERS DEFAULT_COLLATE_CATALOG DEFAULT_COLLATE_SCHEMA DEFAULT_COLLATE_NAME
AdSchemaCheckConstraints Returns the check constraints specified in the catalog that are owned by a given user	CHECK_CONSTRAINTS Rowset CONSTRAINT_CATALOG CONSTRAINT_SCHEMA CONSTRAINT_NAME CHECK_CLAUSE DESCRIPTION
AdSchemaCollations Returns the character collations specified in the catalog that are accessible to a given user	**COLLATIONS Rowset** COLLATION_CATALOG COLLATION_SCHEMA COLLATION_NAME CHARACTER_SET_CATALOG CHARACTER_SET_SCHEMA CHARACTER_SET_NAME PAD_ATTRIBUTE
AdSchemaColumnPrivileges Returns the privileges on columns of tables specified in the catalog that are available to, or granted by, a given user	**COLUMN_PRIVILEGES Rowset** **GRANTOR** **GRANTEE** **TABLE_CATALOG** **TABLE_SCHEMA** **TABLE_NAME** **COLUMN_NAME** COLUMN_GUID COLUMN_PROPID PRIVILEGE_TYPE IS_GRANTABLE
AdSchemaColumns Returns the columns of tables (including views) specified in the catalog that are accessible to a given user	COLUMNS Rowset TABLE_CATALOG TABLE_SCHEMA TABLE_NAME COLUMN_NAME COLUMN_GUID COLUMN_PROPID ORDINAL_POSITION COLUMN_HASDEFAULT COLUMN_DEFAULT

	COLUMN_FLAGS IS_NULLABLE DATA_TYPE TYPE_GUID CHARACTER_MAXIMUM_LENGTH CHARACTER_OCTET_LENGTH NUMERIC_PRECISION NUMERIC_SCALE DATETIME_PRECISION CHARACTER_SET_CATALOG CHARACTER_SET_SCHEMA CHARACTER_SET_NAME COLLATION_CATALOG COLLATION_SCHEMA COLLATION_NAME DOMAIN_CATALOG DOMAIN_SCHEMA DOMAIN_NAME DESCRIPTION
AdSchemaColumnsDomainUsage	**COLUMN_DOMAIN_USAGE Rowset**
Returns the columns specified in the catalog that are dependent on a domain specified in the catalog and owned by a given user	DOMAIN_CATALOG DOMAIN_SCHEMA DOMAIN_NAME COLUMN_NAME TABLE_CATALOG TABLE_SCHEMA TABLE_NAME COLUMN_NAME COLUMN_GUID COLUMN_PROPID
AdSchemaConstraintColumnUsage	CONSTRAINT_COLUMN_USAGE Rowset
Returns the columns used by referential constraints, unique constraints, check constraints, and assertions, that are specified in the catalog and owned by a given user	TABLE_CATALOG TABLE_SCHEMA TABLE_NAME COLUMN_NAME COLUMN_GUID COLUMN_PROPID **CONSTRAINT_CATALOG** **CONSTRAINT_SCHEMA** **CONSTAINT_NAME**

AdSchemaConstraintTableUsage	CONSTRAINT_TABLE_USAGE Rowset
Returns the tables that are used by referential constraints, unique constraints, check constraints, and assertions that are specified in the catalog and owned by a given user	**TABLE_CATALOG** **TABLE_SCHEMA** **TABLE_NAME** **CONSTRAINT_CATALOG** **CONSTRAINT_SCHEMA** **CONSTAINT_NAME**
AdSchemaCubes	CUBES Rowset
Returns information about the available cubes in a schema (or the catalog, if the provider does not support schemas)	CATALOG_NAME SCHEMA_NAME CUBE_NAME CUBE_TYPE CUBE_GUID CREATED_ON LAST_SCHEMA_UPDATE SCHEMA_UPDATED_BY LAST_DATA_UPDATE DATA_UPDATED_BY DESCRIPTION ANNOTATIONS
AdSchemaDBInfoKeywords	IDBInfo::GetKeywords
Returns a list of provider-specific keywords	<None>
AdSchemaDBInfoLiterals	IDBInfo::GetLiteralInfo
Returns a list of provider-specific literals used in text commands	<None>
AdSchemaDimensions	DIMENSIONS Rowset
Returns information about the dimensions in a given cube. It has one row for each dimension.	CATALOG_NAME SCHEMA_NAME CUBE_NAME DIMENSION_NAME DIMENSION_UNIQUE_NAME DIMENSION_GUID DIMENSION_CAPTION DIMENSION_ORDINAL DIMENSION_TYPE DIMENSION_CARDINALITY DEFAULT_HIERARCHY DESCRIPTION ANNOTATIONS

AdSchemaForeignKeys	FOREIGN_KEYS Rowset
Returns the foreign key columns specified in the catalog	PK_TABLE_CATALOG PK_TABLE_SCHEMA PK_TABLE_NAME PK_COLUMN_NAME PK_COLUMN_GUID PK_COLUMN_PROPID **FK_TABLE_CATALOG** **FK_TABLE_SCHEMA** **FK_TABLE_NAME** FK_COLUMN_NAME FK_COLUMN_GUID FK_COLUMN_PROPID ORDINAL UPDATE_RULE DELETE_RULE PK_NAME FK_NAME DEFERRABILITY
AdSchemaHierarchies	HIERARCHIES Rowset
Returns information about the hierarchies available in a dimension	CATALOG_NAME SCHEMA_NAME CUBE_NAME DIMENSION_UNIQUE_NAME HIERARCHY_NAME HIERARCHY_UNIQUE_NAME HIERARCHY_GUID HIERARCHY_CAPTION DIMENSION_TYPE HIERARCHY_CARDINALITY DEFAULT_MEMBER [ALL]_MEMBER DESCRIPTION ANNOTATIONS STRUCTURE
AdSchemaIndexes	INDEXES Rowset
Returns the indexes specified in the catalog that are owned by a given user	**TABLE_CATALOG** **TABLE_SCHEMA** **TABLE_NAME** INDEX_CATALOG INDEX_SCHEMA

	INDEX_NAME PRIMARY_KEY UNIQUE CLUSTERED **TYPE** FILL_FACTOR INITIAL_SIZE NULLS SORT_BOOKMARKS AUTO_UPDATE NULL_COLLATION ORDINAL_POSITION COLUMN_NAME COLUMN_GUID COLUMN_PROPID COLLATION CARDINALITY PAGES FILTER_CONDITION INTEGRATED
AdSchemaKeyColumnUsage Returns the columns specified in the catalog that are constrained as keys by a given user	KEY_COLUMN_USAGE Rowset CONSTRAINT_CATALOG CONSTRAINT_SCHEMA CONSTRAINT_NAME TABLE_CATALOG TABLE_SCHEMA TABLE_NAME COLUMN_NAME COLUMN_GUID COLUMN_PROPID ORDINAL_POSITION
AdSchemaLevels Returns information about the levels available in a dimension	LEVELS Rowset CATALOG_NAME SCHEMA_NAME CUBE_NAME DIMENSION_UNIQUE_NAME HIERARCHY_UNIQUE_NAME LEVEL_NAME LEVEL_UNIQUE_NAME LEVEL_GUID LEVEL_CAPTION

	LEVEL_NUMBER LEVEL_CARDINALITY LEVEL_TYPE DESCRIPTION
AdSchemaMeasures Returns information about the available measures	MEASURES Rowset CATALOG_NAME SCHEMA_NAME CUBE_NAME MEASURE_NAME MEASURE_UNIQUE_NAME MEASURE_GUID MEASURE_AGGREGATOR DATA_TYPE NUMERIC_PRECISION NUMERIC_SCALE MEASURE_UNITS DESCRIPTION
AdSchemaMembers Returns information about the available members	MEMBERS Rowset **CATALOG_NAME** **SCHEMA_NAME** **CUBE_NAME** **DIMENSION_UNIQUE_NAME** **HIERARCHY_UNIQUE_NAME** **LEVEL_UNIQUE_NAME** **LEVEL_NUMBER** **MEMBER_NAME** **MEMBER_UNIQUE_NAME** **MEMBER_CAPTION** **MEMBER_TYPE** MEMBER_GUID MEMBER_CAPTION CHILDREN_CARDINALITY PARENT_LEVEL PARENT_UNIQUE_NAME PARENT_COUNT DESCRIPTION
AdSchemaPrimaryKeys Returns the primary key columns specified in the catalog	PRIMARY_KEYS Rowset TABLE_CATALOG TABLE_SCHEMA TABLE_NAME

	COLUMN_NAME COLUMN_GUID COLUMN_PROPID ORDINAL PK_NAME
AdSchemaProcedureColumns Returns information about the columns of rowsets returned by procedures	PROCEDURE_COLUMNS Rowset PROCEDURE_CATALOG PROCEDURE_SCHEMA PROCEDURE_NAME COLUMN_NAME COLUMN_GUID COLUMN_PROPID ROWSET_NUMBER ORDINAL_POSITION IS_NULLABLE DATA_TYPE TYPE_GUID CHARACTER_MAXIMUM_LENGTH CHARACTER_OCTET_LENGTH NUMERIC_PRECISION NUMERIC_SCALE DESCRIPTION
AdSchemaProcedureParameters Returns information about the parameters and return codes of procedures	PROCEDURE_PARAMETERS Rowset PROCEDURE_CATALOG PROCEDURE_SCHEMA PROCEDURE_NAME PARAMETER_NAME ORDINAL_POSITION PARAMETER_TYPE PARAMETER_HASDEFAULT PARAMETER_DEFAULT IS_NULLABLE DATA_TYPE CHARACTER_MAXIMUM_LENGTH CHARACTER_OCTET_LENGTH NUMERIC_PRECISION NUMERIC_SCALE DESCRIPTION TYPE_NAME LOCAL_TYPE_NAME

`AdSchemaProcedures`	`PROCEDURES` Rowset

Returns the procedures specified in the catalog that are owned by a given user	`PROCEDURE_CATALOG`
	`PROCEDURE_SCHEMA`
	`PROCEDURE_NAME`
	`PROCEDURE_TYPE`
	`PROCEDURE_DEFINITION`
	`DESCRIPTION`
	`DATE_CREATED`
	`DATE_MODIFIED`

`AdSchemaProperties`	`PROPERTIES` Rowset

Returns information about the available properties for each level of the dimension	`CATALOG_NAME`
	`SCHEMA_NAME`
	`CUBE_NAME`
	`DIMENSION_UNIQUE_NAME`
	`HIERARCHY_UNIQUE_NAME`
	`LEVEL_UNIQUE_NAME`
	`MEMBER_UNIQUE_NAME`
	`PROPERTY_TYPE`
	`PROPERTY_NAME`

`AdSchemaProviderSpecific`	<Provider specific>
Used if the provider specifies its own nonstandard schema queries	Specified by the provider
`AdSchemaProviderTypes`	`PROVIDER_TYPES` Rowset

Returns the (base) data types supported by the data provider	`TYPE_NAME`
	`DATA_TYPE`
	`BEST_MATCH`
	`COLUMN_SIZE`
	`LITERAL_PREFIX`
	`LITERAL_SUFFIX`
	`CREATE_PARAMS`
	`IS_NULLABLE`
	`CASE_SENSITIVE`
	`SEARCHABLE`
	`UNSIGNED_ATTRIBUTE`
	`FIXED_PREC_SCALE`
	`AUTO_UNIQUE_VALUE`
	`LOCAL_TYPE_NAME`
	`MINIMUM_SCALE`
	`MAXIMUM_SCALE`
	`GUID`

	TYPELIB VERSION IS_LONG BEST_MATCH IS_FIXEDLENGTH
AdSchemaReferentialConstraints	REFERENTIAL_CONSTRAINTS Rowset
Returns the referential constraints specified in the catalog that are owned by a given user	CONSTRAINT_CATALOG CONSTRAINT_SCHEMA CONSTRAINT_NAME
	UNIQUE_CONSTRAINT_CATALOG UNIQUE_CONSTRAINT_SCHEMA UNIQUE_CONSTRAINT_NAME MATCH_OPTION UPDATE_RULE DELETE_RULE DESCRIPTION
AdSchemaSchemata	SCHEMATA Rowset
Returns the schemas (database objects) that are owned by a given user	CATALOG_NAME SCHEMA_NAME SCHEMA_OWNER
	DEFAULT_CHARACTER_SET_CATALOG DEFAULT_CHARACTER_SET_SCHEMA DEFAULT_CHARACTER_SET_NAME
AdSchemaSQLLanguages	SQL_LANGUAGES Rowset
Returns the conformance levels, options, and dialects supported by the SQL-implementation processing data specified in the catalog	SQL_LANGUAGE_SOURCE SQL_LANGUAGE_YEAR SQL_LANGUAGE_CONFORMANCE SQL_LANGUAGE_INTEGRITY SQL_LANGUAGE_IMPLEMENTATION SQL_LANGUAGE_BINDING_STYLE SQL_LANGUAGE_PROGRAMMING_LANGUAGE
AdSchemaStatistics	STATISTICS Rowset
Returns the statistics specified in the catalog that are owned by a given user	TABLE_CATALOG TABLE_SCHEMA TABLE_NAME
	CARDINALITY
AdSchemaTableConstraints	TABLE_CONSTRAINTS Rowset
Returns the table constraints specified in the catalog that are owned by a given user	CONSTRAINT_CATALOG CONSTRAINT_SCHEMA

	CONSTRAINT_NAME TABLE_CATALOG TABLE_SCHEMA TABLE_NAME CONSTRAINT_TYPE IS_DEFERRABLE INITIALLY_DEFERRED DESCRIPTION
AdSchemaTablePrivileges Returns the privileges on tables specified in the catalog that are available to, or granted by, a given user	TABLE_PRIVILEGES Rowset **GRANTOR** **GRANTEE** **TABLE_CATALOG** **TABLE_SCHEMA** **TABLE_NAME** PRIVILEGE_TYPE IS_GRANTABLE
AdSchemaTables Returns the tables (including views) specified in the catalog that are accessible to a given user	TABLES Rowset TABLE_CATALOG TABLE_SCHEMA TABLE_NAME TABLE_TYPE TABLE_GUID DESCRIPTION TABLE_PROPID DATE_CREATED DATE_MODIFIED
AdSchemaTranslations Returns the character translations specified in the catalog that are accessible to a given user	TRANSLATIONS Rowset TRANSLATION_CATALOG TRANSLATION_SCHEMA TRANSLATION_NAME SOURCE_CHARACTER_SET_CATALOG SOURCE_CHARACTER_SET_SCHEMA SOURCE_CHARACTER_SET_NAME TARGET_CHARACTER_SET_CATALOG TARGET_CHARACTER_SET_SCHEMA TARGET_CHARACTER_SET_NAME
AdSchemaUsagePrivileges Returns the USAGE privileges on objects specified in the catalog that are available to, or granted by, a given user	USAGE_PRIVILEGES Rowset **GRANTOR** **GRANTEE** **OBJECT_CATALOG**

	OBJECT_SCHEMA **OBJECT_NAME** **OBJECT_TYPE** PRIVILEGE_TYPE IS_GRANTABLE
AdSchemaViewColumnUsage Returns the columns on which viewed tables, specified in the catalog and owned by a given user, are dependent	VIEW_COLUMN_USAGE Rowset VIEW_CATALOG VIEW_SCHEMA VIEW_NAME TABLE_CATALOG TABLE_SCHEMA TABLE_NAME COLUMN_NAME COLUMN_GUID COLUMN_PROPID
AdSchemaViews Returns the views specified in the catalog that are accessible to a given user	VIEWS Rowset TABLE_CATALOG TABLE_SCHEMA TABLE_NAME VIEW_DEFINITION CHECK_OPTION IS_UPDATABLE DESCRIPTION DATE_CREATED DATE_MODIFIED
AdSchemaViewTableUsage Returns the tables on which viewed tables, specified in the catalog and owned by a given user, are dependent	VIEW_TABLE_USAGE Rowset VIEW_CATALOG VIEW_SCHEMA VIEW_NAME TABLE_CATALOG TABLE_SCHEMA TABLE_NAME

F A Statistics Primer

Understanding the terms and methods of statistics is useful in data mining, other aspects of business intelligence, and life in general. A solid understanding of statistics helps you better evaluate claims made by others including the government, reporters, competitors, and vendors. A little statistical knowledge can go a long way towards making you a better decision maker. The intention of this appendix is to introduce some of the key concepts in statistics. The foundations presented here are intended as a refresher and not as a complete discussion. For a more comprehensive introduction to statistics, please see one of the references listed at the end of the chapter.

PROBABILITY AND DISTRIBUTIONS

One of the fundamental principles of statistics is that of probability. Probability captures the idea that most situations are not perfectly reproducible—that is that they have some random variation. The amount of variation that surrounds a given situation depends on the situation itself; some things, such as physics or chemistry experiments, are reproducible to a very narrow range. Most business situations have a much broader range of outcomes. Understanding that the data generated by some process comes from some kind of distribution is vital to being able effectively use statistical methods.

Although descriptive statistics have been gathered since biblical times, the first people to study probability were chiefly concerned with games of chance. The basic idea developed by observations of games of chance, such as drawing a card from a well shuffled deck, rolling a die or tossing a coin. Based on their studies of multiple trials of these games, Pierre de Fermat and Blaise Pascal created many of the fundamental ideas behind statistics in the seventeenth century. From there, successive refinements through the centuries have created an analytical model that is used in almost every field of endeavor from agriculture to zoology, and are especially relevant to managerial decision making.

One of the concepts that is simple to develop from observing multiple games is the concept of probability calculations. What is the chance that we will roll a six on the next toss of the die? The probability of this happening is one chance out of six. The chance of it happening on the next roll is also one out of six. Two rolls of a die are *independent* of one another in that the first roll does not influence the chances of the second or subsequent rolls.

On the other hand, if you are looking at drawing cards from a deck when you do not replace the cards after they are drawn, you can see that the chances of drawing a particular card on a particular draw depend on the cards that have been drawn previously. So, the chances of drawing a royal flush in spades in the order ace, king, queen, jack, ten can be calculated by

$$\frac{1}{52} \times \frac{1}{51} \times \frac{1}{50} \times \frac{1}{49} \times \frac{1}{48} = 1 / (52 \times 51 \times 50 \times 49 \times 48) = 1 / 311875200,$$

which isn't very likely at all.

However, in cards, the order in which the cards are drawn is not important. So, a royal flush in spades can be drawn in any order and it is just as good as one drawn in order. To calculate this probability, we need to first figure out how many possible ways there are of drawing a royal flush in spades. In any royal flush, there are five possible cards that can be drawn first, four that can be drawn second, three third and so on. So the number of possible ways to draw the five cards can be calculated by $5 \times 4 \times 3 \times 2 \times 1$, which can also be written as 5! (or 5 *factorial*). So, what we need to calculate is the number of ways of choosing 5 particular cards out of 52, which can be written as

$$\binom{52}{5} = \frac{52!}{5!\,47!} = 2598960.$$

So, our chances of drawing a royal flush in spades in any order are 1/2598960.

When you are looking at coin tosses, it is more interesting to look at the overall numbers of heads or tails rather than observing that each individual toss is a head or tail. The number of heads in the toss of a coin 10 times is a random number in itself, since it depends of the individual outcomes of each coin toss. For 10 tosses of a coin, the number of heads can be any integer number from zero to 10. To introduce a little statistical notation, a random variable X has a ***probability distribution*** that is described by the function $f(x) = P(X = x)$, which can be read as "the function f of x is the probability that the random variable X is equal to the given x)". For the coin toss example, the function is

$$f(x) = \binom{n}{x} p^x (1 - p)^{n-x},$$

which is the *binomial probability distribution* where p is the chance of a particular outcome (heads in this case), n is the total number of tosses, and x is number of heads that turn up.

To put it into more concrete terms, the chances of getting exactly four heads in 10 tosses of a coin is

$$f(4) = \binom{10}{4} .5^4 (1 - .5)^6 = 0.205078125.$$

A plot of the binomial distribution for 10 tosses of a fair coin is presented in Figure F.1.

The binomial distribution is a discrete distribution because it has values that are always integers. It is not possible to throw half a head with a coin, so the count of the number of heads in 10 tosses of a coin will be an integer from 0 to 10. Other important discrete distributions include the geometric distribution, which measures the number of trials until a success, and the *Poisson* distribution, which is used to measure discrete outcomes during a specified time period such as number of new customers, number of orders, and so on.

Instead of being discrete, many measurements are continuous. In actual practice, of course, they will be recorded at a certain precision and so could be measured as discrete, but in practice, we will treat them as continuous variables. As an example, sales in dollars are a continuous measure.

To statistically model continuous data, we need to use real numbers. Because real numbers can have an infinite number of values infinitely close, the probability of any particular number is always zero. So there is no concept of point probability as we had with discrete distributions. Instead of point probabilities, with continuous distributions, we deal with *probability density*. This is the probability of getting the values in a small region around x divided by the size of the region. The cumulative distribution function is the probability that the random variable X will be less than or equal to x. For a continuous distribution, it is defined as

$$F(x) = \int_{-\infty}^{x} f(x)dx.$$

The most prevalent continuous distribution is the uniform distribution, which has a constant density over a specific interval and the normal (or Gaussian distribution). The normal distribution has a density function given by

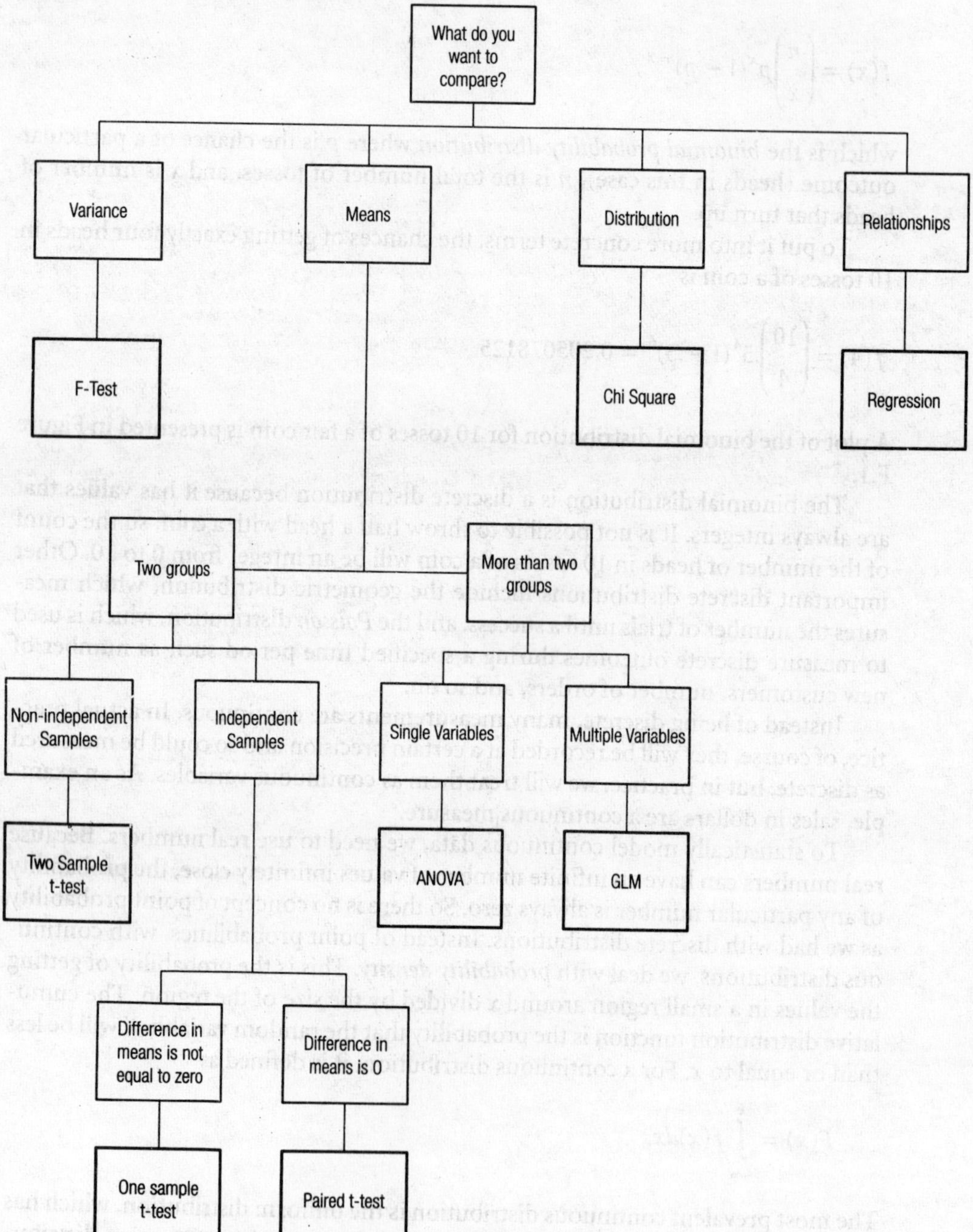

FIGURE F.1 The binomial distribution for 10 tosses of a fair coin.

$$f(x) = \frac{1}{\sqrt{2\pi\sigma}} \exp\left(-\frac{(x-\mu)^2}{2\sigma^2} \right).$$

The normal distribution is parameterized by the mean and standard deviation. The normal distribution is by far the most widely used distribution in statistical models, and it is used to approximate other distributions. One very useful characteristic of the normal distribution is that a certain percentage of the values fall at certain distances away from the mean. Approximately 67 percent of values fall within one standard deviation of the mean, 95 percent fall within two standard deviations of the mean, and 99 percent fall within three standard deviations of the mean. So, the standard deviation (represented by the Greek letter σ, read "sigma") is the dispersion of the normal distribution about the mean (represented by the Greek letter μ, read "mu"). A plot of a normal distribution with $\sigma = 0$ and $\mu = 1$ is presented in Figure F.2.

Decision Based on Sample	Actual Value: True	Actual Value: False
Accept	Correct	Type II
Reject	Type I	Correct

FIGURE F.2 The normal distribution has a characteristic bell-shaped curve.

Often, values are normalized to place them in context of the mean. In many instances, we assume a normal distribution of data. For example, Figure F.3 shows a normal distribution with $\sigma = 5$ and $\mu = 1.5$ superimposed over the binomial distribution from 10 tosses of a fair coin. Since the plot of the normal distribution and the binomial distribution look pretty close, it seems reasonable to approximate the binomial distribution with a normal distribution.

Many physical characteristics, such as height and weight, follow an approximately normal distribution. On many occasions, this is a fine approximation; however there are times when it can be very misleading to assume normality of the data.

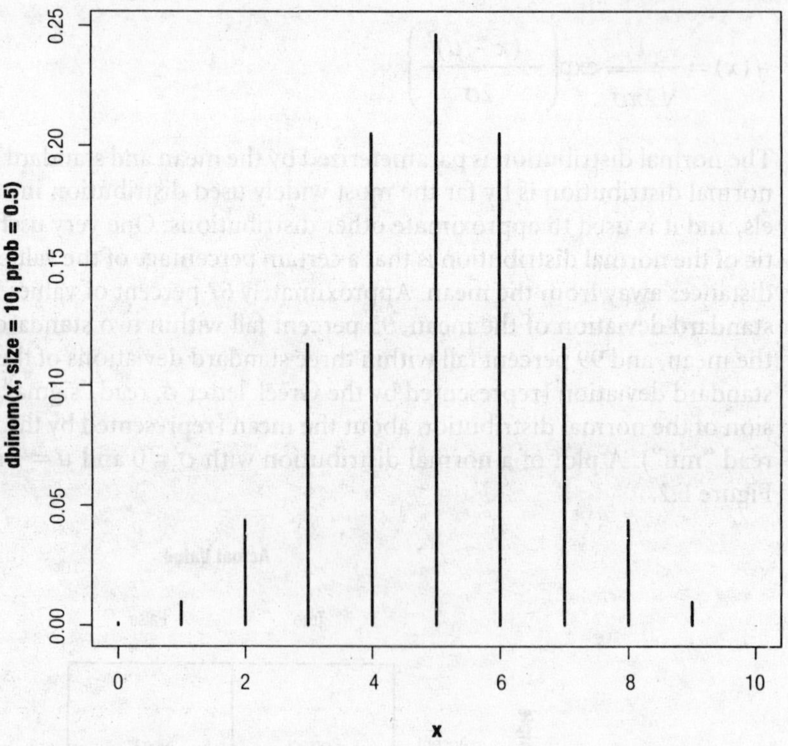

FIGURE F.3 Many distributions can be approximated by the normal distribution.

For example, the pattern of arrival for store customers over time is better suited to a Poisson distribution.

DESCRIPTIVE STATISTICS

Descriptive statistics summarize a set of data and allow you to understand the underlying distribution of the data without having to individually examine all of the data points. To do this, we use a smaller set of statistics that describe the characteristics of the distribution of the data. Of course, representing a large set of data with a smaller set of data can gloss over some important characteristics of the data. But, in many cases, a simple representation of a set of data is very important to understanding it.

One of the most common statistics used to understand data is measure of central tendency. A measure of central tendency uses a single number to represent an entire set of data. The three most common measures of central tendency are the mean, median, and mode.

The *mean* is the arithmetic average of a set of data. This is the most common measure applied to any data and is very useful. You probably use means on an everyday basis. The calculation is very simple: sum up the values and divide by the count of values.

The *median* is the middle value in a set of values that have been ranked in numerical order. If the median does not fall directly on a value (that is, there is an even number of values), it is placed directly between the two middle values. The median is a very robust measure of central tendency because it is resistant to skewed data.

The *mode* is the most frequently occurring value in a set of values. If two values have the same number of occurrences, the data is said to be bimodal. The mode is useful only for discrete variables but is a robust measure of central tendency because it, like the median, is not subject to distortion by outliers.

Although measures of central tendency help place a distribution, measures of variability help understand the dispersion or spread of the data. Understanding the amount of variability in the data is very important to understanding what it looks like. A set of data with a given mean and a small dispersion looks a lot different than a set of data with the same mean and a large dispersion.

The first measure of variability is the range. The *range* is simply the difference between the highest value and the lowest value. The range is useful in understanding where a certain value lies in the overall distribution; it does not identify clumps of data or help understand how evenly distributed the values are.

The *variance* is the variability of scores around the mean. Unlike the range, which uses only the lowest and highest values, the variance uses all of the values. The variance is calculated as the average of the squared deviation from the mean. The *deviation* is simply the observed value minus the mean. Values below the mean will have negative values. Squaring the deviation makes the negative scores positive and assigns a non-linear weight to scores that are considerably above or below the mean.

The *standard deviation* is the square root of the variance. One nice thing about using the standard deviation is that it is in the same units as the values. So it makes assessing the amount of spread in a given distribution more understandable. If you are talking about a normal distribution, a specific value can easily be interpreted as an outlier if you know the mean and standard deviation. For example, if you believe that the average customer service call time is normally distributed with a mean of five minutes and a standard deviation of one minute, you would know that a call of nine minutes was four standard deviations higher than the mean. This exceptional call might be worth investigating further.

DESCRIPTIVE GRAPHICS

In addition to calculating numbers to help represent a set of data, displaying the data in a graphical format often makes it much easier to understand. People are hardwired to react to images and can absorb more information in a graphical format than a tabular format in many cases. Sometimes a picture really is worth a thousand words when describing a set of data.

Before spending a lot of time and effort on statistical analysis, sometimes it is very helpful to simply plot the data in a variety of ways to become more familiar with it. You can learn quite a bit in this way and it can help direct your further inquires into the structure of the data.

However, it is also easy to create graphics that do not capture the salient points in the data, and instead, confuse or obfuscate the meaning of the data. Designing appropriate graphics for data analysis can be quite difficult and you should always make sure to keep the assumptions that you have made in mind when viewing graphical data displays. See some of the references at the end of this appendix for more information on how to effectively create and use graphical data presentations.

STATISTICAL TESTS

In almost every data analysis situation, the big question that needs to be answered is: compared to what? What we are most interested in a set of numbers is not usually a simple description, but a comparison to other similar data. The sales average for January is $50,000 per day. Is that good or bad? Is this set of data different in some way from that set of data or from our expectations? Making assertions about our data is essential be being able to compare it to our experiences and expectations.

One of the most important facets of statistical analysis is this ability to make inferences about populations of data. That is, we can test a sample of data against a theory and see if the data supports that theory. In statistical terms, we call our theory a *hypothesis*. Being able to test a hypothesis is a very powerful tool. Scientists and researches use statistical testing on a regular basis to be able to support their research. You can use the same tools to be able to run your business in a more predictable fashion, with some powerful results. The understanding imparted by statistical analysis can help you make better decisions.

To make their businesses more predictable, many corporations use a technique based on statistical analysis called *Six Sigma*. Six Sigma was developed in the 1980s primarily by Motorola as a process improvement initiative, but was made most famous when General Electric adopted it as a primary initiative in the mid-1990s. Although sometimes viewed as a fad, Six Sigma's longevity and importance to very successful and high-profile businesses has imparted a good deal of credibility to the technique.

The concept behind Six Sigma is to create a closed-loop system to enable con tinuous improvements in business processes. The basic premise is simple: pick a critical customer-related goal that is easily measured, and improve the processes that affect the measurement. The time it takes to deliver a product to a customer might be a good candidate. Then, measure against that goal and make adjustments to the process to improve performance. The key here is to make sure that you are not only measuring in terms of average, but in terms of variation. The focus is to first reduce process variance, since a customer is on the receiving end of each individual outcome, and then improve capabilities.

The objective is to reduce the number of defects to below 3.4 per million opportunities,. *Defect* is a Six Sigma term for missing the goal and can refer to defects in a manufactured product, errors in a computer program, or any other case in which a goal is not reached. The name Six Sigma refers to the area of a normal distribution that is six standard deviations away from the mean, within which 99.9997 percent of the distribution should fall. A table to convert between sigma levels, defects per million opportunities, and process yield is presented in Table F.1.

TABLE F.1 Sigma levels, defects per million opportunities, and process yield.

Sigma Level	*Defects per Million Opportunities*	*Yield*
1	690,000	30.9%
2	308,000	69.2%
3	66,800	93.3%
4	6,210	99.94%
5	230	99.98%
6	3.4	99.9997%

In addition to the use of variance to measure process performance, Six Sigma often includes other statistical and data-analysis techniques. These include control charts and statistical process controls that monitor a process performance over time and can catch unexpected trends in variance before they become problems. *Pareto* diagrams are also used to focus on problems that have the greatest potential for improvement by examining the relative frequency and impact in a bar chart. This kind of analysis is based on the Pareto principle that says that 80 percent of the problems are from 20 percent of all possible sources.

HYPOTHESIS TESTING

In experiments, scientists use inferential statistics to test the null hypothesis. The null hypothesis is that the sets of data are the same. If we can reject the null hypothesis, then we can say that the two groups of data are different. In a well-controlled experiment, that would indicate that the experimental factor is responsible for the difference.

Since the data that we are capturing is random, there is a risk that we reach the wrong conclusion. Given the structure of our hypothesis testing, we can get it wrong in two ways:

Type I error: The hypothesis is correct, but we reject it.

Type II error: The hypothesis is wrong, but we accept it.

The risk of Type I error is the significance level of the test. The risk of a Type II error is dependent on the *power* of the test being conducted. The simple diagram in Figure F.4 helps to illustrate the relationship between the types of error. Suffice it to say that the power is a tradeoff with the significance level of the test. If you raise the significance level, you will reduce the power of the test. This makes sense if you think about it: by raising the significance level, you are raising the bar for the data and you run the risk of raising it too high. The only way to increase the power of a test without compromising on the significance level is to have more data.

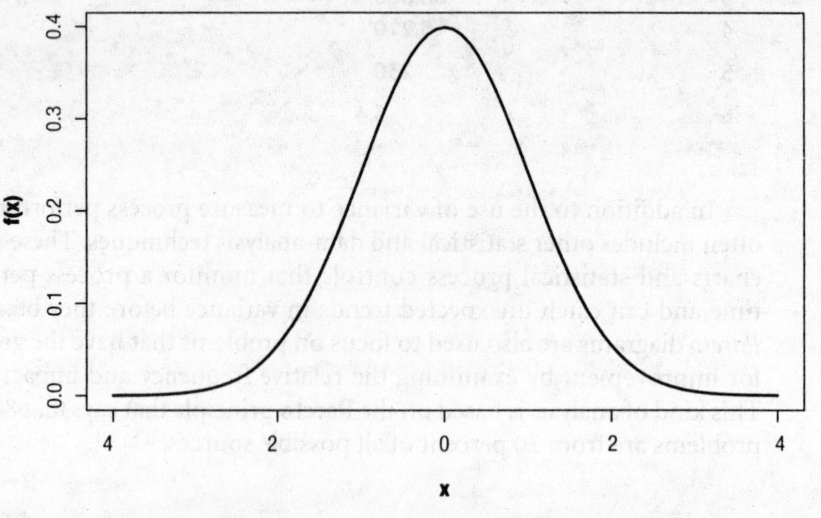

FIGURE F.4 The relationship between the hypothesis and acceptance or rejection.

Another common way of assessing a statistical test is to look at the p-value of the result. A *p-value* provides a measure of the strength of the results of a hypothesis test on a scale of zero to one. A test result with a low p-value indicates that the null hypothesis should be rejected. Table F.2 can help interpret p-values.

TABLE F.2

p-value	*Result*
< 0.01	Strongly reject null hypothesis
$0.01 < p < 0.05$	Moderately reject null hypothesis
$0.05 < p < 0.10$	Some evidence against null hypothesis
$P > 0.10$	No evidence against null hypothesis

The same type of logic applies to almost all types of statistical analysis. The types of tests that you might consider in each situation are presented in Figure F.5. We will go through a simple example of each of these types of analysis and show you how you would go about conducting the analysis with some common tools we have already introduced.

Microsoft Excel is probably the most widely used tool for statistical analysis in business. Excel comes with many powerful features for statistical analysis that you can use to improve your understanding of the information you already have. As good as Excel is as a desktop statistical application, it is not very easy to use as a library in server-based analytical applications. It is atypical (and possibly a security

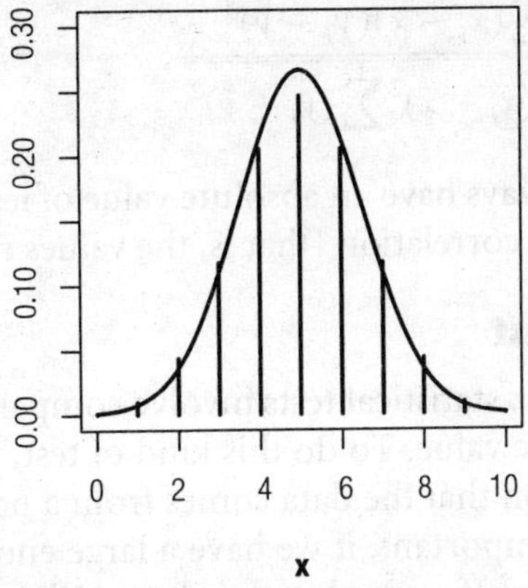

FIGURE F.5 A decision-tree for determining which type of statistical analysis is appropriate.

risk) to install Excel on server machines. To help in those cases in which it is difficult to use Excel, such as on a Web server, the CD-ROM contains a library of statistical routines that you can use in your .NET applications. This library is intended for illustration and prototyping purposes only so you can see how the various statistical tests look in code. The library is not complete and has not been fully tested under a range of conditions. If you are creating an application for statistical analysis, you should strongly consider purchasing a commercial statistics library.

CORRELATION

It is often very useful to understand the ways in which values are related. Correlation assesses the relationship between two or more sets of data. A coefficient of correlation measures the amount that two series move together. A correlation of zero indicates that the two series do not influence each other. A negative correlation means that they move in opposite directions. A positive correlation means that they move in the same direction. The strength of a correlation is dependent on the size.

When assessing correlation, you need to be very careful not to read too much into it. Although correlation is important because it allows you to understand how the data moves together, it does not imply causation. More investigation and understanding is needed to show causation than the basic fact that two series tend to move together.

One of the most common evaluations of correlation is the Pearson correlation coefficient. The *Pearson correlation coefficient* measures the linear correlation between two normally distributed variables. It is calculated by

$$r = \frac{\sum (x_i - \bar{x})(y_i - \bar{y})}{\sqrt{\sum (x_i - \bar{x})^2 \sum (y_i - \bar{y})^2}},$$

which will always have an absolute value of less than 1 with a correlation of 1 indicating perfect correlation (that is, the values move in tandem).

The One-sample t-test

The most basic statistical tests involve comparing a group of data to another group or to a specific value. To do this kind of test, we use a *t-test*. The *t*-test is based on the assumption that the data comes from a normal distribution. Although this assumption is important, if we have a large enough sample size, the relative importance declines. If you plot the data and it does not follow the characteristic bell-shaped curve or you know that the process that generated the data does not follow a normal pattern, or you conduct a test of normality that casts suspicion on the normality of the data, you would be advised to use a *non-parametric* test instead of a *t*-test for making inferences. Deciding when to use a non-parametric test is a contentious issue and beyond the scope of this book.

The simplest *t* test is a one-sample *t*-test. In this test, we are testing the null hypothesis that $\mu = \mu_0$. To do a one-sample t test you first calculate the standard error of the mean with the formula $SEM = \frac{\sigma}{\sqrt{n}}$, then you calculate the *t*-statistic, which is defined as $t = \frac{\bar{x} - \mu_0}{SEM}$, and see if this value falls into the acceptance region. The size of the acceptance region is determined by the chosen significance level of the test. Most often, tests are conducted at a 5 percent significance level and the acceptance region is approximately the range from –2 to 2. If *t* is outside of the acceptance region, we reject the null hypothesis that $\mu = \mu_0$ at the selected significance level.

Sample code that implements a *t*-test is shown here:

```
public class TTest
{
    protected RealVector _rv;
    private double _hyp;
    private TestType _type;

    public TTest(RealVector rv, double hyp, TestType type)
    {
        _rv = rv;
        _hyp = hyp;
        _type = type;
    }
    public double t
    {
        get
        {
            double sem = 0.0;

            sem = _rv.StdDev / Math.Sqrt(_rv.Count);

            return (_rv.Mean - _hyp) / sem;

        }
    }
    public int df
    {
        get
        {
            return _rv.Count - 1;
        }
    }
    public double p
```

```
        {
            get
            {
                // call the cdf for t with df and calculated t
                TDist tdist = new TDist(df);
                switch (_type)
                {
                    case (TestType.NotEqual):
                        return 2*tdist.CDF(t);
                    case (TestType.Greater):
                        return 1-tdist.CDF(t);
                    case (TestType.Less):
                        return tdist.CDF(t);
                    default:
                        throw new Exception("Invalid test type");
                }
            }
        }
    }
    public enum TestType
    {
        NotEqual,
        Greater,
        Less
    }
```

The Two-sample t-test

If we want to compare two distinct groups of data to see if they have the same mean, we use a two-sample *t*-test. A *two-sample t-test* is very similar to a one-sample test, except that the data is drawn from two different groups, x_1 and x_2, that we assume are from distinct normal distributions. The *t* value is calculated by $t = \frac{\overline{x}_2 - \overline{x}_1}{SEDM}$, where the *standard error of the difference of the means* is calculated by

$$SEDM = \sqrt{SEM_1^2 + SEM_2^2}.$$

If the calculated *t*-value is not significant with $n_1 + n_2 - 2$ degrees of freedom, we can reject the null hypothesis and accept the alternate hypothesis that the means are indeed different.

Some sample code that implements a two-sample *t*-test is shown here:

```
public class TwoSampleTTest
{
    RealVector _rv1, _rv2;

    public TwoSampleTTest(RealVector rv1, RealVector rv2)
    {
```

```
        _rv1 = rv1;
        _rv2 = rv2;
    }
    public double t
    {
        get
        {
            // calculate the weighted average of the variance
            double s = ((_rv1.Count - 1)* rv1.Variance+
                (_rv2.Count - 1)*_rv2.Variance)/df;
            // calculate the standard error in difference of means
            double sedm = Math.Sqrt(s*(1.0/_rv2.Count+1.0/_rv1.Count));
            // calculate t as the difference in means over the standard
            //error in difference of means
            return (_rv2.Mean - _rv1.Mean)/sedm;
        }
    }
    public int df
    {
        get
        {
            return _rv1.Count + _rv2.Count - 2;
        }
    }
    public double p
    {
        get
        {
            // call the cdf for t with df and calculated t
            TDist tdist = new TDist(df);
            return 2*tdist.CDF(t);
        }
    }
}
```

The Paired t-test

A *paired t-test* is used to compare two sample measurements taken from the same population. For example, let's say we have data on the number of out-of-spec ball bearings produced by a set of equipment every hour one day that we want to compare against a set of the same measurements against the same equipment the next day (maybe we subtly changed the machine setup and want to see if that makes a difference in the quality). Essentially, this test boils down to a one-sample *t*-test that checks the differences between the measurements against the null hypothesis that the difference is zero. It is important to note that this kind of test needs to be done against data that has the same variance at different levels, since we are testing the means of two samples from that population. So, you might want to plot the data to make sure that the variance between the two groups is the same.

Sample code that implements the paired *t*-test is shown here:

```
public PairedTTest(RealVector rv1, RealVector rv2):
   base(rv1, 0, TestType.NotEqual)
{
    if (rv1.Count != rv2.Count)
        throw
            new Exception
              ("Vectors must be same length for paired test");

    int i = 0;
    foreach(Double d in rv2)
    {
        _rv[i] = _rv[i] - d;
        i++;
    }

}
```

The F-test

To test variances between groups, we use an *F*-test. The *F-test* measures the probability that two independent samples have the same variance. The estimators of the variance are s_1^2 and s_2^2. We define as the test statistic their ratio $F = \frac{s_1^2}{s_2^2}$, which has an *F* Distribution with $n_1 - 1$ and $n_2 - 1$ degrees of freedom. *F*-tests are often used with regression analysis as we will see later in the next section.

Sample code that implements an *F*-test is shown here:

```
public class FTest
{
    double _p;
    int _numDF;
    int _denomDF;
    double _F;

    public FTest(RealVector rv1, RealVector rv2)
    {
        // get variance
        double var1 = rv1.Variance;
        double var2 = rv2.Variance;

        // get ratio of variance
        _F = var1/var2;

        // if the ratio is greater than 1, flip the ratio
```

```
        // to make sure we calculate a meaningful score
        if (_F > 1.0)
        {
            _F = 1 / _F;
            _numDF = rv2.Count - 1;
            _denomDF = rv1.Count - 1;
        }
        else
        {
            _numDF = rv1.Count - 1;
            _denomDF = rv2.Count - 1;
        }
        // a two-tailed test, so we double the region
        _p = 2*CDF(_F);
    }

    public double p
    {
        get
        {
            return _p;
        }
    }

    public int NumeratorDF
    {
        get
        {
            return _numDF;
        }
    }

    public int DenomenatorDF
    {
        get
        {
            return _denomDF;
        }
    }

    public double F
    {
        get
        {
            return _F;
        }
    }
```

```
    private double CDF(double x)
    {
        double u = _denomDF / (_denomDF + _numDF * x);
        if (x < 0) return 0;
        else return 1 - Functions.BetaCDF
          (u, 0.5 * _denomDF, 0.5 * _numDF);
    }
}
```

Regression Analysis

Linear regression analysis allows us to describe the relationship between variables. We talked a little bit about regression in Chapter 3 but this will provide some more details. When we use regression, the term "regression of *y* on *x*" is commonly used. This means that we are looking at the variability of *y* and trying to explain it in terms of *x*. The general linear regression model is given by

$$Y = \alpha + \beta x + \varepsilon$$

where ε is the residual variance, the amount of variability that is not explained by the β. ε is assumed to be independent and normally distributed with a mean of zero. β is the slope of the line showing the change in *Y* for a unit change in *x*. The intercept of the line with the *y*-axis is given by α.

The linear regression parameters can be estimated by using *least squares.* Least squares finds the values of α and β that minimize the sum of squared errors. This is not done by randomly trying variables, but by minimizing the following equations:

$$\hat{\beta} = \frac{\sum (x_i - \bar{x})(y_i - \bar{y})}{\sum (x_i - \bar{x})^2}$$

$$\hat{\alpha} = \bar{y} - \hat{\beta}\bar{x}$$

The error that is left over becomes the residual variance $SS_{res}/(n-2)$ with the residual standard deviation being the square root of that.

Just as you can calculate the variability of a sample mean and conduct a *t*-test to determine if the population mean could be a certain value, you can use a *t*-test to evaluate the significance of the estimated parameters of the regression. One of the most important tests is testing whether $\beta = 0$.

If $\beta = 0$, that means that the value of *y* is independent of the value of *x* and we should discount the premise that *y* depends on *x*. The *t* value for β can be calculated as $t = \frac{\beta}{se(\beta)}$, which follows a *t*-distribution with $n-2$ degrees of freedom.

Similarly, you can test the *v* parameter to see if the equation line does pass through the *x-y* intercept, but you should be careful about doing this unless you have a particular reason to believe that the value should go through the origin and have data that covers the region in question. For example, if you are trying to estimate the number of defects based on the number of units produced, you might have a reason to test whether the regression line goes through the intercept because without any production, you cannot have defects. However, in many cases the relationship between the variables will not be so clear.

Another value of importance when evaluating the results of a regression analysis is the value of R^2. Roughly, R^2 is a measure of the correlation between *x* and *y* in the regression equation. Simply adding variables to the equation will increase the level of R^2, so there is a more refined calculation called adjusted R^2 that takes this effect into account and provides a more accurate measure of the amount of variability explained by the regression equation.

Lastly, an important test for a regression is an *F*-test in which the regression coefficients are not zero. In the case of a single variable regression, this will be the same as the square of the *t*-test for B. For multiple regression, the *F*-test will indicate how likely it is that the relationship between *x* and *y* could be by chance and have nothing to do with the given regression parameters.

Sample code that calculates a least-squares regression and some of the descriptive statistics is sas follows:

```
/// <summary>
/// LeastSquares calculation.
/// </summary>
public class LeastSquares
{

    Matrix _beta;
    double _r2;
    double _ssr;
    double _sse;
    double _f;
    double _p;

    public Matrix Beta
    {
        get
        {
            return _beta;
        }
    }

    public double R2
    {
        get
```

```
        {
            return _r2;
        }
    }

    public double SSR
    {
        get
        {
            return _ssr;
        }
    }

    public double SSE
    {
        get
        {
            return _sse;
        }
    }

    public double F
    {
        get
        {
            return _f;
        }
    }

    public double PValue
    {
        get
        {
            return _p;
        }
    }

    /// <summary>
    /// Creates a least-squares estimate.
    /// </summary>
    /// <param name="y">A one-column dimension of y-values.</param>
    /// <param name="x">
    ///   The x-values in a matrix. The first column represents the
    ///   intercept coefficient.
    /// </param>
    public LeastSquares(Matrix y, Matrix x)
    {
```

```
//transpose the x matrix
Matrix xprime = x.transpose();
// calculate the least squares estimate for beta
_beta = xprime.times(x).inverse().times(xprime.times(y));
// get the number of observations
int n = y.getRowDimension();
// get the number of estimates
int p = _beta.getRowDimension();
// calculate ybar
double ybar = 0.0;
for(int i = 0; i < n; i++)
{
    ybar += y.get(i, 0);
}
ybar /= n;

// calculate SSE and SSR
_sse = 0.0;
_ssr = 0.0;
for(int i = 0; i < n; i++)
{
    // get the estimated y
    double yhat = 0.0;
    for (int j = 0 ; j < p; j++)
    {
        yhat += _beta.get(j, 0) * x.get(i, j);
    }
    // get the squared error
    _sse += Math.Pow(y.get(i, 0) - yhat, 2);
    // get the SSR
    _ssr += Math.Pow(yhat - ybar, 2);
}
// calculate R2
_r2 = _ssr/(_ssr+_sse);
// calculate mean squared error (estimate of sigma-squared)
double MSE = _sse/(n-p);
// calculate the MSR
double MSR = _ssr/(p-1);
// covariance matrix
Matrix C = xprime.times(x).inverse();
// standard errors and t-scores for the estimators
RealVector BetaSE = new RealVector();
RealVector BetaT = new RealVector();
for(int i=0; i < p; i++)
{
    double se = Math.Sqrt(MSE*C.get(i, i));
    double t = _beta.get(i, 0)/se;
    BetaSE.Add(se);
    BetaT.Add(t);
```

```
        }
        // calculate F statistic
        _f = MSR/MSE;
        // calculate p-value
        _p = 1- new FDist(p-1, n-p).CDF(_f);

    }
```

Tests of Proportion

Proportion tests are used to analyze tabular data. Tests of single proportion are based on the binomial distribution of size N with probability p. For large samples, this can be well approximated with the normal distribution with mean Np and variance $Np(1-p)$. The rule of thumb that is often used is that you need at least five successes and failures to make the assumption of normality.

We can test the hypothesis that $p = p_0$ by calculating

$$u = \frac{x - Np_0}{\sqrt{Np_0(1-p_0)}}.$$

This will have an approximately normal distribution with a mean of zero and a standard deviation of 1. Alternately, we can test using u^2 which has approximately χ^2 distribution with 1 degree of freedom.

As an example, consider the case where 39 of 215 randomly selected orders had rush delivery and we want to test the hypothesis that 15 percent of orders have rush delivery. Calculating u^2 we get a value of 1.425. This has a p-value of 0.2326 on a χ^2 distribution with one degree of freedom, so we can reject the null hypothesis that the real probability parameter is 15% at a 95% significance level.

This test can be generalized to test among multiple categories. If we have multiple classes, we can organize the data into the following $r \times c$ matrix:

$$\begin{array}{ccc|c} n_{11} & n_{12} & n_{1c} & n_{1\cdot} \\ n_{21} & n_{22} & n_{2c} & n_{2\cdot} \\ & & & \\ n_{r1} & n_{r1} & n_{rc} & n_{r\cdot} \\ \hline n_{\cdot 1} & n_{\cdot 2} & n_{\cdot c} & n_{\cdot\cdot} \end{array}$$

If there is no relation between the rows and columns, then the expected value of each cell can be calculated by distributing each row total according to the proportions in each column by

$$E_{ij} = \frac{n_{i\cdot} \times n_{\cdot j}}{n_{\cdot\cdot}}.$$

The test statistic calculated over the entire matrix

$$X^2 = \sum \frac{(O - E)^2}{E}.$$

has an approximately χ^2 distribution with $(r-1) \cdot (c-1)$ degrees of freedom where O is the observed values and E is the expected values over the entire table.

Analysis of Variance (ANOVA)

The goal of analysis of variance (ANOVA) is to compare groups. To understand ANOVA, we will first define some variables. We will say that x_{ij} is the ith observation in group j. So, x_{62} is the 6th observation of group 2. Let's further define $\bar{x}$ as the mean of all of the observations in all of the groups and $\bar{x}_i$ is the mean for group i. So, we note that

$$x_{ij} = \bar{x} + (\bar{x}_i - \bar{x}) + (x_{ij} - \bar{x}_i)$$

where the first parenthesis $(\bar{x}_i - \bar{x})$ is the deviation of the group mean from the overall mean and the second parenthesis $(x_{ij} - \bar{x}_i)$ is the deviation of the observation from the group mean.

The sum of the squares of the deviations from the group mean is the *variation within groups* written as

$$SSD_W = \sum_i \sum_j (x_i - \bar{x})^2.$$

The sum of the squares of the deviations from the overall mean is the *variation between groups* and can be written as

$$SSD_B = \sum_i \sum_j (\bar{x}_i - \bar{x})^2 = \sum_i n_i (\bar{x}_i - \bar{x})^2.$$

We can show that the total variation is divided between the two kinds variation. If we have meaningful groupings, the difference between the groups will be larger than when the groups are not as meaningful. We can write the sum of the variations as

$$SSD_B + SSD_W = SSD_{total} = \sum_i \sum_j (x_{ij} - \bar{x})^2.$$

If we have irrelevant groups, the variation between groups will still be positive because it is a sum of squares. It turns out that if the groups are random, the sum of squares will be divided between the groups depending on the degrees of freedom in each. Normalizing the sum of squares, we calculate the mean squares for each as

$$MS_W = SSD_W \,/\, (N - k)$$
$$MS_B = SSD_B \,/\, (k - 1)$$

where N is the total number of observations and k is the number of groups.

Since MS_w is the pooled variance of each of the group variances, it is an estimate of σ^2. If there are no meaningful groupings, MS_B will also be an estimate of σ^2. If the groups are meaningful, then the differences between the group means will be larger and MSB will also be larger. So, we can test for the significant differences between the group means by testing the ratio of the two variance estimates. This ratio will have an F distribution with $k - 1$ and $N - k$ degrees of freedom. You reject the null hypothesis that the means are identical if F is larger than the 95% in the F distribution. If F is very small, then we accept that the means between the groups are identical.

Since the t-test also tests the difference between groups, it is a legitimate question to ask if it is acceptable to conduct t-tests for each of the pairs. The difficulty with this is in the number of tests required. As the number of pairs grows, the number of t-tests that would be needed grows rapidly. So if you have seven distinct groups, you would need to do 21 t-tests on the possible pairs. Since it is quite possible to observe things that happen 5 percent of the time in a group of 21, a .05 significance level is suspect and leads to an inflation of the Type I error rate. ANOVA analysis lets us put all of the data in one test and gives us one result to consider, which minimizes the chance that we reject a true hypothesis. A sample class to produce an ANOVA analysis is presented here.

```
/// <summary>
/// Class to do analysis of variance
/// </summary>
public class Anova
{
    double _SSDB;
    double _SSDW;
    double _MSB;
    double _MSW;
    int _dfb;
    double _F;
    double _pValue;

    public double SSDB
    {
        get
        {
            return _SSDB;
        }
    }
```

```
public int DFB
{
    get
    {
        return _dfb;
    }
}

public double MSB
{
    get
    {
        return _MSB;
    }
}

public double F
{
    get
    {
        return _F;
    }
}

public double PValue
{
    get
    {
        return _pValue;
    }
}
/// <summary>
/// Anova creates a single-factor Analysis of Variance
/// </summary>
/// <param name="depend">
/// A single-column matrix with the dependent variables
/// </param>
/// <param name="factors">
/// A single-column matrix with the group number
/// </param>
public Anova(Matrix depend, Matrix factors)
{

    // calculate the overall mean and sum of observations
    double xbar = depend.average();
    double grandSum = depend.sum();
```

```
// get the total number of observations
//int N = factors.rows;
int N = factors.getRowDimension();
// get the total number of factors
int k = (int)factors.max();

// get a count of each of the factors
int[] factorCount = new int[k];
// and a sum of each of the factors
double[] factorSum = new double[k];
// collect the factor sums and counts
for(int i = 1; i <= k; i++)
{
    for(int j = 0; j < factors.getRowDimension(); j++)
    {
        if (factors.get(j, 0) == i)
        {
            factorCount[i-1]++;
            factorSum[i-1] += depend.get(j, 0);
        }
    }
}

// calculate the factor degrees of freedom
_dfb = k-1;
// calculate the overall degrees of freedom
int dfw = N - k;

// calculate variation between groups (SSDB)
_SSDB = 0.0;
for (int i = 0; i < k; i++)
{
    _SSDB += factorCount[i]*
      Math.Pow((factorSum[i]/factorCount[i]-xbar), 2);
}

// calculate total variation(SST)
double SST = 0.0;
for (int i = 0; i < depend.getRowDimension(); i++)
{
    SST += Math.Pow(depend.get(i, 0) - xbar, 2);
}

// calculate varation within groups (SSDW)
// since we know SST = SSDW + SSDB
_SSDW = 0.0;
_SSDW = SST - SSDB;

// get the mean sqare for each
```

```
            _MSW = _SSDW/(N-k);
            _MSB = _SSDB/(k-1);

            _F = _MSB / _MSW;


            // calc p-value wit F-dist with k-1 and N-k degrees of freedom
            _pValue = 1.0 - (new FDist(_dfb, dfw)).CDF(_F);

        }
    }
```

END NOTES AND REFERENCES

Arsham, Hossein. "Topics in Statistical Data Analysis: Revealing Facts from Data." Available online at *http://ubmail.ubalt.edu/~harsham/stat-data/opre330.htm*. Accessed 8/20/2003.

Johnson, R.A. *Miller & Freund's Probability and Statistics for Engineers, 5th ed.* Prentice-Hall. 1994.

Goulden, C.H. *Methods of Statistical Analysis, 2nd ed.* New York: Wiley, 1956.

G About the CD-ROM

The CD-ROM included with *Building Business Intelligence Applications with .NET* includes all the code and projects from the various examples found in the book.

CD-ROM FOLDERS

All of the code and data from examples in the book are organized by chapter on the CD-ROM.

Chapter 2

PretzelCo.cab
Sales.mdb
CustomTask
- AssemblyInfo.cs
- CustomTask.sln
- SampleCustomTask.csproj
- SampleCustomTask.csproj.user
- SampleCustomTask.snk
- SimpleTask.cs

PackageList
- App.ico
- AssemblyInfo.cs
- Class1.cs
- PackageList.csproj
- PackageList.csproj.user
- PackageList.sln

PackageLoad
- App.ico
- AssemblyInfo.cs
- Class1.cs
- PackageLoad.csproj
- PackageLoad.csproj.user
- PackageLoad.sln
- PackageSaveApp.ico
- AssemblyInfo.cs
- Class1.cs
- PackageSave.csproj
- PackageSave.csproj.user
- PackageSave.sln

Chapter 4

DsoTest
- App.ico
- AssemblyInfo.cs
- Class1.cs
- DsoTest.csproj
- DsoTest.csproj.user
- DsoTest.sln

Mdequis
- App.ico
- AssemblyInfo.cs
- Class1.cs
- DsoTest.csproj
- DsoTest.csproj.user
- DsoTest.sln

Chapter 5

XMLA
- App.ico
- AssemblyInfo.cs
- FormXmla.cs
- FormXmla.resx
- Xmla.cs
- XMLA.csproj
- XMLA.csproj.user
- XMLA.sln

Chapter 6

ReportSvcViewer
- App.ico
- AssemblyInfo.cs
- ReportListForm.cs

ReportListForm.resx
ReportSvcViewer.csproj
ReportSvcViewer.csproj.user
ReportSvcViewer.sln
ReportViewForm.cs
ReportViewForm.resx
Revenue
AssemblyInfo.cs
dynamic_images
Global.asax
Global.asax.cs
Global.asax.resx
revenue.csproj
revenue.csproj.webinfo
revenue.sln
revenue.vsdisco
RevenueReport.cs
RevenueReport.resx
RevenueReport.rpt
Web.config
WebForm1.aspx
WebForm1.aspx.cs
WebForm1.aspx.resx
RWS_Revenue
AssemblyInfo.cs
Global.asax
Global.asax.cs
Global.asax.resx
rws_revenue.csproj
rws_revenue.csproj.webinfo
rws_revenue.sln
rws_revenue.vsdisco
Web.config
WebForm1.aspx
WebForm1.aspx.cs
WebForm1.aspx.resx

Chapter 7

DMXMLA.xml
Pmml.xml
StoreMining.xls
DMXMLA
App.ico
AssemblyInfo.cs

        - DMout2.xml
        - DMXMLA.csproj
        - DMXMLA.csproj.use
        - DMXMLA.sln
        - DMXMLA.suo
        - DMXMLA.xml
        - FormXmla.cs
        - FormXmla.resx
        - Web References
        - Xmla.cs
- **Chapter 8**
    - MDGrid
        - AssemblyInfo.cs
        - Global.asax
        - Global.asax.cs
        - Global.asax.resx
        - MDGrid.csproj
        - MDGrid.csproj.webinfo
        - MDGrid.sln
        - MDGrid.vsdisco
        - Web.config
        - WebForm1.aspx
        - WebForm1.aspx.cs
        - WebForm1.aspx.resx
- **Chapter 9**
    - MdxPart
        - AssemblyInfo.cs
        - Manifest.xml
        - MdxPart.csproj
        - MdxPart.csproj.user
        - MdxPart.sln
        - MdxReportPart.cs
        - MdxReportPart.dwp
    - MdxPartCab
        - MdxPartCab.vdproj
    - MdxReport
        - AssemblyInfo.cs
        - MdxReport.csproj
        - MdxReport.csproj.user
        - MdxReport.sln
        - MdxReportControl.cs

SYSTEM REQUIREMENTS

To use the sample applications, you will need to have access to the following software:

- Windows 2000 or later
- Microsoft SQL Server 2000
- Microsoft Analysis Services
- Microsoft Visual Studio .NET 2002 or later

The minimum processor requirement for running the sample applications is a 450-megahertz (MHz) Pentium II-class processor with a 600-MHz Pentium III-class or better processor recommended. Memory requirements vary by operating system with 160MB of RAM as the minimum requirement for Windows Server 2003 or XP Professional, 192MB of RAM for Windows 2000 Server, and 96MB of RAM for Windows 2000 Professional. More RAM will yield better performance. In addition to the space required by the prerequisite applications, the sample applications require 25MB of free disk space.

Note that the sample applications were written using Microsoft Visual Studio .NET 2002 and can be converted to the 2003 version of that application when they are opened. Once they have been converted to the 2003 format, they can no longer be opened using the 2002 version.

In addition to the baseline requirements, some chapters have additional requirements to use all the samples in the chapter. The use of the specific applications and, where necessary, installation instructions are included in the individual chapters. Chapter 3 uses Microsoft Excel 2002 to examine cube data. Chapter 5 uses the Microsoft XML for Analysis. Chapter 7 uses Crystal Reports for Visual Studio .NET (included with Microsoft Visual Studio .NET). Chapters 6 and 9 use the ADOMD.NET Beta. In addition, Chapter 9 uses Microsoft Windows SharePoint Services. Please note that SharePoint Services requires Windows Server 2003 and more processing power and memory than specified by the baseline requirements. To use SharePoint Services, Microsoft recommends an Intel Pentium III-class processor and 512 MB of RAM.

Glossary

.NET framework A software platform that supports component-oriented development and relies on a virtual machine that is independent of operating system and programming language. It is intended as a replacement for the *Component Object Model.*

Active Server Pages (ASP) A programming environment for Microsoft Internet Information Server where HTML, scripts, and ActiveX server components are used to create a program that returns dynamic Web pages. See also *Internet Information Server* and *Common Gateway Interface.*

ActiveX The catchall name for a set of COM-based technologies. See also *Component Object Model.*

ActiveX Data Objects Multi-dimensional (ADOMD) ActiveX Data Objects Multidimensional (ADOMD) provides a set of COM object that can be used to manipulate multidimensional data. ADOMD is based on the OLE DB for OLAP specification, which defines a set of COM objects and interfaces to allow OLE DB to access multidimensional data stores.

ADOMD See *ActiveX Data Objects Multi-dimensional.*

aggregation A pre-calculated summary of data. Aggregations are intended to improve query response time by reducing the amount of computation that needs to be done when queries are run.

analytic applications *Analytic applications* are designed to automate data-intensive business processes, assisting end users with complex data analysis and manipulation. These applications help speed the process and increase the reliability and availability of information for decision-making purposes. Analytic applications are domain-specific solutions that enable decision makers to access, analyze, and act on information in the context of a specific business area.

API See *Application Programming Interface.*

Application Programming Interface (API) The interface by which an application accesses services provided by other programs.

ASP See *Active Server Pages.*

ASP.NET The version of Active Server Pages that is integrated with the .NET Framework. See also *.NET Framework* and *Active Server Pages.*

axis A set of tuples. Each tuple is a vector of members. A set of axes defines the coordinates of a multidimensional data set.

balanced scorecard The balanced scorecard is a management technique that was developed in the early 1990s by Edward Kaplan and David Norton. A balanced scorecard allows a company to translate strategy into action by setting goals and measuring activity from a variety of viewpoints. There are four perspectives in the canonical balanced scorecard:

- Learning and growth perspective
- Business process perspective
- Customer perspective
- Financial perspective

business intelligence Business intelligence allows you to pull data together to help form a unified view of your enterprise that executives and analysts can use to generate insights and make better decisions.

calculated member A dimension member that is calculated at run-time using stored expression. Calculated members can be used as measures.

case A record used in data mining. A case can be used to train a model or to make a prediction. See also *training* and *prediction.*

cell Data at the intersection of axis coordinates contained in a Cellset.

Cellset The `Cellset` is retrieved as the results of an MDX query and contains the collection of `Cells` organized into `Axes` and `Positions` which can be retrieved in the form of a multidimensional array or by navigating down the axes.

CGI See *Common Gateway Interface.*

changing dimension Those dimensions with a tendency to evolve over time.

clustering In data mining, a process in which an algorithm separates records into groups based on similar attributes. See also *case* and *decision tree.*

COM See *Component Object Model.*

Common Gateway Interface (CGI) A standard for running external programs from a World Wide Web HTTP server. CGI specifies how to pass arguments to the executing program as part of the HTTP request and return a Web page to the browser.

Component Object Model (COM) A Microsoft technology for software components used to enable cross-application communication. See also *ActiveX.*

CRM See *Customer Relationship Management.*

Crystal Reports A product produced by Crystal Decisions that can be used for creating and distributing reports.

cube Cubes are the logical storage structures for OLAP databases. They combine dimensions and measures into a model that users can query. A cube defines a set of related dimensions that form an *n*-dimensional grid or cube.

Customer Relationship Management (CRM) A system that enables a company to better serve its customers by providing automated customer service and integrated customer profile tracking.

data cleaning See *data cleansing.*

data cleansing Data cleansing checks data for errors such as duplication, incorrect spelling, and unrecognized abbreviations. Also known as *data cleaning.*

data mart A data mart is a subset of a data warehouse that is focused on a specific area of interest.

data mining Data mining uses statistical techniques and artificial intelligence algorithms to discover patterns that are hidden deep in your data. Data mining enables you to discover previously unknown facts present in your business data.

Data Transformation Service (DTS) A tool included with Microsoft SQL Server that supports data extraction, translation, and loading. DTS provides capabilities to import, export, and transform data among one or more data sources.

data warehouse The purpose of a data warehouse is to be a repository for consolidated and organized data that can be used for analysis. This data can come from a large variety of sources including on-line transaction processing (OLTP) databases, legacy systems, spreadsheets, and external sources. Data warehouses range from very, very large with many terabytes of data to smallish collections of a few megabytes. A *data mart* is a subset of a data warehouse that is focused on a specific area of interest. The term "data warehouse" is often used broadly to encompass both of these meanings.

decision support systems Systems optimized for querying data that are used for making business decisions. Because decision support systems are focused on retrieving data, not updates, transactional issues are not important. The data contained in the decision support system is typically updated by a scheduled task that preprocesses, indexes, and organizes the data.

decision tree For data mining, a set of nodes in a tree structure that represent decision values and can be used to categorize a case that is generated by an algorithm. See also *clustering* and *case.*

digital dashboard A user interface that presents information in an easy-to-read format. In many cases, a dashboard will integrate data from multiple sources and allow end-user customization of the display.

dimension Dimensions represent the categories that provide context to the numeric measures. These categories should be derived from the classifications that are important to your business. A dimension is made up of *levels* and *members.*

dimensional modeling Dimensional modeling is the process of creating a logical model that is optimized for query and analysis performance.

DLL See *Dynamic Link Library.*

dimension table A dimension table establishes the context of the facts in the fact table. In a *star schema,* they are joined to the fact table by *key columns.*

drill down Drilling down allows you to focus on specific data to explore details that underlie a higher-level member.

drill up When you drill up on a member or group of members in a hierarchy, you collapse the detail so that you see only the summary information for the parent. Drilling up allows you to see a bigger picture with fewer details.

drillthrough Retrieves the source data from the fact table for a selected tuple.

DTS Package DTS solutions are bundled as packages. A package can contain any of the four types of objects:

Connections: Specify the source and destination for the data to be moved with DTS.

Tasks: Specify the actions that occur during the package execution.

Transformations: Map data from the source to the destination.

Workflow: Specifies the precedence and constraints of the tasks in the package.

DTS See *Data Transformation Service.*

Dynamic Link Library (DLL) A library of compiled code that is linked to applications when they are loaded rather than during compilation. The advantage of this is that the DLL can be shared between several tasks rather than each task containing copies of the library.

Enterprise Resource Planning (ERP) A system that is designed to integrate and automate many business processes within a company. Typically, the system is cross-functional and deployed throughout the company.

ERP See *Enterprise Resource Planning.*

ETL See *Extract, Transform, and Load.*

eXtensible Markup Language (XML) As the name implies, XML is a markup language that allows the development of user-defined types. See also *schema.*

Extract, Transform, and Load (ETL) Source data from transactional systems is brought together in data warehouses though the process of extraction, transformation, and loading.

fact Facts are the measurements of interest to the business.

fact table A fact table is the primary table in a dimensional model. The fact table is where the numeric data that is the focus of analysis is stored.

flattened recordset Multidimensional data that is retrieved as an ADO `Recordset`. This data can be directly bound to a grid without any special considerations. However, the multidimensional structure of the data is not present.

hierarchy A way in which the members of a dimension can be aggregated or "rolled up" to higher levels. Dimensions can have multiple hierarchies, representing different paths of aggregation.

HOLAP See *Hybrid OLAP.*

HTTP See *Hypertext Transfer Protocol.*

Hybrid OLAP (HOLAP) Fact data is stored in a relational database and aggregations are stored on the OLAP server in a proprietary format that is optimized for multidimensional use.

Hypertext Transfer Protocol (HTTP) The primary method for communicating on the World Wide Web. HTTP is a request/response protocol that is used between clients and servers, typically over TCP/IP port 80. There is also a secure version of HTTP called HTTPS that encrypts the connection between client and server.

IIS See *Internet Information Server.*

Internet Information Server (IIS) Microsoft's Web server for Windows. IIS also provides FTP and SMTP services.

Internet Server Application Programming Interface (ISAPI) Microsoft's programming interface between applications and Internet Information Server. ISAPI is used to create the same kinds of applications as CGI but uses dynamic link libraries (DLLs) for greater efficiency. The server loads the DLL the first time a request is received and the DLL then stays in memory, ready to service other requests until the server decides it is no longer needed, reducing overhead from executing applications many times. See also *Dynamic Link Library* and *Internet Information Server.*

ISAPI See *Internet Server Application Programming Interface.*

key columns Used to join the *fact table* to the *dimension tables* in a star schema. The fact table will contain multiple foreign keys that are joined to the primary keys of the dimension tables.

Key Performance Indicator (KPI) A measurement or metric used to evaluate performance. KPIs assess objectives in financial or physical units that can compare performance over time or between different entities.

knowledge management *Knowledge management* is another area of business intelligence that is a little different from the areas discussed so far. Instead of focusing on numeric data that is extracted out of either relational or OLAP databases, knowledge management focuses on the unstructured information that is so important to daily business activities. Knowledge management technologies, including portals, are often used to communicate information, and are valuable tools for any business intelligence effort.

KPI See *Key Performance Indicator.*

leaf Member with no children are said to be at the *leaf level.*

level A *level* is a group of dimension members that share a common meaning. Levels map to dimension table columns.

lift A measure of the effectiveness of a predictive model calculated as the ratio between the results obtained with and without the predictive model.

MDX See *Multidimensional Expressions.*

measure Measures are the numerical data values, or facts, that users analyze.

member An element in a dimension.

metadata describes the data that exists in the data warehouse so that decision makers can use the data effectively.

MOLAP See *Multidimensional OLAP.*

Multidimensional Expressions (MDX) MDX is a full-featured query language that is designed specifically to work with multidimensional data.

Multidimensional OLAP (MOLAP) Fact data and aggregations are stored on the OLAP server in a proprietary format that is optimized for multidimensional use.

neural networks In data mining, a set of non-linear equations that mimic the operation of neurons in the brain.

Object Linking and Embedding DataBase (OLE DB) COM-based data access layer that provides uniform access to different types of data.

ODBC See *Open Database Connectivity.*

OLAP See *Online Analytical Processing.*

OLE DB COM-based data access layer that provides uniform access to different types of data.

OLE DB for Data Mining (OLEDB DM) A protocol based on the SQL language that provides software vendors and application developers with an interface to integrate data mining tools into business applications.

OLE DB for OLAP OLE DB for OLAP is published by Microsoft and establishes an API standard for multidimensional data access that is broadly used for OLAP on the Windows platform. OLE DB for OLAP consists of a set of objects and interfaces that extends the relational database access provided by OLE DB to include multidimensional data. The use of OLE DB as the core of OLE DB for OLAP allows the reuse of the interfaces that provide common data handling and manipulation and minimizes the number of multidimensional specific objects and interfaces that have to be added to the architecture. The language used to access data through OLE DB for OLAP is *MDX.*

OLTP See *Online Transaction Processing.*

Online Analytical Processing (OLAP) Provides analysts with tools for exploring patterns and trends in multidimensional business data. OLAP analysis is often used to get a better understanding of patterns and trends in historical data and to analyze business performance across a variety of metrics and functional areas.

Online Transactional Processing (OLTP) Online Transaction Processing applications are optimized for managing frequently changing data. Primary concerns for OLTP applications are the ACID properties of atomicity, concurrency, independence, and durability.

Open Database Connectivity (ODBC) A standard for database access. ODBC has interfaces defined for almost every programming language and database, as well as a number of other storage formats (Excel, text, and so on).

partition The separation of a large database up into smaller pieces on different servers. This is done to optimize performance for very large databases.

PMML See *Predictive Model Markup Language.*

portal A Web site that provides a gateway to other information either on the Internet or within a corporation. Portals help to present information in categories so that it can be more easily discovered.

prediction With respect to data mining, prediction is the process of applying cases to a trained mining model to obtain a forecast. See also *training.*

Predictive Model Markup Language (PMML) An XML schema, backed by the Data Mining Group, that describes statistical and data-mining models to facilitate model interchange.

probability A number expressing the likelihood of a specific event, expressed as a number between 0 and 1 that represents the ratio of the number of actual occurrences to the number of possible occurrences.

relational database Relational databases are one way of organizing data. In a relational database, data is organized into tables. A table represents some class of objects that are important to an organization. Each table is built of columns and rows. Each column represents some attribute of the object represented by the table. Each row represents an instance of the object represented by the table.

Relational OLAP (ROLAP) A method of storing OLAP data where the fact data and aggregations are stored in a relational database. See also *Online Transaction Processing.*

report A formatted publication of information. Often produced according to a schedule and containing detailed information.

Return on Investment (ROI) The value generated by an investment over time.

risk management A range of activities undertaken by an organization to control the threat of loss from various factors. Risk management includes the identification and categorization of threats as well as deciding what action to take to reduce their potential impact.

ROI See *Return on Investment.*

ROLAP See *Relational OLAP.*

schema In OLE DB, the schema for an object is a description of the object's structure (that is, the contents of that object's metadata). In XML, a schema is a formal specification of the rules of an XML document describing which elements are allowed in a document and in what combinations.

set An ordered collection of tuples. A set can contain zero tuples, in which case it is an empty set.

SharePoint A set of Microsoft products and technologies that provide services for information sharing.

Simple Object Access Protocol (SOAP) SOAP is a lightweight XML-based protocol for exchanging structured and type information on the Web.

slice A member or group of members that are evaluated across other dimensions. You can think of a slice as being a subset of a cube.

snowflake schema Like a star schema, except one or more dimension tables are not joined directly to the fact table. Instead, they must be joined through other dimension tables.

SOAP See *Simple Object Access Protocol.*

source database The origin of data in a data warehouse.

sparse cube In many cases cubes do not have data for all intersections. This is called a *sparse cube.* Sparse is not a negative term; it simply means they there are missing data points for a majority of the cells.

standard deviation A statistic used to describe dispersion in a distribution, equal to the square root of the arithmetic mean of the squares of the deviations from the arithmetic mean. See also *variance.*

star schema A distinguishing feature of a dimensional model is a set of business facts surrounded by multiple dimensions that describe those facts. In most cases, a data warehouse is organized in a *star schema* with central *fact tables* surrounded by *dimension tables* and joined by *key columns.*

training With respect to data mining, training is the process of applying cases to an algorithm to create a model that describes the cases. See also *prediction.*

tuple An ordered collection of one member from one or more dimensions. The tuple identifies specific sections of a cube where these dimensions intersect.

variance The square of the standard deviation. See also *standard deviation.*

Web parts A Microsoft technology that allows the construction of reusable components that contain Web-based content, such as eXtensible Markup Language (XML) code, HTML pages, or script, and support a set of standard properties that determine how they are rendered.

Web Server control A reusable component implemented in ASP.NET that allows the server to process the component and return HTML to the browser.

Web Service Definition Language (WSDL) An XML document that provides information about a Web service, including information about the types of messages a service understands, the protocols that a service supports, and the destination for outgoing messages. See also *Hypertext Transfer Protocol, Simple Object Access Protocol,* and *eXtensible Markup Language.*

Web Services A method of integrating applications through publicly available open APIs, primarily over the HTTP protocol. See also *Hypertext Transfer Protocol, Simple Object Access Protocol,* and *Web Service Definition Language.*

Windows controls In .NET, refers to a reusable client control that is displayed in a user interface, typically a Windows form.

WSDL See *Web Service Definition Language.*

XML for Analysis (XMLA) XMLA is a standard proposed and supported by Microsoft, Hyperion, and SAS to provide an XML schema that can be used to standardize the way OLAP services are called over the Internet or intranet. It provides a standard data access API to remote data access providers that can be used universally on the Internet or intranet for multidimensional data. XMLA supports technologically independent implementations using any tool, programming language, technology, hardware platform, or device. XMLA allows building on open Internet standards, such as SOAP, XML, and HTTP. It also permits use and reuse of successful OLE DB design concepts, so that OLE DB for OLAP applications and OLE DB providers can be easily enabled for XML for Analysis.

XML See *eXtensible Markup Language.*

XMLA See *XML for Analysis.*

Index